Egypt and the Bible

by

Nicholas Thom

**Grosvenor House
Publishing Limited**

This book is published by
Grosvenor House Publishing Ltd
28-30 High Street, Guildford, Surrey, GU1 3HY.
www.grosvenorhousepublishing.co.uk

A CIP record for this book
is available from the British Library

ISBN 1-905529-97-x

Preface

In an age where so many are desperately seeking meaning in life, the Bible is coming under scrutiny as never before. Rationalists point to the absurd nature of some of the Bible stories; a worldwide flood, characters who live far beyond the age of today's oldest humans, seas becoming dry land, the sun standing still in the sky. Ancient historians point out the serious discrepancies between their understanding of historical events and those given in the Bible. Even theologians regularly speak of the illogical and contradictory nature of certain passages. To a Christian – or for that matter a Jew – these are worrying issues. There would seem to be but two alternatives: either blind faith or acceptance that traditional belief needs to be cast aside.

Fortunately, I believe in neither course! Faith that is wilfully blind is not worth having. That road leads to the certainty of disappointment. Nor am I prepared to cast my beliefs aside on the say-so of others. To accuse something of being 'absurd', 'illogical' or 'factually wrong', the case for the prosecution needs to be backed up by hard facts – and this book is an examination of some of those facts, namely those related to ancient history. The result has certainly surprised me. I confess that I was mentally prepared to adjust my belief in the Bible's basic trustworthiness, since it is difficult to imagine that generations of historians could be so thoroughly wrong. But they have been!

Of course I don't expect anyone to take my word for it at the outset, so please read on. The principal subject I will be dealing with is the dating of ancient history and the place of the Bible stories within the historical framework which emerges. The underlying subject – whether the Bible is to be trusted – is of vital importance, but it is a bigger subject than that of ancient history alone. However, if the history told in the pages of the Bible proves to be reliable, then this at least means that the book should not be discarded straight away!

I hope that as well as fulfilling the serious purpose of 'sorting out' historical dates, I have also provided an interesting voyage of historical discovery for those for whom the subject is new – and a surprising voyage for those who think they know the subject already.

Finally, I invite your comments and criticism since I have no interest in propagating untruth.

Nick Thom
University of Nottingham
December 2006

Contents

1

Introduction

To some the subject of this book may seem infinitely remote. I will be visiting days when the seemingly timeless monument of Stonehenge in southern England hadn't even been conceived, when the wind still blew uninterrupted across the Giza plateau where today the Great Pyramid stands, and elephants roamed the well-wooded countryside of Syria. Yet this was only 200 generations ago! Do you really imagine you have 'evolved' significantly in just 200 generations? You may not have been able to understand the speech of your ancestor of 200 generations past, but that would only be because of the ever-changing nature of human language. That ancestor could easily have learnt modern English and conversed with you about all manner of things familiar to you both – the weather, cookery, house construction, the price of bread. We have certainly gained in knowledge since those days (electricity, steel, nuclear fission, anti-viral drugs) but could we honestly say we have gained in wisdom? Our brains are not appreciably different; we are subject to just the same hopes, fears, pleasures, anxieties and traumas. It is only the material world around us that has changed.

The fact is that the world I wish to introduce you to is a world just like our own in the crucial sense that the central players, human beings, are just like us. Their problems are just like ours (earning enough to live on); they organise themselves in similar ways (government, organised religion); they have the same human weaknesses (pride in their various cultures, distrust of foreign ways). Family life is similar, probably village life too – although relatively few of us live in villages nowadays. The job market may not look quite so familiar, with a preponderance of agricultural employment, but there is industry already in the shape of tool manufacture, construction (of houses and roads), mining, shipbuilding. In short, this is not a remote world at all; it is in many ways like looking through a distorted mirror and seeing people who, though different in appearance, are actually images of ourselves. And since these people are so like

1

ourselves, it is hardly surprising that so much of modern thought can be traced back to these ancient times. If you happen to follow a religion, you will realise that the teachings of that religion are rooted in the distant past. If you are a Jew, Muslim or Christian then you should want to know about the world of Noah, Abraham and Moses. These characters, assuming they were as real as so many of us believe, didn't exist in a vacuum. They interacted with the rest of society, sometimes with kings and governors, yet for the most part we are content to read the stories of the Bible or the Koran and not to ask too much about the context, about the political situation of the time, who was ruling or what the economic realities of the day might have been. But I want to know! I want to know which of Egypt's pharaohs gave his daughter in marriage to Solomon – assuming for a moment that the story is true; I want to know the identity of the earlier pharaoh who set his will against that of Moses; and his even earlier predecessor who made Joseph his vizier. If I could, I would like to know what the world was like in the days of Noah when, according to the Bible and the Koran, a great flood engulfed the world. In this book I shall have to leave this last wish unfulfilled since, whether the flood was real or not, I will not be voyaging far enough back in time to find out, but I hope you will come to see that my other wishes and many more can indeed be satisfied – but only if we can date the past properly!

Dating the Distant Past

Useful and fascinating though a study of the past may be, its worth would be sadly diminished if we had no clear idea of when things happened. It would be impossible then to understand the sequence of events in any given land, or the interrelationships between events in different lands. Dating recent history is obviously no problem. Our current records are really very good indeed so we know with absolute assurance for example that the Second World War started in 1939 and finished in 1945. We even know the day, the hour and the minute.[1] But how do we know that Christopher Columbus 'discovered' America on October 12th 1492?[2] Again, the mystery is not great. The system we use to designate dates giving us years such as 1492 has been in existence since the 6th Century when a Roman monk named Dionysius Exiguus worked out (approximately) the year in which Jesus of Nazareth had been born, so as soon as we come across a quoted date according to this system, that anchors the event described firmly in time.

But how on earth can we know that the Mayan king known as '18 Rabbit' (for want of a better translation of the glyphs denoting his name), one of the greatest rulers of the city of Copan, now in western Honduras, met his untimely end (captured and sacrificed by a neighbouring king) in the year 738?[3] The answer this time lies in the Mayan calendar, which has been known and understood by specialists for just about 100 years and which, once correlated with the Christian calendar, gives equally absolute and reliable dates.

OK; but what about times before the birth of Jesus? How do we know that Julius Caesar invaded Britain in 55BC? How do we know that Alexander the Great captured Persepolis, the capital of the Persian Empire, in 331BC? What was the dating system used? Well, the normal way in which events were dated throughout the ancient world was either with respect to the regnal year (year since coronation) of a particular ruler, or else the number of years since some defining event in a people's past, for example the founding of a city or an empire. Thus, on the death of a king, say in the 29th year of his reign, the count would often start again with Year 1 of his successor. This makes life a little more tricky for historians since they have to do a bit of simple addition and subtraction but I guess you can see that, so long as there are plenty of records, specifically so long as we know in what year each king or queen died, then there are no insurmountable problems. Certainly throughout the Roman period (dated with respect to the supposed founding of Rome in 753BC)[4] and of the city states of Greece (dated from the first Olympic Games in 776BC) there is plenty of evidence. Occasionally an undated text may cause difficulties if it contains insufficient reference to known events but the overall sequence of history is well known.

So, we know with some confidence that king Nebuchadnezzar II of Babylon conquered Jerusalem in 586BC (plus or minus a year perhaps), sending many of the Israelites into exile. Babylonian records are hardly extensive but there are enough to correlate with Egyptian and Jewish records and thence with those of ancient Greece. There are plenty of things we don't know about Nebuchadnezzar's reign of course, but there is certainly enough information to give us the overall chronological framework.

But what if we go back slightly further? Greece was the centre of literacy and is the source of much of our knowledge of the Middle East in the 1st Millennium BC but the Greeks only took up writing seriously some time around 700BC.[5] True, record keeping was in progress further east, for example in Babylon and also in Egypt, not to mention China. Babylonian records are datable by experts with a high degree of confidence back to the year 747BC when a certain king Nabonassar instigated a system of record keeping tied in with astronomical observations. In Egypt, confidence evaporates once we go further back than the traumatic sack of Egypt's spiritual capital Thebes by Assyrian armies in 664BC. In China, where astronomical records were kept, it is sometimes possible to go further but only a few scraps of information survived the first emperor's book-burning edict of the late 3rd Century BC.

Yet last night I heard a television documentary which stated with apparent confidence that pharaoh Akhenaten of Egypt came to the throne in 1338BC!

How is it possible to be so certain? Well, I guess the first thing to say is that it was only a television documentary and that a check with some of the available reference books on ancient Egypt[6] reveals a rather lower level of confidence (alternatives of 1352, 1348 and 1344BC given), but how do we even know what century we are in?

As an academic I have to say that the level of confidence itself is no mystery at all. In my own field, and I am sure the same applies to all academic disciplines, there is a tendency to follow a strong lead whether it's right or wrong! We like to project certainty so, when a respected academic presents a view, this view can easily take on the appearance of fact. Once widely accepted it becomes almost impossible to question the matter further without losing 'academic credibility'. My view and the view of a large number of others is that just such a solidifying of academic opinion has occurred in the field of ancient history, specifically Egyptian history, and that it is high time that this opinion was seriously questioned – and even overturned.

Questions begin to be asked

Firstly, why does it matter so much? Well, the trouble is that the Egyptian sequence of history, the basic framework for which was worked out well over 100 years ago,[7] has now become the standard to which all other histories have to conform. In some cases (Greek history for example), the requirement to tie in with accepted Egyptian history has left a very uncomfortable gap, almost devoid of either archaeology or written record. In others (the Bible record for example), it has led to the rejection as unreliable of those elements which do not conform. For our understanding of the ancient world, it is hard to overstate the importance of Egyptian history and of the particular dates which historians have worked out. Ancient Middle Eastern history is like a building with but a single supporting column, Egypt. And the consequence is that it is ever more difficult to question the correctness of Egyptian history because too many other things depend on it. It is simply too dangerous to too many reputations to even think of dismantling it!

Yet several brave individuals have tried. In 1952 Immanuel Velikovsky, a psychiatrist by profession, became a hate figure among ancient historians when he published the first volume of his work *Ages in Chaos*. To read Velikovsky is an amazing experience. His boldness in completely re-interpreting historical evidence is quite breathtaking and the fact that his story is woven brilliantly into a brand new and exciting version of history, all supported – so it seems – by numerous references to genuine evidence, makes the experience exhilarating. His approach is scholarly, always referring back to original sources and often quoting the views of those who first excavated key archaeological sites. Essentially, he proceeded to completely rewrite history. He drew seemingly outrageous parallels between Egyptian history and the Bible, assigning the well-known Egyptian queen Hatshepsut a role as the queen of Sheba who is said to have visited king Solomon in Jerusalem, all plausibly supported by Egyptian inscriptions, while the greatest of Egypt's conquering pharaohs, Tuthmose III, played the part of another Biblical character, pharaoh Shishak, who, the Bible tells us, conquered Jerusalem shortly after king Solomon's reign. By the time Velikovsky reached the days of king Ahab of Israel, dated by all historians to the 9th Century BC, he had managed to shunt Egyptian history forward by over 500 years!

Now I do not wish to belittle Velikovsky's achievements in any way, despite my total disagreement with his conclusions. His great achievement was to open up for debate a subject which had been closed for 100 years. Even today, Velikovsky has a strong following – but it is not one which includes serious historians. Enough holes have been found in his interpretation of history to reassure the academic world that they can still sleep easy at night.

So, Velikovsky disposed of to the satisfaction of the 'establishment', the traditional view continued to dominate. There were other revisionists, for example biochemist Donovan Courville,[8] who is still well known among sections of the American religious community, but their followers were relatively few until, in 1991, Peter James and four colleagues produced their work, *Centuries of Darkness*. This scholarly work grew out of a feeling shared by the five authors that something was wrong somewhere around the centuries from 1200BC to 900BC. The traditional view, based on Egyptian chronology (with significant support from Babylon and Assyria), is that civilisation went through a very sticky patch around this time. In Egypt, there are records of invasions by mysterious foreigners; in Greece, the civilisation of those who fought the Trojan War is supposed to have collapsed; the Hittite Empire in Turkey came to a sudden and mysterious end; in Babylon there were several dynasties of kings assigned to this period, none of which left the smallest obvious mark on history. James and the others formed the view that some 250 years of supposed history, conventionally termed the 'Dark Ages', simply never happened! The problem was that, while removing these dark ages from the histories of several countries seemed to make sense, there was still the great rock of Egyptian history to deal with and, to be honest, the authors never really gave enough detail concerning Egypt to convince other scholars that the theory was viable. In fact, James' proposals didn't go down at all well with Egyptologists, foremost among whom was Kenneth Kitchen, professor at Liverpool University. He had spent much of his working life on the subject of the so-called 'Third Intermediate Period', the period of Egyptian history which had become the main victim of James' theory, and had produced his own widely-respected textbook on the subject.[9] Kitchen's has been one of the most strident voices among those supporting a conventional chronology. He had been dismissive of Velikovsky and he placed James' work firmly – some would say abusively – in the same dustbin.

However, while James and others were doing their best to shorten history and get rid of unwanted dark ages, there has also been pressure in the opposite direction and this all relates to the eruption of a volcano on the Greek island of Santorini (previously known as Thera) in the Aegean Sea. Perhaps the name means little to you; perhaps you have read or seen a television documentary about it. I'll be saying quite a bit about Thera in due course but here you should know that there is plenty of physical evidence for there having been a gigantic volcanic eruption, almost destroying the island, at some time in the 2nd Millennium BC and that a growing number of voices have been claiming as fact that the eruption can be dated quite precisely to 1628BC – based on tree ring evidence. Foremost among these voices, at least as far as history is concerned, has been that of Sturt Manning of Reading University, England.[10] As an archaeologist, he used this date to draw conclusions based on the large amount of pottery and architectural evidence on Santorini/Thera itself, dating from just before the eruption. And the inescapable conclusion, if the 1628BC date is correct, is that the chronology of the ancient world needs extending somewhat, not reducing! In fact Manning now prefers an even earlier though slightly less precise date, 1650–1645BC, based on Greenland ice core evidence and, if he is correct, the consequence for ancient history is that new and even longer dark ages start to appear.[11]

Forgive the details. I just want to get across the fact that the chronology of the ancient world is being pulled in both directions for differing reasons, in both cases by respected researchers, and that those believing in a traditional chronology are caught in the cross-fire. And it is into the midst of this turbulent situation that the most vocal of the modern revisionists has now set out his stall. David Rohl, another English archaeologist, has written an excellent and highly persuasive book, *A Test of Time* (same main title as Manning's book incidentally), as well as generating a three-part television series, in which he has proposed his own rewriting of history. And with his more recent publications, *Legend: the Genesis of Civilisation* and *The Lost Testament*, he has now woven his reconstruction of Egyptian history into a massive reworking of the history of the entire Near East and Middle East area, in particular relating this history to events and characters described in the Bible. His books are well written, well illustrated and extremely well argued, and they suggest a shift in Egyptian history of up to about 350 years in places! As you can imagine, if Kenneth Kitchen and others were unhappy at James knocking 250 years off Egyptian history, then Rohl's 350 years went down like a lead balloon! If Kitchen was dismissive of James' work, he was even more so of Rohl's.[12]

Personally, I am hugely indebted to the efforts of all the authors I have mentioned. As I see it there are five main chronologies on offer, which I could illustrate crudely as follows:

+ 200 years   Manning (based on dating of the eruption of Thera)

The Conventional or Orthodox history of the ancient world

− 250 years   James (*Centuries of Darkness*)
− 350 years   Rohl (*A Test of Time*)
− 500 years   Velikovsky (*Ages in Chaos*)

Where do we go from here?

In my view none of these schemes should be disregarded. Each author has brought valid evidence to bear on the issue but clearly they cannot all be correct in their interpretation of the evidence! What is needed is a view from outside the battlefield, seeking out the truth as to what should and should not be believed, because the truth is certainly out there somewhere. That is the task which I set myself and this book is my report. It does not present any new facts; it is primarily a work of logic, taking the available evidence – all of it produced by the excellent work of historians, archaeologists and other specialists and some of it highlighted by the various authors mentioned – and piecing it together to discover where the real truth lies. I would particularly like to single out David Rohl's contribution to the ever-growing mountain of evidence despite my profound disagreement with much of his version of history.

The motivation for this book comes from a desire to see events and characters placed properly in their right historical setting. I am among a very large number of people who have been disillusioned by the lack of apparent agreement between the Bible and history as it is conventionally told and I freely admit that I have, at least subconsciously, been affected by my desire to see the Bible in some sense vindicated. Of course that is not something I can arrange; all I can hope to achieve is to come up with a correct order of events and a broadly correct set of absolute dates and to check whether the events of the Bible make sense within that framework. If the Bible is wrong so be it; but I want to know the truth.

What I intend to do therefore is to check ancient history out from scratch. It is really quite important that the history which is used as a standard is correct and, as you will see, I believe that an extremely serious error has indeed been made, a view which many before me have also taken. However, the hard task is not simply to produce reasons for believing that an error has occurred but to find it, and to put it right! You will have to be the judge of whether or not I have succeeded.

However, I'm first going to spend a chapter journeying back in time, following in the footsteps of those who first worked out what has now become the accepted orthodox view of ancient Middle Eastern history – and I hope you'll be able to see for yourself how shaky its foundations really are. This then begs the question:

just what can we trust? – and I want to spend a chapter checking out the mysteries of Carbon 14 dating, tree rings, ice cores etc. Obviously if a true and reliable course is to be charted through the treacherous waters of the 2nd and 3rd Millennia BC it is of paramount importance that we know what information is reliable – and, equally important, what is not; and believe me, there is plenty of information being used, quoted and re-quoted which is very far from being reliable!

However, the major part of the book, from Chapter 4 onwards, will be devoted to telling anew the epic and absorbing story of the Middle East from the founding of the Egyptian Empire through to a time in the 1st Millennium BC when history really does become well known and accurately dated. I will be galloping rapidly through the 3rd Millennium BC, a consequence of our relative lack of data, slowing to a canter during the early 2nd Millennium, reaching a trot during the mid 2nd Millennium and, finally, slowing to a careful walk as I approach the really tricky bit, the bit where I have to tie into dates which are genuinely known. At the end of each chapter I will include two short additional sections. The first, entitled 'What does the Bible have to say?', is included for those who are interested in seeing how the Bible stories fit in – and you may end up surprised at just how well they do fit in – and I have then included a paragraph or two entitled 'What was going on in the rest of the world?', because we should never lose sight of the bigger picture.

I hope you enjoy the journey; I did. You most certainly do not need to be a specialist to read this book, simply someone with an interest in the truth about our past.

2

Winding Back the Clock

If we look at the general Middle Eastern scene through the centuries of ancient history, the picture is one of successive great empires. Last, greatest and longest-ruling were the Romans and it is with the Roman conquest of Egypt in the summer of 30BC that I shall begin this journey back in time. The incorporation of Egypt into the Roman Empire stemmed from a civil war fought between the two most powerful Romans of the day, Mark Anthony and Octavian. Mark Anthony had persuaded much of the eastern part of the empire to support him – together with his wife, queen Cleopatra of Egypt. Octavian on the other hand had the support of Rome itself. It was a fateful moment for the history of the world. When Mark Anthony was defeated, this left Octavian with absolute authority over the Roman world. The following years saw his position grow from that of Consul under the constitution of the Roman Republic to emperor, the Emperor Augustus, the first emperor of the new Roman Empire. In contrast, Mark Anthony's fate, and that of his wife Cleopatra, was suicide. The fact that Egypt thereby slipped quietly under Roman control was just a side effect.

The Hellenistic Era

Now we know without any significant doubt that these events took place in the summer of 30BC. We have extensive documentation, histories written by Roman and Greek historians, even quoting letters from the principal participants.[1] We also have confidence that just over 300 years earlier, in 332BC, the armies of Alexander the Great rolled virtually unopposed into Egypt and that for the whole of those 302 years Egypt was ruled by Greek-speaking kings and queens.

Alexander changed the face of the Middle East more completely than any before or since. He grew up during days when his home country Macedonia was just a small state at the northern end of the Greek-speaking world. And the Greek-speaking world, though significantly more widespread than it is today, was still a relatively small entity. To the east, as far as any traveller could venture, the world was the province of a single empire, that of Persia, the greatest empire the world had ever known; yet Alexander swallowed it whole! As soon as he came to the Macedonian throne in 336BC he set about the grand task of conquering the world. He commenced with Greece, obliterating the ancient city of Thebes in the process, and within a year he had effective control. His launch pad was in position; he was ready for his great adventure. In 334BC he crossed the Dardanelles Strait from Europe into Asia and was on his way. The first Persian force sent to intercept him he swept away at the battle of Granicus in western Turkey. This left the door open for Alexander to move through Turkey until, in early 333BC, he crossed the Taurus Mountains and entered Cilicia in south-central Turkey, a rich land of significant economic importance to the Persians. You have to imagine that the Persian emperor Darius III still felt reasonably confident. He had been busy raising a vast army to deal with this threat from the west and he still had a great empire behind him. But, confident or not, he was soon to learn that Alexander meant business. At the battle of Issus on the Orontes river in northern Syria, Alexander's army gained a decisive victory, overwhelming the superior numbers of the Persian force by a combination of good tactics and more appropriate weaponry.

Alexander then moved down the coast of Syria, Lebanon and Palestine, taking city after city, most notably the almost impossibly well fortified city of Tyre, before finally entering Egypt, where he was proclaimed both pharaoh and god! There is no doubt that Alexander looked upon his conquest of Egypt as one of the pinnacles of his career. The city he founded, named Alexandria as so many other cities were, was to endure and become a serious rival to Athens as a centre of Greek learning and culture. The Macedonians were in Egypt to stay.

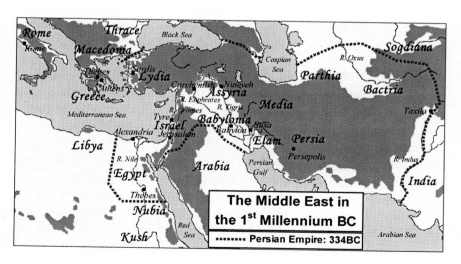

However, Alexander was not in Egypt to stay! He was still 400 miles from the Persian heartlands; Darius III was still emperor of Persia and he was not particularly happy about losing a large part of his territory to a young upstart Greek, so he set about raising another mighty army, this time largely of the feared Persian cavalry. Battle finally came in late summer of 331BC on the plains to the east of the Tigris River, the battle of Gaugamela. Once again, Alexander's tactics were superior; he seized his opening when it came and pulled off yet another famous victory. And that was the end for Darius. Though he managed to flee the battle, Alexander's forces eventually caught up with him and killed him. The Macedonian army then set out to conquer the heart of Persian power, Persepolis in southern Iran, where the looting was on such a scale that modern excavation has revealed almost nothing of the fabulous wealth which is known to have been accumulated during the centuries of Persian might.

Alexander continued – there was no stopping him despite the protests of many of his army commanders. He mopped up the remainder of Persian territory and then advanced north-east through what are now the states of Turkmenistan, Uzbekistan, Tajikistan and Kyrgyzstan, conquering and founding cities as he went. He turned south, through Afghanistan and on into Pakistan and India. He had an insatiable thirst to conquer ever more and more lands. His territory stretched for 3000 miles and if his troops had been willing to go further I am quite sure he would have reached China. But, in 326BC, somewhere to the north of Delhi, India, after eight long years of marching and fighting, the army finally convinced him that enough was enough. There may have been other worlds to conquer but they had no intention of conquering them.

Thus did one man change the world! Of course he didn't win the battles by himself, but his will was the determining factor. Because of his will power – and not a little skill – the Middle East changed at a stroke from being a Persian dominated zone to being Greek dominated – hence the term 'Hellenistic' from 'Hellas', the Greek word for Greece. On Alexander's death in Babylon in 323BC, the vast empire started fraying at the edges, but Iraq, Turkey, Syria, Palestine and Egypt remained firmly under Greek (or more correctly Macedonian) control for centuries. Egypt became the province of one of Alexander's commanders, Ptolemy, and he soon set about creating for himself a lasting dynasty of kings.

The Persian Era

While the Hellenistic world was well documented by the highly literate Greek society of the time,[2] the same cannot be said for that of the Persians. Indeed much of what we know of the Persian Empire comes via the Greeks. The Persians were literate; they used the cuneiform script, suited to impressing lines into a wet clay tablet, but they had no history of writing at the time they took on the mantle of world superpower. In fact they employed their neighbours the Elamites, a people from south-west Iran, to form the scribal class, those responsible for such writing as was necessary. One could even suggest that the Persians suffered from a slight inferiority complex. They were in charge – no doubt about that – but they recognised that they would have to join forces with other nationalities in order to achieve a working empire. They needed the Babylonians with their long history of administration; they needed the Phoenicians, the inhabitants of the Syrian and Lebanese coasts, because of their mastery of world trade and of seafaring; they needed the Greeks because of their high level of scientific knowledge. In contrast, when the Macedonians took over, bearing Greek culture, they suffered from no such inferiority complex; they believed in their hearts that Greek society was the most developed in the known world and, as far as they were concerned, they needed little of the skills of other nations. Thus, whilst the Persians presided over a multi-cultural society and were proud of it, the Macedonians presided over a Greek society and they expected the world to conform!

Two different attitudes, two different routes to success; and the Persian Empire was certainly successful. When the first Persian emperor Cyrus was growing up, Persia was just a small state in southern Iran dominated by its larger neighbour Media, centred on north-west Iran. Yet, under Cyrus, Persian power exploded across the map. Media was absorbed as a junior partner in 549BC; next the combined forces of the Medes and the Persians headed west and defeated the major power in Turkey at the time, known as Lydia. With the momentum behind him, Cyrus then took on the premier Middle Eastern power of the day, the empire of Babylon, taking the city by stealth in 539BC. With this one coup, Cyrus found himself master of the entire Middle East right to the border of Egypt. This border was then crossed in 525BC by Cyrus' successor Cambyses, and Egypt was incorporated into the Persian Empire.

But can we really be sure that these dates are correct? Certainly; the evidence is largely derived from Greek sources, which are excellent throughout this period.[3] There is also a certain amount of documentation from Egypt and from Babylonia. Details may often be obscure but the overall scheme of things is known, at least to the year.

The Babylonian Era

King Nebuchadnezzar of Babylon is famous as the king who conquered Jerusalem in 586BC – or perhaps it's just the sheer unlikeliness of the name Nebuchadnezzar that makes him stick in the memory![4] Nebuchadnezzar had conquered Jerusalem once already, in 597BC, but in 586BC he more than conquered it, he destroyed it. And, once again, we can have a high level of confidence that the year in which Jerusalem fell was genuinely 586BC. Babylonian records are admittedly sparse, particularly from the second half of Nebuchadnezzar's long reign, but these are supplemented by reliably dated Greek and Egyptian records.[5] And in case any doubt remains we also have the benefit of an absolute, scientifically-determined date. Two of Babylon's great rivals, the Medes and the Lydians, had come to blows over ownership of eastern Turkey and we are most fortunate to have a record of the battle, much the most memorable aspect of which was a total solar eclipse, interrupting the best laid plans of the generals on either side. Everyone was so shocked by this miracle that they even stopped killing each other long enough to agree an armistice and for peace to break out – enough to make believers of the most hardened sceptics! Anyway, the key point is that scientists can actually calculate, based on the known movements of the Earth, sun and moon, just when solar eclipses have occurred in the past. They have to be careful to take proper account of matters such as the change in the speed of the Earth's rotation which, though measured in milliseconds over a single year, adds up to a considerable potential error over the course of two and a half millennia, but the business of calculating the dates (and times) of past eclipses is now a respected part of historical research. In this case the calculated date according to our modern calendar is 28th May 585BC.

The total period of Babylonian domination over the Middle East was relatively short-lived. It commenced in 612BC when Babylonian forces, acting in cooperation with those of the Medes, annihilated the city of Nineveh, the capital of the country then known as Assyria, located in northern Iraq. Then, when Nebuchadnezzar succeeded to the throne in 604BC he immediately set about enlarging the kingdom. He fought and defeated the Egyptian pharaoh Necho II at the battle of Carchemish in northern Syria, giving him effective control of Syria and Palestine as far as the Jewish kingdom of Judah; it was rebellion by Zedekiah king of Judah which led to his destruction of Jerusalem. Nebuchadnezzar succeeded in making Babylon the greatest city the world had ever known; the world-famous 'hanging gardens' are the stuff of legend and the subject of continuing debate amongst historians as to exactly what they consisted of. Babylon today, once you strip away the bricks commemorating the somewhat more recent and less glorious rule of Saddam Hussein, still reveals to archaeologists the remains of palaces and temples on a truly magnificent scale.

But Babylon was not the first great empire of the Middle East.

The Assyrian Era

To readers of the Bible the name 'Assyria' is a familiar one, but you could certainly be forgiven for not knowing too much about the Assyrians today. The problem is that the very name of Assyria has disappeared off the face of the map. When the forces of Babylon and Media destroyed Nineveh, situated on the outskirts of the modern Iraqi city of Mosul, they destroyed for ever one of the most dominating civilisations the world has ever known.

In their day the Assyrians were a very serious power. They were also literate. The language they spoke (or at least the language they wrote) was Akkadian, a Semitic language quite closely related to modern Arabic and Hebrew, the same language as was in use in Babylon and throughout Iraq. As we push back into the 7th Century BC, we are coming to times when the Greeks, so far our main source of ancient historical knowledge, were only just learning (actually re-learning) to write. The Persians had hardly registered their presence, appearing only as 'Parsuash' in Assyrian records. And at the time that the Babylonians and Medes were putting Nineveh to the sword, Rome was still controlled by the Etruscan king Tarquin I; it would be over a hundred years before the Roman Republic came into being.

But the Assyrians were not only literate but writing was an essential part of their culture and had been for well over a thousand years. Their last great king, Ashurbanipal, developed a taste for literature and for history, and he set up a magnificent library at Nineveh. There, thousands of priceless documents lay buried in the ruins for two and a half millennia before being discovered in a frenzied series of archaeological excavations during the second half of the 19th Century. Most fortunately for us the inhabitants of ancient Iraq were writing not on paper – as was often the case in Egypt – but on clay tablets, tablets which, if subjected to heat, would become as hard as brick and which would then survive the ravages of the centuries, ready to be read by the practised eye of a modern 'Assyriologist'. Among many great finds at Nineveh and at several other sites in Iraq a king list has been discovered, listing the sequence of Assyrian rulers and their reign lengths right back through a period of well over a thousand years! Now one should never believe a king list unquestioningly; the documents we now possess were compiled long after the reigns of most of the kings listed and one has to question the accuracy of the information available to the compiler. So an ultra-cautious approach is the only sensible one to take. However, the *Assyrian king list* is supplemented by a pretty impressive array of other documentation (to use the term in its broadest sense). Many of the more successful kings trumpeted their achievements on walls, pillars or commemorative plaques of one shape or another. They proclaimed their victories, their public building works, their treaties and their laws. But most useful of all have been astronomical observations recorded on the so-called *Limmu list*, a list of Assyrian state officials which can be directly tied to the king list. These match similar observations listed on a 2nd Century BC document from Alexandria known as *Ptolemy's Canon* and, more importantly, they also tie in with retro-calculation of actual events, notably a solar eclipse in 763BC. So, through a combination of the king list, the Limmu list and other supporting documents, scholars have worked out to the satisfaction of both themselves and the wider historical community the sequence of reigns of Assyrian kings right back to the year 911BC – and I have no intention of challenging it!

The Assyrian Empire therefore provides the backbone to Middle East history over a period of about 300 years, a strong enough backbone from which to hang the histories of the other peoples with which they came into contact. For instance, we know from Assyrian records that the state of Elam was effectively snuffed out by king Ashurbanipal's attack in the year 646BC. Similarly, we know that Ashurbanipal sacked the Egyptian capital Thebes[6] (not to be confused with Thebes in Greece – destroyed by Alexander the Great) in the year 664BC, an event which is readily identifiable from historical documents and inscriptions from Egypt itself. From the 4th year of king Sennacherib (701BC) comes evidence in broad support of the Bible's telling of history, notably a text telling us of the capture of 46 cities from Hezekiah king of Judah; the Bible agrees by stating that Sennacherib took "all" the fortified cities of Judah.[7] In 722BC, the demise of the northern Jewish kingdom, Israel, and the deportation of many of its inhabitants, described in some detail in the Bible, is confirmed by Sargon II's readily datable annals, in which he boasts that he conquered Samaria and led away some 27000 of its citizens.[8] Earlier still the Bible records the activities of Tiglath Pileser III of Assyria (744–727BC), who annexed large chunks of the kingdom of Israel, as well as destroying the Aramaean-speaking kingdom of Damascus. Tiglath Pileser's annals tie in well, adding that when Israel overthrew its own king, Pekah, he (Tiglath Pileser) placed Hoshea on the throne of Israel. These names are duly found in their correct sequence in the Bible.

As we journey back into the 9th Century BC we have to remember that Greece is an illiterate society firmly stuck in the period we know as the 'Dark Ages'. Rome has not even been founded. The first mention of the Medes and the Persians occurs in records dated to the Assyrian king Shalmaneser III, who reigned from 859 to 824BC. On Shalmaneser's famous black obelisk[9] we also find a depiction of a subservient king whose followers bear tribute, identified in the text as "Jehu son of Omri", with a date of 841BC. Now, according to the Bible, Jehu king of Israel was not actually the son of Omri, but he was nevertheless the occupant of the throne of Israel in Samaria, a city founded some 40 years earlier by king Omri, so the designation "son of Omri" is reasonable, from an Assyrian point of view. Another stela (inscribed stone) from earlier in Shalmaneser III's reign describes the battle of Karkar on the Euphrates river, dated to 853BC, where Shalmaneser met a coalition of Syrian and Palestinian forces, together with some from Egypt, and among them according to the stela were "2000 chariots and 10000 infantry of Ahab the Israelite" – a very considerable force. Now Ahab really was the son of Omri and the Bible indicates that he was one of the most successful of the kings of Israel (as well as being just about the most wicked!). The mention of Egypt is less helpful unless specific reference can be found in Egyptian documents to this sending of a (relatively small) Egyptian force to support the Syrians and Palestinians at Karkar and, to date, this is lacking.

Before Shalmaneser III we can date three earlier Assyrian kings with confidence, giving datable evidence for certain events in Babylon also. This takes us back to the coronation of Adad Nirari II in 911BC, but the incomplete state of the *Limmu list* means that we can go no further with any certainty. Historians believe that it was the reign of Adad Nirari which set the Assyrians on the road to greatness, reviving their fortunes after many years of total obscurity. The king list continues back in time – but that is all. There are no annals, land registries, trade records or archives of any kind for the previous 150 years or so, just a handful of inscriptions to lighten the darkness. The map leads on, but can we trust it?

Probing the Secrets of the Dark

Yet, despite this wall of darkness, a pretty comprehensive scheme of ancient history was worked out well over 100 years ago right back to the early 3rd Millennium BC, and it is based largely on Egypt. Let me explain the way it was done, at least in outline.

Egypt is rich in historical texts, on walls, monuments and papyri. Ever since 1824, the year that Jean François Champollion, a young Frenchman, announced to the world that he could now read Egyptian hieroglyphs, historians have had plenty of material to work with. Suddenly they knew that a certain pharaoh Usermaatre Setepenre Ramesses[10] (known to us now as Ramesses II) had been responsible for a quite staggering number of construction activities throughout the length and breadth of Egypt. Vast expanses of temple wall were devoted to describing his prowess in battle and to enumerating the peoples he claimed to have vanquished. Other names which were read on the monuments could be matched to the names known from Greek historical documents, in particular the various versions of an Egyptian king list (with supporting descriptive text), stemming originally from the pen of a certain Egyptian priest-turned-historian named Manetho who lived in the 3rd Century BC, but preserved only as quotations by other classical authors.[11] Egyptian history came alive – though it didn't all immediately make sense! Manetho had broken his list of rulers into a series of 30 dynasties, some with the individual kings and their reign lengths listed, and these could be matched to inscriptions found on monuments which gave references to important events, often dated to the specific year of a specific king. Another important source of knowledge was an ancient papyrus, now known as the *Turin Canon*. This document is also a king list, like Manetho's, but written some thousand years earlier. Unfortunately maltreatment in transit led to its current fragmentary condition, but it still contains invaluable data. It wasn't easy, but it gradually became possible to reconstruct a plausible sequence of events. It was quite another matter, however, to state when events took place in absolute terms. Simply adding up the (often conflicting) reign lengths was obviously not going to work since it was apparent that there were times when dynasties ruled in parallel (i.e. Egypt was divided) and there may have been other times when no king ruled at all; what was needed was some sort of independent yardstick.

The first breakthrough was made by finding the name of an Egyptian pharaoh which matched that of 'pharaoh Shishak' in the Bible, who is said to have conquered Jerusalem about 5 years after the death of the fabulously wealthy king Solomon. Now, with a pretty high level of confidence in the dates of the kings of Israel back to Ahab (873–851BC approximately), based on correlations with Assyrian history, it was a reasonable move to trust the Bible back another 50 years and to date Shishak's attack on Jerusalem to around 925BC. Scanning down the list of Manetho's kings an obvious match was found with the name 'Shoshenq' and, although there were several Shoshenqs, luckily one stood out. A wall at the great temple to Amun at Karnak (near Thebes) had been devoted to the military achievements of a certain 'Hedjkheperre Shoshenq'. The wall tells us that in his 20th year he had campaigned in Palestine and some of the names of the cities he conquered could easily be read, such as Megiddo, Taanach and Bethshan, cities on the Esdraelon plain in northern Israel. Then, on his one and only visit to Egypt, Champollion came and inspected the famous wall. As he scanned the rows of cities listed, his eyes lighted on one of several which could not be placed, and he pronounced to the world (wrongly as it turned out) that the name should be read as 'Judah the kingdom'. The case seemed to be solved; pharaoh Shishak was Hedjkheperre Shoshenq (known to us as Shoshenq I) and the 20th year of his reign was therefore 925BC, plus or minus a year or so.

However, the really big breakthrough came with the reading of a document recovered from Thebes known as the *Ebers Papyrus* and the realisation that it provided a potential key to absolute dating. That key lay in the Egyptians' use of a 365 day calendar with no adjustment for the extra quarter of a day or so – i.e. no leap year. The result was a set of months which would drift gradually through the seasons. This 365 day calendar (12 months of 30 days + 5 additional days) was divided up into three 4-month seasons, known as 'flood', 'emergence' and 'dry season', reflecting the realities of the Egyptian climate, and the fact that Day 1 of the flood season fell, according to the calendar, about a day earlier every four years didn't put the Egyptians off continuing to use this system, so it is believed, throughout their history. One would however presume that, when the calendar first came into use, Day 1 of the flood season according to the calendar really was the first day of the Nile flood (generally some time in mid July). We now come to a crucial error, and one that continues to be repeated to this day. The assumption was made that the journey through the seasons would have taken 1461 years (4 × 365¼). This is not correct; the length of our year is not exactly 365¼ days, but around 365.24 days, which means the Egyptians lost a little less than a day every 4 years and which also means we have to skip a leap year every so often (the year 1900AD was not a leap year for example, though 1896 and 1904 were).

I have to say that I find it quite extraordinary that the figure of 1461 years has continued to be quoted and used by Egyptologists right up to the present day.[12] The correct figure is 1507 years, and as you will see this makes an appreciable difference to the dating of ancient history.

To return to the *Ebers Papyrus*: it contains a year date, Year 9 of a pharaoh known to us as Amenophis I,[13] and it was believed that the document also referred to the 'heliacal rising' (appearance just before dawn) of the bright star Sirius on the 9th day of the 3rd month of the dry season. Sirius was important to the Egyptians; its heliacal rising occurs on around July 19th (depending on which part of Egypt you are in) and heralds the arrival of the Nile flood, so vital for Egyptian agriculture. Now, as it happens, in a much later document written by the Roman author Censorinus in the 3rd Century AD, there is reference to the heliacal rising of Sirius having occurred on the 1st day of the 1st month of the flood season in the year 139AD. If true, this means that the calendar matched reality in 139AD. Working this through, but using the erroneous 1461 year period for the journey through the seasons (known as a 'Great Sothic Year' after Sothis, the Greek name for Sirius), it was thought that Year 9 of Amenophis I had to have been the year 1542BC (or else a millennium and a half earlier). Here then was another and much earlier anchor to history. There have since been arguments as to exactly where the observations might have been made from – and the difference translates to a commonly quoted date of 1517BC – but in principle the dating derived in this way (known as Sothic dating) has ruled ever since. As a confidence-boosting bonus, this date seemed to tie in pretty well with those that Assyriologists were working to based on the *Assyrian king list*. Of course, if the correct length of the Great Sothic Year is used then the date for Year 9 of pharaoh Amenophis I would have to be amended, to something between 1568 and 1593BC depending on your view of the most likely observation point for Sirius, and the tie-up with Assyria then becomes much less convincing.

The *Ebers Papyrus* has since been supplemented by another found at El Lahun in the Faiyum region of Middle Egypt, appearing to refer to the heliacal rising of Sothis/Sirius and giving a day and month which were thought to translate to 1872BC (1933BC with the correct Sothic cycle length). The *El Lahun Papyrus* is dated to Year 7 of an unnamed monarch; however, Sesostris III is the usual choice made by historians, based on the form of the characters used in the script.[14] Here, then, was another anchor – and it tied in acceptably well with the *Ebers Papyrus* date. Please don't worry if you have no idea at this stage who these characters were; I simply want to get across the way that Egyptian history has been 'constructed'. Please also forgive me if the versions I use for the names of the various personalities I introduce are not the ones you are used to. It is particularly true of Egyptian names that numerous variant English renderings exist.

Anyway, having obtained a supposed absolute date as far back as 1872BC, it was just a matter of filling in the gaps with reference to the king lists and the texts on monuments and papyri. Compared to what could be deduced for other parts of the ancient world, Egyptian history became very confidently dated indeed, and the basic chronology established by means of these anchor points has remained dominant for over 100 years. Of course, with such confidence in Egyptian chronology, all other histories for peoples around the Near East and Middle East have naturally had to be tied back to Egyptian history in order to determine absolute dates. Thus, the discovery of a large cache of inscribed tablets, basically diplomatic correspondence, at El Amarna in middle Egypt meant that the histories of Babylon, Assyria, the Hittite lands and Palestine were anchored to Egypt at that point, with conventionally assigned dates of 1360 to 1320BC, representing the reigns of pharaohs Amenophis III and Akhenaten, the authors or recipients of the correspondence.

Quite commonly, of course, the details of ancient history have to be deduced without the help of written records. Archaeology reveals the remains of generation after generation of human habitation thanks to our enduring habit of never throwing things away properly. Ancient cities are basically great rubbish heaps rising ever higher from their foundations as each new generation builds on the rubbish of their predecessors. Archaeologists painstakingly sift through the debris, piecing together fragments of pottery and stone and building up a picture of life through the ages. By taking careful note of the types of pottery, architecture, weaponry etc found at each level of a site, it is possible to relate the type of find to a particular period and in this way to cross-reference between sites. But, for absolute dates, everything still has to relate back to Egypt. Most useful are inscribed texts, whether on pottery, weapons, monuments or tablets. So, when excavators at Megiddo in northern Israel found a victory stela of Shoshenq I, they should have been able to date the level from which it came to the time of that pharaoh. Unfortunately they found it in a dump from earlier excavation! They were more fortunate with a silver pen case bearing the name of pharaoh Ramesses III.

Question Time

I guess the point I am trying to make is pretty obvious. If so much depends on Egyptian history we had better be absolutely sure we have got it right! For a century the general correctness of Egyptian history was rarely questioned, which I find impressive testimony in itself – but it is certainly being questioned now; in fact, it seems to be 'open season' nowadays on traditional Egyptology! The reliance on Sothic dating has been quietly eroded for several decades. The need to revise dates upwards in line with the correct Sothic cycle length is particularly embarrassing and has not been widely acknowledged; scholars working on the histories of nations reliant on cross-checks with Egyptian history certainly do not seem to have been informed. The preferred course among Egyptologists has been to deny the need to rely on Sothic dating at all. Besides incorrect mathematics, a further fundamental problem lies in the *Ebers* and *El Lahun papyri* themselves. If the *Ebers Papyrus* only had two lines (one to give the king's name and the year of his reign and one to tell us about the date of the heliacal rising of Sirius) we would probably be happy, but the problem is the next 11 lines, which appear to repeat the phrase "going forth of Sothis" – i.e. Sirius – for each month of the year (using ancient Egyptian 'ditto' marks).[15] As many have pointed out, this makes a nonsense of the traditional interpretation. It has also been remarked that the date in question, the 9th day of the 3rd month of the dry season, just happens to be the anniversary of Amenophis I's coronation, which suggests that, though the year may be in some way special, there is no additional significance in the date. The *El Lahun Papyrus* is more straightforward – assuming that the unnamed king at the time really was Sesostris III – and the traditional explanation therefore more reasonable, except that the same phrase, "going forth of Sothis", is used; and if it doesn't refer to a heliacal rising in the *Ebers Papyrus* what's to say that it does in the *El Lahun Papyrus*? Some have suggested, quite reasonably, that the expression relates to a ceremonial event, particularly since the *El Lahun Papyrus* was part of a temple register.[16] Unsurprisingly, Egyptologists who now 'do not rely on Sothic dating' still tend to maintain basically the same actual dates as before, claiming that internal dating provided by the available documents is now sufficient to give the same level of confidence as previously, which I have to say is a very typical academic reaction, probably a very typical human reaction, but unfortunately is quite untrue! By the way, the level of confidence claimed for Egyptian history is commonly of the order of 5 years back to the early 2nd Millennium BC, rising to 20 years or so for the 3rd Millennium.

The identification of Shoshenq I as 'Shishak' has been less frequently questioned, even by those who would rather not rely on anything from such a controversial source as the Bible. However, in this case the problem is not so much the Bible as the Shoshenq inscription at Karnak. As I intimated above, it is now recognised that there is no reference to Judah or Jerusalem on the wall in question, although it is clear from the list of towns given that Shoshenq must have passed close by. For many, an indirect reason for continuing to believe in the identity of Shoshenq I and Shishak is that Shoshenq's immediate successor, Osorkon I, who came to the throne a year or two after the Palestine campaign, managed to dedicate (to various Egyptian temples) 170 Tons of gold and 210 Tons of silver, according to an inscription at Bubastis in the Nile delta. One wonders where this vast wealth could have come from in those days, unless it was recovered as booty. In support, the Bible says first that Solomon was the wealthiest ruler of his time (measuring gold income in tens of Tons per year) and secondly that Shishak "took everything". The supposition is that Shishak/Shoshenq was 'paid off', which could just explain why his Palestinian campaign appears to have been waged mainly against the northern kingdom of Israel rather than the kingdom of Judah where Jerusalem was located. Plausible? Maybe; but I for one remain to be convinced.

With such low confidence nowadays in Sothic dating and some disturbing discrepancies between Shoshenq's and Shishak's campaigns, I hope you will agree that Egyptian history is now in a very fragile state. It is like a building whose main columns have corroded away completely and which is now held up solely by a mass of additional brickwork! If the bricks have been soundly placed, then the edifice may yet remain standing; if not, disaster looms – and a disaster for Egyptian history would reverberate around the whole of the ancient Near and Middle East, forcing a rewriting of histories from Greece to Iran. The stakes are high; treasured parallels with events in the Bible are at risk. Egyptology is now a battle ground.

So what can we trust? I have no problem with the Assyrian evidence back to the accession of king Adad Nirari II in 911BC, with trustworthy correlations to both Babylonian and Israelite history in the 9th Century BC. Real certainty in Egyptian history, however, is only possible back to the year 664BC, at which point it is underpinned by Assyrian evidence. If we want to go further back with any confidence, it is obviously going to be extremely important to know just what else we can believe. The next chapter is therefore a crucial one. In it I will be taking a good hard look at the various rival methods of absolute dating on offer, methods such as Carbon 14 dating, tree rings and astronomical retro-calculation, before deciding just what should and should not be trusted.

3

The Dating Game

Carbon 14 Dating

The use of C14 dating has transformed archaeology since the technique first came in during the 1950's. When Kathleen Kenyon, one of the most famous of the archaeologists of Palestine, neared the base of the great mound of Tell Es-Sultan, otherwise known as Jericho, she found yet another city wall and watchtower, together with well-built circular houses. She had gone down through successive Middle and Early Bronze Age city layers, then a so-called proto-Urban period, followed by a couple of quite distinct Neolithic (i.e. Late Stone Age) towns. Next, surprisingly, came a level of rather more impressive development, certainly as far as the building structures went, although these were now times before the appearance of even hand-made pottery. And here, lower still, was an even earlier town, but still one with a significant wall and tower. But when might this town have actually been inhabited? It would be possible to arrive at a crude estimate based on the number of construction levels, making some allowance for periods, one probably of over a hundred years, when the site appeared not to have been occupied at all judging from the erosion that had clearly taken place. But, most fortunately for us, one of the houses during the several-hundred-year period of occupation of this earliest town at Jericho had burnt down, leaving a charcoal deposit, ideal for the newly-introduced technique of C14 dating. The result was a jaw-dropping 6850BC,[1] a figure which would now be rounded up (i.e. become even older) quite significantly by a procedure known as 'calibration'. In fact, Kenyon was able to date an even earlier deposit (7800BC uncalibrated) from a period when the site was used by people dwelling in rudimentary shelters rather than permanent houses. There is no doubt about it; C14 dating has made a big difference – but can it really be trusted?

The principle is sound enough. During their life-time, growing plants absorb two different isotopes of carbon from the atmosphere, known as Carbon 12 and Carbon 14 (C12 and C14), the '12' and '14' referring to their different atomic weights.[2] The relative quantities of the two isotopes depend on the prevailing conditions in the Earth's atmosphere. However, as soon as an organism dies, the already small C14 fraction starts to decay. This process occurs at a known rate, the quantity of C14 halving every 5730 years, which means that, by measuring the present ratio of C14 to C12, the time since death can be established. The only slight unknown is the initial ratio in the atmosphere whilst the organism was alive. However, to a first approximation this problem can be ignored and today's conditions can be assumed to have prevailed in the past also. This gives the un-calibrated dates quoted above. William Libby of Chicago University, who developed the technique, found an extremely impressive match from tests on various artefacts from Egypt between their (uncalibrated) C14-dated ages and 'known' Egyptian history.[3]

One has to be a little careful in interpreting the results of course. The time resulting from the analysis is the time since the organism died, not necessarily the time since a particular structure burnt down. It is reasonable to assume that timber would be used and reused, as it is today, before reaching the end of its useful life. Thus, the date of a structure may be significantly more recent than the C14 date would indicate. C14 dating of such products as seeds would, however, be expected to give a realistic date since they would not be stored for long between cropping and usage.

Tree Ring Dating and C14 Calibration

So, in principle, C14 dating is a really useful tool in the archaeologist's armoury. Indeed, it should be even more useful nowadays because of the calibration which is possible based on tree ring evidence. Tree ring studies have become a key part of the dating process. We all know that a tree forms an annual ring during each growing season as it spurts during the summer and rests during the winter. You probably also know that trees can live to a ripe old age – several thousand years for the Californian Redwood and the Bristlecone Pine for example. Trees can be 'cored' non-destructively these days, recovering a thin cylinder of wood right through to the heart of the tree without doing any significant damage. Similarly, tree rings can be obtained from dead bits of wood wherever they can be found and, for really ancient times, this often means at the bottom of a peat bog, where they are preserved from decay by the combination of chemicals in the peat, a sort of embalming fluid for trees.[4] In fact you may have seen or read something of 'bog bodies', remarkably preserved corpses from two or three thousand years ago who for one reason or another (usually human sacrifice) ended up in a peat bog. It seems the embalming effect works for both humans and trees. The trick with ancient bits of timber, wherever they come from, is to match up the sequences of tree rings from different sources according to how thick each ring is (the better the growing season, the thicker the ring), on the assumption that a poor growing season for one tree would probably be reflected in a poor growing season for all trees of that species in that region.[5]

This process has now been conducted on several species of tree from different parts of the world and a master sequence of rings developed for each. This is useful in its own right since any fresh piece of timber which appears – for example timbers from a ship found at the bottom of the Mediterranean Sea – could in theory be dated with reference to the appropriate sequence. This exact scenario in fact occurred in 1994 and it has been claimed that samples from a shipwreck can be dated from their combined ring sequence to 1316BC, almost precisely.[6] The samples, one from the ship itself, the other from the cargo, were retrieved from a wreck off the coast of Turkey which also contained a scarab (beetle shaped ornament) with the cartouche (an oval with a name inside, used by Egyptian royalty) of Nefertiti, the wife of the 18th Dynasty pharaoh Akhenaten. If the date is correct then I am sure you can appreciate the significance of this finding; it gives us a much needed time anchor in the middle of the 2nd Millennium BC. However, this particular claim is, in my view, quite spurious – which is unfortunate to say the least since the claim now seems to have developed a momentum of its own, appearing in text after text as proven fact! The most significant problem (of several[7]) is that cedar of unknown provenance but most likely Lebanon is being compared to pine from central Turkey; there is absolutely no hope of a genuine match! The same fundamental objections must be levelled at claims that charred oak specimens from a Hittite fort on the Euphrates river can be dated to 1101BC with reference to the same Turkish pine sequence.[8] In fact, my advice is: don't even think of trusting any tree ring dating claim from the Middle East region unless it specifically relates to pine wood specimens from Turkey – which unfortunately leaves us with very little to go on.

Never mind; let's return to C14 dating. Genuine, reliable interpretation of tree rings, wherever they might be found, gives the opportunity to develop a planet-wide calibration for C14 dates. Once the age of a certain specimen of wood is determined from its rings, the same specimen can be subjected to C14 dating and the results compared. The tree ring determined age can be taken as exact, providing an adjustment factor for the C14 date. The result, now that many such comparisons have been made, is a calibration line, albeit one which seems to jump around quite a bit, presumably a consequence of fluctuating atmospheric carbon conditions through the ages. Generally speaking, the calibration doesn't have much effect on C14 dates from the last 2000 years. There is then increasing divergence such that C14 dates become significantly older after calibration. For example, a 'raw' C14 date of 2000BC would be calibrated to around 2300BC.

This is all excellent science and should provide a really first class dating system. Unfortunately many ancient historians find themselves quite unable to trust it! For a start, the excellent agreement obtained by William Libby when he compared his original C14 dates with 'known' historical dates from ancient Egypt becomes decidedly *less* excellent after calibration. And archaeologists continue to experience quite inexplicable results. Let me give you an example. David Ussishkin was the archaeologist excavating Lachish, an important town in southern Palestine, during the 1970s.[9] It was a successful excavation, leading to a pretty clear picture of occupation at the site through the Bronze and Iron Ages. Particularly clear were the levels relating to destructions of the city by Nebuchadnezzar II of Babylon in 588BC and by Sennacherib of Assyria in 701BC, both very well established dates. Samples of charred wood were analysed from each destruction level, giving uncalibrated dates of 880 and 990BC respectively (mismatches of 292 and 289 years). On calibration, the dates became 1048 and 1187BC (mismatches of 460 and 486 years). Uncalibrated, the mismatch is nearly 300 years and calibration only seems to make it worse! Of course some or all of this discrepancy could in theory be explained by the timbers already being hundreds of years old when they were burnt, but it nevertheless exemplifies the frustration felt by archaeologists at the unreliability of C14 dates.

Recognising anomalous results like these, a project known as the Pyramids Radiocarbon Dating Project was launched in 1984.[10] In this study organic material (straw, reed fragments and charcoal) was analysed, which had been obtained from various of the tombs and pyramids built for the pharaohs of the Egyptian Old Kingdom (3rd Millennium BC). The first round of results produced an inexplicable average discrepancy of 374 years compared to the traditionally accepted chronology of Egypt, the (calibrated) C14 dates being much older than the traditional chronology would suggest. A second round of testing in 1995, including material from Middle Kingdom (early 2nd Millennium BC) sites, produced further wildly inconsistent results. Admittedly, the Middle Kingdom data was, on average, much closer to expectations, but that for the Old Kingdom was still coming out significantly too old – according to conventional wisdom. Not only so, but there was a high level of scatter in the results from any one site.

Let me state my position. I am firmly on the side of the ancient historians. C14 dating most definitely has a problem! The good news is that the source of the problem has, I believe, now been identified[11] – although I am not sure it has yet been widely accepted, perhaps partly because it is not at all easy to understand. Let me try to explain. The key issue seems to be that the C12:C14 ratio in the atmosphere varies not only through the centuries but also according to location. Specifically, the interaction between the oceans and the atmosphere is an important element in the carbon cycle. In most of the world's oceans, the water slowly circulates, which means that no water mass remains in the depths for more than a few hundred years before making it back to the surface. However, that is not always the case in inland seas. It is not the case in the Black Sea today and, from about 8500 to 4500BC, it was not the case in the eastern Mediterranean. Water at depth simply stagnated[12] and one result was a steadily reducing C14 content. Then, from about 4500BC, the waters of the eastern Mediterranean started to circulate once more, feeding low-C14 carbon into the atmosphere above and affecting the C14 content in carbon in all living organisms in that part of the world. Organic matter would have appeared to be old even while it was still alive! Naturally this would lead to overestimation of age based on C14 dating, and the effect apparently continued for several millennia while the low-C14 water slowly worked its way out of the system. Douglas Keenan, who formulated this explanation, estimates that 'normal service' was only resumed from about 1000BC.

It is hard to overstate the importance of this issue for archaeologists. If Keenan is right, then the awe in which C14 dates are held by many is badly misplaced! And the consequence is that we should expect erroneously (but unquantifiably) high C14 dates all around the eastern Mediterranean during a key phase of ancient history. This will be hard for experts to accept – but it certainly explains results such as those from the Pyramids Radiocarbon Dating Project.[13]

So, if we can't trust C14 dates, and I have also warned against believing any tree ring date from the Middle East, is there anything we can trust?

Ice Cores, Volcanoes and the Eruption of Thera

Fortunately there are other techniques besides C14 dating and tree rings. Another of the Earth's absolute dating systems is found in the ice caps of Greenland and Antarctica. Ice caps are like giant white tree ring series[14]. The appearance of the ice varies depending on the amount of snow lost to evaporation, which in turn depends on the season at the time the snow fell. This makes it possible to pick out annual bands in much the same way as annual rings in trees. The count cannot be considered as accurate as that for tree rings as the distinction between bands is less marked. Depending on the exact weather conditions during a season, there may even be two bands or, if little snow falls, none at all. None the less, the vast majority of years are thought to be accurately represented. Several cores have now been extracted from the ice sheets of both Greenland and Antarctica to depths measured in kilometres and they have been analysed for all manner of things. For example, tiny bubbles formed within the ice are preserved and contain minute samples of the atmosphere at the time the ice was formed. So, for instance, we can check on carbon dioxide levels over tens of thousands of years. However, for our purposes the key measurement is the acidity level within the ice. There is a definite correlation between high acidity and the occurrence of volcanic eruptions. For example an acidity peak is regularly found in around 44BC, the year in which Plutarch states that: "the sun rose pale and without radiance". This suggests some kind of dust veil in the atmosphere, a phenomenon associated with major volcanic eruptions. Similarly, Chinese records give unusual quantities of snow in April of that year and a "pale blue sun that cast no shadows".[15] But the clinching evidence comes from tree rings; the American Bristle Cone Pine series shows narrow bands and summer frost damage for the years 44 through to 41BC.[16]

Now, interesting though the 44BC event is, it doesn't really add much to our historical knowledge. The same is true of a similar event in 208BC, showing a similar coincidence of evidence from ice cores, tree rings and both Chinese and European records. However, earlier ice core acidity peaks in approximately 1120 and 1645BC which, given the error margin in ice core interpretation, may plausibly be associated with tree ring events in 1159 and 1628BC, could be more useful. Some experts believe that both dates are also supported by dust cloud observations in China. The speculation for the ancient historian is, of course, whether either event relates to the violent eruption of the Greek island of Thera, known to have occurred at some time in the 2nd Millennium BC. Archaeological excavations on what is left of the island (now known as Santorini) have uncovered a major Bronze Age town, Akrotiri, buried almost intact in a similar way to the Roman cities of Herculaneum and Pompeii, which were buried by ash from Mount Vesuvius in 79AD. And the message from the archaeologists is as clear as daylight; Akrotiri was abandoned, presumably because of volcanic activity, stuffed full of what is known as 'Late Minoan 1a' pottery but with no 'Late Minoan 1b'. In Egypt, according to most researchers, though with the notable exception of Sturt Manning, the same types of Late Minoan 1a pottery can be found up until the time of the 18th Dynasty pharaoh Tuthmose III,[17] giving an eruption date, according to the conventional chronology of Egypt, of around 1450BC. But, if the eruption of Thera was proved to be large enough to have caused the same sort of effects as seen in 44BC and 208BC, then we would have no option but to re-date the whole of Egyptian history, either upward to match the 1628BC date or downward to match 1159BC. Expert after expert has stood up and stated that the eruption must indeed have been large enough, based on the sheer size of the remaining under-sea crater, but experts have been wrong before – I sometimes wonder whether a pronouncement by an expert isn't the kiss of death! Anyway, adherents to more conventional thinking can always draw comfort from the fact that lesser ice core acidity peaks have been noted in 1594, 1454, 1327 and 1284BC,[18] giving enough alternative options to suit almost every palette!

Undoubtedly the most common view taken by those vulcanologists who have looked into the Thera question has been that a date of 1628BC is the most plausible, although a statement by researchers analysing ice cores that volcanic glass fragments found in a layer of ice dated approximately to 1623BC (close enough to 1628BC considering the expected error in ice layer recognition) "could not have come from Thera" is beginning to change a few minds.[19] In any case, most ancient historians resist the 1628BC identification resolutely. There is no way they could find enough history to pad out the extra couple of centuries. The leading alternative of 1159BC is rejected even more firmly by most, although with the keen exception of David Rohl. For him, 1159BC is not bad. However, for most historians there is only one conclusion to draw and that is that neither the 1159BC nor the 1628BC event can represent the Thera eruption. They would be most likely to grab the 1454BC option despite the acidity peak being lower and the lack of any noticeable associated tree ring evidence. Perhaps I should add that most of the calibrated C14 dates from Akrotiri (some of them from short-lived species) range from about 1530 to 1630BC[20] – but this of course only makes archaeologists suspect that the real date is rather more recent! The bottom line seems to be that ice cores can only be expected to provide approximate supporting evidence, not the kind of firm date we need in order to reconstruct history with confidence.

Ocean Sediments

Yet another dating technique derives from cores taken through ocean floor deposits. The exact make-up of the sediments can be evaluated, for example for the mix of different crustacean species which are found and the chemical composition of their shells, and conclusions made regarding ocean temperature and salinity and, consequently, climate. There may even be debris dropped from melting icebergs or ash layer deposits from volcanic eruptions. The Thera ash deposits are particularly clear right across the eastern part of the Mediterranean but unfortunately not in a context which can be accurately dated. However, a potentially significant finding related to our understanding of ancient history is that a severe climatic shift began to take place around the year 2200BC, leading to the probability of drier conditions across much of the region under consideration in this book.[21] It is rather a vague point though and hardly likely to help us much with accurate dating. We could really do with something more precise…….

Sothic Dating

……which brings me back to the method originally used to establish Egyptian history, namely Sothic dating. As I have already indicated, it appears to have been more or less shelved by Egyptologists because of the uncertainties in the meaning of the *Ebers* and *El Lahun papyri*. However, I can see no justification whatsoever for shelving the concept. If the Roman historian Censorinus was correct in his assertion that 139AD marked the beginning of a new 'Great Sothic Year', when the official calendar once more matched the real seasons, then the previous one would have started 1507 years earlier (using the correct cycle length), which would be 1369BC (there was no Year 0); and the one before that would have started in 2876BC. There is every reason to utilise the system as a means of deriving absolute dates but it is necessary firstly to use the correct Great Sothic Year length and secondly to find inscriptions whose meaning is clear. If such inscriptions can be found however, then Sothic dating provides an immensely powerful tool and one which it would be foolish to ignore.

Astronomical Retro-Calculation

Finally, I would like to introduce what should be a highly fruitful source of absolute dates, astronomical observation, and for this I am thoroughly indebted to the excellent work of Wayne Mitchell for his retro-calculations relating to eclipses and lunar month lengths (whether 29 or 30 days).[22] Now, eclipses of the moon affect half the planet at the same time and so are seen relatively frequently; we are therefore forced to give them much less weight than other types of observation because there is almost always more than one possible date to choose from. Solar eclipses on the other hand affect much smaller areas and are therefore much less commonly seen as well as being much more dramatic (and therefore much more likely to be recorded). I have already illustrated their potential by referring to the eclipse which occurred on the day of the battle between the Medes and Lydians in 585BC, and another recorded both in the *Assyrian Limmu list* and in *Ptolemy's Canon* and dated to 763BC. All we need therefore is adequate documentation of such events, preferably together with dating information such as reference to the reign of a particular king. Failing such dating information, we at least need the archaeological context of the 'document' concerned.

Mitchell reports two sets of early solar eclipse calculations. I'll quote one here to illustrate both the power of the method and also the difficulties. It relates to an eclipse seen at the port city of Ugarit on the coast of Syria and described in a tablet found in the ruins of a palace there. The archaeological context is 'Late Bronze IIa' (archaeologists divide major eras like the Late Bronze Age into numerous sub-divisions), conventional dates for which would be about 1400 to 1350BC. As is often the case, variant translations of the tablet have been offered, but all agree that it states that "in the month of Hiyaru the sun went down '*b-t-t*', its gate-keeper was Rashap". Now since the sun 'goes down' every day, it is presumed that the reference in this case is to an eclipse and some suggest that the word *b-t-t*[23] should be translated *was put to shame*. This would reinforce the impression of an eclipse and allow *went down* to refer to the eclipse occurring at sunset. Others prefer the equally possible meaning of *at the sixth hour* (i.e. at midday) for *b-t-t*. Furthermore, there is a choice of months for *Hiyaru*, either February/March if an Egyptian-based calendar was in use or April/May following the Babylonian calendar![24] Finally, *Rashap* is usually identified as the planet Mars although some have suggested Venus. Mitchell has identified five possible eclipses, dated to 1375, 1223, 1138, 1084 and 1012BC. Clearly 1375BC (3rd of May) would match conventional thinking acceptably well, but it suffers from the drawback that the eclipse occurred just after dawn and that neither Mars nor Venus were anywhere near. Mitchell selects 1012BC (9th of May) since it is the only one which occurred near sunset and Mars, along with Jupiter and Mercury, would not have been far away. The most likely alternative appears to be 1223BC (5th of March), a midday eclipse first proposed by de Jong and van Soldt[25] when Mars would have been very close indeed – some would say invisible due to the sun's corona, but that remains speculation. The other two options were also midday eclipses (approximately) but in neither case was Mars or Venus particularly close. The Late Bronze IIa context of the tablet puts it at a time when Ugarit lay broadly within the Egyptian cultural sphere, which suggests to me that March 1223BC is marginally the more likely date since it relates to *Hiyaru* according to an Egyptian-based system. However, you can see from the ongoing disagreement that it is not possible to be 100% certain either way.

I am also aware that we have to treat astronomical retro-calculations with a little caution. However brilliant the mathematics used, the calculations rely on correct assumptions regarding such matters as the gradual slowing of the Earth's rotation (a matter highlighted by Mitchell) and the slight fluctuation in the path of the Earth's orbit around the sun, not to mention the not insignificant change in tilt of the Earth's axis. All these are thought to be understood sufficiently but, particularly in the case of solar eclipse predictions, the calculations are highly sensitive to all such factors.

However, there is one further type of observation which lends itself to retro-calculation with a fairly high degree of confidence and that is the length of a lunar month. The real average length is approximately 29.55 days, which means that an observer on Earth will either record a 29 or a 30 day month length depending on whether the new moon is just visible or not quite visible on the 29th night. Now, a single observation is clearly useless. However, a series of observations can be extremely useful so long as we can work out their relative chronology and this is possible where such observations are dated with the year and month of a particular king's reign. It is a little bit like the probability of guessing a sequence of heads and tails when tossing a coin. If you get one right, that's no big deal; even four or five correct guesses on the trot could easily be just coincidence. But if you guessed correctly ten times in a row I would suspect that you really knew something. Similarly if a set of ten predicted lunar month lengths matches observations when a particular year is assumed, then I would have to concede that the year chosen is quite likely to be correct. However, 'quite likely' is as far as I could go since the lunar month length sequence is not really as random as tossing a coin. There is a pattern to the observations which means that a very similar though not quite identical sequence appears every few years and that a set of many more than ten observations is needed to achieve a high level of confidence, preferably over a period of several decades. However, as we shall see in due course, it seems that two such observation sequences have indeed survived, from two different eras and two different parts of the Middle East.

The dating game is getting more promising!

Summary

That is just about as far as I think we can go in terms of absolute dating using scientific techniques. I have summarised what I see as the potential of each technique in the following table.

The conclusion is clear. Since we really need precise data – even ± 50 years just isn't good enough – *Sothic dating* and *astronomical retro-calculation* are the methods that hold out the greatest hope. The dating of worldwide climatic events using *tree rings* may also be helpful. We cannot realistically expect other techniques, including C14 dating, to give anything more than approximate supporting evidence.

OK; we now know what to believe; but the question is: where to start? Before the accession of king Adad Nirari II of Assyria in 911BC my canvas is completely blank. I need some fixed date to build on, preferably a precise date. Most fortunately I believe such a date exists and that it can be found not long after the founding of the Egyptian Empire under the kings of the so-called 1st Dynasty. That, therefore, is where my journey has to begin.

Technique	Precise (± 5 years)		Approximate (± 50 years)		Very Approximate (± 500 years)	
	Local events	World-wide events	Local events	World-wide events	Local events	World-wide events
C14 (before about 1000BC)					✓	
C14 (after about 1000BC)			✓			
Tree Rings	don't trust!	✓				
Ice Cores				✓		
Ocean Floor Deposits				✓		
Sothic Dating	✓					
Astronomical Retro-calculation	✓					

I hope you enjoy the story which unfolds. While my underlying purpose is to get the dates right, I also want to give you a flavour of events in these ancient times. I want to take you through times of peace and war, of stability and collapse, of boom and bust. I hope to show you that people were essentially exactly the same then as now. There never was any golden era of peace and harmony; nor was there any age of savagery and deprivation. The struggle between good and evil, sense and foolishness is as old as human nature itself.

Let's pick the story up in the year 3000BC.

4

Let There Be Light: 3000–2500BC

Egypt is Born

Ancient Egypt was always two lands. Throughout the millennia of pharaonic rule, the country was subdivided into Upper (i.e. southern) and Lower (i.e. northern) Egypt. The chief symbol of royal power was the so-called 'double crown', an amalgam of the white crown of Upper Egypt and the red crown of Lower Egypt. And these were very ancient symbols indeed. The red crown appears on pottery and in rock art from the 4th Millennium BC.[1] The ancestry of the white crown is less clear – it may even have been a foreign import[2] – but what is clear is that kingly authority operated in both Lower and Upper Egypt from well before the first unified state.

I am going to dive straight in at the very close of the 4th Millennium BC, a period which archaeologists know as 'Naqada III'. Firstly, how do we know the date? In truth, we don't – not precisely. For such times, a lot of reliance has to be placed on C14 dates, of which a few have been published from the Naqada I-III phases from both Upper and Lower Egypt. In the case of Lower Egypt, situated close to the eastern Mediterranean, I expect the dates to be artificially high for the reasons given in the last chapter, but Upper Egyptian dates should be more trustworthy and I certainly feel able to use the rather vague expression 'at the very close of the 4th Millennium BC' with reasonable confidence.[3]

There were two Egypts because two different languages and cultures inhabited the two lands.[4] We don't have proper written records from these times, just early pictographs and, in Upper Egypt, the first few hieroglyphs, but historical lin-

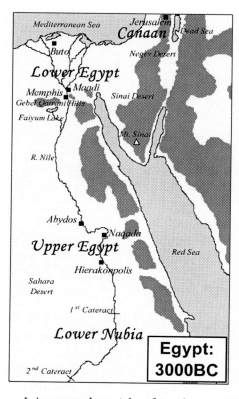

guistics, the study of the spread of languages across the planet, combined with archaeological evidence, lets us know that the people of Lower Egypt in those days were 'Semitic'; their language and culture were related to those of Palestine, the land known in ancient times as Canaan. We can see this relationship archaeologically; Nile delta sites such as Maadi and Buto show strong similarities with sites in Palestine, with a similar agricultural economy. In contrast, the language of Upper Egypt was directly ancestral to that of pharaonic times. It had arrived from the west, from the Sahara, in days when the Sahara was fertile grassland supporting herds of elephant, giraffe, ostrich etc, very like the plains of East Africa today, and unsurprisingly therefore Upper Egyptian culture was strongly pastoralist.[5]

It is easy to lose sight of just how civilised human society was in those days. There is a tendency to equate lack of writing with lack of everything else, but this is far from correct. Houses, palaces and temples had been constructed for thousands of years; stone, timber and, where appropriate, mud-brick architecture was well developed. So was agricultural production. So, undoubtedly, was state organisation. Just because we don't have names or records, just because tools and weapons were still mainly made of wood and stone,[6] we must never lose sight of the fact that the principal component of society, mankind, was pretty much exactly the same animal as you or I today. While archaeology can only reveal the remains of towns and villages, giving us clues as to the general economy, we can be quite sure that these remains conceal the fact that kings, nobles, priests and civic authorities governed the population, armies were recruited and fought battles, laws were made and lawyers were probably paid handsomely to administer them! We should also not be deceived into forgetting the international dimension. Certainly long-distance travel was a serious undertaking; equally certainly it was common-place. We can see the evidence for this in Naqada III Egypt, in Buto in the north and also in Upper Egypt. In both regions several distinctly Mesopotamian (i.e. Iraqi) artefacts and influences have been unearthed. In Buto, architectural practices, notably the use of terracotta cones for exterior decoration, have been uncovered which directly parallel those of the city of Uruk, then the leading city in southern Iraq. In Upper Egypt, the 'Jebel-el-Arak knife' is the best known of several artefacts which are clearly of Uruk style. So, if nothing else, this is evidence of trade and communication over surprisingly long distances. And how could such trade have been achieved? No real problem; by long-distance donkey![7]

In reconstructing history, cross-cultural connections such as these are invaluable. It isn't possible to date these Uruk-style artefacts with any precision, but it certainly is possible to state that they are typical of the stage in Uruk's long and distinguished history known as Uruk III.[8] This was a particularly exciting period of development as it happens, since the very first writing had recently appeared in Iraq, initially just symbols representing commodities used in trade (e.g. sheep, bushels of wheat etc) together with a full set of numerals. In fact this earliest Uruk style of writing had already spread widely. The first script of Iran, usually termed 'proto-Elamite', was almost identical and its use has been revealed by archaeology to have stretched right across Iran to Afghanistan, presumably accompanying the then flourishing trade in precious stones. So it is an interesting coincidence that this Uruk influence was also present in both Upper and Lower Egypt just as the Egyptians themselves were making their own first attempts at writing.[9]

But can we be a little more specific about the date? Well, I believe so, but for that we have to take a few steps forward. In these earliest days of the written word, all we can see are a handful of rulers' names, barely readable, from the tombs of Upper Egypt, but things become rapidly clearer following the country's unification. Archaeologically, we know that Upper Egyptian culture spread steadily north during the second half of the 4th Millennium BC and that it finally took over the Nile delta, where Buto is situated, some time around the end of the millennium.[10] In terms of historical records, Manetho, the 3rd Century BC Egyptian chronicler, begins his history with the unification of the country under king 'Menes', the first king of the 1st Dynasty, usually equated by modern historians with the hieroglyphic name 'Aha', since the two names appear together on an ivory label from the tomb of Aha's mother Nithotep in Naqada in Upper Egypt. Aha was the founder of the city of Memphis – or at least a city very close to where Memphis would one day be. Under Aha, Egypt became for the first time a large, politically strong, unified empire.

Aha's successor was Djer and he too was evidently an able ruler. He extended Egyptian control down to the second Nile cataract, more or less the modern Egypt/Sudan border, thereby incorporating the land known as Lower Nubia into the Egyptian empire. And please don't think he was dealing with a bunch of uncivilised savages! Nubians shared close cultural ties with Upper Egyptians and they would certainly have had their own political organisations and armies, albeit on a smaller scale. However, the key point for this history comes from an ivory tablet of Djer's reign which, experts are reasonably confident, portrays the adoption of a solar calendar, the same famous Egyptian calendar which has led to so much grief in relation to the *Ebers* and *El Lahun papyri*. But, grief or not, this presents a golden opportunity for dating Djer's reign. As I said before, we can be quite sure that the calendar, when first introduced, matched the realities of Egyptian life, i.e. that Day 1 of the flood season really fell more or less at the time of year when the Nile flood actually commenced. In fact, it's pretty certain that Day 1 of the flood season in the calendar was chosen to coincide with the heliacal rising of Sothis, also represented on the same ivory tablet.[11] Furthermore, I find it hard to believe that the Egyptians ever forgot the official observation point for Sothis (it was almost certainly Memphis), in which case the start of the calendar must be dated to a multiple of 1507 years (the Great Sothic Year length) prior to 139AD, the date given by Censorinus as the start of another Great Sothic Year. Basically, this gives but one option; the Egyptian calendar began life in 2876BC, which means that Djer was on the throne in that year. I see no other realistic possibility.

Absolute date: 2876BC
Start of the Egyptian calendar, celebrated on an ivory tablet from the reign of Pharaoh Djer, second king of the 1st Dynasty

---

Now admittedly we can't be certain how long either Aha or Djer reigned since the different versions of Manetho's history disagree. However, the most believable reign lengths are the 30 and 27 years quoted by Eusebius,[12] which would put the start of Aha's reign some time a decade or so prior to 2900BC – say 2920BC. It's not a firm date, but the error margin is unlikely to be more than about 20 years, which is pretty good!

So why don't all historians make this very obvious link? The answer is that they can't. They know all about Djer's ivory tablet of course and they know about the Egyptian calendar. Unfortunately, almost all seem still to be labouring under the misapprehension that the length of the Great Sothic Year is 1461 years, which would give a date of 2784BC for the start of a Sothic cycle, but even 2876BC is much too late for most historians to think about accepting as a date within Djer's reign; the range 3100–3050BC is typically found in the literature.[13] Never mind; I have a blank canvas and an open mind, so I am quite prepared to accept 2876BC for Djer and to see where it leads. This, then, represents my first brush-stroke on my otherwise empty canvas! It represents the first ray of light illuminating the ancient history of the Middle East.

The Great City of Uruk

If, as I have suggested, Aha's reign commenced in about 2920BC, his predecessor Narmer who, Egyptologists agree, was the man that actually unified the country, ruled during the previous couple of decades or so[14] and the period of Uruk III evidence in Egypt is therefore datable from about 2950BC. It's far from precise, but we need all the help we can get when dating ancient history and at least this gives us a ball-park figure to work from in Iraq.

Let me say a word or two about Uruk. It was quite simply the most magnificent city on the planet and was clearly at the centre of a very extensive trading empire. So-called Uruk culture can be seen in archaeological layers from towns right across Iraq, northern Syria and southern Turkey as far as the Mediterranean, and a point remarked on by several researchers is just how uniform it is. Sometimes, 'mini-Uruks' were constructed as quarters in other cities. It all speaks for a considerable empire and I find it hard to believe that such an economic empire could possibly have been held together without actual military and governmental control. Perhaps the control was relatively loose, but I am sure that it was nevertheless real enough.

So who lived in Uruk? Well, the people were 'Sumerians', inhabitants of the land then known as 'Sumer', now southern Iraq. Sumerian was the first identifiable written language of Iraq. The earliest script appeared during the Uruk IV phase and consisted purely of symbols for commodities and numerals, so it could have been used to write almost any language, but that of the succeeding Uruk III period was different and clearly ancestral to the later Sumerian script. So

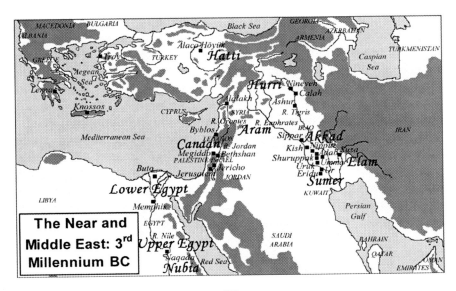

The Near and Middle East: 3rd Millennium BC

a reasonable question would be: just who were these clever people, the Sumerians, and where did they come from?

Unfortunately I am not sure that anyone can really answer that question. Archaeologically, Sumerian culture descends from that of the very first cities of southern Iraq, some of them founded before 5000BC (based on C14 dating evidence). Sumerian legends are all set in a land of plain and marsh – matching southern Iraq's geography. Linguistically, most would say that Sumerian is unrelated to any other tongue; I wouldn't go quite that far, but I would certainly agree that it had seen well over 10000 years of independent development. There can be little doubt that Sumerian was a truly ancient Middle Eastern language and culture, in contrast to Semitic which was then spreading eastwards and northwards from Palestine, having arrived a thousand years or so previously from northern Egypt.[15] The pre-eminence of Uruk itself began in about 3800BC, not necessarily with any sudden event but with a recognition that Uruk had become the strongest city in Sumer. I say "not necessarily with any sudden event", but we do know that an absolutely massive flood must have taken place at just about that time, the evidence for which was first uncovered by the renowned archaeologist Leonard Woolley at the city of Ur,[16] about 50 miles south-east of Uruk and, at that time, close to the waters of the Persian Gulf.[17] The flood deposits mark a clear boundary at Ur between an earlier culture known as 'Ubaid' and the onset of what has become known as Uruk culture, and it seems quite plausible that it was this flood which turned the political map of Sumer on its head. Ur and the former leading city of Eridu[18] may well have been much harder hit than other centres, giving the rulers of Uruk their chance to take over top spot.

Still, never mind Uruk's pedigree; the point is that much of the Middle East was, in Uruk III times, under the sway of the lords of Uruk and that Uruk influence was felt as far away as Egypt. By about 2900BC, based on my dates for Egypt, Uruk was absolutely at the zenith of its power, with magnificent temples, palaces and ziggurats. The great mound of the city, built up from generations of earlier construction and demolition waste, rose some 90 feet above the plain of the Euphrates river. The ruler of Uruk, whoever he or she was, was a very powerful individual indeed, who could call upon armies of labourers, artisans and soldiers.

But then things began to change; it would not be correct to term it a collapse – it was more of an economic down-turn. Why? Well, increased salinity of the land due to over-exploitation may be one reason, and we can see this in that whereas approximately equal quantities of wheat and barley were grown in the Uruk III period, this had become a 6:1 ratio in favour of the more salt-tolerant barley by the end of the 3rd Millennium BC.[19] However, increasing pressure from Semites, Hurrians and Hattians (see later in the chapter) was probably a more immediate cause. And the upshot of it all was that there was a steady loss of Uruk influence right across the region, which was of course reflected at Uruk it-

LET THERE BE LIGHT: 3000–2500BC

self by a loss of cash![20] Other cities began to dream of independence and, before long, those dreams were reality. The changing political scene is graphically illustrated by the fact that defensive city walls appear at Uruk in the second half of the Uruk III period. We are now entering a new archaeological era, known as 'Jemdet Nasr' after a particular site in southern Iraq, an era of reduced wealth, of increasing dilapidation at Uruk itself, and an era in which Iraqi cities such as Kish, Adab, Umma, Ur, Nippur and Sippar grew greatly, from glorified villages to genuine cities. And with the growth of rival cities came the inevitable competition and warfare. The Jemdet Nasr period, approximately 2850-2650BC according to this dating scheme,[21] is a confused time with no written historical records. It was a time of small city states, of shifting alliances and petty wars. And, as has tended to happen the world over in this sort of political environment, the number of 'players' was slowly whittled down as lesser cities finally acknowledged the overlordship of one or other of the larger states. It is best seen as a transitional period, and certainly one of reduced wealth compared to Uruk III days.

The Dynasties of Egypt

At Uruk and the other cities of Iraq we have archaeology but no significant records, and so no historical detail; in Egypt, however, we have real history. Manetho's king list gives an excellent framework and this is supplemented by increasing numbers of contemporary texts, both in stone and on papyrus. So, with the reigns of Aha and Djer established within reasonable error margins, we can now assign approximate dates for the next several kings (and one queen – Meryetnit) of Egypt. Admittedly, there is still plenty of scope for error because of the lack of agreement between sources but the following list broadly reflects main-stream opinion regarding reign lengths (although not absolute dates of course).

1st Dynasty:	Aha (Menes)	2920–2890BC	*first of Manetho's kings*
	Djer	2890–2863BC	*calendar adopted 2876BC*
	Meryetnit, Wadjit, Den, Anedjib, Semerkhet, Ka'a	2863–2700BC	
2nd Dynasty:	Hetepsekhemwy, Reneb, Nenetjer, Sekhamib, Sened, Neterka, Neferkara, Khasekhem, Khasekhemwy	2700–2520BC	
3rd Dynasty:	Nebka	2520–2500BC	

39

After Aha and Djer, the 1st Dynasty continued with six further rulers. The strong cultural difference between Upper and Lower Egypt is still apparent from archaeology, and each ruler had two separate tombs, one in the north and one in the south.[22] And the tombs bring us to a slightly disturbing feature, namely the number of subsidiary burials (sometimes over 100) in each tomb, which many have interpreted as sacrificial victims selected to accompany the monarch in the next life. Inevitably, many argue against this interpretation and we will certainly never know the truth, but I have to say that the sacrificial victim theory is the one I am inclined to believe. There is certainly plenty in later human history to remind us that otherwise civilised societies, for example the Phoenicians, can quite happily accommodate human sacrifice.

This was still a prosperous time. Although commercial contacts with Uruk came to an end soon after the start of the 1st Dynasty, doubtless due to the economic down-turn in Iraq, there was still plenty of trade with Canaan and the Lebanese coast. Throughout Egyptian history, Lebanon was a key source of timber and strong trade links were maintained with the port city of Byblos. But as we move into the 2nd Dynasty, friction between Upper and Lower Egypt seems to have increased to the point of civil war at times. The pot-luck of archaeology means that we have less information on the 2nd Dynasty than the 1st, but the general picture is one of decreased security, much reduced trade and, inevitably, less wealth to go round. It was only with the last 2nd Dynasty ruler, Khasekhemwy, that the land was properly re-united again under a strong, centralised leadership and prosperity returned once more. Egypt now stood at the threshold of one of the most incredible passages in all its long history, the age of the great pyramids. For now, however, we must leave the land of the Nile in the capable hands of Khasekhemwy's successor, Nebka, the first king of the 3rd Dynasty.[23]

The City States of Canaan

Although Egypt and Iraq were the two great cultural centres in the early 3rd Millennium BC, the lands where writing first took root, the rest of the region was hardly a cultural vacuum! Let me take you on a quick tour.

Canaan (i.e. Palestine) is the land in which much of the Bible is set – but not in the early 3rd Millennium BC. The Uruk III period coincides with the phase known to archaeologists as Early Bronze I in Palestine, giving way to Early Bronze II after the first phase of the Egyptian 1st Dynasty. Dates are based on correlations with Egypt; for example a type of jug with a fine burnished red glaze known as 'metallic ware' occurs both in Early Bronze II Palestine and in Egyptian tombs. This was a period during which the great Canaanite cities were in their formative phases. Cities such as Megiddo, Bethshan and Jericho had all been founded (or in some cases re-founded) during the so-called 'Proto-Urban' period at the end of the 4th Millennium BC, at which time the culture of Palestine paralleled that of northern Egypt,[24] and they continued to thrive throughout the Early Bronze I and II phases. The Canaanites were Semitic speakers, and we know from the fact that Semitic names and language would shortly appear right across Syria and Iraq that Semitic culture was a very successful one.

But then, in about 2600BC, everything changed. The settlement of Khirbet Kerak near the Sea of Galilee gives its name to a particular and very distinctive type of pottery which suddenly makes its appearance right across northern Palestine, marking a complete change in culture and the start of the Early Bronze III phase.[25] It is always accompanied by burning of the previous town's structures and is very clearly foreign in origin. For those who like to think that early humans were peace-loving folk and that war is a modern invention this evidence is unwelcome, as it most certainly indicates conquest by a hostile people. And we can trace the evidence of Khirbet Kerak ware north through western Syria and eastern Turkey over a period of many centuries. These invaders were the people we know as 'Hattians', descended from the inhabitants of the land known in ancient times as 'Hatti', now a large chunk of east-central Turkey.

South of the areas conquered by the Hattians, however, Canaanite society remained in charge and there is ongoing evidence of relations with Egypt. For example, at Et Tell near Jerusalem alabaster and stone bowls typical of the 2nd and 3rd Dynasties of Egypt appear in Early Bronze III layers.[26]

Hatti

Most people associate the land of Hatti with the people we call the 'Hittites' – but not in the 3rd Millennium BC. At that date, the cultural ancestors of the Hittites were still living in Europe, probably Romania or Bulgaria,[27] and no Hittite voice would be heard in Hatti for many hundreds of years. The people in residence during the 3rd Millennium BC were the makers of Khirbet Kerak ware, the people we call 'Hattians'. Since the 4th Millennium BC they had occupied the region south of the Caucasus Mountains (modern Georgia and Armenia) and then spread south and west.[28] We have fragments of Hattian language from later Hittite records, enough to suggest that Hattian and Hurrian (see below) were related languages. Archaeologically, the major settlement of Alaca Höyük, a little north of the later Hittite capital Hattusas, was certainly Hattian. To the south, on the upper reaches of the river Euphrates and also on the Amq plain near the mouth of the Orontes river, the archaeological sequence shows a long period during which Khirbet Kerak ware was in use before the arrival of Hurrian culture.[29] It may have been pressure from the Hurrians that then prompted the rather violent Hattian migration south into Palestine.

Hurri

Like Hattian, Hurrian language has no descendants today but is distantly related to those now spoken in the northern Caucasus (e.g. Chechen). However, I believe the evidence of archaeology is that both the Hurrians and the Hattians (and the Chechens) arrived from the east via northern Iran during the 4th Millennium BC. The Hurrians made their home in what is now northern Iraq, south-eastern Turkey and northern Syria.[30] Jumping to what would become the western limit of their domain, there is impressive continuity of culture at the city of Alalakh in southern Turkey from the time of its founding in the early 3rd Millennium BC (my estimate is 2900BC based on archaeological parallels with Uruk III and Jemdet Nasr)[31] until times for which real evidence of a Hurrian population is found. The logical conclusion is that even in Alalakh XVII, the lowest and therefore oldest level, the population was already Hurrian. In fact, it is clear from other excavations in the region that the founding of Alalakh represented the arrival of a new and highly cultivated people, introducing a period of relative wealth and prosperity to the area as well as, quite probably, displacing the Hattians south towards Palestine.[32]

The Aegean

Just as there were no Hittites in Hatti, so there were no Greeks in Greece in the early 3rd Millennium BC. In fact, I would be so bold as to say that the Greek and Hittite languages, both members of the Indo-European language family, only separated in about 3000BC – such is the remarkably high rate of change which some languages experience. Ancestral Greeks, like ancestral Hittites, were still in Romania and Bulgaria.[33] Greece and the whole Aegean were inhabited by a quite different civilisation, the civilisation which included that of ancient Crete, the so-called 'Minoan' civilisation. The direct origin of this civilisation lay to the north. Long before the Indo-Europeans arrived on the scene, the 'Vinča' people of Serbia and Romania were world leaders. Not only did they have efficient agriculture, impressive architecture and advanced metallurgy (experimenting with bronze as early as 4000BC), but tablets have been found with what looks like a very early form of writing. Archaeologically, the culture spread steadily south through Bulgaria to the Aegean, where similar written signs have been found in early levels at the city of Troy in western Turkey and also in Crete.[34] Thus, even at this early date the Aegean was a centre of high culture. We know nothing about state organisation because of the lack of readable records, but one would expect that a wealthy city like Troy, founded not long after 3000BC, would have been at the centre of a sizeable kingdom.

Crete's importance is also clear from archaeology. Trade between Crete and Lower Egypt is revealed by the presence of Egyptian goods and styles in Crete even before Narmer unified the land of the Nile. One would presume that the merchants who facilitated this trade were Cretan rather than Egyptian because of the obvious need for sea travel and the fact that Cretans have always had to be a maritime people. The fact, noted by Flinders Petrie, one of the founding fathers of modern archaeology, that many of the earliest north Egyptian signs bore a striking resemblance to those of Vinča culture sites may therefore have been more than mere coincidence. Although these early signs were not directly ancestral to the Egyptian hieroglyphic script – that moved north with Narmer's armies – they make the point that Cretan culture was already influential. Certainly the period known on Crete as 'Early Minoan I' was a time of growth and steadily increasing prosperity throughout the Aegean and it takes us right through to about 2500BC.

Cyprus

Cyprus and Crete are much the largest eastern Mediterranean islands and the economies and cultures of the two countries will frequently prove to be related – but not in 3000BC. In 3000BC the population of Cyprus was still firmly in the so-called Chalcolithic Age, i.e. they were farmers and their toolkit included copper (for which Cyprus was famous) but not bronze. The culture had evolved over a period of about 1500 years[35] without any dramatic change, simply steady and largely independent development. However, by about 2500BC, evidence from western Cyprus[36] tells us that significant cultural changes were occurring, including the arrival of new elements in the population. And, on pottery evidence, the source was western Turkey or the Aegean. The expansion of Vinča-derived culture looks by then to have covered the whole of western Turkey and spread along the southern coastal region. It looks as though an adventurous few had then crossed the sea to the island they knew lay just below the horizon.

Elam

My final port of call in this round-up of 3rd Millennium BC civilisations is the enigmatic land of Elam. The Elamites are yet another mysterious ancient people. Like Sumerian, Elamite language is not closely related to any known today; like Sumerian, it already had a good 10000 years of separate development behind it.[37] The Elamite lands, now south-west Iran, lay immediately east of Sumer, and Elamite culture was very similar to that of the Sumerians. They quickly adopted the same writing technique as was used in Uruk IV and the fact that it spread rapidly across Iran and beyond implies that Elamite influence was, in those days, quite extensive. It is impossible to talk confidently of an Elamite state because of the lack of written records but, as with Uruk, I find it hard to imagine that such economic influence could have been achieved without some form of statehood.

Certainly Elam appears in the *Sumerian king list*[38] as a political entity of similar standing to cities like Uruk.

Iraq emerges from the Doldrums

As the Jemdet Nasr period in Iraq gave way to the so-called 'Early Dynastic', so the regional economy slowly recovered. With ever fewer and larger city states, the opportunities for trade steadily improved, but competition between states also provided an excellent environment for innovation, and the Early Dynastic period in Iraq is rightly seen as one of tremendous development. Many of the great pieces of Sumerian literature are rooted in Early Dynastic times, and I will conclude this section by referring to the best known of all, the *Epic of Gilgamesh*.

Gilgamesh is a name found in the *Sumerian king list* as a ruler of Uruk. Now it is simply not possible to read this part of the king list as literal history because of the quite unbelievable reign lengths given for many of the earlier kings (126 years for Gilgamesh himself for example) and also because many of the dynasties listed are known to have ruled in parallel. But archaeology tells us the hard facts. The city of Kish is prominent in the king list and Kish was founded during the Jemdet Nasr period, so it is reasonable to assign the first kings of Kish in the king list to the Jemdet Nasr/Early Dynastic transition, somewhere around 2650BC. Gilgamesh is listed as the fifth ruler of Uruk, a king who fought Kish and was victorious, and he therefore probably reigned some time in the 26th Century BC. Of Gilgamesh it is said that he rebuilt the walls of Uruk after "the flood", and we have genuine evidence of another great flood in the archaeology of Shuruppak, a little north of Uruk, some time in the first phase of the Early Dynastic period. So, while I would not claim that the *Epic of Gilgamesh* is a true story, it almost certainly has a foundation in fact. And this means that we can leave this epoch of history as we found it, with Uruk once again on top of the pile in Iraq, ruled by the heirs of the semi-legendary Gilgamesh.

Summary

I hope that you have been getting a picture of a world which was far from backward, a world where some at least could live in relative luxury, a world of cities and kingdoms and of merchants and traders. It was a very international world. No land was isolated and the role of trade meant that no land was truly self-sufficient; each depended on goods or products made or grown elsewhere in order to maintain the lifestyle that the upper echelons of society had become accustomed to, with trickle-down effects to most other sectors of society. The problem is that prosperity depends on peace and peace depends on human good will – and that is sometimes in short supply! Thus, the break-up of the Uruk empire

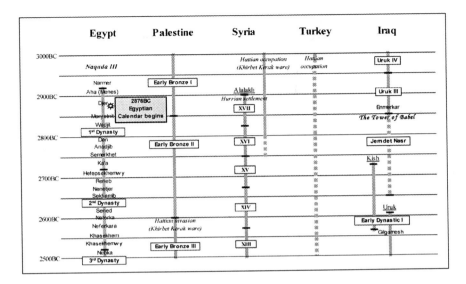

in about 2850BC meant less trade and therefore less wealth, and this continued during the politically fragmented Jemdet Nasr period. In Egypt, the 2nd Dynasty represents this less prosperous phase, during which intermittent civil war took hold. Fortunately, both Egypt and Iraq are now rapidly emerging from recession and the good times seem to be returning once more!

As far as our story goes the key point is that we have an anchor in time, with a highly plausible date (2876BC) for an event which took place in the reign of king Djer, the second king of the 1st Dynasty of a united Egypt. Not only that, but the clear inter-relationships between the different advanced peoples of the Middle East in those days mean that we can be pretty sure which phase of history this date relates to in Iraq, Palestine, Syria, Turkey and the Aegean. The single shaft of light which fell initially on the Egyptian 1st Dynasty has now brought a degree of illumination to wider Middle Eastern history through the first half of the 3rd Millennium BC.

What does the Bible have to say?

Before the days of Abraham, Isaac and Jacob, it is very difficult to date events in the Bible. You may look at your copy and tell me that's not true, that there is a clear and dated line of descent from Noah to Abraham, but you may not be aware that what you read in your version of the Bible is just one of the options which the translators had before them. Most modern translations make principal use of the oldest Hebrew version we have, known as the Masoretic text, supplemented by Dead Sea Scroll evidence where it exists. On the other hand texts from the oldest Greek translation, known as the Septuagint, are much older than those of the Masoretic Bible, and the Septuagint often gives different numbers as well as a different form of expression. This applies to the line from Noah to Abraham. So, where I mention evidence of great floods at Ur and Shuruppak in Iraq, my advice is not to get too excited! You are entitled to your opinion of course, but personally I am quite confident that neither flood represents the flood of Noah.

I would say that the only parts of the Bible which fall in the 3000-2500BC time window are elements of Genesis chapters 10 and 11. Genesis chapter 10 describes the many and varied descendants of Noah; it includes peoples throughout the Middle East from Elam to Greece,[39] and there is nothing which this history can add to it to prove anything one way or the other. Chapter 11, in addition to Abraham's genealogy, also includes the well-known story of the tower of Babel.

The Sons of Shem *(Genesis 10:21-31)*

Our word 'Semite' derives from Shem, one of Noah's sons, but it is important to realise that it is just a borrowed word, now used to describe one branch of one of the world's many language families. It is the branch which includes Hebrew. However, if you think Noah spoke Hebrew, then I would say you are on completely the wrong track! The fact that some of his descendants did is totally irrelevant; my ancestors probably once spoke a Celtic language, whereas I speak English, but that doesn't make me any less their descendant. Language is not inherited! Genesis lists the sons of Shem, from whom Abraham was descended, as Elam, Ashur, Arpaxhad, Lud and Aram, representing peoples in an arc from south-west Iran (Elam) through northern Iraq (Ashur, Arpaxhad[40]) and eastern Syria (Aram) into Turkey (Lud[41]). The Bible then states that they lived "from Mesha to Sephar". The identification of Mesha is not agreed but Sephar we know well enough; it is Sippar, a little north of the later city of Babylon in central Iraq. The descendants of Shem were therefore 'easterners' and 'northerners'. Some will have spoken Sumerian, some Elamite, Hurrian and many other languages too, but in 3000BC they would certainly not have spoken Hebrew. By the way, Abraham's line is traced through Arpaxhad.

Nimrod *(Genesis 10:8-12)*

Nimrod, a descendant of another of Noah's sons, Ham, is singled out as both a "mighty warrior" and a "mighty hunter", with a kingdom in the land of "Shinar". The cities of his kingdom are named as "Babylon, Erech, Akkad, Calneh, Nineveh, Rehoboth Ir, Calah and Resen". From the many occasions on which it occurs, we know that Shinar is Sumer, i.e. southern Iraq. We can also recognise some of the cities. Erech is Uruk for instance. Calah is a city in northern Iraq which would later be named after Nimrod himself. Nimrod could therefore quite plausibly be a ruler from the days of Uruk IV or III, when the city dominated the whole of Iraq as far north as Nineveh. Babylon, by the way, probably isn't the Babylon we know since the city didn't exist until much later times; the name is effectively the same as 'Babel'.

The Tower of Babel *(Genesis 11:1-9)*

The story of the tower of Babel is set in the plain of Shinar, i.e. Sumer. It is the story of a people who decided to build a massive tower but whose plans were in some way thwarted by God, who then dispersed them, forming separate nations with separate languages. Now, let's be honest; this is a difficult story to take at face value. Linguistics is not an exact science but there is no way that any linguist would accept that Sumerian, Elamite, Hurrian, Canaanite and Egyptian all descend from a single language spoken some time within the period of mankind's tower-building capability; in some cases (Egyptian and Canaanite) it is possible to see that they do indeed stem from a common tongue – but one spoken in much earlier times. May I therefore suggest that the original meaning of the passage is not quite what it now appears to be. That a single people with a single language was in some way dispersed and broken up is quite reasonable – that happens all the time when great empires collapse – and that would then allow other peoples with other languages to move in, breaking up the previously uniform language map. And we have seen that just such an event took place in around 2850BC, at the end of the Uruk III period. The impressively uniform Sumerian culture which covered Iraq and beyond suddenly came to an end, allowing Hurrians, Elamites and Semites to muscle in. This, then, is a logical time setting for the tower of Babel story, just as it was a logical setting for Nimrod. It is also a logical setting for the Sumerian epic tale 'Enmerkar and the Lord of Aratta', a story which, among other things, tells us that the god Enki stopped a temple building project and "changed the speech in their mouths".

But where was Babel? I can do no better than recommend David Rohl's explanation in his book 'Legend: The Genesis of Civilisation', in which he argues that both Babylon and Babel are translations (into Akkadian) of the Sumerian 'Nunki', a name that was applied both to Babylon and also to the sacred city of Eridu. In the context of Uruk III, Eridu is the more likely setting. The city lay some 60 miles south-east of Uruk and, since its founding back in the 6th Millennium BC, it had always been the site of a great temple. During Uruk times the city of Eridu was hardly inhabited any more, but its temple complex certainly was; it had become a truly magnificent structure, towering above the flat plain of the Euphrates. Then, following collapse (or demolition) of the great Level VI structure, preparations were apparently made to build yet another temple, at an even higher level, a structure which was never completed.[42] Was this the tower of Babel? The time frame is about right, and Eridu was certainly one of the key ceremonial centres of the Uruk empire. It is much the most likely suggestion I have come across, and I am indebted to David Rohl for publicising it.

What was going on in the Rest of the World?

It's easy to get the impression that everything outside the Middle East lay in total darkness until much more recent times and undoubtedly the lack of written records is a key contributor to this impression; but it's a false impression. By

3000BC wheat and barley based agriculture had been practised for 5000 years or more and it had spread from its origins in Turkey, Syria or Iran to a zone which stretched from Scotland to central India and from the Aral Sea to the Sudan. The Vinča culture of Serbia and Romania was paralleled across central Europe by several advanced societies of villages and farmsteads. These were settled people leading civilised lives. They traded in agricultural produce, metals, precious stones and amber and, for such long-distance contacts to function, they certainly had their own unidentifiable political structures, probably in the form of numerous small clans and statelets. In England there was sufficient centralisation of authority at a regional level for undertakings such as Stonehenge to be commissioned; 3000-2500BC represents the earliest stages of that structure, but several earlier 'temples' of various sorts had already been planned and constructed. Archaeologists find little evidence for warfare amongst these European societies, which suggests that their political organisation was on a very local level, since I see no evidence that human nature was any purer then than now!

If we turn east from the areas of Sumerian and Elamite civilisation, here too the light burns bright. The Elamite trade zone of Iran, Afghanistan and Central Asia consisted of advanced societies throughout the region. Northern Iran hosted peoples related to the Hurrians and Hattians; they too were organised into towns and villages and they too participated in trade with the Elamites.

And still further to the east, in modern Pakistan, the Indus valley civilisation was just getting its act together in 3000BC, a civilisation which would soon produce its own cities, its own metal industry and its own, ultra-conservative form of statehood. The great 3rd Millennium BC cities of Harappa and Mohenjo Daro would soon outshine Memphis and Uruk, at least in terms of their structural engineering and plumbing.

Eastward again: in 3000BC, China was a land of many cultures. In the north the millet-growing Yang Shao civilisation, a culture which has given much (e.g. cuisine) to modern China, was already 2000 years old and was about to be superseded by another culture, known as Lung Shan. We know nothing of political organisation until the Shang emperors emerge from the mists in about 1600BC, but I think we can be pretty sure that city states and small kingdoms already existed in 3000BC, carrying out trade, diplomacy and, as ever, war. Certainly many sites show a violent transition from Yang Shao to Lung Shan culture. And in parallel with these events in northern China, the south was a giant patchwork quilt of various rice-growing peoples, the idea of rice agriculture having spread steadily across the land from its origins three or four thousand years previously in the middle reaches of the Yangtze river.

Finally, it's worth glancing at the coasts and islands of South-East Asia, because a quite stunning technological advance had recently taken place in southern Taiwan, namely the construction of ocean-going ships! For two or three thousand years there had been coastal travel and trade around the coasts of Malaysia, Thailand, Cambodia, Vietnam and southern China,[43] but now a people we know as 'Austronesians' were taking seamanship to new heights and setting out across the South China Sea, first to the Philippines, then to the islands of Indonesia. Their descendants would one day reach Hawaii and Easter Island. These people did not write but they were every bit as capable as a citizen of Memphis!

5

Pyramids and Ziggurats: 2500–2000BC

The Old Kingdom of Egypt

The 'Old Kingdom' is the term used to describe the long and glorious epoch of Egyptian history from the 3rd Dynasty to the 6th. Our sources include Manetho's histories in their different versions and the *Turin Canon*, which also gives reign lengths for much of this period. Another source, which should have been a lot more useful than it actually is if it hadn't been broken and substantially lost, is the so-called Palermo stone.[1] This monument dates from the 5th Dynasty and probably once listed the achievements of all the preceding rulers; the fragments we now have unfortunately only give details for a few of the kings. We also have several tomb inscriptions and, as the centuries pass, an ever-increasing number of other texts, shedding real light onto the lives of the population at large. Following on from the deductions in the last chapter, here are my suggested dates for the rulers of the Egyptian 3rd and 4th Dynasties.[2]

3rd Dynasty:	Nebka	–2500BC	
	Sanakht	2500–2494BC	
	Djoser	2494–2474BC	*constructor of the Step Pyramid*
	Sekhemkhet	2474–467BC	
	Neferkare	2467–2459BC	
	Huni	2459–2435BC	
4th Dynasty:	Snofru	2435–2397BC	*constructor of 3 large pyramids*
	Khufu	2397–2373BC	*constructor of the Great Pyramid*

Djedefre	2373–2365BC	
Khafre	2365–2341BC	*constructor of 2ⁿᵈ Giza Pyramid*
Baefre	2341–2339BC	
Menkaure	2339–2320BC	*constructor of 3ʳᵈ Giza Pyramid*
Shepseskaf	2320–2300BC	
Djedefptah	2300–2298BC	

Pharaoh Nebka had inherited a strong and united land with the resources at its disposal to do something a bit special. And the special idea which emerged was the concept of a pyramid.[3] It was during the 3ʳᵈ and 4ᵗʰ Dynasties that all the great pyramids were built. It was the 3ʳᵈ Dynasty king Djoser who was responsible for setting the fashion with what is now known as the 'Step Pyramid', a structure so impressive that its architect, named Imhotep, was later deified as the god of architecture and medicine! The challenge was then taken up by the first ruler of the 4ᵗʰ Dynasty, king Snofru. Snofru had not one but three major pyramids constructed and they involved some serious innovations in engineering. His first was another massive step pyramid, at Meidum a little upstream of Djoser's. Not content with this, his next project, at Dahshur near Memphis, is now known as the 'Bent Pyramid' since the angle of slope had to be changed half way up to avoid collapse of the foundations. But it seems that Snofru was determined to construct a large and truly shaped pyramid before he died and this he achieved with his 'Red Pyramid', just a couple of miles north of the Bent Pyramid, and it was here that he was eventually laid to rest. The pyramid age then reached its climax with the work of Khufu, Snofru's son, whose 'Great Pyramid' at Giza near modern Cairo is the largest of all the famous burial houses of the pharaohs, one of the seven wonders of the ancient world; and the picture was completed by Khufu's son Khafre, the occupier of an adjacent pyramid only slightly less impressive than Khufu's. Pyramids remained popular for many centuries but the era of really massive construction ended with Khafre. This frenzy of giant pyramid building had lasted barely 150 years, from 2500BC to 2350BC if my dating of Djer's reign was correct.

Of course all this tells us little about Egyptian society at large. The Greek historian Herodotus tells us of the virtual enslavement of the whole population in order to construct the Great Pyramid – but most historians are firmly of the opinion that Herodotus' information was completely false and that even working-class Egyptians were far from being slaves in those days. In fact, we read on the Palermo stone that Snofru brought back 7000 prisoners from the land of Nubia and a further stela tells us that they were put to work on his three pyramids.[4] Egypt, it seems, had no need to make slaves of its own people!

The Dynasties of Sumer

Meanwhile, in the east, the year 2500BC saw Sumer (i.e. southern Iraq) once more in the hands of the lords of Uruk, the dynasty of Gilgamesh. But there were now many rival cities challenging Uruk's right to rule. The *Sumerian king list* tells us that power lurched from one city to another, from Kish to Uruk, to Ur, to Awan and back to Kish, to Hamazi, Uruk, Ur, Adab and Mari, and again back to Kish. In fact the regularity with which Kish reclaimed the leading role led to the title 'King of Kish' being used for centuries afterwards to denote the ruling power in southern Iraq. I am not going to speculate too much here about the exact history of the times; that would blow me too far off course, and we certainly don't have a full picture of events. The famous royal burials unearthed at Ur, containing wealth on a quite magnificent scale, not to mention a large number of sacrificed attendants,[5] date from the so-called 1st Dynasty of Ur, the period when Ur (aided by Elamite armies) wrested control of the region from Kish and Uruk. Archaeologically, the phase is denoted Early Dynastic II and, working forward from 2650BC, the date I suggested for the start of the Early Dynastic period, the 1st Dynasty of Ur probably ruled around 2500-2400BC. A confusing succession of cities and dynasties followed until Ur's second spell at the top was brought to an end by Adab, where king Lugalanemundu is said to have ruled from the Zagros Mountains of Iran to the Taurus Mountains of Turkey and from the Persian Gulf to the Mediterranean. Another powerful city during the Early Dynastic III period was Lagash near the Elamite border, from which we have numerous documents. Over a period of about 100 years, the kings of Lagash fought successful campaigns against Kish, Uruk, Umma and, on several occasions, against the Elamites. But no one city was dominant for long during this phase and the Early Dynastic III period ends with the reign of king Lugalzagesi of Umma, another whose rule is said to have reached the Mediterranean.

We have no reliable written evidence for the overall length of the Early Dynastic period. From archaeology we can see that it must have been approximately 500 years, but the error margin on this is probably at least a century! We clearly need more evidence – and for that we will have to leave Iraq and head west to Syria.

The Lost World of Ebla

From the number of Sumerian rulers who claim to have conquered as far as the Mediterranean you would expect Sumerian influence to be highly visible in Syria, and Alalakh, today just over the border in Turkey, shows this expectation to be fully justified. An Early Dynastic I style cylinder seal turned up in Level XIII and there were further Early Dynastic seals in the long-lasting and prosperous Level XII. The columns of the Level XII palace were in a style similar to those at

Kish and Uruk. Only the temple was definitely non-Sumerian, implying that the religion and culture of the people were distinct, presumably Hurrian.

And just 50 miles south-east of Alalakh lies the famous site of Ebla, a city which generations of historians knew existed but which was not discovered until comparatively recently. Archaeologist Paolo Matthiae may have suspected that the mound of Tell Mardikh which he was excavating concealed the remains of the mysterious city of Ebla but he had no proof for the first four years of excavation. That changed in 1968 with the finding of a statue inscribed with a king's name, Ibbit Lim, together with the name of the city itself, Ebla. But what made the Ebla excavation something rather special was the discovery in 1974 of a royal archive containing literally thousands of inscribed clay tablets, the first really major discovery of its kind for several decades. And the icing on the cake, so to speak, was the fact that the tablets were written in a brand new language, now known as 'Eblaite'. You might think that a new and unknown language would pose something of a problem for those studying the texts but, to put this into context, Eblaite is a Semitic language, closely related to other well-known variants. In fact, tablets found at Nabada in north-east Syria, inscriptions from Mari on the middle Euphrates, and other texts from central Iraq are all in languages very similar to Eblaite, proving that Semitic cultures had come to cover most of Syria and large parts of Iraq by the second half of the 3rd Millennium BC.

The reading of the Ebla tablets suddenly transformed a barren heap of debris into the memory of a living, vibrant and clearly important city. Its very size

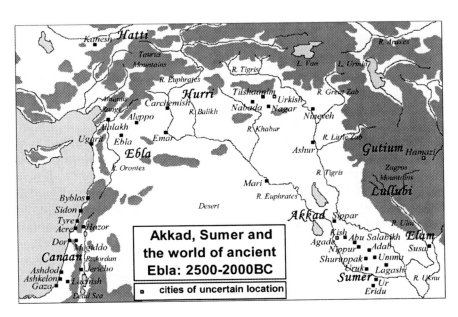

Akkad, Sumer and the world of ancient Ebla: 2500-2000BC

cities of uncertain location

meant that it had to have been important. Although estimates differ widely of course, a typical figure suggested for the population of Ebla during the days of the royal archive would be about 40000 in the city itself, with quarter to half a million living in the surrounding villages. And out of the archives sprang the record of a dynasty of five kings, Igrish Halam, Irkab Damu, Ar Ennum, Ebrum and Ibbi Sipish, who reigned over a period of about 70 years according to the original translator of the texts.[6] Many of the tablets recorded administrative details, for example concerning the distribution of food, temple offerings, commodity prices, the slave trade etc, all extremely revealing for those studying ancient society, and the picture to emerge was of an authoritarian central government combined with a strong capitalist culture. Facts such as the use of standard weights of silver in lieu of coinage are of the utmost importance to our understanding of the ancient world. On the international front, the Ebla tablets tell of numerous Middle Eastern towns and cities, many of which cannot be placed with confidence, but which include Kish, Adab and Mari as well as more local cities like Alalakh, Aleppo,[7] Carchemish, Emar and Byblos.

It is clear from the archive that the status of Ebla was a very important one indeed. Cities as far away as Carchemish appear to be under some degree of Eblaite control. The king of Ebla made a treaty with the king of far away Ashur and there was a gathering of learned scribes at Ebla with participants from the Sumerian city of Kish. Then there is the direct evidence from the tablets themselves regarding the wealth of the city, measured in cattle, sheep and metal goods. Perhaps of keenest interest to historians is the record of a victorious military campaign fought during the reign of Ebrum, the fourth king of the dynasty, against the city of Mari (whose king, Iblul Il, is also known from inscriptions found at Mari itself), and which ended with the capture of Mari, some 200 miles from Ebla, and the installation of a military governor. Ebla clearly ruled a significant kingdom and it seems certain that all the surrounding cities of northern Syria acknowledged Ebla's overlordship.

But just when did all this take place?

In the treaty between Ebla and Ashur, the king of Ashur is named as 'Tudia' and this name turns up right at the top of the *Assyrian king list*; he was the first founding father of the Assyrian rulers. But since the *Assyrian king list* gives no reign lengths for the first 23 kings, this is of limited help. Another clue lies in the mention of Kish, Mari and Adab (but not Uruk, Ur or Umma). Furthermore, the name 'Mesalimu' appears, and Mesalim king of Kish, though not in the *Sumerian king list*, is known from a boundary stela; he is thought to have reigned shortly before the time that Lagash came to the fore, i.e. in the mid Early Dynastic III period.[8] It has also been noted that the style and script of the Ebla tablets themselves are quite close to others discovered in the ancient Sumerian cities of Shuruppak and Abu Salabikh, which are known to be of Early Dynastic III date. The Ebla script, much of which consists of Sumerian logograms, was clearly derived directly from that in use in Sumer, and if anything one would therefore expect that the Ebla archive dates from a few years after the Shuruppak and Abu Salabikh texts. Putting all this together, it seems that the period covered by the archives at Ebla coincided with the second half of the Early Dynastic III period in Sumer, the phase which ended with the reign of Lugalzagesi of Umma. A final clue comes from the claim that a name found in the Ebla archive is actually that of the Egyptian pharaoh Pepy I, whose dates I will shortly be estimating as 2130-2081BC.

But what happened to Ebla? The archives stop without warning, without any mention of any danger or any warfare other than the successful campaign against Mari. True, the treaty with Ashur and another with Hamazi, thought to lie in western Iran, may mean that a danger was foreseen, but there is no specific mention of it. However, the mere fact that the tablets were found in a good enough condition to transport and read says something; it says that the palace in which they were stored was burnt to the ground, firing the tablets to the texture of concrete, and the evidence of archaeology is that this was no accidental fire!

Sargon the Great and the Rise of Akkad

As well as the title 'King of Kish', the chief ruler in Iraq would become known as the lord of 'Akkad and Sumer', which reflects the fact that, ethnically and culturally, Iraq was changing. It seems that the spread of Semitic speakers had, by around 2500BC, reached central Iraq, where many of the rulers of Kish had Semitic names. The first inscription in the Semitic language known as 'Akkadian' (which used the same writing system as Sumerian) was found in a royal grave from the 1st Dynasty of Ur (probably around 2450BC) and by the end of the Early Dynastic III period most commentators believe that Akkadian had taken over as the 'common tongue' in central Iraq, while Sumerian continued in the southern cities.

But it was a single individual who really brought Akkadian language and culture to the fore. The Early Dynastic period was brought to a dramatic end by one of the greatest kings of the ancient world, Sargon the Great, a man who literally became a legend in his own time and a man about whom we have quite a bit of information thanks to the faithful copying of royal inscriptions carried out by scribes in the city of Nippur several hundred years after Sargon's time. Of Sargon it is told that he was abandoned by his parents in a reed basket and left to float down river, but that he was rescued and brought up by a humble gardener. He then entered the service of Ur Zababa king of Kish, where he is said to have risen to the position of cup-bearer. Somehow, at some time, he seized power for himself – and he never looked back. King Lugalzagesi of Umma was then the most powerful force in Iraq, claiming to have "brought peace from the Mediterranean to the Persian Gulf" – but Sargon defeated him and humiliated him publicly by putting him in the stocks at Nippur. Sargon then proceeded to bring all the city states of Iraq under his authority, creating the first ever Akkadian-speaking empire. He founded a new capital city, Agade (from which the words Akkad and Akkadian derive), the site of which is unfortunately still not known;[9] he conquered Mari; there is a suspicious destruction between Levels III and II at Tilshaanim, the city in north-east Syria also known as Chagar Bazaar, and, most importantly for this reconstruction of history, the inscriptions also claim that he conquered Ebla. For centuries to come he was known as the king who was able to cross the mighty Euphrates river. In Level XI at Alalakh a seal of Sargon type was found, suggesting that his dominion reached the Mediterranean. A later tale from the Hittite archives and another found in Egypt both tell of Sargon's conquests deep into central Turkey against the most powerful city in Turkey at the time, Purushanda, although we simply don't have hard information as to whether there is real truth in the story.

With Sargon's empire, the Tigris/Euphrates plain was once more in the hands of a single state, just as it had been centuries before when Uruk was in charge, but this time we know much more detail due to the presence of written records, monuments etc.[10] Regarding absolute date, the fact that Sargon defeated Lugalzagesi of Umma means that his empire follows directly on from the Early Dynastic III period. Then there is the Ebla evidence, where there is no mention of Sargon or Agade and the end of Ibbi Sipish's reign appears to have arrived as a bolt from the blue. There seems no reason to disbelieve Sargon's claim that he conquered Ebla, a feat which was achieved in a campaign that also included conquest of Mari and which took him to the "forests of cedar and the mountain of silver". The 'forests of cedar' are surely those of the Amanus range situated immediately north of Alalakh, the source of much of the timber used in Iraq in those days, while the 'mountain of silver' must have lain in the adjacent silver-rich region of Cilicia in southern Turkey. The date for the start of Sargon's reign is therefore likely to be the late 22nd or early 21st Century BC, the end of the Ebla archive period.

With your indulgence, and because I know what is coming in the next chapter, I will pluck a date out of the air. I suggest that Sargon defeated Lugalzagesi of Umma in 2117BC and that his campaign against the kingdom of Ebla took place very soon afterwards (in his 3rd year according to one inscription), which means that the Ebla kings would have ruled from about 2185BC to 2115BC. The quality of the records we have for the kings of Agade then allows me to assign dates as follows:

Sargon	2117 – 2062BC
Rimush	2062 – 2053BC
Manishtushu	2053 – 2038BC
Naram Sin	2038 – 2001BC
Shar Kali Shari	2001 –

Reassuringly, I am still a good 200 years out compared to most conventional dating! Never mind; let's continue. Following Sargon's death, the next two kings of Agade, Rimush and Manishtushu managed to hold the empire together. However, both met their ends in palace revolts. The fourth king, Naram Sin, is very well known indeed. He extended the empire further still, conquering Elam and the Lullubi people of the Zagros Mountains, as well as claiming to have conquered both Ebla and Aleppo ("never before achieved" in his words). He also had a fine new palace built at Nagar.

So what about Naram Sin's claim to have conquered Ebla – again? Well, archaeology offers a degree of support. The torching of the royal palace, which I have just suggested was the work of Sargon, was followed some considerable time, perhaps around a century, later by a thorough destruction of the city, bringing to an end the whole phase of occupation known as Ebla II. Naram Sin's inscription brackets Ebla and Aleppo together, but it is Aleppo which is recorded first and whose king (Rida Hadad) is named; Aleppo had clearly become the more important city, something which would not have been the case at the time of the Ebla palace archive, and it was probably the conquest of Aleppo to which the words "never before achieved" applied. The century that had passed since Sargon's time had seen a complete change in northern Syria and Aleppo was now the principal player.

Most commentators suggest a weakening of Agade's dominance during the latter part of Naram Sin's reign.[11] After all, his was a large empire and difficult to hold together. And so the millennium ends with the empire still more or less intact but under pressure, ruled by Naram Sin's successor Shar Kali Shari.

The Early Kings of Elam

Elam had been an important country during the Early Dynastic period, with long-distance trade connections through to Afghanistan and Central Asia.[12] It was also 'in the mix' with the city states of Sumer, sometimes conquering and sometimes being conquered.[13] From Elamite records we know of a dynasty of twelve kings who reigned in Early Dynastic and Agade times, but we know little of actual events until Sargon managed to defeat the eighth king of the dynasty, Luh Ishshan, and to incorporate Elam into his empire. Sargon's successor Rimush then crushed a rebellion in Elam, and Manishtushu in his turn is reported to have conquered 'Anshan' and 'Sherihun', which were southern Elamite lands; a statue of him was dedicated by Eshpun, Agade's viceroy in Elam. That Elam had become a tributary kingdom to Agade is emphasized by a treaty between Naram Sin and king Hita of Elam, the eleventh from the dynasty. Thus, in 2000BC Hita's successor Kutik Inshushinak still served Agade – but he was most definitely dreaming of independence!

In the Shadow of the Pyramids

Back in the land of the Nile there had been no let-up in Egyptian power. The kings of the 5th Dynasty didn't go in for large pyramids in the way their predecessors had, but Egypt remained a united and prosperous land. The first recorded trading expedition to the fabled land of Punt (see Chapter 10) took place in the time of Sahure, the second ruler of the dynasty. In fact Sahure's reign (2290-2271BC according to this book) produces further evidence of far flung trade in the form of a chair with his name on it found (but now lost[14]) in a royal burial in north-western Turkey, near the Sea of Marmara. The same group of royal graves is also reported to have contained a finely crafted silver blade showing ocean-going ships, giving an insight into the advances in seafaring which had already taken place.

But, as the 5th Dynasty gives way to the 6th, archaeologists tend to remark on what they see as a weakening of Egyptian society, a decadent phase in which, for example, old forms of architecture and pottery are continued but in a lazy and formulaic way, without the dynamism and willingness to experiment which marks a society on the up. Bureaucracy was on the increase; initiative was on the decline – rather as it is in our 21st Century world! And then came the extraordinary reign of king Pepy II, awarded 94 years by Manetho. For better or worse, I have reduced this to 64 years since only 33 censuses are recorded and these generally took place at intervals of no more than two years. A very long reign is certainly correct, but 94 years, 30 more than Queen Victoria of England, is stretching credulity more than a little! Thus, rightly or wrongly I am suggesting the following dates for the 5th and 6th Dynasty rulers.

5th Dynasty:	Userkaf	2298–2290BC	
	Sahure	2290–2271BC	*first expedition to Punt*
	Neferirkare	2271–2261BC	
	Shepseskare	2261–2259BC	
	Neferefre	2259–2240BC	
	Neuserre	2240–2216BC	
	Menkauhor	2216–2201BC	
	Isesi	2201–2173BC	
	Wenis	2173–2143BC	
6th Dynasty	Teti	2143–2132BC	
	Userkare	2132–2130BC	
	Pepy I	2130–2081BC	
	Merenre I	2081–2072BC	
	Pepy II	2072–2008BC	
	Nitocris	2008–2000BC	

It has to be acknowledged that the evidence permits a range of views as to the total length of the first six Egyptian dynasties; a glance at three relatively recently published histories reveals opinions between 916 and 970 years. My estimate here is 920 years, and is typical of those who doubt the veracity of Pepy II's 94 years in office.

As Pepy's reign dragged on and on so the life drained out of the Egyptian monarchy. First his children and then his grandchildren began to die off, and the clear line of succession which is so important to the strength of a hereditary monarchy was lost. The result was political paralysis. By 2000BC the mighty land that had thrived for nearly a thousand years was beginning to look seriously shaky.

Palestine and the Coming of the Amorites

And in Palestine, on Egypt's north-eastern frontier, worrying events had taken place. The cosy world of the Early Bronze Age Canaanite (and Hattian) cities had been dramatically overturned in about 2100BC. Egyptian artefacts, mainly stone or alabaster bowls, turn up in southern Palestinian sites from throughout the 3rd and 4th Egyptian Dynasties, suggesting stability and trade. The Ebla archives confirm that the cities of Palestine were still flourishing in the 22nd Century BC, for instance describing a trade route running along the Palestinian coast through Byblos, Sidon, Acre, Dor, Ashdod and Gaza. Trade is also recorded with the cities of Megiddo and Hazor, both in northern Palestine. But then, suddenly, nothing! Almost every city in Palestine was destroyed and largely abandoned, certainly left with a much reduced population. In Jericho, the situation is graphically illustrated by the fact that the last Early Bronze Age city wall was hurriedly thrown together using old bricks and rubble; but it didn't last long before being destroyed by fire.[15] Whoever was responsible for these destructions, it seems they didn't care much for cities!

Experts are agreed; the conquerors of Palestine were 'Amorites'. In the archives of Ebla they appear as 'Martu', a word which means 'westerner' in Sumerian, and a bronze Martu dagger was evidently a sought-after commodity, worth about 15 silver shekels, almost as much as a child slave! A gold Martu dagger was more than twice the price. The Amorites (or Martu) were therefore already known as craftsmen in the 22nd Century BC. They were a nomadic Semitic-speaking people, from the semi-desert of eastern Jordan. Later texts from Iraq describe the Amorites as "raiders of settled lands" and "a people who know not grain". But it would be a mistake to think of the Amorites as a disorganised rabble. Their traditional lifestyle was quite different from that of the settled people of Iraq, northern Syria, Palestine and Egypt, but that was simply a function of the territory they inhabited. The Amorites will certainly have had their own political organisation, based around their tribal structure; and every tribe will have had its leader and its council of elders. They had their own laws and customs and doubtless administered their own justice. In short, the Amorites were by no means uncivilised; they were just different.

For the Amorites, at a time when the regional climate was drying significantly, Palestine was excellent pasture land for herds and flocks and there is plenty of evidence that the Canaanites and Hattians may have actually created this pasture by their prolific deforestation of the country. The Amorite invaders simply pitched their tents among the ruins of the Canaanite cities, making use of each city's water supply, but leaving very little for the archaeologist to uncover. We can see that many cities were still inhabited from the evidence of pottery (of a totally different form from that of the Canaanites) and domestic rubbish, but there is very little evidence of structures. However, though the Amorites may have preferred tents to brick or stone, there was one type of construction activity they took very seriously indeed – their tombs. Amorite tombs were varied in nature and often magnificent in size. The quite different types of tomb architecture found across Palestine (and also Jordan) are thought to represent the traditions of the different tribes, and it is the changing fashions seen in these tombs more than anything else which indicates that the period of Amorite occupation of Palestine was centuries long. Six feet of solid rock eroded from the cliff face at Jericho during this period![16]

The Aegean and the Arrival of the Indo-Europeans

And while Amorite tribes were undoing the progress of centuries in Palestine, another warlike collection of peoples were doing something very similar in the far west. One of the really big stories of the last few thousand years is the way in which Indo-European language speakers have taken control of large sectors of the planet and the process was well under way during the 3rd Millennium BC. In Greece the arrival of Greek-speaking tribes from the north is marked by the destruction of settlements such as Lerna, a previously prosperous town on the Aegean coast, in about 2100BC. This is paralleled in western Turkey, where the ancestors of the Hittites are the most likely culprits behind the destruction of Troy II,[17] also in about 2100BC. Nearly a century later, during Naram Sin's reign, come reports that a fierce and mysterious people had conquered the Turkish city of Purushanda.[18]

But the Indo-Europeans couldn't reach Crete and the other Aegean islands. On Crete, the Early Minoan II period flourished from about 2500BC, giving way to Early Minoan III in about 2100BC, without any particular change other than changes in pottery fashion. This is the time that the first true Cretan script appears, a development of earlier individual signs; it is a hieroglyphic script which has not been read and probably never will be. There is plenty of evidence of trade too. Seals of this time in Crete were commonly made from ivory and, since there were no elephants, walruses or mammoth carcasses on Crete, the

ivory must have been purchased from elsewhere; Syria is the most likely source since the Syrian elephant would survive down until the early 1st Millennium BC. Furthermore, many of the designs used on the seals are also paralleled in 6th Dynasty Egypt, which many have taken to imply Egyptian influence in Crete but which I am more inclined to take as a sign of Cretan influence in Egypt. We know from many Cretan illustrations of the importance of sea travel in the Early Minoan period, and the fact that Early Minoan copper daggers have been found in Italy, and Lipari Island obsidian in Early Minoan Crete, reinforces Crete's role as initiator of trade contacts, perhaps even coloniser of foreign lands.[19]

Cyprus

On Cyprus, the other large eastern Mediterranean island, another significant influx of population arrived during this period. The usual date quoted is about 2300BC based on C14 dating evidence which, I suggest, means that 2000BC may be closer to the truth. Judging from the pattern of settlement found on the island, not to mention similarities in tools and weapons, this new bronze-using people clearly arrived from the north, i.e. from southern Turkey;[20] but who were they? The date is still too early for the Hittites; the pottery suggests they were neither Hattians nor Cretans; the connection with Turkey rules out Eblaites. This seems to leave only the virtually unknown kingdoms of southern and western Turkey, whose people were distant cultural kin to the Cretans. The chief city of the region was Purushanda, the city which Sargon fought – according to legend – and which Naram Sin later reclaimed from an invading (probably Hittite) army. This region is the most likely source of Bronze Age Cypriot civilisation, and the invasion of Cyprus may have been partly in response to Hittite pressure from the north. The earlier people of Cyprus were not eliminated, but several sites were burned and many more were abandoned. For Cyprus, this was certainly a very significant invasion.

The Kingdoms of Early Bronze Age Turkey

Well to the north-east of Purushanda, the flowering of Hattian civilisation can be seen in the magnificent royal tombs of Alaca Höyük in north-central Turkey, where each burial was accompanied not only by sumptuous wealth in gems and precious metals but also by a single piece of Khirbet Kerak ware pottery. This hand-made ware, by then many hundreds of years old, was clearly somehow still seen as a defining element in Hattian culture. But of names and events we know nothing. A similar silence hangs over the Hurrian kingdoms although we read of Hurrian individuals in the Ebla archives[21] and that the cities of Urkish and Carchemish had Hurrian rulers. The early kings on the *Assyrian king list* also had non-Semitic and possibly Hurrian names. But the Hurrians were now clearly under Sumerian/Akkadian influence. We have the physical evidence of Iraqi architecture at Alalakh; we also have the story of Sargon's conquests in southern Turkey which, if true, must have seriously affected the Hurrian kingdoms; and we have the story of a rebellion against Naram Sin by seventeen kings, including the Hattian kings of Hattusas and Kanesh.[22] According to an inscription, Naram Sin restored his authority and re-conquered as far as Purushanda and 'Ulisum',[23] which suggests that, at its height, his empire must have extended right across the Hurrian lands, through Hattian territory and even further to the west. It is a timely reminder of how little we know of kingdoms and empires when all we have to go on is archaeology.

Summary

Much has happened since 2500BC. In Egypt, the seemingly indestructible Old Kingdom staggers uncertainly on, now under the rule of queen Nitocris, successor to Pepy II; in Iraq, supremacy has swapped from city to city and now lies with Agade. But in both cases the original vigour has departed. The nomadic Amorites have now dominated Palestine for 100 years or so and sit restlessly on the borders of both Egypt and Iraq. The Hattians and Hurrians remain an ever-present threat to the northern parts of Agade's empire; similarly, the Elamites to the east, not to mention the tribes of the Zagros Mountains. In Turkey the powerful kingdom of Purushanda has come under attack from the north-west, where Indo-Europeans are taking over city after city. Troy has fallen; likewise much of mainland Greece. Only Crete, the Aegean islands and parts of western Turkey remain as beacons of 'old world' Mediterranean civilisation. It wouldn't take a clairvoyant to suggest that more big changes might be just around the corner!

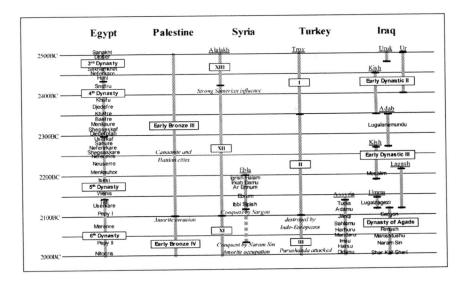

What does the Bible have to say?

There is very little to report under this heading. We are now in times which appear to be covered by nothing more than the genealogy of Abraham's ancestors! I will therefore confine myself to pointing out the parallels between the language and names in the Ebla archives and those of ancient Hebrew times. The Biblical sounding names Abramu, Ishmail, Ishrail and Mikail all appear in the archives – and there is a good reason for that. Eblaite is a West Semitic language and it was probably spoken throughout northern Syria and Lebanon until the fall of Ebla to Sargon's armies in about 2115BC. The 2nd Millennium BC West Semitic language which we know as Canaanite sprang from the Byblos region of Lebanon and was therefore probably a direct descendant of Eblaite – and Hebrew is essentially a development of Canaanite. It would therefore be remarkable if Hebrew and Eblaite were not closely related. This seems to be an embarrassment to modern Syrian politicians, but with absolutely no good reason. The fact that Arabic separated from the Eblaite/Canaanite branch a little earlier, and is therefore not quite so close, has no more relevance today than the fact that the ancestor of Turkish was still being spoken in Siberia in 2000BC!

What was going on in the Rest of the World?

The Indo-European threat is drawing ever closer to the lands of the Middle East. In the west, the Greeks and Hittites have already made their presence felt; and in the east, sites such as Anau in Turkmenistan and Hissar in northern Iran inform us of the arrival of yet another Indo-European group not long after 2500BC (based on C14 dating – which should be reliable so far from the Mediterranean).[24]

These particular Indo-Europeans were speakers of the Indic branch of the family and they quickly spread their culture across northern Iran and Afghanistan. Meanwhile, 2000BC sees the Indus valley civilisation of Pakistan at its height, at the far end of an extensive trade network reaching out from Sumer via the Persian Gulf. A key port of call was copper-rich Oman. The island of Bahrain (ancient Dilmun) was both a trading partner and a giant cemetery, in use for many hundreds of years during the Early Dynastic period and later; it seems that the island was associated in some way with the after-life in Sumerian mythology.

In distant Britain, 2000BC sees the finishing touches being put to Phase II of the great temple to the heavens which we call Stonehenge, not to mention the construction of other monuments such as Silbury Hill and Seahenge – datable to exactly 2049BC from tree ring evidence. There has clearly been continuity of culture for a considerable period of time.[25] The only possibly significant archaeological change has been the spread of a particular type of pottery known as 'bell beakers' across Spain, France and Britain, and then also into Central Europe, although whether this was anything more than trade I will not speculate; there is simply insufficient data.

Finally, let's take a quick glance across the water to America where agriculture based on maize is really taking hold in 3rd Millennium BC Mexico. This is paralleled in South America, notably Ecuador and northern Peru where agriculture has also been developed, again making use of maize, supplemented by potatoes. Furthermore, some sort of political organisation can clearly be discerned in the monumental constructions which have appeared in both regions. Already, the famous ceremonial designs with sunken plazas, often known as ball-courts, are found in northern Peru, later to be paralleled in Mexico.

The Middle East is far from being the only centre of human civilisation!

6

Ur of the Chaldeans: 2000–1800BC

The Collapse of the Egyptian Old Kingdom

In 2000BC Egypt was weak, fatally weak. We don't know entirely why. Many blame Pepy II's over-long reign, although this can hardly be the sole cause. Probably custom had bred corruption, complacency and the paralysis of bureaucracy. The empire had been a dominant force for so long that any change in the established order was simply outside anyone's imagination – rather like the days preceding the collapse of the Roman Empire. But in about 2000BC Egypt simply imploded. Suddenly, out of nowhere, an unstoppable tide of Amorite fighters overran the Nile delta, upsetting the balance of centuries! The situation is vividly described in one of the key documents of the time, the *Admonitions of Ipuwer*, and the description is one of a ravaged land and a total breakdown of law and order.[1] During this period, known to Egyptologists as the 'First Intermediate Period', the Egyptian priest/historian Manetho lists two dynasties of which almost nothing is known, the 7th and 8th. He says of the 7th Dynasty that there were "70 kings in 70 days"! The 8th Dynasty seems to have been the official line, descendants of Pepy II, and they still ruled what they could from Memphis – but the economy had been shattered; the pharaoh was neither to be feared nor respected so, inevitably, each city and province made its own way as best it could.

The Fall of Agade

Under Shar Kali Shari, the Agade empire was almost as weak as Egypt. The major cities of the south, Lagash, Uruk and Ur, were now more or less self-governing. King Kutik Inshushinak of Elam declared unilateral independence – and there was no response from Agade. A rock inscription in Akkadian cuneiform tells of victories over Agade by the Lullubi people of western Iran.[2] We have a record of a battle against invading Amorites, which demonstrates just how broad Amorite territory had become. Agade's Amorite frontier would have been at least 400 miles from Palestine and 600 miles from the Nile delta. Fortunately for Shar Kali Shari, he won that one. But for Agade the real problem lay in the east. Once independent, Kutik Inshushinak of Elam started to conquer north-west along the Zagros range, claiming[3] to defeat the lands of 'Simaski' (populated by Elamite speakers) and 'Gutium', as well as territories down on the Tigris plain but, whatever the truth of these claims, it is certain that the people of Gutium were not long under the thumb of the Elamites. The *Sumerian king list* records the dwindling of Agade's authority and the coming to power of a new force in Iraq, the Gutians. Shar Kali Shari had fought and won battles against the Gutians before, but he was quite unable to stop their inexorable advance. His reign was followed by a 3-year period during which, so the *Sumerian king list* tells us, four kings reigned, one of whom had a Gutian name. It was a time of chaos and, though Agade itself recovered, the empire was lost for ever.

At this point let me introduce some overdue evidence in support of my dates for the Agade dynasty. Amongst a collection of astronomical observations gathered together by some unknown official many hundreds of years later[4] is a record of a lunar eclipse (on the 14th day of the 1st month, i.e. some time in early spring) written in the form of an omen concerning the death of the king of Agade and the fall of the kingdom into a time of anarchy – which is as good a description of the situation at the end of Shar Kali Shari's reign as you could wish for. What makes this particular lunar eclipse potentially datable is the fact that the text also speaks of the planet 'Dilbat' being in the moon's '*shurinnu*', a word of uncertain meaning but, judging from other eclipse texts, referring to the area immediately around the moon. This is where it gets a bit complicated and, it would be fair to say, somewhat debatable. Dilbat is generally taken to refer to the planet Venus – but it is physically impossible for Venus to be anywhere near the moon during a lunar eclipse since its orbit lies nearer the sun than that of the Earth, while the moon is on the far side of the Earth from the sun during a lunar eclipse. Even if Venus were visible, it would be on the opposite horizon to the moon! So, if the text has any reliability at all Dilbat refers to some other heavenly body in this case, and the obvious alternative is Jupiter, almost as bright as Venus in the night sky. Wayne Mitchell has carried out a thorough investigation[5] of early spring eclipses in which Jupiter could possibly have been in the close vicinity of the moon and can find none over a 250 year period until the year 1976BC (March 4th according to our present calendar) – hence my suggested dating of Shar Kali Shari's death, and therefore of the whole Agade dynasty. Now, I would freely admit that there is some uncertainty in this identification, not least questions as to the reliability of the text, so I will just pencil it in for now on the understanding that it can only stand if supported by further data.

> **Possible absolute date: 1976BC**
> Lunar eclipse reported as an omen of the death of the king of
> Agade and the collapse of the kingdom

The eclipse text goes on to speak of the recovery of the kingdom, which could be seen as a reason to doubt that it applied to Shar Kali Shari's time, but in a sense the kingdom did recover. As a much smaller entity, Agade survived for another 39 years after the 3-year period with four kings, before finally succumbing to the Gutians. After that we hear almost nothing of Agade; it seems that the city, if not totally abandoned, became nothing more than a rather insignificant town.

So who were these Gutians? Good question! They were herders and arable farmers from the valleys of the Zagros Mountains, but we have no idea of their language. As to why they felt the need to spill out across the Tigris and Euphrates plain, perhaps the real culprit was Naram Sin of Agade. He conquered the whole Zagros region; and he was followed by Kutik Inshushinak of Elam, who also defeated Gutium. Perhaps this unlooked-for attention from the outside world prompted the Gutian kings to join in the conquering game. On the other hand, it may just have been the age-old tendency of kings and rulers to exploit a weakness in a neighbour, in this case the unfortunate Shar Kali Shari of Agade. The Akkadians and Sumerians almost certainly thought of the Gutians as savages – texts from Sippar speak of "Gutian slaves" being traded in exchange for exotic oils – but they were nevertheless well enough organised to defeat the armies of Akkad and Sumer in battle! The Gutian period may not have been a time of high culture,[6] but the 'savage' Gutians still continued to honour the various Sumerian gods and goddesses; it was not quite the disaster that had overtaken Egypt.

The Amorite Lands

Westward from Gutian-controlled Iraq, nomadic Amorite tribes continued to dominate a very wide stretch of territory indeed; northern Egypt was just one small corner of their domain. In Palestine there is continuing archaeological evidence of their presence, and at some stage during their occupation some at least of the Amorites abandoned their tents and started to build conventional houses. This is apparent at Jericho and Megiddo,[7] and it is also their building activities which give away their presence as far north as Ebla. After Naram Sin's destruction of Ebla, it was the Amorites who were the next occupiers of the site, erecting their rather crudely fashioned houses against the ruined walls of what had once been Ibbi Sipish's royal palace. Even at Ugarit on the Syrian coast, Amorite graves have been found. In fact it looks as though Amorite rule now covers all of Palestine, Lebanon, Syria and Jordan, as well as northern Egypt. Other peoples clearly survived, but it was the tent-dwelling Amorite kings who were most definitely in charge – and so it continued throughout the 20th Century BC. Civilisation in the traditional sense had been put firmly on hold!

Egypt rises from the Ashes

Egyptologists generally estimate around 40 years for the appallingly chaotic 7th and 8th Dynasty period, a period during which royal authority seems to have broken down completely, allowing the Amorites unfettered access to the Nile delta. Slowly however, from the depths of social anarchy, two rival Egyptian cities rose to prominence, namely Herakleopolis in middle Egypt, and Thebes in the far south. Manetho's 9th and 10th Dynasties reigned consecutively in Herakleopolis, while the 11th ruled at the same time in Thebes. Thebes, so it seems, had remained loyal to the 8th Dynasty kings of Memphis but, when the first 9th Dynasty ruler Khety I of Herakleopolis became *de facto* pharaoh in about 1960BC, Montuhotep of Thebes refused to play ball. He may not have realised it at the time, but his opposition to Khety's claims would lead to his becoming the first of Manetho's 11th Dynasty kings.

Egypt's emergence from chaos was slow and painful. It would be another two or three generations before Khety III of the 10th Dynasty finally oversaw the expulsion of the Amorites from Egypt. According to the dates in this book, this took place in the early years of the 19th Century BC; the Amorites had pastured their flocks in the lush land of the Nile delta for over 100 years! But Khety III was the last significant ruler of Herakleopolis and it was probably (opinions are divided) in the time of his son Merikare that the 11th Dynasty Theban king Montuhotep II finally brought the land under united rule once more. Thereafter, he and his successors began to rebuild the country and to strengthen its borders; the Amorite episode was certainly not one that anyone wanted to see repeated!

Assuming I am right in my dating of the first six dynasties, and assuming that 40 years is a good estimate for the 7th and 8th Dynasty period, the Theban kings of the 11th Dynasty can be dated approximately as follows.[8]

Montuhotep I	1960 – 1939BC	
Inyotef I	1939 – 1917BC	
Inyotef II	1917 – 1868BC	
Inyotef III	1868 – 1860BC	
Montuhotep II	1860 – 1809BC	*unification in 1839BC*
Montuhotep III	1809 –	

Sumerian Revival

Amorite dominance over Egypt is neatly paralleled by Gutian dominance over Iraq. I would suggest that the beginning of the Gutian dynasty given in the *Sumerian king list* follows directly from the three years of chaos after Shar Kali Shari's death in 1976BC. In fact, according to the *Sumerian king list* the Gutian dynasty starts with a 3-year period during which "no king was famous" – which sounds very like the "three years with four kings" in the Agade dynasty. There are then approximately 85 years of Gutian rule,[9] taking us down to about 1889BC, when Utu Hegal king of Uruk finally defeated them.

It seems a strange coincidence that the period of Gutian rule in Iraq should correspond so closely with that of the Amorites in Egypt – but of course it isn't coincidence at all. Even in 2000BC the Middle and Near East was a single organic society, each part relying heavily on trade with the rest. Collapse in Egypt spelt inevitable problems for Iraq; regeneration in Egypt made recovery in Iraq that much easier. And when recovery came it was the historic city of Uruk which led the way. But this was no repeat of earlier Uruk empire days – it seems unlikely that Lagash, for example, was in any way subservient to Uruk – but for a brief period Uruk gained supremacy once more. It would not last long! King Utu Hegal of Uruk was too trusting of his associates. He had appointed an able man named Ur Nammu as his military governor in the city of Ur and, in Utu Hegal's 8th year, 1881BC according to this chronology, Ur Nammu saw his chance; he seized control of Ur for himself, ushering in the 3rd Dynasty of Ur, a very well documented period indeed.

The 3rd Dynasty of Ur represents the final flourish, and a highly spectacular flourish, of true Sumerian civilisation. Ur Nammu was a vigorous and charismatic figure who united all of Iraq and even beyond into a single trade network with Ur as the city at the centre of the financial web, a city which reached its zenith in his day, with an immense ziggurat at its centre. Ziggurats had long been a popular feature in religious architecture in Iraq. It seems they were basically artificial mountains created as suitable dwelling places for a city's god or gods, understandable in a land where all that can be seen is a seemingly infinite expanse of billiard-table-flat plain. The ziggurat at Ur was revealed in all its magnificence by Sir Leonard Woolley in the 1920s[10] and, though it continues to crumble, not least due to its location in a war zone, it still towers over the surrounding flat landscape today. In its time it must have been truly spectacular. However, it was the bureaucratic administration set up to control the entire financial and commercial network which was the most remarkable legacy of the 3rd Dynasty of Ur. We have literally tens of thousands of administrative texts preserved in Sumerian cuneiform on clay tablets[11] and they tell the story of a very tightly controlled system. But it worked; the times were prosperous to judge by the very extensive public building works undertaken in most of the cities of Iraq. The roads were good, the police force did its job and the economy boomed.

The extent of the empire can be seen as far away as Nagar in north-east Syria, which was one of the largest cities in that region at the time, and where a building inscribed with Ur Nammu's name has been found. There are also plenty of references to dealings with Ebla in western Syria and "tribute" is mentioned, suggesting that the supremacy of Ur was recognised by Ebla's Amorite rulers. Closer to hand, Ur maintained an army at Mari on the middle Euphrates. On the military front, it is known that Shulgi, who reigned for a majestic 48 years and who was extremely active in building up the magnificence of the city of Ur itself, subjugated Elam rather thoroughly and formed a sort of Elamite foreign legion, an army which the Ur kings used to police their large and lucrative empire. Regarding dates, the reign lengths of the Ur kings are very well known so, if I am right in suggesting that Ur Nammu came to power in 1881BC, the remaining 19th Century BC rulers of Ur can be dated as follows:

Ur Nammu	1881 – 1864BC
Shulgi	1864 – 1816BC
Amar Sin	1816 – 1807BC
Shu Sin	1807 –

So, although both Egypt and Iraq had suffered collapse in the early 20th Century BC, both lands experienced revival during the 19th Century BC and the restoration of commercial activity – but what about the rest of the region?

Elam

It is a recurrent theme of Elamite history that wealth and riches flow to Elam when the Iraqi powers are in trouble! During the divided time of the Early Dynastic period Elam was a power of equal standing to the city states of Sumer, and it thrived; during the Agade empire period it was conquered more than once and wealth flowed out rather than in. Then, when the Gutians upset the apple-cart, came boom times and the building of new temples and palaces. But when Gutian power subsided so did the power of Elam and king Shulgi of Ur incorporated Elam into his vast empire. So, by the time of Shu Sin of Ur, the Elamites were seen as little more than a source of revenue for the royal coffers and mercenary soldiery for Ur's armies.

The Hurrian World

As far as we know there was still no large Hurrian state. Alalakh, Carchemish and Urkish were all important Hurrian-ruled cities; Assyria may have had Hurrian kings[12] – but Assyria was now firmly part of the Ur empire and under direct control of an appointed governor. As we approach the year 1800BC, it looks as though the frontiers of the Hurrian world have become a little blurred and Hurrian names are common in texts from various cities of the Ur empire. By now the uniformity of Hurrian culture, which had been spread across northern Iraq and northern Syria for over a thousand years, would certainly have broken down, an inevitable consequence of there being no unifying state. By 1800BC I very much doubt whether an eastern Hurrian from Assyria could have understood the speech of a westerner from Alalakh; the languages would have been as different from each other as French and Italian are today.

Hittites and Hattians

The tentacles of the Ur empire were both long and strong, engulfing Elam and the Hurrian lands – but they never engulfed Hatti. Here a different tale was unfolding. Indo-European culture had made steady progress across Turkey. In the south the language was developing into what would be known as 'Luwian'; in the north it would become 'Palaic', and in central regions the tongue we know as 'Hittite' – although the Hittites actually called it 'Nesili'. Only parts of western Turkey preserved the culture and language of the earlier Aegean-related civilisation.[13] But, as the Hittites pushed ever east, they inevitably ran up against the Hattian people, the proud descendants of the makers of Khirbet Kerak pottery and the bearers of a mature culture. In all truth, we can't really say what happened. What we do know is that when written records eventually appear most of the leading people of Hatti have Hittite names; just a few are Hattian. On the other hand, we also know that less than half of Hittite vocabulary is of Indo-European root; the majority is foreign, some of it almost certainly Hattian. Furthermore, we know that the Hittites had a certain reverence for Hattian ways since some of the texts from Hattusas, though dating from Hittite times, are written in Hattian, and these texts are all of a religious or ceremonial nature. In short, whatever happened – and we can be sure it was by no means entirely peaceful – the resulting culture of Hatti was a composite. This was actually very common among Indo-European peoples as they conquered civilisations which were in all respects other than warfare more advanced than their own. In Greece, Greek culture was really a composite containing many elements from earlier Minoan-related civilisation, and the Greek language has numerous non Indo-European words, words which are most likely to be related to ancient Cretan.

The Aegean

Speaking of Crete, this was an exciting phase in Cretan history. Since the arrival of Vinča culture late in the 4th Millennium BC, Crete had always been a place of high civilisation and, notably, trade. Following the arrival of the Greeks in the region toward the end of the 3rd Millennium BC, Cretan culture can be seen soon afterwards influencing the new lords of the mainland, where Cretan goods became popular. And Cretan influence is still easily recognisable in Egypt – and *vice-versa*. A particular style of seal with rectilinear and spiral motifs, one of the typical Early Minoan III types, had suddenly become popular in 6th Dynasty Egypt and the popularity of the style continued through the First Intermediate Period. Conversely, a seal of this period has been found in Crete, in undoubtedly Cretan style, showing a man playing draughts, which was an Egyptian game!

So, while Egypt and Iraq both suffered collapse, Crete continued to thrive, and it seems that trade around the eastern Mediterranean remained active. With the recovery of both Egypt and Iraq and the growth of international commerce, the wealth of Crete grew substantially further – which brings us to the archaeological phase known as Middle Minoan I. This was the first palace-building phase on Crete and impressive structures sprang up at Knossos, Mallia and Phaistos, tied into the construction of considerable cities. It's pretty clear that Crete was now a lot more than a collection of enterprising merchants; it was almost certainly under a strong centralised government. It was a rich land in a world which was fast emerging from the traumas of the 20th Century BC.

And although the Mediterranean island of Cyprus retained its own culture and its own pottery styles, it was also very much part of the Cretan trading network, with Cretan products turning up throughout the Early Minoan III and Middle Minoan I phases. In fact, strong Cretan influence can reasonably be inferred in coastal communities from Turkey all the way to northern Egypt.

Summary

The 20th Century BC saw the passing of an ancient order, swept away by Amorites in the west and by Gutians in the east. In both Egypt and Iraq the shock to the system must have been considerable and people who grew up in a stable world of agriculture, town life and reasonable affluence suddenly found their world turned on its head. Both lands took many decades to recover. The complex inter-relationships between cities, between town and country and between nation states had been shattered, destroying trade networks and so destroying the livelihoods of those who lived by trade. The inevitable consequence was insecurity, poverty and a general lack of resources.

Yet the world recovered. Cretan civilisation had remained a bright spark in an otherwise gloomy universe, and it seems that Cretans played no little part in maintaining standards of living around the coasts of the eastern Mediterranean. Slowly but surely the settled peoples of Egypt and Iraq sorted themselves out once more, until in each land a single city state had enough power to throw the invading forces out, although in neither case was this city state destined to rule the whole land. In Egypt, Herakleopolis was superseded by Thebes; In Iraq, Uruk was superseded by Ur. But the key point for the population was that, as the

	Egypt	Palestine	Syria	Turkey	Iraq
2000BC	Memphis / Amorite invasion		Alalakh	XI	Assyria / Didanu — Dynasty of Agade
	7th & 8th Dynasties				Ilushu / Shar Kali Shari / 1976BC Lunar Eclipse
	Herakleopolis | Thebes				Zuabu
	Khety I / Montuhotep I	Amorite occupation			Nuabu
	9th Dynasty				Abazu
	Inyotef I				Belu / Gutian Kings
	10th Dynasty				Azarah / Birth of Abraham
1900BC	Khety III / Inyotef II		X		Ushpia / Uruk
	11th Dynasty				Utu Hegal / Ur / Apiashal
					Conquest by Ur / Ur Nammu
	Inyotef III	Cretan colonies? (Philistines Perizzites)	Abraham's family in Harran		Shulgi
	Merikare				
	Montuhotep II				
	Unification / Abraham arrives in Canaan				3rd Dynasty of Ur
	Abraham in Egypt / War against Sodom / Birth of Ishmael			IX	Zariqi (as governor)
	Birth of Isaac				Amar Sin / Shu Sin
1800BC	Montuhotep III				

19th Century BC progressed, a single strong state emerged in each country. After a break of 100 years or more, order was restored and the serious business of creating wealth could be resumed.

And a key point for this story is that I have a second absolute date, 1976BC, the date of a lunar eclipse with a likely connection to the end of the reign of Shar Kali Shari of Agade.

What does the Bible have to say?

This is an important phase in Bible history. We have now reached the days of Abraham, according to the dating information which the Bible supplies. We read in I Kings 6:1 that king Solomon's temple was founded either 440 or 480 years (depending on which translation you have) after the Israelites left Egypt; I am going with 440 years since that is derived from the earlier Septuagint translation rather than the more recent Masoretic text. And by the way, in case you think it is ridiculous to imagine that a people can keep track of time over a period of over 400 years, we have a parallel and seemingly accurate example from Egypt where pharaoh Ramesses II is said to have celebrated the 400th anniversary of the temple of Seth in the city of Avaris. Besides, the Israelites were counting from a date which they considered to be the very beginning of their existence as a nation.

We then read in Exodus 12:40 that the Israelites left Egypt after 430 years[14] in Egypt and Canaan (again following the Septuagint in its inclusion of Canaan as well as Egypt). Finally, Genesis 12:4 tells us that Abraham travelled to Canaan at the age of 75. Therefore, adding these figures together, Abraham was born about 945 years before the founding of Solomon's temple. And when was that? The answer is "in the 4th year of his reign",

73

and the date given by Biblical scholars is around 965BC, plus or minus a year or so, which then gives us an approximate year in which Abraham son of Terah was born, 1910BC.

Abraham's early years

For Jews, Christians and Muslims alike, Abraham is a key historical character. From his first son Ishmael a large section of the Arab nation traces its lineage and Ishmael is an important figure in Muslim tradition. From his second son Isaac the Jewish race is said to be descended. And the Bible states (Genesis 11:28) that Abraham's native city was Ur. Now you may have read that the Ur of the Bible is really to be identified with a city now called Urfa in southern Turkey – the inhabitants of Urfa would certainly make the case forcibly and they may be right – but there is no escaping the fact that the writer of the book of Genesis in the Bible, or more likely a later editor, inserted the words "of the Chaldeans" by way of explanation as to which city was intended. There is also no escaping the fact that the Chaldeans, when they eventually turn up in 9th Century BC records from Assyria, are to be found in southern Iraq and it is in southern Iraq that the renowned ancient city of Ur is located, a city which, in 1910BC, was once more on the threshold of greatness.

So the straightforward interpretation of the Bible is that, as a young man, Abraham was a citizen of the greatest city in the Middle East, arguably the greatest on Earth. Under the kings of the 3rd Dynasty, Ur was a cultivated place, a place where education would have been the norm. Archaeology reveals the relatively sumptuous standard of accommodation available to the wealthy citizen – not that Abraham's family were necessarily near the top of the social tree!

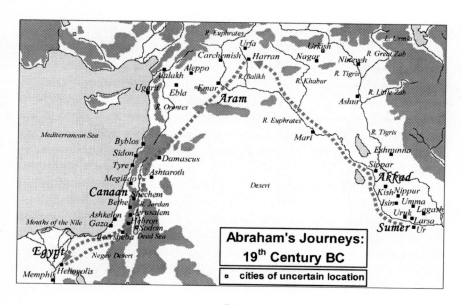

Journey to Canaan

Abraham and his brothers grew up, married and, in one case, died in Ur. Then, for an undisclosed reason, they upped sticks and migrated about 500 miles north-west to Harran in northern Syria, a very important city in Ur empire days and the second centre (after Ur) for worship of the mood god Sin. Harran would have been a mixed Akkadian and Hurrian city at that time. But for Abraham the call of God took him much further still and, at the age of 75, in 1835BC, he set out with his nephew Lot for the land of Canaan, at that time still dominated by Amorite tribes. And the picture of Canaan given in the Bible is definitely compatible with what we know of Amorite times. It was a land where Abraham could lead a nomadic pastoralist life; it was populated by Canaanites, Perizzites, Amorites and Hittites – in fact Abraham's closest colleagues seem to have been Amorites (Mamre, Eshcol and Aner – Genesis 14:13). I am not aware that the identity of the Perizzites has been established[15] but the presence of both Canaanites and Hittites (actually Hattians) is quite consistent with what we would expect.

A Trip to Egypt *(Genesis 12:10-20)*

An unspecified time after his arrival in Canaan, but probably just a few years, the Bible reports that there was a famine in the land and so Abraham and his wife Sarah travelled down to Egypt. The date would have been about 1830BC. Next we read that Sarah, then nearly 70 years old, was taken into the pharaoh's palace as a concubine! Unlikely though this sounds, it is worth noting that Montuhotep II of Egypt was no longer a young man, being in the 30th year of his long reign, so perhaps we shouldn't rush to dismiss the story. Anyway, Sarah's kidnapping proved to be a misunderstanding (of Abraham's own making according to the Bible) and things were sorted out to everyone's satisfaction; in fact, Abraham became a very rich man doing business in Egypt.

Sodom and Gomorrah

One of the few Bible tales which is known by almost everyone is the story of Sodom and Gomorrah, or at least the part of the story where Sodom and Gomorrah are destroyed by fire from heaven (on account of their great wickedness).[16] However, it is not the destruction of the cities which is of direct interest here. Rather, it is a fascinating event recorded in Genesis 14 as having taken place some time after Abraham's trip to Egypt in about 1830BC but before the birth of his first son Ishmael in 1824BC. Abraham had by this time separated from his nephew Lot, who had gone to live in Sodom, while he himself lived with the Amorites near Hebron on the high ground west of the Dead Sea. The Bible records that the cities of Sodom, Gomorrah, Admah, Zeboiim and Zoar were attacked by a confederation of four kings from very distant lands. The attack is initially a success and Lot is abducted along with an unspecified number of the other inhabitants of Sodom. Abraham himself then sends out 318 trained men from his own household (I told you he had become rich!), joining with others from some of the local Amorite chiefs, and the upshot is that the four kings are defeated, Lot and the others are rescued and Abraham earns the undying gratitude of the king of Sodom. The names given in the Bible for the four invading kings are:

> Amraphel king of Shinar
> Arioch king of Ellasar
> Kederlaomer king of Elam
> Tidal king of Goiim

Of these, Shinar we know as Sumer, i.e. southern Iraq. Elam, east of Sumer, is also very familiar; the other two lands are more obscure although Ashur, the capital city of Assyria, has been suggested for Ellasar[17] and Goiim sounds suspiciously like Gutium to me. Turning to the names of the kings, the all-powerful king of Sumer at the time was Shulgi, the second ruler of the 3rd Dynasty of Ur, then about 60 years of age, and his name is clearly not among those mentioned in the Bible. Amraphel king of Shinar/Sumer (probably 'Amar Piel' in Akkadian) may have been a vassal ruler under Shulgi's authority.[18] Kederlaomer is recognisable as 'Kuter Lagamar', a good Elamite name, though no king of Elam of this or any other name is known from the time. However, I mentioned earlier the fact that Shulgi created an Elamite foreign legion, which would explain the presence of Elamite troops in the armies of Sumer. Indeed, this short period in history is just about the only conceivable time when Sumerian and Elamite forces could possibly have been found fighting together so far from home. So, even without a definite understanding of the other two kings and their lands,[19] we have a quite plausible sounding force under the leadership of Ur, arriving in the region of the Dead Sea for some unstated purpose. And a genuine enough purpose is not hard to find; it would most likely have been to secure the interests of the Ur empire in maintaining salt supplies, the Dead Sea region being a key source of salt. The nearby copper mines may also have been of more than passing interest.[20] Unfortunately, no record of such an expedition has been found at Ur or elsewhere in Iraq – not surprising in view of its unsuccessful outcome – but the setting is highly plausible, the names look genuine and, not least, it is hard to see why anyone should make up such a story!

So we leave Abraham in 1800BC, a very old man of 110 years, but a very wealthy man – for a nomadic herder. It was a life he had voluntarily chosen, a life quite unlike that of his forebears. By now he had moved again and was living in Beersheba in the Negev desert region and was energetically engaged in bringing up his second son Isaac.

What was going on in the Rest of the World?

Doubtless many important events were taking place from America (the civilisation of Ecuador spreading south into Peru as a period of higher rainfall begins) to Britain (the Wessex culture – barrow burials etc), but I will confine my remarks here to Hungary and northern Romania. This had been the seat of a stable and apparently peaceful society of farmers and town-dwellers since the 6th Millennium BC. It wasn't quite within the Vinča cultural sphere but it was closely related. It seems that, for about 1000 years, the Carpathian Mountains formed the frontier between this so-called 'Hungarian Tell' culture and the Indo-Europeans of the Ukraine, but that this frontier was crossed in around 2000BC.[21] This was the very beginning of what would later become the 'Urnfield' culture, due to the practice of burying cremation urns, and this was yet another example of a composite society, a blend of new and old. The languages which would emerge from the plains of Hungary would be Indo-European (Celtic and Italic), but the culture was almost a continuation of the old Hungarian Tell culture. You couldn't really claim that all the conquering urges had drained out of these Indo-Europeans when you remember what the Romans went on to achieve, but it was a relatively peaceful phase and quite a contrast to society in contemporary Greek or Hittite lands.

7

Middle Kingdom:
1800–1600BC

We are now over a thousand years into the Bronze Age. Bronze technology has been steadily developing, producing ever harder metals but also leading to lower production costs and therefore greater affordability. During the 3rd Millennium BC, although the Middle East was technically in the Bronze Age, it would have been rare to actually find much bronze! Most of the armies would still have been equipped with flint tips to their spears; most agricultural or domestic implements would have been of wood, antler and flint. Nevertheless, this in no way means that living standards were poor. Luxury in the form of good food, wine and beer, fine cotton or woollen clothing and beautifully crafted woodwork would still have been possible; in many societies house construction was sophisticated, wooden beams on neatly-plastered brick or stone walls and columns allowing multi-storey buildings to be constructed. And now, with the greater availability of bronze, things could only get better!

Trouble in Sumer

In 1800BC life in Sumer was good and the country appeared to be far from any sort of trouble! The 3rd Dynasty of Ur, in the hands of king Shu Sin, ruled a vast area and dominated its neighbours, Elam, Gutium, Assyria and the Hurrian lands. Nevertheless, storm clouds were gathering. The western frontier had become highly unstable; Amorite bands attacked frequently and the Ur regime even built its own 'Great Wall' to keep them out of southern Iraq, although it doesn't seem to have been any more successful than its more famous Chinese counterpart. Then, during the reign of Shu Sin's successor Ibbi Sin, the storm broke. In his 2nd year, 1797BC, he lost control of the important eastern city of Eshnunna. The

Elamite king Lurak Luhhan immediately sensed a weakness and rebelled – but he was too rash; Ibbi Sin defeated him and dragged him back to Ur. Next he had yet another Amorite invasion to contend with; again he was successful. Once more the Elamites revolted; once more, after a hard campaign, Ibbi Sin managed to quell them. But in 1786BC came what would ultimately prove to be a fatal blow when one of Ibbi Sin's own commanders rebelled and set himself up as a rival king in the city of Isin, about 90 miles up-river from Ur. His name was Ishbi Erra, formerly commander of the garrison at Mari, and at a single stroke he had cut away a large proportion of Ibbi Sin's empire. Ur would never recover.

In about 1773BC (if earlier deductions were correct) the Elamites finally administered the *coup de grace*. Under their new king Hutran Tempt they launched a full invasion of southern Iraq and this time they were successful, taking possession of several cities including Ur itself, which they garrisoned and held for many years. As you can imagine, the defeat of Ur, the city that had ruled so absolutely for so long, opened the door to any number of claimants to the right to be lord of Akkad and Sumer. The Elamites had staked their claim in the far south and archaeology attests to the real wealth and power of Elam during Hutran Tempt's reign. Ishbi Erra had siezed the middle ground, while in the north Assyria had become an independent Akkadian-ruled kingdom in about 1790BC. And in the west, Amorite chiefs were pushing forward the frontiers of their land whenever they had the chance.

When the dust settled however it was Ishbi Erra, ruling from Isin, who showed himself to be the most powerful man in the land. He won a significant battle against Elam in about 1760BC and his successor Shu Ilishu finally drove out the Elamite ruler of Ur in about 1752BC. It had been a hard fight, and Isin's kingdom was considerably smaller than that of the Ur empire, but peace and stability could return to the region once more. Isin now held the kingship of Akkad and Sumer and, although other cities had their own rulers, it seems they all acknowledged the primacy of Isin.[1] Trade and prosperity broke out once more. In fact the Isin period saw a tremendous flowering of Sumerian literature; it was the age during which many of the well-known tales and sagas of Sumerian myth were first set down in writing, though of course their origins may go centuries or even millennia back in time, having previously been transmitted purely orally.

The Increasing Power of Egypt

Meanwhile, Montuhotep II's re-unification of Egypt (in about 1839BC in this chronology) had ushered in the so-called 'Middle Kingdom', a long period of sustained power and wealth. By 1800BC, his son Montuhotep III was on the throne, followed in 1797BC by the 7-year reign of Montuhotep IV – "seven empty years" according to the *Turin Canon*, but nevertheless years in which Egyptian trade continued to expand. However, Montuhotep IV had no direct descendants and so the throne passed to his vizier, a man named Amenemes, the first ruler of Manetho's 12th Dynasty. Of course there were plenty of objections to this from Montuhotep's surviving friends and relatives, not to mention a little civil war in the south of the country, but the upshot was that Amenemes was eventually confirmed as king of the two lands (Upper and Lower Egypt) and the dynasty he founded was to be a very successful one indeed. He showed the break with the 11th Dynasty by moving the capital north once more, not to Memphis but to a new city in the Faiyum region of middle Egypt called Itj-tawy.

Unfortunately the precise chronology of the 12th Dynasty rulers is still subject to disagreement between experts. The problem is that, in response to Amenemes I's assassination, a system was introduced of co-regency between rulers and their heirs, which means that there is continuing debate as to whether the reign lengths given in the king lists and deduced from dated texts are to be counted from the start of co-regency or from the date of sole rulership. Estimates for the duration of the whole dynasty therefore range from about 178 years to over 200 years; my own estimate is 190 years, which would mean that the 12th Dynasty fills the period from 1790BC down to 1600BC according to this chronology. However the bottom line is that a decade or so of uncertainty is present and the following reign dates can therefore only be considered approximate.[2]

Amenemes I	1790 – 1761BC
Sesostris I	1761 – 1727BC
Amenemes II	1727 – 1694BC
Sesostris II	1694 – 1677BC
Sesostris III	1677 – 1639BC
Amenemes III	1657 – 1612BC
Amenemes IV	1612 – 1605BC
Sobekneferu	1605 – 1600BC[3]

The reigns of the 12th Dynasty kings marked a dramatic rise in the fortunes of the country and a period during which Egyptian influence again spilled out well beyond her borders. Both Sesostris I and II were particularly active in opening up trade with the Lebanese port of Byblos and the evidence for trade with Crete is also strong.[4]

The Aegean and the Supremacy of Crete

In fact, the wealth which flowed into Egypt during this whole period was unsurprisingly reflected in the growing wealth of Crete. There still seems every reason to believe that Crete dominated the sea lanes of the Mediterranean. Cretan goods from this period (Middle Minoan I, early Middle Minoan II) have been found in Cyprus, Byblos, Egypt and even Hattusas. In Egypt a famous stash of

150 silver cups from Crete was found in the foundation of a temple from the time of Amenemes II; Cretan pottery has been found at Kahun, a town founded by Sesostris II, and numerous 12th Dynasty seals have been found in Middle Minoan I Crete. Cretan goods have also turned up in southern Italy, Sicily and Malta, which leads many to suspect that Cretan trade stretched as far to the west as it did to the east.

On Crete itself, this period saw an ever-increasing magnificence in the great palaces of Knossos, Phaistos and Mallia, as well as in the surrounding cities. Cretan influence in the form of goods is evident on several islands in the Aegean, although without records it is impossible to know whether the relationship was one of friendly co-operation or actual Cretan control. And when I say 'without records', what I mean is without records we can read, because this was the period in which the old hieroglyphic script was superseded by the syllabic script known as 'Linear A'; and when I say 'without records we can read' what I really mean is without records we can translate, because we know with some confidence what the sound values of most of the characters were.[5] Linear A stands as one of the great remaining challenges to linguists. My tip is: try to crack Etruscan first and Linear A will follow with much less effort!

Mainland Greece was full of Cretan culture throughout this period. At the Greek city of Mycenae a famous group of shaft graves containing rich royal burials began use during the Middle Helladic I phase and continued through the whole of this period, and each contains a large number of Cretan products as well as amber, which must have been traded from the Baltic Sea, over 1000 miles to the north. But the lack of Egyptian goods in mainland Greece, contrasting with the relative abundance in Crete, tells us that sea trade was still firmly in Cretan hands.

Cyprus was also a clear beneficiary of Cretan trade, although the construction of fortifications and the presence of an increasing amount of weaponry suggest that all was not entirely peaceful. In fact, the signs are that a new people were starting to make their home on Cyprus. I suggested earlier that the culture and language of Cyprus had, since about 2000BC, been related to that of southwest Turkey. However, Cyprus has always been in a very vulnerable position in relation to the Syrian coast, where the great port of Ugarit lay just 70 miles away. Nothing can be proved, but I strongly suspect that a resurgence in the fortunes of the Canaanites in the 18th Century BC (see below) led to colonisation of their neighbours' land across the water, bringing with them their own brand of northwest Semitic culture.

Canaanites and Amorites

By 1800BC Amorite kings had ruled Palestine for 300 years[6] – but things were about to change. Amorite construction activity has been limited to rather poor quality houses of ill-fired bricks, visible in places such as Ebla, Megiddo and Jericho – but these were not the palaces of kings; Amorite kings dwelt in magnificent and doubtless luxurious tents and, just because there is of course no record of such things from archaeology, it is important not to dismiss the Amorites as uncultured. But, cultured though they may have been, their comfortable world was about to be rudely disturbed.

Archaeologically the change is as clear as daylight and it is seen in the appearance of a quite different culture, Canaanite culture, starting from the Lebanese coastal region around Byblos in about 1750BC (following the dates in this book) and then spreading right across Palestine. These Canaanites were technologically advanced and you have to guess that it was contact with Sesostris I's Egypt that was responsible for this. Their pottery was of a finer nature (wheel-made) and, probably of most significance with regard to their success in defeating the Amorites, they used bronze-tipped weapons, something which had been too costly previously. Canaanite culture spread remarkably rapidly across all Palestine west of the river Jordan, as far as the city of Jericho, while the Amorites were pushed back to the central hill country, where the terrain was less suited to urban development and settled agriculture, and also back east, across the Jordan. A mobile people can disappear as quickly as they arrive, and it looks as though the Amorite nobility simply packed up their tents and looked for pastures new, well to the east of the troublesome Canaanites. And once freed from Amorite shackles, cities soon sprang up from the ruins, or from Amorite shanty towns. Megiddo, Hazor, Lachish, Debir and Jericho all became important centres, trading (and sometimes fighting) amongst themselves and with surrounding lands. As far as culture and beliefs go, there are strong similarities between the religion of these Canaanites and that of Ebla some 400 years earlier judging from the names of gods, which makes perfect sense since Byblos, about 130 miles south-west of Ebla, was closely associated with the old empire of Ebla, quite possibly even part of it.

This was the start of the Middle Bronze Age in Palestine and Middle Bronze Age Canaanite civilisation was destined to endure for a long time. Archaeologists term the first 80 years or so 'Middle Bronze I' but there is no clear break between Middle Bronze I and the succeeding Middle Bronze II, only continuing changes in pottery style. Some confirmation of relative date is found in the fact that the names of pharaohs Amenemes III and IV have both been found at Byblos in an archaeological context equivalent to early Middle Bronze II.[7]

The Settling of the Amorites

The end of Amorite rule in Palestine was a catalyst for change in wider Amorite society, and the influx of refugee kings from Palestine seems to have had a destabilising influence on the Amorite heartland of modern Jordan. Amorite tribes began to pour eastward across the poorly protected border of Iraq and, despite the initially fairly successful attempts of the Isin government to stamp their control on the region, the land gradually became once more unsafe for ordinary farming folk. But times had changed. This time the Amorite kings were not simply looking for pasture for their livestock; they were looking for power-bases, for real kingdoms to rule, and it seems they now had the military muscle to compete with Sumerian and Akkadian armies – and to win. Amorite-controlled city states began to appear all over Iraq. Larsa, just 15 miles north of Ur, is the first we know of, where an Amorite chief named Gungunum seized control during the reign of Lipit Ishtar of Isin. The date was 1702BC according to this chronology (some 230 years later than the most commonly quoted date). Gungunum's rule was apparently accepted – or at least not challenged – by Lipit Ishtar, and it extended to (temporary) control over the ancient city of Ur. In fact, international trade picked up considerably under Gungunum, notably sea trade across the Persian Gulf to Bahrain, Oman, the Iranian coast and even India. Gungunum and his entourage seem to have thoroughly enjoyed taking on the mantle of civilised rulers and they became almost as Sumerian as the Sumerians themselves!

Larsa was followed in about 1660BC by a hitherto little-known town in central Iraq called Babylon. Here, an Amorite leader named Sumu Abum traded his tent for four walls and a roof, founding his own dynasty. The same happened at Eshnunna in the east and Mari in the west, both already important cities, all of which left Isin with much reduced authority. And exactly the same process was under way in Syria, where Amorite kingdoms were founded at Qatna in southern Syria and Aleppo in the north (the kingdom known as 'Yamkhad'). The old days of the Amorite terror were vanishing fast; the new Amorite elite were careful not to antagonise their relatives still living under canvas in the desert[8] but they were as protective of their new-found agricultural base as any native Sumerian or Akkadian could be.

The Assyrian Free Trade Zone

Powerful though the Amorite advance was, the Akkadian-ruled kingdom of Assyria stood firm. When the Ur empire crumbled, Assyria had successfully regained its independence under Puzur Ashur I, and it remained an independent northern kingdom throughout the Isin period, centred on its traditional capital Ashur on the Tigris river. It was not under threat and, released from the dominance of others, the country soon became a centre of international trade. By way of explanation, we have an inscription of king Erishum I (about 1720-1680BC) to the effect that certain goods had been made exempt from taxes, a sure way to stimulate trade,[9] but the key physical evidence has been found many hundreds of miles from Ashur, deep in the upland region of central Turkey.

Archaeologists have uncovered evidence that a substantial quarter of Kanesh, a city about 700 miles from Ashur, was given over to a colony of Assyrian merchants, and this is known because a stash of some 15000 cuneiform tablets was found there, written in Akkadian and detailing the business activities of the merchants. It seems that these merchants controlled a vast network of trade between Ashur and numerous cities in Turkey and that Kanesh acted as a regional headquarters. Many different materials were traded, but the prime products which attracted Assyria were gold, silver and iron,[10] and these they purchased by exchange for woollen goods and tin. However, business was business, and many merchants simply concentrated on the business generated between the different Turkish cities; some also traded with the Hurrian regions of southern Turkey and northern Syria,[11] notably with the cities of Ursu, Carchemish and Alalakh. The impression given by the Kanesh tablets is that Assyria was now the key economic power throughout the Hurrian lands; indeed, Assyria would itself have had a large Hurrian population.

Assyrian commerce was a real success story and you can be very sure that the rulers of Ashur saw a proportion of the profits despite their generous tax policies. But a rather important question might be: just who were the Assyrians trading with beyond the Hurrian lands?

The First Kings of the Hittites

As you can see from the heading, the short answer is "the Hittites". The majority of the non-Assyrian names mentioned in the Kanesh tablets are identifiably Indo-European which, in Turkey, means Hittite. Some are Hattian – as I said, Hittite culture was really an amalgam of Hattian and Indo-European. By the late 18th Century BC, much of Turkey was divided into numerous Hittite-ruled city states of which Kanesh was one. Hattusas, the later capital of the Hittite empire, was another, and one or two tablets relating to Assyrian trade have turned up there too. Experts disagree on the location of most of the other cities mentioned

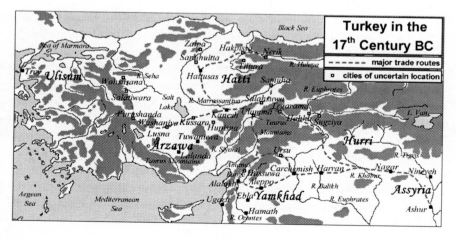

in the texts; personally I believe the network extended far to the west. Besides detailing trade, the tablets also give us a window onto the political situation, including the inevitable rivalry which was developing between the various Hittite states. For example, we read of trouble in the land of 'Purushanda', which meant that journeys to the cities of 'Salatiwara' and 'Wahsusana' were temporarily abandoned. But overall this was a time of peaceful development, of growing economic power and a formative phase in Hittite political life. For nearly a century the Assyrian trade was sufficiently important to stifle what might otherwise have grown into dangerous conflicts; peace suited everyone – for a while.

However, that peace was shattered in about 1620BC.[12] Archaeology tells us quite unequivocally that the Assyrian merchant colony at Kanesh was burnt to the ground, along with much of the rest of the city. A later Hittite document recalls the sack of Kanesh by Uhna king of Zalpa, a city somewhere in northern Turkey, at least 100 miles from Kanesh. Of course we cannot be certain why this took place,[13] but jealousy of Kanesh's favoured status with the Assyrian merchants is likely to have played a part. Whatever the underlying causes, this act of aggression had the effect of sending the merchants packing and putting a halt to the flow of Assyrian luxury goods into Turkey.

The Peak of Middle Kingdom Egypt

Meanwhile, back in Egypt, the people had never had it so good! The two greatest rulers of the 12th Dynasty were undoubtedly Sesostris III and his son Amenemes III. Sesostris III, who came to the throne in about 1677BC, was responsible for a major reorganisation of the state, drastically reducing the power of the regional aristocracy by dividing the land into three divisions, each with a vizier at its head. He also strengthened Egypt's international position by sending military expeditions against Kush, the land to the south of Egypt, and reinforcing the southern frontier with a string of new forts. In Palestine he is reported to have captured Shechem and mention is also made of Ashkelon and Jerusalem.[14] At home, he undertook major canal building activity to allow the easier passage of Egyptian shipping up the Nile. The result of all this was that, when Amenemes III took sole command in 1639BC, after 18 years of joint rule, Egypt was at the height of its powers, as strong as at any time under the great pyramid-building monarchs of the Old Kingdom. Amenemes carried out large numbers of building projects, many of them in the region of the Faiyum, a large lake in middle Egypt not far from the capital Itj-Tawy and basically an overspill for the Nile floods. The whole Faiyum region saw tremendous development during the 12th Dynasty.[15]

And so the good times rolled on, through the reign of Amenemes III's son Amenemes IV and then the rule of queen Sobekneferu, who was probably either the sister or widow of Amenemes IV. Archaeology reveals no significant break and absolutely no sign of any trouble right through to the end of Sobekneferu's reign. Yet a very significant change was about to take place, a change for which Egyptologists have no ready explanation at all – but a change that will have to wait until the next chapter!

Summary

To look at the Middle East in the 17th Century BC, you could be forgiven for thinking that mankind had developed a serious case of common sense! Of course there were still wars, but these were of limited extent and duration and the periods of peace were long and prosperous. Egypt was on a particularly marked high; so was Crete. Assyria had been developing nicely until its valuable Turkish trade network was smashed by the rather unpredictable Hittites. But perhaps best news of all, the dreaded Amorites were now much less dreadful than they had been, preferring the route of civilisation and the domesticated life to that of warfare and hardship. True, blood was certainly spilt as they took over much of Iraq and northern Syria, but Amorite rule was now bringing real prosperity. The fact that so many countries enjoyed simultaneous periods of thriving commerce and increasing wealth is eloquent proof of the way that the economies of all parts of the region were inextricably linked. If you had tried to read the tea-leaves in the late 17th Century BC, you could hardly have refrained from a real feeling of optimism!

What does the Bible have to say?

Both Abraham (Genesis 21:22-34) and his son Isaac (Genesis 26) are reported to have made treaties with a gentleman called Abimelech king of "Gerar", also referred to as "the

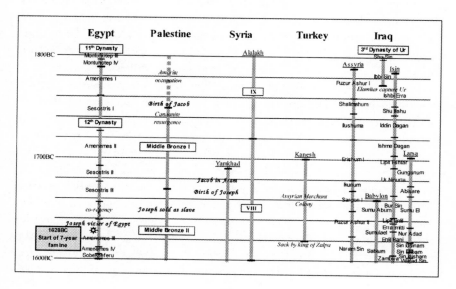

land of the Philistines". It is clear that the land of Gerar lay on the coast of southern Palestine, the modern Gaza strip and neighbouring parts of Israel. So who could these Philistines have been?

The Origin of the Philistines

To almost all historians this mention of the Philistines at such an early date is anachronistic – which means it just shouldn't be there! The problem is that the Philistines have become strongly associated with a particular type of pottery which turns up in the region many hundreds of years later, a pottery known informally as 'Philistine ware'. But it isn't stamped as such! I will reach that episode of history in several chapters' time, but the Bible makes it very clear that, as far as several of its writers were concerned, "the Philistines came from Crete" (Jeremiah 47:4; Amos 9:7).[16] And it could well be true. It is quite certain that Cretan seafaring took Cretan ships and Cretan produce right around the coasts of Syria and Palestine to Egypt and it did so from the time of the Egyptian Old Kingdom onwards. After the Amorites had been thrown out of Egypt in about 1890BC the southern Palestinian coast would have been weak, and it may well be that Cretan settlers took possession of some of the ancient sites such as Ashkelon and Gaza. Their language certainly didn't survive, just as the French of William the Conqueror didn't survive in England, but part of their culture may well have done so. Abimelech is a Semitic name but he may well have presided over a kingdom which had been put in place by Cretans.[17]

The Hattians of Hebron

The ethnic make-up of Palestine is emphasised when Abraham negotiates the purchase of a field near Hebron from a people who usually translate as 'Hittites' (Genesis 23). This is of course quite consistent with the known presence of Hattians in the land – they had now been there for around 800 years – and, if the Bible story is correct, it implies that some town life continued through the centuries of Amorite control, since Hebron is clearly identified as a Hittite (or Hattian) town.

The Land of Aram

When Abraham's servant heads off in search of a wife for Isaac (Genesis 24), he goes to the house of Abraham's brother Nahor in the land of "Aram". Is this reasonable? Well, it is certainly interesting. Outside the Bible the world will not be hearing of Aram for many centuries, but when they do it will be found in eastern Syria, a little to the south of Harran, and you will remember that Abraham left his family behind at Harran when he set out for the land of Canaan. Whether a distinct Aramaean people already existed at this early date[18] or whether the references are simply made by later authors who then knew the region as Aram[19] is an open question. I suggest the truth is most likely to be that the land had been known as Aram for as long as anyone could remember and that whoever lived there would therefore be known as Aramaean, in just the same way that Hatti and

Canaan also transferred their names from the land to the inhabitants. In fact Abraham himself is later referred to as a "wandering Aramaean" (Deuteronomy 26.5).

Isaac and his sons

Isaac lived out his days in southern Palestine and the neighbouring Negev desert. His eldest son (of twins) Esau married two "Hittite" (i.e. Hattian) women (Genesis 26:34), elsewhere referred to as "Canaanite", which doubtless reflects a blurring of the distinction between the two peoples. The younger son Jacob left home and travelled to Aram, to the land of his relatives, where he too married (four different women) and fathered twelve children, from whom the twelve tribes of Israel take their names (Genesis 28-30). The Bible's picture of the land of Canaan and its inhabitants is consistent with the period during which Canaanite dominance was becoming re-established. The fact that Isaac lived on the fringes of Canaan could have been in part because nomadic pastoralism was becoming more difficult in the new Canaanite society.

Joseph the Dreamer

Joseph was the second youngest of Jacob's sons. According to the Bible, Abraham fathered Isaac at the age of 100, which would be in 1810BC; Isaac then became the father of Jacob at the age of 60, say 1751BC.[20] The unknown factor is Jacob's age when Joseph was born. He left for Aram some time after his brother Esau's marriage, at which time they were both 40 years old, but there is little clue as to how long after – long enough for Rebekah, Isaac's wife, to become thoroughly fed up with Esau's Hattian wives! However, in Genesis 47:9 Jacob tells the Egyptian pharaoh that he is 130 years old (!) and the context allows us to estimate that Jacob's son Joseph was then in his early 40's. On this evidence Jacob travelled to Aram at the ripe old age of 72 and he was about 86 years old at the birth of his eleventh son Joseph. Thus Joseph would have been born in roughly 1666BC. If you are not an implicit believer in the Bible, you may be rather shocked that I appear not to question the remarkably slow ageing rate with which Abraham's family seems to have been blessed. However, that subject lies wholly outside the scope of this book. All I will try to do here is to deduce the historical context of the Bible if it should turn out to be true. Its truth or otherwise is of course an enormously important subject upon which I have strong views – but not here!

To continue: you probably know something of the story of Joseph (Genesis 37 and 39-41), how he dreamed his dreams and thoroughly annoyed his brothers to the extent that they actually sold him to a bunch of passing traders ('Midianites' – from the region of Medina according to Arab tradition), pretending to their father that he had been killed. They got a good price for him too, 18 silver shekels – more than the going rate in 22nd Century BC Ebla (13 shekels) or 19th Century BC Ur (11 shekels). The 17-year old Joseph was then sold on into Egypt, at that time (1649BC) under the joint rule of Sesostris III and his son Amenemes III. It was the height of the Middle Kingdom and there was a lively market in foreign slaves, particularly bright young slaves like Joseph, and so he found himself *taken on as a steward in the house of an important Egyptian official. So far nothing too remarkable; there were probably many such slaves brought to Egypt from foreign parts and I am sure that several of them did very well for themselves. But what propels Joseph into a unique category, according to the Bible, is the fact that he actually rose to be vizier of the entire land of Egypt! Pharaoh dreamed a dream and, to cut a long story short, only Joseph could tell him the meaning; and the meaning was that there would be 7 years of bumper harvests in Egypt followed by 7 years of famine. Pharaoh was so impressed at Joseph that he entrusted the young (30-year old) foreigner with the task of getting Egypt through the famine, which he duly did. But are we really to believe such a tale? Is there any independent evidence?*

Seven years of Bumper Harvests

Several researchers have drawn attention to a unique set of measurements which were made during the reigns of Amenemes III and his immediate successors, namely records of the maximum height reached by the Nile flood where the river passes through the Semna gorge on Egypt's southern border. Only fourteen of the height markers have been found still in position from a period of some 50 years duration, but that is enough to give a general impression of what was happening. The first point to note is that the average height recorded is some 6 metres above recent historical levels (before the Aswan dam was constructed). This sounds dramatic, but when one considers the fact that the river bed has been eroding over a period of nearly 4000 years, in turn reducing the water surface level, the average volume of water coming down the river may actually have been similar to that today. However, the key point is that over a period of 13 years, between Amenemes' 20th and 32nd years inclusive (1638-1625BC), all remaining height markers show flood levels about 3 metres higher than those before or after. This additional flood volume would have irrigated a very wide area indeed and the likely result would have been bumper harvests.

Seven years of Famine

The bumper harvests should have continued until 1625BC. However, this was not to be. In 1628BC, or possibly the previous year, something dramatic occurred somewhere on the planet, something which would have worldwide repercussions. Many believe it to have been the eruption of the volcano on the island of Thera. It may quite possibly have been a volcanic eruption but definitely not Thera, which was then a thriving island and probably a directly controlled part of the Cretan empire. However, for purposes of this discussion it matters not a jot what the event actually was; it simply matters that it was significant enough to cause a worldwide reduction in tree growth as deduced from the widths of annual rings in bristlecone pine trees in America and Irish oaks in Europe,[21] relating to the years from 1628 to about 1622BC; and if trees were so dramatically affected, all living plants would also have been similarly affected. No matter how good the Nile flood, dust in the atmosphere meant that the quality of sunlight reaching the crops was inadequate and it led to greatly reduced harvests, in Egypt, Palestine and in every other coun-

try on Earth. It has always been difficult to explain why a famine in Egypt should also have been felt in Palestine where Joseph's brothers lived, since the sources of fertility of the two lands are so entirely different, but a global reduction in sunlight answers the point very well indeed.

Absolute date: 1628BC
The first of several years of poor harvest due to atmospheric dust
of unknown origin

The evidence, both for bumper harvests and for famine, is fully in accord with the Bible record. If Joseph became vizier in 1636BC as the numbers in the Bible suggest, there would have been 7 further years (1635-1629BC) of above-average floods and excellent crop yields followed by about 7 years (1628-1622BC) of poor vegetation growth world-wide. The Egyptian records do not mention Joseph by name, but neither do they mention many high officials. However, it is undeniable that the Bahr Yussuf (waterway of Joseph) is the name of a major waterway linking the Nile with the Faiyum, the centre of activity for Amenemes III and many of the other 12th Dynasty rulers.

So, the tie-up between the Bible and known history does indeed look pretty good at this stage, with the rather dramatic shift in dating of world events which I am propos-ing. The 17th Century BC would have come to an end with Joseph, his brothers and his entire extended family living in Egypt, having stayed there after the famine. As the next chapter will indicate, they were living in or around the city of Avaris in the Nile delta, the major northern administrative centre founded by the 12th Dynasty pharaohs and a city where Asiatic-type burials have been discovered dating from the late 12th Dynasty pe-riod.[22] Joseph would have been a respected elder statesman of 66 years of age, an hon-orary Egyptian citizen.

What was going on in the Rest of the World?

This time I am going to look east because this was a very significant period in the history of India. Just as Indo-European tribes had overrun Greece (and the rest of the Balkans) and Turkey, so they were now moving into India. Speakers of the Indic branch of the family had already filled eastern Iran and Afghanistan, and they now started to descend onto the plains of the Indus, modern Pakistan. This is actually a very touchy subject area for some historians, although from a lin-guistic point of view the very fact that Indic languages like Hindi and Bengali made it to India means that Indic culture must have entered the country some-how. There are very few linguists who believe that the Indo-European family began life in India. Put this evidence alongside ancient Indian tradition contained in the epic tales of the Rigveda and I personally find it hard to come to any conclusion other than that Indo-European invaders began the conquest of northern Pakistan in the 18th or 17th Century BC. These were the 'Aryans' of the Rigveda and their victims were the 'Dasyas'. Of course, history is written by the winners, so it would be unreasonable to expect the Rigveda to present a balanced picture of events, but the clear message is of a series of wars between the two peoples, culminating in victory for the Aryans.

Much has been made of the lack of archaeological evidence for this invasion, but the truth is that the prosperous and long-lasting Indus valley civilisation fell at around this time, at least in northern Pakistan, and that it was replaced by a culture which showed strong affinities with Central Asia, a culture which brought the horse to the subcontinent.[23] It is true that many aspects of the Indus valley culture survived and still survive in Hindu religion, but then that is exactly typical of all the lands where Indo-European speakers went. Greek culture was largely Cretan, Hittite culture was largely Hattian, but there is no denying the fact that Indo-Europeans physically invaded and conquered both Greece and Turkey.

The upshot of all this for the Middle East would eventually be the decline of the long-distance trade to India. It still continued in Gungunum's day (1702-1675BC), but it would be reducing shortly thereafter.

8

The Rise of Babylon: 1600–1500BC

The Turbulent World of the Amorites

By 1600BC Amorite dynasties ruled Larsa in southern Iraq, Babylon in the centre of the country, Eshnunna in the east and Mari in the west. In Syria, they had expanded the city state of Aleppo into the large and powerful kingdom of 'Yamkhad'. They also ruled Qatna to the south of Yamkhad and Carchemish to the north. The only non-Amorite ruling houses in Iraq were at Isin and Ashur – and both would soon fall.

But this was no unified Amorite empire. Each king was independent and often in conflict with his neighbours, no matter their common cultural stock. Besides, these rulers had by now almost forgotten their Amorite roots and saw themselves as Akkadian and thoroughly civilised. But nomadic Amorites still roamed the fringes of the settled lands, and among them were the descendants of a certain king Hale, who once pitched his tent in the Khabur river region of north-east Syria.[1] And so we pick up the story in the early years of the 16th Century BC with one of king Hale's successors named Shamsi Adad setting himself up in the city of Terqa on the Euphrates river, well within Mari's sphere of interest. Yaggid Lim king of Mari had no intention of standing for this and he was powerful enough to drive Shamsi Adad out. But this only served to teach the young Shamsi Adad the arts of politics and war, and he looked around, as Amorite leaders tended to do, to see if he could carve out an opening for himself elsewhere. His eye lighted upon the rich land of Assyria, in his eyes ripe for the taking since suffering a serious defeat at the hands of the Amorite king of Eshnunna. Shamsi Adad promptly seized and held onto the town of Ekellate north of Ashur. The details are vague,[2] but we know that the kingdom of Assyria was soon in the hands of Shamsi Adad the Amorite. If the dates deduced so far are correct, Shamsi Adad came to power in Ashur in about 1582BC.

Meanwhile, Shamsi Adad's father Illakhabkabu had actually succeeded in driving Yaggid Lim out of Mari, before the tables were turned and Yaggid Lim's son Yahdum Lim was able to retake the city and sit on the throne of his father.[3] By the way, a lot of the evidence we have for this phase of Iraqi history comes from the palace archives of Mari, together with large numbers of records from Sippar near Babylon; it is just the luck of the archaeological draw that we have so much excellent information from this period. We are also blessed with a respectable number of documents from Alalakh and they reveal that in about 1600BC the Hurrian city of Alalakh had been taken over by the Amorite-controlled state of Yamkhad with its capital at Aleppo. The Alalakh documents are written in Akkadian, as all official records in the region seem to have been, and we learn that Yamkhad was strongly allied to Mari.

The next major act took place in approximately 1570BC. It was the murder of Yahdum Lim of Mari on the orders, so it is thought, of Shamsi Adad of Assyria, and the 'acquisition' of the city and all its lands. Shamsi Adad now controlled a large empire stretching across northern Iraq and north-east Syria, and south west to the river Euphrates. He put his second son Yasmah Adad in charge of Mari, a thoroughly worthless individual if the evidence of the Mari archives is to be believed. He may have been the son of a great warrior chief but he had developed

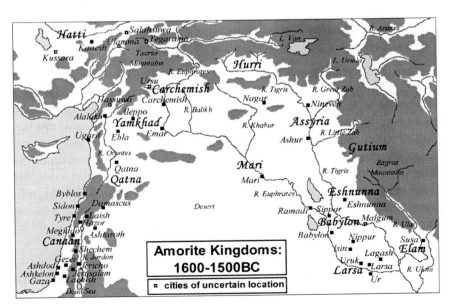

an undying liking for the easy life; we have several letters from his father and elder brother back in Ashur complaining of his laziness.

Keeping rather quiet in this brutal world of Amorite politics were the rulers of Babylon in central Iraq. They had strengthened their position over the years, taking control of neighbouring cities including Sippar. But, when Hammurabi took over the throne of his father Sin Muballit in 1562BC, Babylon was still a comparatively small player sandwiched between the powerful southern king-dom of Rim Sin of Larsa and the growing domain of Shamsi Adad of Ashur. Babylon survived by making shrewd alliances, sometimes with Eshnunna to the east, also with the claimant to the throne of Mari, Yahdum Lim's son Zimri Lim – and, by extension, Yamkhad. Shamsi Adad countered this by developing strong ties with Carchemish in the north-west and Qatna south of Yamkhad, alliances which brought about a nice balance of power. A few years previously, Rim Sin of Larsa had finally extinguished the life from the last remaining non-Amorite power in the region, namely Isin – only to lose it again, to Hammurabi. In fact Rim Sin's capture of Isin in 1564BC is the key event which allows us to date these times relative to what went before, since the reign lengths of the Isin kings are well recorded and can be fairly confidently tied to the end of the 3rd Dynasty of Ur some 200 years previously.[4]

And so the stalemate continued, except that Hammurabi strengthened his hand with the capture of Ramadi from Shamsi Adad's son and also Malgum from Eshnunna. The situation is summed up in an oft-quoted text from the Mari archives:

> There is no king who by himself is strongest. Ten or fifteen kings follow Hammurabi of Babylon; as many follow Rim Sin of Larsa, Ibal Piel of Eshnunna and Amut Piel of Qatna, while twenty kings follow Yarim Lim of Yamkhad.

Then, in 1550BC, Shamsi Adad, the most powerful man in the Middle East, died. Within a year or so his son Yasmah Adad had been ousted from Mari (with the support of Yamkhad and Babylon) and Zimri Lim was back in the palace he grew up in. The balance shifted. Shamsi Adad's eldest son Ishme Dagan, the new king of Ashur, was now under pressure from Eshnunna, whose rulers sensed blood. They had the close co-operation of their eastern neighbours the Elamites as well. But Ishme Dagan held out and stalemate was restored once more. The 1540s came and went; so did half the 1530s. Unstable though the nature of Amorite politics most certainly was, power was just too finely balanced for any single ruler to break the deadlock.

The Growing Power of the Hittites

While the Amorite kings jockeyed for position in Syria and Iraq, a new power was steadily emerging in Turkey. In Kanesh, archaeology tells us that the city was resettled some 40 years after its sack (in about 1620BC) by armies from Zalpa and the consequent suspension of Assyrian commercial relations. In the next archaeological phase (Level 1b) cuneiform tablets tell us of a certain king Inar and his son Warsama, and of conflict with an adjacent kingdom known as 'Mama',[5] and the picture which emerges is one of relatively small kingdoms, diplomatic alliances and conflicts. Kanesh, Mama, Hattusas, Zalpa and Purushanda were five of the larger states. Kanesh Level 1b, which coincides with Shamsi Adad's reign in Ashur, also provides evidence that the Assyrian merchants were active once more. However, trade never regained the levels seen a generation or so earlier[6] and the merchant colony was abruptly snuffed out again after another 30 to 40 years, probably early in the reign of Shamsi Adad's son Ishme Dagan; but by whom?

In the archives of Hattusas, three fragmentary copies of an inscription have been found which tell of a Hittite king named Pithana. He came from a city called Kussara (perhaps located just outside the modern city of Aksaray, about 70 miles west of Kanesh[7]) and we read that he conquered Kanesh and became its king, and it is presumed by most that this is the conquest which put a final end to the Assyrian merchant colony.[8] Pithana's son Anitta[9] then proceeded to conquer much of Turkey. The inscription tells us that he defeated Zalpa in the north and that he razed Hattusas to the ground; his domain also included Ulamma, well to the south-east of Kanesh.[10] He fought two campaigns against the city of Salatiwara, which I suggest was probably far to the west, and he finally received the submission of Purushanda, whose ruler had previously been known as 'king of kings' and which had for centuries been the leading city in all of Turkey. Admittedly there are as many opinions on the extent of his territory as there are students of Hittite history, but the key point is that, by around 1530BC, Anitta had set up the first true Hittite empire that we know of, and with the capture of Ulamma that empire bordered directly onto the Amorite-ruled lands to the south.

Of course just because Anitta's empire is the first to be documented in Turkey, that doesn't mean there weren't any earlier empires! Before the recent interpretation of Mayan glyphs, the conventional academic position was that Mayans were peace-loving folk who concerned themselves with matters of religion and art. Now we know that they were as vicious as any other race of humans and fought as many wars as anyone else. We can also see the extent of their empires and kingdoms. Logic strongly suggests that the traditional title of the king of Purushanda, 'king of kings', was given for a good reason and that reason can hardly be anything other than that Purushanda had previously been at the centre of a genuine empire in Turkey, unfortunately an empire which had not appreciated the value of writing things down for the benefit of future generations of archaeologists and historians!

The Hurrian Lands

This last point also very much applies to the Hurrians. Writing was just not part of their culture. Hurrian names appear extensively in the Mari archives[11] as well as in texts from Kanesh, but we know little of Hurrian states. The records of Alalakh VII give us a window onto one small corner of the Hurrian world – but only after it had been absorbed into the Amorite-ruled kingdom of Yamkhad. Most of the names in Alalakh VII texts are Hurrian but the texts are all in the Akkadian language. The majority of the texts relate to the rule of Yarim Lim, the king who was overlord to 20 other kings, compared to 10-15 each for Babylon, Larsa, Eshnunna and Qatna; a smaller number of texts date from the reign of his son Niqme Epuh.

Alalakh VII also brings me to a well-known but much abused tie-up between events in Syria and Turkey. A certain general in Yamkhad's army named Zukrasi is mentioned both in a tablet from Alalakh VII and in a Hittite record found at Hattusas. The Alalakh reference puts the date some time during Yarim Lim's rule, roughly 1550-1520BC; the Hittite reference relates to a battle between Hittite forces (king unnamed) and those of Yamkhad at a city called Hassuwa whose location was not far north of Alalakh[12]. The date allows me no other conclusion than that the Hittite ruler who fought general Zukrasi at Hassuwa was either Pithana or, much more likely, his son Anitta. Yet commentator after commentator has attributed this Hittite attack to the well-known king Hattusili I, whom we shall meet in the next chapter, so far as I can see for no better reason than that he is known to have fought at Hassuwa. There is absolutely no way that this interpretation is correct; the relative date range is fixed[13] and the choice of Hittite ruler is limited to either Pithana or Anitta, kings of Kanesh.

There are very clear signs that Yamkhad's rule was not at all popular in Alalakh. The palace had to be remodelled at some stage to make it more readily defensible against attack from the city and, when the palace was de-stroyed at the end of Level VII, the site was used as a refuse tip and was not built on again for well over a century. Similarly, the site of the temple sanctuary, which had been in use for hundreds of years, was abandoned after Alalakh VII. And perhaps the clearest evidence of all is that the old pottery forms from the Level VIII city, which had completely disappeared during Level VII, were carefully resurrected following the destruction of Niqme Epuh's palace and the other official buildings in the city. All the signs are that Alalakh had thrown off the unwelcome yoke of Yamkhad's rule (perhaps with the co-operation of Anitta's Hittite armies) and regained its independence as a sovereign Hurrian state. The date would have been some time in the last two decades of the 16th Century BC.

The Mediterranean World

One of the questions debated by archaeologists is whether inspiration for the architecture and decoration of the great palaces at Mari and Alalakh was derived from Crete or whether the influence was the other way round, because the parallels are far too strong to be coincidental. Great palaces had been built on Crete since the 19th Century BC (according to my chronology) and naturalistic frescos have been found dating to the Middle Minoan II period, which started around the time of Sesostris II of Egypt, judging from the discovery of Cretan pottery fragments at Kahun and Harageh in Egypt, i.e. around 1680BC. On the other hand, Zimri Lim's palace at Mari most closely matches the subsequent Middle Minoan III phase. In short, I won't pretend I can settle the issue. Communication by sea would have been in the hands of Cretans, so I guess the logical interpretation is that Cretan travellers saw things they liked and put them into practice back home, but perhaps the real point is not who had the ideas first but the fact that ideas travelled at all. It reinforces the message that Cretan commercial power was still extensive. Tablets at Mari speak of imports from Crete and Hammurabi-style seals have been found on Crete itself.

But Crete was about to get a nasty shock from nature. The great Middle Minoan II palace at Knossos, together with the rest of the city, was shaken to the ground by a large earthquake and the other cities of Crete also suffered considerable damage. Dating can only be approximate, marked by the Middle Minoan II/III transition, but the earthquake must have occurred some time between 1550 and 1500BC. However, the palaces and cities were soon rebuilt and Cretan power hardly suffered more than a blip.[14]

In mainland Greece the material culture (notably pottery) was becoming ever more Cretan in appearance and the general picture is quite compatible with a Cretan empire of some sort, although without readable records this has to remain purely conjectural.

In Cyprus, the century from 1600 to 1500BC sees no significant change. There still appear to be real differences between different sections of the population, which probably reflects the presence of peoples originating from both western Turkey and Syria.

Egypt's Bold Experiment

Meanwhile Egypt had most certainly experienced major change! The Egyptian 13th Dynasty, which started life in about 1600BC, is a real nightmare for historians. It was a unique period in the history of the country. Whatever your views on the desirability of a hereditary monarchy for good government, there can be no doubt of its usefulness for historical research! There is just no substitute for having a reliable list of rulers to refer to. The problem is that, for some as yet undiscovered reason, Egypt decided to completely change the way in which it was governed and, during the first phase of the 13th Dynasty, there was a bewildering succession of very short-reigning pharaohs, a year being a typical reign length. We have a fragmentary king list on papyrus (the *Turin Canon*) but not enough surviving detail to give us more than a rough estimate of the duration. Most historians assign about 50 years to the first phase of the 13th Dynasty before three slightly longer-lasting pharaohs, Neferhotep I, Sobekhotep IV and Sobekhotep V, signal a temporary return to the more usual way of operating.[15] These three rulers were then followed by another long and nearly illegible list of remarkably short-reigning pharaohs. I have not come across any convincing explanation as to why Egypt should have experimented with this new and quite different system of government and indeed we don't know what that system really was except that it was highly bureaucratic and that there is evidence that continuity was provided by a dynasty of viziers rather than by the pharaohs themselves.[16] It may have been that rulers were in some way elected to serve a short term, as we elect presidents and prime ministers today, but the terms of office are unusually short even for this. Perhaps votes of no confidence were permitted rather more regularly than seems to be the case in our modern democracies!

However, this complete change of government style was not accompanied by any immediate loss of wealth; if anything, the graves of the early 13th Dynasty are even richer than those of the 12th.[17] Nor was there any reduction in trade. Egyptian products are found in Crete as well as at cities like Ugarit and Byblos throughout this period. In fact, an early 13th Dynasty style scarab was found in the same level of votive offerings at the sacred cave of Psychro on Crete as a Hammurabi-style seal, providing some confirmation of relative dating. Relations with Lebanon are exemplified by a limestone slab discovered at Byblos bearing a readable part of the cartouche of Neferhotep I of Egypt, and which also gave the name of the king of Byblos at the time, Yantin Ammu. Fortunately the name Yantin Ammu also appears in the Mari tablet archive (he gave a gift to king Zimri Lim of Mari) and so a Byblos king of the same name must have been a contemporary of Zimri Lim. The straightforward deduction is that Neferhotep I's rule fell within the reign of Zimri Lim (about 1550-1531BC). Relative dating therefore looks to be just about spot on.

But what about absolute dating? It is a long time since the start of the Egyptian calendar and the only supporting evidence for absolute dating I have given you since then (other than tree ring evidence in support of Biblical dates) has been an eclipse sighting in Iraq. Fortunately, however, the 13th Dynasty brings us a further clue, and we have the Egyptian calendar to thank once more. David Rohl is among those who draw attention to a fragmentary stela from Karnak of an otherwise unknown king Sobekhotep, commemorating the coming of the king just as the flood waters of the Nile inundated the floor of the temple and it is dated to one of the 5 additional days (to make up the 365) right at the end of the calendar year. Now, a high flood is most likely to have occurred in late August or early September, between 30 and 50 days after the start of the actual flood season. Since the inscription date is close to the start of the calendar year (i.e. the start of the calendrical 'flood' season), the mismatch between the calendar and reality would also have been approximately 30 to 50 days, equating to a date about 120 to 200 years before the start of a Great Sothic Year. As the next Sothic cycle was due to begin in 1369BC, this gives a likely date range for this particular king Sobekhotep somewhere between 1570 and 1490BC. Now Sobekhotep is an uncompromisingly 13th Dynasty name (there are 7 known kings Sobekhotep in addition to this one) and there are several very short-reigning kings listed in the *Turin Canon* for the second half of the 13th Dynasty whose names are completely indecipherable, so the king commemorated on the stela was almost certainly one of these.

> **Absolute date range: 1570-1490BC**
> Stela commemorating an unknown king Sobekhotep from the second half of the 13th Dynasty

This date range fits perfectly with the chronology proposed here – and not at all well with conventional wisdom. In the conventional chronology, the 13th Dynasty ends in about 1675BC, over 100 years before the likely date range for this flood stela. This one silly little piece of evidence is enough to cast very serious doubt on conventional thinking.[18]

The Deadlock is broken in Iraq

The balance of power between the Amorite kingdoms lasted until 1534BC. In that year Eshnunna and Ashur, long time enemies, opted to gang up rather than fight each other all the time and, with the support of Elamite armies, they decided that the time had come for Babylon to be 'taken out'. They miscalculated very badly indeed! Hammurabi was a good general as well as a good political strategist and with the support of his friend Zimri Lim of Mari the battle was won. With the northern and eastern threats lifted, and with the venerable Rim Sin of Larsa approaching the 60th year of his remarkable reign, Hammurabi took the opportunity to do the unexpected. In 1533BC he carried out a lightening campaign in the south, took Larsa and all Rim Sin's kingdom and returned to Babylon very much the biggest player on the board. The year 1532BC saw Hammurabi take the battle to Eshnunna and Ashur, defeating them both and incorporating their territories into his now sizeable empire.[19] In two years Hammurabi had gone from being a candidate for extinction to undisputed lord of

Akkad and Sumer. However, when he looked at the map, he couldn't help noticing an area in west-central Iraq which was still outside his control and that irked him! Technically Zimri Lim was a friend and undeniably he had been a big help in the struggle against Ashur and Eshnunna, but all is fair in love, war and Amorite politics so, in 1531BC, Hammurabi completed his bid for world domination by conquering and later burning down Zimri Lim's palace – and the whole city of Mari – snuffing the life for ever out of one of the greatest cities of the ancient world. There, under the gathering dust of millennia, the scorched tablets of the royal archive waited patiently for the archaeologist's spade to unearth them in the 20th Century AD! Without those tablets our knowledge of these times would be immeasurably poorer.

Let me mention briefly the other reason why Hammurabi is so famous. It is his law code, inscribed in Akkadian cuneiform on a large black basalt statue, the longest surviving text in the Akkadian language of the Old Babylonian era. It is not the only such law code from the ancient world, nor is it the first (we have quotations from Ur Nammu's laws for instance), but it is certainly the most complete. We are indeed fortunate that the famous statue containing Hammurabi's laws was looted by the Elamite king Shutruk Nahhunte during his conquest of southern Iraq some hundreds of years later and taken to Susa, the Elamite capital, where it was later buried in the ruins of that city. It currently resides in the Louvre Museum in Paris. The statue was looted from Sippar rather than from Babylon itself, which implies that there may well once have been several copies of the law code spread around the cities of Hammurabi's empire. Basically, apart from an introduction and a postscript, it consists of a set of conditional sentences, for example: "If a woman has brought about the death of her husband because of another man, they shall impale that woman on stakes". In fact, there are numerous such laws describing the punishment to be applied for a given offence. The 'eye for an eye' principle is enshrined: "If a free man has put out the eye of another free man, they shall put out his eye". On the other hand distinctions in relation to class are apparent: "If a free man has put out the eye of a bondsman, he shall pay one mina of silver". According to the text, the laws were set down "that the strong may not oppress the weak and to give justice to the orphan and the widow" – laudable enough aims you'd have to agree even if you would like to have changed some of the details!

Elamites, Gutians and Kassites

The Elamites suffered by backing the wrong horse! Eshnunna was a part-Elamite city and a natural ally of the Elamite kings in Susa and, had the war against Babylon turned out differently, Elam would doubtless have gained significantly. So would the Gutians since they too had allied themselves with Eshnunna. As it was, Hammurabi soon followed up the conquest of his immediate neighbours with a further attack against Elam and we next read that Siwe Palor Hupak of Elam only carried the title 'governor' not king. It was only when Hammurabi died in 1519BC and his son Samsu Iluna took charge that Elam, in the hands of the vigorous Kuter Nahhunte I, became independent once more.

The reign of Samsu Iluna also introduces us to a new people – the 'Kassites'. In Samsu Iluna's 9th year (about 1511BC) it is recorded that he fought a battle against a Kassite army. So who were they and why were they fighting against Babylon? Well, it is thought most likely that their homeland, like that of the Gutians, was in the Zagros Mountains somewhere[20] but, tellingly, the names of their rulers are identifiably Indo-European. Just as the Hittites had taken over Hattian society and the Greeks had taken over the pre-Indo-European society of Greece, so the Indo-European speakers of Iran had somehow worked their way into Kassite society. Although the Kassites held onto their own language, they had somehow been transformed from a remote tribe that no-one had heard of into an effective fighting force!

However, they were not yet effective enough to significantly dent the power of Samsu Iluna, who remained in control of much of his father Hammurabi's empire. In the Sumerian south there was rebellion which led to Samsu Iluna's sacking of the historic city of Ur, and in the north Ashur regained its independence some time during Samsu Iluna's reign. But the central part of the country remained securely under Babylon's control.

Middle Bronze Age Palestine

The problem with Palestine during these times is exactly the same as the problem with the Hurrian lands. We have archaeology, plenty of it, but we don't have written records. Writing just wasn't part of the Canaanite psyche. The clearest chronological sequence which archaeology has to offer comes from rock tombs at Jericho, where Kathleen Kenyon was able to divide the whole Middle Bronze II/III period into five phases based on the pottery sequence found in the tombs. Others have reinterpreted the data and some find themselves unable to agree with the fineness of Kenyon's original sub-division, but for our purposes here it provides a useful check on relative dating. Phase (i) has already passed; in Phase (ii), we find another Hammurabi-style cylinder seal together with a scarab of pharaoh Hornedjeratef, who reigned about 30 to 40 years after the start of the 13th Dynasty, i.e. somewhere between 1570 and 1560BC according to this dating scheme.[21] Hammurabi reigned from 1562 to 1519BC. The two are certainly close enough to end up being represented in the same pottery phase at Jericho, and I suggest that Phase (ii) covers the years from about 1610 to 1550BC. In Phase (iii) we are rewarded with another scarab, this time of Sobekhotep V, whose date would be roughly 1530BC, so it would be fair to say that the chronological picture being painted is a consistent one.

But what about the political picture? We know that Hazor was an important north Palestinian centre, not just from its impressive archaeological remains[22] but also because we read about it in the Mari archives (king Ibni Hadad of Hazor hosted ambassadors from Babylon). Megiddo was another important centre, dominating the Esdraelon plain. So were Jericho in the Jordan valley and Lachish in the southern hills. However the political relationships between them, their alliances and their wars, are unknown. But we do know that this was not a peaceful time. The cities were all fortified; several suffered destruction. In Byblos, instances of buried hoards of 'treasure' are datable to 13th Dynasty times (by the presence of typically 13th Dynasty faience work), and hoards are always a sign of trouble, often invasion or occupation by foreigners. Moreover, we can be quite certain that one particular Palestinian power eventually became strong enough and organised enough to invade, conquer, occupy and rule northern Egypt!

The Hyksos Invasion of Egypt

As we reach the second string of short-reigning and pretty much unknown 13th Dynasty Egyptian rulers so our knowledge dwindles. By 1530BC or shortly thereafter, the authority of the kings, now based at Memphis, had reached such a low ebb that a parallel line, Manetho's 14th Dynasty, started ruling from Avaris in the eastern delta. But 'ruling' doesn't seem to have meant much for either dynasty and real power clearly lay with the bureaucrats – which means there wasn't much real power at all! The Middle Kingdom was well and truly over; the country had entered what historians term the 'Second Intermediate Period'. Egypt was effectively paralysed, an easy target.

The Egyptian historian Manetho gives us a particularly dramatic passage, quoted by the Jewish writer Josephus. Manetho talks of a great disaster befalling the land during the days of the 13th Dynasty pharaoh Dudimose (a legible late 13th Dynasty name in the *Turin Canon* – dated here to around 1505BC), a "blast from God", following which invaders from the east, "people of an obscure race", were able to seize the land without striking a blow. Their first leader is named "Salitis". To the Egyptians these invaders were known as the 'Hyksos', a mysterious Asiatic people who appeared from nowhere (from an Egyptian perspective) and settled throughout the Nile delta, dominating the whole land.[23] The name *Hyksos* has variously been translated *kings of foreign lands*, *kings of the desert uplands* or *king shepherds*. That a significant new population had appeared is evidenced by the excavations at Tell ed Daba in the Nile delta,[24] the site of Avaris, an important administrative centre since the late 12th Dynasty and now the Hyksos capital. Here, Stratum G corresponds to the 13th Dynasty period and it comes to an end with a series of mass graves, suggesting a serious disaster of some kind.[25] In the subsequent stratum, F, totally different (and certainly Asiatic) burial practices were found, together with quite different building techniques.[26]

Looking at it rationally, without the Egyptian perspective of mystery, the Hyksos can only have been rulers from one of the major Palestinian power-blocks. We read later that their Palestinian base was Sharuhen, a city south of Gaza, so it's a reasonable guess that this had also been their territory immediately prior to the invasion. However, their earlier origins remain unknown and the subject of fierce debate.[27]

Summary

Perhaps the optimism which I spoke about at the end of the previous chapter was a little premature! Egypt has tried out a totally new system of government, which has ended in political paralysis and foreign invasion. Kingdoms and empires have come and gone in Amorite-ruled Iraq and we are left with Babylon trying desperately to hold onto the gains made under Hammurabi, while Elamites, Kassites, Assyrians and new-age Sumerians do their best to shake off the yoke. In Syria, Amorite dynasties still rule much of the land but Alalakh has been lost and the Hittite threat has drawn uncomfortably close with the forming of Anitta's empire. All in all, the Middle East situation looks to be much less stable in 1500BC than it had looked a century earlier. It is anybody's guess how things will turn out but there seems little prospect of lasting peace – except perhaps in Crete and the Aegean.

As far as dating goes, the Sobekhotep flood stela gives a strong indication that I am still on the right track and there is plenty of evidence that my relative dating of Egypt and Iraq is still approximately correct.

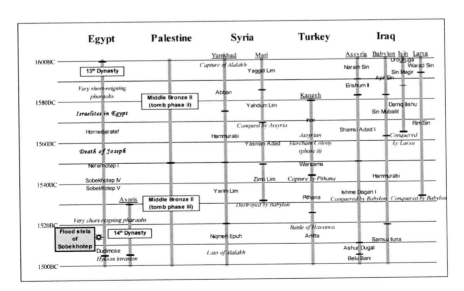

What does the Bible have to say?

The whole century covered by this chapter spans just a few lines here and there in the Bible where genealogies are given linking the time of the patriarchs (Abraham, Isaac and Jacob) to the time of Moses. The first book of the Bible, Genesis, ends with the death of Joseph (in 1556BC according to my reading of the Bible's dating information) and with the Israelite people living in the land of 'Goshen' in Egypt; the second book, Exodus, starts with the birth of Moses – some time in the future still. Nevertheless, we can at least ask the question as to whether there is any evidence for there having been a foreign population living in the Nile delta during the 13th Dynasty. And the answer is a definite "yes", although of course no-one can prove that the evidence relates to the Israelites. At Tell ed Daba, where such clear evidence for the arrival of the Hyksos invaders has been found, there is also evidence for the earlier presence of a different Asiatic people.[28] This can be seen in their houses, pottery and burial customs. Whoever these people were, they lived alongside the Egyptians, apparently peacefully and with their approval throughout the 13th Dynasty. Now the Bible tells us that the Israelites were settled in the land of Goshen but it doesn't tell us exactly where that was. But it was somewhere in the eastern delta region – that is deducible from later events – so it is likely to have been somewhere near the city of Avaris, now the archaeological site of Tell ed Daba.

There is one further matter which I wish to draw to your attention. I have already mentioned that there was a powerful family of viziers during the 13th Dynasty who wielded a more effective authority than that of the short-reigning pharaohs, providing the continuity which would otherwise have been lacking. Let me pose a simple question. Could these have been Joseph and his descendants? I am going beyond the Bible here since it makes no claim for any governmental role for Joseph after seeing Egypt through the years of famine. Yet it does portray him as continuing to be a very important person in Egypt. When his father Jacob died (1604BC), the Egyptian pharaoh provided an honour guard to accompany Jacob's body to the family burial ground near Hebron in Palestine. When Joseph himself died at the ripe old age of 110, the Bible tells us that he was embalmed. My guess would be, if the story is generally true, that Joseph did indeed retain an important government role, in which case he could hardly have failed to be involved in setting up the system part of which was the scrapping of hereditary monarchy. That doesn't mean he was right to do so of course – none of the characters in the Bible except one are portrayed as infallible!

What was going on in the Rest of the World?

While the soldiers of Hammurabi, Anitta, Yarim Lim and all the other warlords of the Middle East were slogging it out on foot on battlefield after battlefield, a revolutionary development was taking place far away on the plains of Central Asia; people were beginning to ride horses. It was already 2500 years since the horse first made the transition from an item on the menu to an indispensable aid to modern life, and horses had been used as pack animals, drawers of ploughs and carts right across the plains of Asia and Europe. Indo-Europeans had tended to be strongly associated with use of the horse ever since they first domesticated the great beasts out on the Ukrainian steppe. Part of the reason for the success of the Indic tribes in Pakistan was undoubtedly their use of horses as drawers of chariots. But now, somewhere near the Aral Sea, some persistent individual had actually managed to tame a horse to such an extent that he could both ride it and control it; the potential was enormous. That individual spoke a particular brand of Indo-European quite closely related to the language of the Indic tribes of Pakistan and Iran and his particular brand of Indo-European would soon spread from Hungary to China and south to the Indian Ocean, becoming known as 'Iranian'. Such would be the impact of horse-riding on human society.

Horses were not indigenous to the Middle East. Transport was still by donkey or camel.[29] But things were about to change. It would be a while before the art of horse riding would make it to Iraq and Egypt, but chariot warfare had now arrived. The plains of Cilicia in southern Turkey had always been valuable agricultural land; they would now become ideal horse-breeding territory.

9

The Lights Go Out: 1500–1400BC

This will be a shorter chapter – at least in its main part. That's not because less events took place in this century than in the previous or succeeding centuries, but the fact is that we simply have much less information to go on. The archives at Alalakh, Kanesh and Mari survived because someone decided to burn down the buildings in which they were housed. Had that not been the case the history related in the last chapter would have been a great deal vaguer. You see, just burying clay tablets isn't good enough; you have to heat them in a furnace to harden them off ready for the millennia of environmental attack in the ground, and that really means torching the relevant building. And it seems that no-one was obliging enough to do that for more than a very few records from the century between 1500 and 1400BC. Even Egypt, where much of our information comes from inscriptions painstakingly etched into stone, is a disappointment because, as chance would have it, it was largely in the hands of the nearly illiterate Hyksos kings. And to cap it all, the one rock of stability, Crete, spoke a language which we still don't understand, so no joy there! Never mind, the darkness is far from absolute so let's see what can be seen and, since Crete does seem to be a lot more stable than most other countries, let's start there.

The Aegean

Despite the problems afflicting Egypt, some commercial contact with Crete continued; an alabaster lid inscribed with the name of one of the Hyksos kings, Khyan, has been found at Knossos. And there was certainly plenty of trade around the Aegean itself, generating sufficient wealth for the palaces and cities of Crete to be maintained and improved. Additional palaces at Gourmia and

Zakro now join the large edifices at Knossos, Phaistos and Mallia. It would be wrong to imagine that Crete was a sort of idyllically peaceful world though, despite the wonderful naturalistic artwork, often with idyllically peaceful themes, associated with Cretan interior decorators. Plenty of swords, shields and helmets have been recovered and even an imported battle-axe. The question we can't answer is what these weapons were used for. There doesn't seem to be any evidence for warfare on the island itself, in which case one would have to assume that the weaponry was a necessary part of maintaining Cretan dominance in the Aegean and beyond. By now the Greeks had been civilised to the extent that their culture had come to very closely resemble that of Crete itself, and that of course brought the danger that the pupils would one day rise up and overthrow their teacher. There was no immediate threat but the government in Knossos needed to be strong to maintain its position.

But Cretan history suffers from a total lack of readable records. All dating is therefore relative to that of other lands, and to find another land with datable records in the 15th Century BC we must travel far to the east.

The Heirs of Hammurabi

In Babylonia a handful of written records survive from this period. Most are business documents and among other things they demonstrate that the business climate in Babylon and its surrounding kingdom was a stable one. The names they contain also give a clue as to the ever-changing population of Iraq. Most are still Akkadian but several are now Kassite, revealing a steady influx of settlers from the east. Regarding the kings themselves, the descendants of Hammurabi, we have a widely trusted king list[1] which, if my dating of Hammurabi's reign was correct, furnishes the following dates for his successors:

Samsu Iluna	– 1483BC
Abiesha	1483 – 1455BC
Ammiditana	1455 – 1419BC
Ammisaduga	1419 –

The reigns of Samsu Iluna and Abiesha saw the extent of the kingdom shrink quite rapidly back to cover only the central part of Iraq, the area known as Akkad. From Susa we hear of an Elamite invasion of Akkad late in Samsu Iluna's reign and the "levelling of 30 cities" under their king Kuter Nahhunte I. Since the same story appears in an Assyrian document there was probably a fair degree of truth to it. We also find plenty of reference to warfare against the rulers of what is known to scholars as the 'Sealand' Dynasty, kings who controlled the southern land of Sumer, and from Abiesha's time onwards it seems to have been accepted that Babylon no longer had any claim over Sumer. The Sealand kings saw them-

selves as upholders of true Sumerian culture and, although Sumerian had probably not been spoken as a first language for some 300 years, they adopted it as
their official tongue. In fact, Sumerian had taken on a status very similar to that
of Latin in mediaeval Europe; it was the language of culture, the language which
betrayed real education and learning.

Both northern and western Iraq had also been lost to Babylon. Nomadic
Amorites still pastured their flocks in the western desert and we hear of a battle
to keep them back towards the end of Samsu Iluna's reign. However, the main
western threat was a growing concentration of Kassite settlement; the king of
Terqa, close to the ruins of Mari, had a Kassite name[2] during Abiesha's time. To
the north, Assyria had regained its independence by 1500BC, although we don't
hear very much about it. The *Assyrian king list* gives us names – but there is little
evidence of actions. Similarly, the scarcity of evidence from Elam suggests a
dwindling of Elamite power following the death of Kuter Nahhunte I.

However, the documents which most excite historians of this period of Babylonian history come from the reign of king Ammisaduga. His reign has long provided one of the key pieces of evidence with which to date the ancient world and
this evidence is to be found in the so-called *Venus Tablets*. These cuneiform tablets
record observations of the comings and goings of the planet Venus as it switches
from being the morning star to being the evening star and back again, every 1.6
years or so, and experts have realised for the best part of a hundred years that
they allow the dates of king Ammisaduga to be narrowed down to certain specific options – a function of the peculiarities of Venus' motion.[3] In the current
conventional view of ancient history, the favoured options for Year 1 of king Ammisaduga based on the evidence of the *Venus Tablets* are 1702, 1646 and 1582BC
(giving what are colloquially known as the 'long', 'medium' and 'short'
chronologies), and there are continuing battles amongst ancient historians as to
which represents the truth. My impression is that Egyptologists favour the short
chronology while specialists on Babylon and the Hittites often plump for the
medium or long options.

It has also been realised for a long time now that the choice as to which option should be selected could potentially be further refined with reference to
other astronomical observations made on the *Venus Tablets*. These observations
consist of the lengths of 22 specific lunar months (either 29 or 30 days) which, in
theory, should be checkable through retro-calculation. This task has been carried
out by a number of researchers over the years and, of the three solutions traditionally favoured by historians, it seems that 1702BC gives the best match to the
month length data; however researchers rarely consider solutions either earlier
than 1702BC or later than 1582BC because of the presumed historical difficulties
this would cause. Once released from this constraint, much the best solution I
can see is Wayne Mitchell's well-argued case for 1419BC.[4] Mitchell, after careful

consideration of the real slow-down of the Earth based on well-corroborated 1st Millennium BC eclipse records, came up with a slight advantage for 1419BC with just three bad mismatches to the month length data (compared to four for its nearest rivals, including 1702BC). This was reduced to just one bad mismatch after adjusting the Earth's slow-down rate based on evidence from a solar and lunar eclipse combination which I will present in the next chapter. His clear conclusion, therefore, was that 1419BC was much the most likely year for Ammisaduga's coronation, based on the *Venus Tablets*.

Absolute date: 1419BC
Year 1 of king Ammisaduga of Babylon based on the evidence of the *Venus Tablets*

As you can see, this places the history presented here fully 163 years later than any conventional date. It also means that I can now feel much more confident about the direction things are taking – and pencil in the earlier lunar eclipse date (1976BC) marking the end of Shar Kali Shari's reign rather more firmly.

Egypt under Hyksos Rule

If the light is dim in Iraq, it has been virtually extinguished in Hyksos-ruled Egypt! Archaeology tells us a certain amount. It reveals that the new Hyksos capital Avaris was a splendid city and militarily very well defended. It also reveals that a number of other towns and cities were built up as defensible sites. We can see that the Hyksos were clearly somewhat in awe of the culture they had inherited and almost tried to 'become Egyptian'. One of the hallmarks of Hyksos presence is an object which at first glance is archetypically Egyptian, the 'scarab', a beetle-shaped inscribed stone, but the Hyksos version is distinctive in that the designs tend to be pseudo-Egyptian, sometimes with made-up characters rather than genuine hieroglyphs. These scarabs have been found in large quantities all over Hyksos-controlled Egypt and also Palestine. However, archaeology can tell us little of the actual nature of Hyksos rule and its impact on the Egyptian population. Later histories tell a consistent picture of Hyksos cruelty and Egyptian suffering – as I mentioned earlier, Manetho speaks of the Hyksos as being a "blast from God" – and, although it is fashionable to dismiss this nowadays as wild exaggeration, we weren't there!

But the question of just how long Hyksos rule lasted is not a straightforward one, not least because of the large number of different dynasties which Manetho records. Although Dudimose, in whose time the Hyksos invaded, was the last 13th Dynasty king to be attested in Upper (southern) Egypt, the *Turin Canon*'s list of 13th Dynasty rulers continues for another 40 years or so. The same is true of the 14th Dynasty, based at Avaris.[5] Manetho's 15th Dynasty (to which he assigns 250 years) are the Hyksos 'great kings'[6] and he also lists a large number (32) of 16th Dynasty rulers, usually taken to be minor Hyksos chiefs. All in all it is a very confusing picture indeed.

So the question remains: how long did Hyksos rule last? Well, the *Turin Canon* gives six indecipherable lines for the Hyksos great kings with a legible "108 year" total, which ties in reasonably with the answer from archaeology, which is approximately a century. Another estimate can be derived from the final overlapping dynasty, the 17th. This was an independent line of Egyptian rulers based at Thebes in the south of the country, but the trouble is that the records here are hardly great either. We have ten names of kings on monuments, nine on a 'table of kings' at the Karnak temple near Thebes and eight tombs, so at best the duration is an estimate, about 75 years.[7] The dynasty was founded by Rahotep and we know from inscriptional evidence that he was a contemporary of a Hyksos king named Yaqub Har, and the upshot is that the Thebes evidence ties in broadly with the *Turin Canon* and with archaeology. Majority opinion therefore gives the Hyksos just over a century of rule, and I see no justification for taking a different view. The following are my suggested approximate dates for the 15th Dynasty kings:[8]

Salitis	1505 – 1496BC
Sheshi	1496 – 1480BC
Yaqub Har	1480 – 1472BC
Khyan	1472 – 1446BC
Apopis	1446 – 1406BC
Khamudy	1406 –

Hyksos power was strong until late in the reign of Apopis. It is an open question to what extent Palestine was part of the same state as northern Egypt – most believe that direct rule was limited to southern Palestine – but it is certainly the case that very close trading ties existed between Hyksos Egypt and the Canaanite world.[9] The Hyksos also allied themselves with the state of Kush to the south of Egypt, which meant that when the independent 17th Dynasty arose in Thebes they were effectively boxed in. However it is clear that relations between Avaris and Thebes were generally peaceful and there may even have been a marriage alliance at one point between two great leaders, Apopis of the Hyksos north and Inyotef VII of the Egyptian south.[10]

The Palestinian Territories

Meanwhile, in Palestine Canaanite culture was pretty much identical to that of Hyksos Egypt, at least as far as archaeology goes. It wasn't a particularly wealthy society, probably because international trade was much less active now than in times past, but neither was it a time of great hardship. As long as you survived the frequent conflicts between the different power blocks in the region, you could look forward to a reasonably satisfying life with enough food and well built accommodation. According to Kathleen Kenyon's sub-divisions based on the Jericho tomb record, this century includes the latter part of Phase (iii), all of Phase (iv) and part of Phase (v), but there is little to assist with dating other than relative dating within Palestine and also tying Palestine to Hyksos Egypt, primarily by means of the many dozens of Hyksos scarabs which have turned up.[11]

Syria

Syria is even more of a blank slate than Palestine I'm afraid. The state of Yamkhad survived right through the 15th Century BC, but as far as we know it grew no further. Unfortunately Aleppo, the seat of the Yamkhad kings, is a closed book to archaeology for the excellent reason that it is still densely inhabited. At Ebla the last city walls must have been built during this period but we have absolutely no way of knowing whether the city was independent or whether, as seems more likely, it was part of Yamkhad. South of Yamkhad, Qatna survived as the centre of another small Amorite state and, on the coast, Ugarit also remained the centre of an independent kingdom, trading with Crete, Cyprus and Hyksos Egypt.

The Land of Hatti

Nor do we have any more data from Hatti for most of this century than we have from Palestine and Syria. We have no idea when or under what circumstances Anitta's empire came to an end; all we know is that it was little more than a legend by the time further information becomes available. Light only begins to dawn with the activities of a man named Hattusili (Hattusili I to us), who took over the land of Hatti some indeterminate time after Anitta and who made Hattusas his capital (rebuilding it after Anitta's destruction of the site and cursing of the ground on which it stood!). This we know because a written record was made of some of his achievements, a record which survived for archaeologists to find. Furthermore, references to Hattusili have also survived in the records of later Hittite rulers. We read that Hattusili, like Pithana and Anitta before him, was from the city of Kussara, which strongly suggests a continuity of dynasty. We also read of Hattusili's father Labarna (who "made the sea his frontier") and a rebellion which occurred against Labarna's rule in the city of Sanuhuitta, probably quite close to the then ruined site of Hattusas. Hattusili also speaks of rebellion against his grandfather and, if a name is required, a seal of appropriately antiquated style bearing the name Huzziya has been found. But in truth all we know for sure is that a significant time elapsed between Anitta and Hattusili, long enough for Hattusili not to worry too much about the curse which Anitta is said to have put on Hattusas! Anitta's reign must have come to an end in around 1500BC or shortly thereafter and it looks as though Hattusili was at least the third generation after Anitta. As it happens, and for reasons which will not appear until the next chapter, I am actually quite confident about the approximate date for the beginning of Hattusili's reign – it is 1420BC – and I am pleased to see that this gives an appropriately long interval between Anitta's time and his.

We read that Hattusili conquered the Hittite heartland, including Zalpa and Sanuhuitta, from his home city of Kussara, although uncertainty remains as to the precise order and timing of events.[12] He also took Kanesh, Salahsuwa and Ulamma in the south-east, towards Syria, and Hupisna, Tuwanuwa (classical Tyana), Lalanda, Lusna (classical Lystra?) and Purushanda, in the south and south-west. His territory therefore covered much of southern and central Turkey, more or less the same area that Anitta had once controlled, and, when Hattusili decided he needed a new and prestigious capital from which to govern his empire, he chose Hattusas, rebuilt it and fortified it – and its fortifications would soon be tested!

A Sleeping Giant Awakes

Since the dawn of history there had never been a large Hurrian state. After gaining independence from Yamkhad late in the 16th Century BC, Alalakh reverted very much to the culture prevailing previously, and Alalakh was probably typical of the Hurrian world. The archaeology of Level VI is not at all spectacular and it reinforces the more general picture of an age without a great deal of spare wealth to go around.

Nevertheless, the spread of a pottery type known informally as Khabur ware (named after the Khabur river in eastern Syria, a tributary of the Euphrates) betrays the fact that something big was afoot. The origin of Khabur ware is to be found in the east, in the northern Zagros Mountains of Iran, and its use had now spread across the great plain of northern Iraq and eastern Syria. It has been found at sites such as Nagar and Tilshaanim and there was even some at Mari before it was destroyed by Hammurabi. Now, there is a big difference between a pottery type and a nation state, but the most likely explanation for this spread is that it accompanied a real spread of Hurrian culture and, possibly, statehood. And when we reach the last two decades of the 15th Century BC we know for sure that the Hurrians were organised enough to fight a serious war against the Hittite king Hattusili I, and there is absolutely no way that could have been achieved without a state administration of some sort – which leaves us wondering what had led to this dramatic change in Hurrian society. And the slightly surprising answer supplied by all historians is: Indo-European influence!

A mysterious people known as the 'Umman Manda'[13] now make their appearance in the records, fighting alongside Hurrian armies against the Hittites, and it is strongly suspected that the Umman Manda represent Indo-European tribes. Although we have no Hurrian records from this era, the names of their kings when they appear out of the darkness are, like those of the Kassites, Indo-European – and one of the known Hurrian kings is referred to in a later inscription as "king of the Umman Manda".[14] In fact, we can be pretty confident that the Umman Manda were an Indic-speaking people since the names of the Indian gods Indra, Varuna and Mitra are all found in later Hurrian documents and also because a Hurrian text (found in the ruins of Hattusas) uses words for numerals and a couple of other technical terms almost identical to those of the Indic language Sanskrit.[15] The language of the resulting state was still Hurrian – the Indic language of the Umman Manda died out – but the Indo-European ethos of conquest and war had been thoroughly instilled into the people. It must have been a nasty shock for the Hittites suddenly to be confronted with their own kind!

The Hittite Wars

Hattusili's annals tells us that, once his empire was in place, his next act was to head south, where he attacked the city of Hassuwa north of Alalakh. Here he met and defeated the combined armies of Yamkhad, the Hurrians and the Umman Manda, and we read that he then succeeded in taking Alalakh. Experts have of course looked for the evidence for this in the archaeology of Alalakh and regularly come up with the end of Level VII, the level which relates to king Yarim Lim of Yamkhad and Hammurabi of Babylon. But it is now 100 years since the deaths of both Yarim Lim and Hammurabi, at least 80 years since the end of Level VII, and I see absolutely no possibility of a connection between Level VII and Hattusili. However, the Level VI citadel was destroyed on two occasions and I suggest one of these destructions was almost certainly Hattusili's work. He then continued his campaign by attacking the city of Ursu, thought to be situated about 130 miles north of Aleppo; we have a nice description of the siege on a Hattusas tablet.

Hattusili obviously liked nothing better than a good fight, so he next decided to launch a campaign into central-southern Turkey, the land known as 'Arzawa', to reinforce his control over the area. But he soon learnt that you can't do that sort of thing with impunity. The Hurrians, with their Indo-European minders the Umman Manda, seized the opportunity to launch a full-scale assault on Hatti. While Hattusili was busy in the south-west, they took almost every city in the Hittite heartland area of central Turkey, being thwarted only by the well-built fortifications of Hattusas. They withdrew as soon as Hattusili returned but they left Hatti in turmoil with rebellion in several Hittite cities where local warlords decided this was the time to assert their independence. Hattusili had to painfully retake Kanesh, Ulamma, Salahsuwa and, finally, Sanuhuitta, obliterating the last three for ever. He needed to show he meant business! He also needed to show the outside world that he was not a man to be trifled with, and to that purpose he launched yet another offensive against Yamkhad's territory, taking and destroying cities in Cilicia and northern Syria as far as the Euphrates river (which he was inordinately proud of having crossed) and bringing their kings back to Hattusas.[16]

For all we know there may have been many more wars than we have records for, but we know for sure that by 1400BC Hattusili was once again firmly in control of a very large empire indeed. He had tasted battle and victory against both Yamkhad and the Hurrians and he had placed the Hittite nation firmly on the international map.

The Growing Egyptian Resistance to the Hyksos

As war raged in Turkey and northern Syria, the uneasy (and unequal) peace between the Hyksos rulers of northern Egypt and the native Egyptian kings in Thebes also broke down. Late in the reign of the Hyksos king Apopis, probably around 1415BC, a titanic struggle developed between Apopis and the southern Egyptian king Seqenenre Ta'a (described in a rather strange tale known as the *Quarrel of Apopis and Seqenenre*) and, judging by Seqenenre Ta'a's mummy, he died in that struggle. His son Kamose continued the war – still fighting the long-reigning Apopis according to a stela at Karnak near Thebes – and succeeded in liberating a good chunk of the Nile delta region. Then, in approximately 1403BC (if my chronology is right), Kamose died and his teenage son Ahmose took up the fight, now against the Hyksos king Khamudy – which is where we have to leave things for now! Hyksos control is clinging on by its toe-nails but has become restricted to the Nile delta and probably not even all of that. Avaris is under real threat.

Summary

This has been a difficult century to live through. The traditional centres of civilisation, Iraq and Egypt, have both suffered serious division and external assault, and the result has been a dramatic reduction in trade and commerce, leading to a very real reduction in wealth. The overwhelming impression from the evidence is that life throughout most of the 15th Century BC was hard work; it was a struggle to make ends meet. However, as the year 1400BC approaches, there are signs that things are changing. Both Hittites and Hurrians are now organised into major states under vigorous leaderships. They, the Greeks and the Kassites have taken into their consciousness a large dose of Indo-European self-belief, and it looks as though this culture from the north is about to have a real impact on the Middle East, possibly as big an impact as that from the desert culture of the Amorites.

	Egypt	Palestine	Syria (Yamkhad)	Turkey (Kanesh)	Iraq — Assyria	Iraq — Babylon
1500BC	Saïtis	Middle Bronze II (tomb phase iii)		Aratta	Beli Bani	Samsu Iuna
	Sheshi / *Birth of Moses*				Libaja	
1480BC	Thebes, Yaqub Har, Rahotep			Terua	Sharma Adad I	
1460BC	15th Dynasty (Hyksos kings) / Khyan / 17th Dynasty	Middle Bronze II/III (tomb phase iv)	Hurri	Hatti / Kassite settlement / Huzziya / Kashtiliash	Iptar-Sin	Abiesha / Sealand Dynasty
1440BC	*Moses flees to Midian* / Inyotef VII			Labarna	Bazaja	Ammiditana
1420BC	Apopis / Seqenenre Ta'a	Middle Bronze II/III (tomb phase v)	*Umman Manda take control* / *War against Hatti (Hittites capture Alalakh)*	Hattusili I	Lulaja / Shu Ninua	Ammisaduga / 1419BC Venus tablet date for Year 1 of Ammisaduga
1400BC	Kamose / *Israelites leave Egypt* / Ahmose, Khamudy				Sharma Adad II / Erishum III	

In Egypt times have been very hard, but as the century closes there are signs here too that the country is about to break free from the hundred-year yoke of Hyksos domination. It is not yet clear exactly which way the winds of change will blow but they are certainly blowing, and with increasing force. A new age looks to be just around the corner.

Finally, on the dating front, the evidence of the *Venus Tablets* is 100% supportive of the chronology in this book. It is not yet enough to dispel all doubt but it is certainly enough to give real confidence.

What does the Bible have to say?

The book of Exodus commences with the Israelites in serious trouble in Egypt. The days of Joseph, the famous vizier who earned the undying gratitude of the Egyptian population, are long gone and, as the Bible (Exodus 1:8-16) says, "a pharaoh who knew not Joseph" was now on the throne. He had imposed hard labour on the Israelite people and had now decided that the only answer to the high Israelite birth rate was infanticide. This was the situation into which Moses was born.

Moses in Egypt

So when was Moses born? The calculation is not too difficult, using the figures given in the Bible. If you accept my recommendation of 440 years (rather than 480) as the time from the Israelites leaving Egypt to the founding of Solomon's temple (1 Kings 6:1), and if we further accept a date of 965BC for the founding of the temple in Solomon's 4th year, then we only have to add Moses' age when he led his people out of Egypt (80 years) to arrive at a date of 1485BC for his birth. The 13th Dynasty no longer wielded authority; Egypt was in the hands of the Hyksos pharaoh Sheshi, a pharaoh who 'knew not Joseph'.

According to Exodus 2:1-10 (and according to more than one modern film) Moses was saved from infanticide by the pharaoh's own daughter and brought up in the royal palace, which would have been at Avaris. One would imagine that the young Moses, brought up as a prince, would have had access to all the knowledge of the ancient world. This would have included the knowledge of Egypt, learnt from the priests of Amun, Ptah and the other Egyptian gods; it would also have included international best-sellers like the Babylonian law code devised 50 years earlier but still current in Babylon.[17]

The Bible tells us nothing further about Moses until he reached 40 years of age.[18] *However, there is a story told by the Alexandrian writer Artapanus*[19] *that Moses grew up under a certain pharaoh "Khenephres", and that he carried out military activities on Egypt's behalf in Kush. According to the scheme in this book Khenephres was Khyan, who would have become pharaoh when Moses was 13 years old. However, since we later find Kush allied to the Hyksos state, any trip which Moses may have made on behalf of pharaoh Khyan is more likely to have been of a diplomatic nature than military.*[20] *Besides, the Bible simply records the adoption of Moses as a baby by the pharaoh's daughter and we are told nothing further until the day he kills an Egyptian slave master (Exodus 2:11-15).*

Moses and the Exodus *(Exodus 5-14)*

Moses fled Egypt aged 40 after killing the slave master and went to live in 'Midian', probably the north-west corner of Saudi Arabia or southern Jordan.[21] *Apopis had recently ascended the Egyptian throne. Thirty-nine years later Apopis died – and all memory of Moses died with him. According to the Bible, however, Moses returned the following year and, after many most remarkable events, he finally led the Israelite people out of Egypt (the event known as the 'Exodus'). It was 1405BC; Kamose king of Thebes was battling his way north and Apopis' successor Khamudy was under serious pressure.*[22]

I am very sorry if you have unquestioningly believed the cinematic version where Moses grows up alongside a totally different set of pharaohs, namely Seti and Ramesses! As far as I can see the Hyksos period makes a much more plausible backdrop to the story of Moses. It means that the Bible record of appalling cruelty to the Israelite slaves matches the Egyptian record of appalling cruelty to the Egyptian population at large. It also provides a pharaoh with a name plausibly matching Artapanus' story. Unfortunately there are no names given in the Bible for any of the Egyptians of Moses' time, so no direct check on this conclusion is possible. However, Hyksos unpopularity could explain why in the Bible, even when plague after plague had devastated the land, the Egyptians are said to have been "favourably disposed" toward the Israelites (Exodus 12:36). The native Egyptians would have been desperate to overthrow the Hyksos regime and the resistance to the Hyksos being offered by Moses would therefore have gone down very well indeed.

Finally, the geography is also right for the Hyksos period. It would appear from the book of Exodus in the Bible that the pharaoh of Moses' day resided in the same general region as the Israelite slaves, who were labouring at two cities, named (Exodus 1:11) as *"Piramesse"* and *"Pithom"*. *Piramesse is the later name for Avaris in the eastern Nile delta, while Pithom is a neighbouring city. Prior to the Hyksos, the 13th Dynasty kings were based further south, in middle Egypt and then at Memphis; later, in the 18th Dynasty, the capital was moved back to Thebes in the far south. Only during the Hyksos period, and much later during the 19th Dynasty, was the capital to be found in the eastern delta.*

The Law of Moses *(parts of Exodus, Leviticus, Numbers, Deuteronomy)*
The enduring legacy of Moses is his law code. The Law of Moses has governed the Jewish people ever since it was written, and also forms an important element in the Christian religion. A large chunk of the Bible spells out laws which, traditionally, were first set down by Moses as the people were camped at the foot of Mount Sinai. And there are striking parallels with the law code of Hammurabi. The same style is adopted. The 'eye for an eye' concept is repeated more than once, and in a similar context to Hammurabi's laws. There is even a similar discrimination between an offence committed against a free Israelite and one against a slave, where freedom for the slave is the price required. The concept of delivering justice to the weak, the orphan and the widow also appears strongly. Of course there are many aspects to Moses' law which are certainly not found in Hammurabi's law, aspects concerning the relationship between God and his people for instance, but my clear impression is that a knowledge of Hammurabi's laws was in the mind of whoever wrote the Law in the Bible. So is Moses a myth? Someone wrote the 'Law of Moses', someone who had the education to know about Hammurabi's law code, and that would have been a rare person indeed amongst a backward nomadic people.

One final point relates to the language and likely script originally used for the Law of Moses. It is worth noting that this is just about the time that someone started inscribing rocks in the Sinai desert with characters which are clearly ancestral to our modern alphabets – including Hebrew! Of course it could have been anyone, but the fact remains that the Sinai characters are certainly based on Egyptian hieroglyphs so an Egyptian education is implied; yet the language is Canaanite, at that time indistinguishable from ancestral Hebrew. The location was the Serabit El Khadum[23] turquoise mines about 50 miles north-west of Mount Sinai, not thought to be in use during late Hyksos times. This may be just a coincidence – but it is certainly circumstantial evidence in support of the Israelites having passed that way.[24]

What was going on in the Rest of the World?

It is easy to forget that Egypt is part of Africa. Egyptian language and culture was a product of the Sahara, and before that East Africa.[25] When reading about the achievements of ancient Egypt it often appears that everything south and west of its borders is utter darkness, a home of uncivilised and ignorant peoples. This is not entirely true!

When the pastoralist people of the Sahara settled on the banks of the Nile in around the 6th Millennium BC, their cultural remains can be seen spreading both north and south. In the north the eventual result was the state of Upper Egypt, which then went on to conquer the Semitic-speaking state of Lower Egypt; in the south the eventual result was the kingdom of Kush, with settlements, later to be cities, centred on what is now northern Sudan. When Egypt was strong, during the Old Kingdom of the 3rd Millennium BC and, more recently, during the Middle Kingdom, they managed to conquer and control as far south as the modern Egyptian-Sudanese border and sometimes beyond, but they did not control Kush. During Hyksos times the Kushite capital was Kerma about 150 miles south of the modern border, and a very significant increase in wealth is apparent in a series of royal burials there. Kushite-style burials also appear at this time in Nubia (the land between Kush and Upper Egypt) and even in Upper Egypt itself, and stelae reveal that Nubia was now under the authority of the king of Kush. There is also a famous stela from the reign of the Theban king Kamose which tells of the interception of a letter from the Hyksos king Apopis to Kush and it is clear that Kush was allied to the Hyksos state. In short, Kush was now a serious power and had been able to conquer previously Egyptian-controlled territory.

Elsewhere, part of East Africa probably lay within the borders of the land of Punt, the fabled trading partner of Egypt (discussed in the next chapter). Now I can be no more certain where Punt actually was than anyone else, but let's just take a look at the Red Sea region for a minute. As northern Semites moved into Palestine and then Syria and Iraq, so southern Semites moved south down the Arabian coast of the Red Sea to Yemen, where descendent languages are still spoken today.[26] At some stage they also crossed the Red Sea and colonised the African coast; this we know simply from the fact that several modern Ethiopian languages are South Semitic. My guess (based on the language evidence) is that Semitic colonisation of Ethiopia began as early as the 3rd Millennium BC, the time that intensive agriculture and irrigation first appear in the Yemeni coastal region known as the Mahrib.

Beyond the lands controlled by South Semites lay much less advanced societies. Somalia was inhabited by pastoralists in some parts, but also by hunter-gatherer tribes. And from Kenya to South Africa the land would have been sparsely populated by hunter-gatherers similar to today's Bushmen. Much has changed since those days. Bantu people now inhabit almost all of southern Africa, for example the Swahili people of Tanzania, but in the 2nd Millennium BC the Bantu were simply one small tribe living somewhere in the Congo basin. The remnants of the East African population of 1500BC can be seen in the Hadza and Sandawe tribes of inland Tanzania, a quite different race, smaller and lighter-skinned, a much more primitive race who stood no chance once the Bantus had got hold of Kushite technology. That hadn't happened yet – but it would.

10

The Growth of Empire: 1400–1300BC

The Fall of Babylon

In 1400BC Iraq was a land divided, but relatively peacefully divided. Babylon was the centre of Akkadian culture and learning and cities such as Sippar and Nippur lay within Babylon's modest little kingdom, but she had long since given up any thought of regaining the southern part of the country, where the Sealand Dynasty ruled and maintained something of the old Sumerian culture. To the east, Elam doesn't appear to have posed much threat to either kingdom. In the west the Kassites were now an organised force, occupying more or less the lands that once formed the old Amorite kingdom of Mari, but it was in the north that the biggest threat lay, a threat that had been growing steadily for several decades. This threat came not from Assyria but from the newly invigorated Hurrian nation. If Samsuditana king of Babylon perceived any danger it would most likely have been from that angle.

Samsuditana had taken over from Ammisaduga in 1398BC (confidently dated based on the observations contained in the *Venus Tablets*) and he had a long and peaceful reign. But the omens were not all they should have been. Babylonian astronomers seem to have adopted the same approach to interpreting signs in the heavens as those of Agade, Ur and Isin before them, which is to say that every sign had a meaning – usually a bad one! There have been various so-called 'omen tablets' over the centuries, some involving lunar eclipses, which I have omitted to mention because I consider the information contained to be much too imprecise for confident dating.[1] However, Samsuditana's reign brings us to another and this time it is a very precise observation, namely a lunar eclipse followed 14 days later by a solar eclipse, and it is stated that it portended the fall of Babylon. Whether this interpretation was made before or after the event is immaterial; the point is that we have a potentially very useful piece of astronomical data.

You may imagine that such an observation would be unique; but not so. As you know, the moon is directly between the Earth and the sun during a solar eclipse – meaning that we can't see the sun. As you also know, the moon goes around the Earth every month (29 or 30 days from the point of view of an observer on Earth), which means that it is pretty much on the far side from the sun 14 or 15 days later (or earlier) and, depending on the details of the moon's orbit, it may be close enough to being exactly opposite the sun and therefore in the shadow of the Earth, which would produce a lunar eclipse. So, eclipse pairs 14 days apart happen – but not that often, and the dating information supplied in the tablet (14th and 28th days of the 11th month – February/March by our calendar) narrows the options considerably. In fact, of all the possibilities in the conceivable date range (1950-1150BC) only two have the right combination of time of year and degree of totality for the solar eclipse, namely 1713BC and 1362BC, and both imply a slightly greater effect from the slowing down of the Earth's rotation than scientists usually consider, by about three quarters of an hour over the intervening three and a half millennia. Assuming one of these two dates is correct – and either would be a difficult pill for any traditionally-minded scholar to swallow – then this extra slow-down effect must have been real, and this was the evidence Wayne Mitchell used to refine his choice of 1419BC for Year 1 of Ammisaduga based on the *Venus Tablets*.[2] And clearly, if 1419BC is the correct date for Year 1 of Ammisaduga, then 1362BC looks very promising for the date of this omen tablet. When this is added to the fact that Samsuditana is reported to have reigned for 36 years (1398-1362BC), then the picture is so consistent as to be very difficult to ignore. In fact the combined evidence of the *Venus Tablets* and this omen tablet looks to me to be almost irrefutable – but for most ancient historians quite impossible to believe!

Absolute date: 1362BC

The year of a double eclipse, an eclipse of the moon followed 14 days later by an eclipse of the sun; portending the fall of Babylon

---

So who was it that put an end to the dynasty made famous by Hammurabi? The southern Sealand rulers? The Kassites? The Hurrians? We have a record of a message sent to Samsuditana by the governor of Sippar warning of an imminent attack – but from whom?

The Long Arm of the Hittites

In 1400BC king Hattusili of Hatti was lord of a very great empire indeed. Admittedly he had a few problems within his own family, banishing his two sons when they were involved in rebellion against him, but as he lay on his deathbed back in his home city of Kussara surrounded by his most loyal friends (we have the text of a deathbed testament) he could feel comfortable in the knowledge that he was giving his chosen successor, his grandson Mursili, the best start a king could want.

Mursili was just a teenager when, somewhere around 1390BC, he took on the mantle of great king of Hatti, but he was well supported and he soon got into the swing of conquest and war. Indeed, his rule was remembered many times in later annals as a time when Hittite power shone at its brightest, although we have to admit that our detailed knowledge of his activities is not bright at all! What we know is that he maintained his grandfather's empire, fighting successfully against both Yamkhad and the Hurrians, and at some stage he actually took Aleppo and put a final end to Yamkhad's existence. The city of Ebla was also destroyed and consigned to oblivion at approximately the same date; Hamath, about 40 miles further south, suffered similar destruction. I think we can deduce that this was much more than a hit-and-run raid and that Mursili placed Aleppo either directly or, more likely, indirectly under Hittite authority, which meant that his empire stretched far to the south-east from Hatti. To his east, the Hurrian kingdom was his neighbour with a frontier running approximately along the line of the Euphrates for about 250 miles. To his west, he could see only the tributary kingdoms of Turkey, subdued by his grandfather. To the south lay the Amorite lands of west-central Syria, the country which would soon be known as 'Amurru'. We don't know how many wars he had to fight to maintain and strengthen this position, but we can be quite sure that in 1362BC, some 28 years after he first became king, he felt very secure indeed, so secure in fact that he risked all and marched his army for hundreds of miles south-east down the Euphrates river.

You have to think that this action was in some way in sympathy with the Kassites since they controlled the middle reaches of the Euphrates. Probably the two nations had co-operated in the overthrow of Yamkhad and were now pooling resources against their other powerful neighbours, Babylon and the Hurrian state. Who knows? Whatever the rationale, a Babylonian document known as the *Chronicle of early kings* clearly states that the land of Akkad suffered an attack by the "man of Hatti". A later Hittite document also speaks of Mursili as "destroyer of Babylon". The Hittites marched many tiring miles though foreign lands with the single objective of sacking Babylon; they succeeded, took what they could lay their hands on (including Babylon's gods), and left for home, cheered all the way by the Kassites. And it was this event, dated by means of an eclipse tablet,

which gave me the confidence I expressed in the last chapter regarding the date of Hattusili I's kingship.

Egypt is Reborn

Meanwhile, the year 1400BC had seen a youthful king Ahmose son of Kamose in control of all Egypt south of the Nile delta, while the Hyksos king Khamudy clung desperately to power in the delta city of Avaris. And in Ahmose's 10th year, 1393BC, he and his general – also named Ahmose and from the walls of whose tomb we learn about many of the events of these times – had thrown themselves into the task of defeating the hated Hyksos foe. This time the game was finally up; the Hyksos were simply unable to hold out any more and they were forced to abandon Avaris and flee east to their Palestinian stronghold Sharuhen, just south of Gaza. General Ahmose describes both the siege of Avaris and then the 3-year battle for Sharuhen. The city was eventually taken and razed to the ground; the Egyptians wanted to obliterate all memory of their late occupiers.

Egypt had finally rejoined the field as a great power. Ahmose went on to re-open the valuable turquoise mines of the Sinai and then to extend Egyptian rule south into Nubia, with the enormous benefit that the massive gold resources of that country could be accessed, greatly enriching the Egyptian treasury. Egypt was back and, although Ahmose was manifestly the son of Kamose, Manetho assigns him a new dynasty number, the 18th, and historians refer to the era he inaugurated as the 'New Kingdom'. Fortunately the reign lengths of the 18th Dynasty rulers are very well known indeed. In fact, many events of Egyptian history from these times are very well documented since this was a wealthy period which has left us many monuments and inscriptions, for example in tombs where it was Egyptian custom to depict whole histories on the walls. So, if I am right in suggesting that Ahmose came to the throne in 1403BC then we can be quite sure that his son Amenophis I ruled from 1377BC to 1357BC.

Amenophis I was to become one of the most venerated of Egyptian rulers, looked upon by all subsequent generations as something of a saintly figure. He inherited a strong kingdom and set about increasing the economic power of the country. He re-instated trade links with the ports of Syria and Lebanon, particularly the port of Byblos, historically a key ally of Egypt and also a key supplier of the timber which Egypt so desperately needed. But the matter which I now wish to draw to your attention concerns Year 9 of Amenophis I's reign, 1369/68BC in this chronology and the year in which the famous and controversial *Ebers Papyrus* was written. As I said in Chapter 2, it is a document of obscure meaning, traditionally taken to describe the heliacal rising of the star Sothis (Sirius) on a certain day (the 9th day of the 3rd month of the dry season). However, the fact is that its use of ditto marks suggests that the expression used, "the going forth of Sothis", applied to the 9th day of *every* month of the year, not a physical possibility if the heliacal rising of the star is really what is meant. So what does it actually mean?

Well, dare I say that the date should be a dead give-away. It is the exact year in which the first Sothic cycle was completed and the second one started. Egyptian culture had seen 1507 years, one 'Great Sothic Year', since the calendar had first been introduced during the reign of king Djer of the 1st Dynasty. The court astronomers must have been beside themselves with excitement and a year of celebration was most certainly called for. The appropriate ceremony was known as 'the going forth of Sothis' and it was decided that the celebrations should start on the 8th anniversary of the king's coronation, the 9th day of the 3rd month of the dry season in the year 1369BC, and that it should then be celebrated on that same day of each month throughout the entire auspicious year. This simply has to be the true meaning of the *Ebers Papyrus* if my dates are correct, and I hope you will find it a lot more persuasive than the extremely suspect original interpretation.

Absolute date: 1369BC
The end the first Great Sothic Year and the start of the second; commemorated in every month of Amenophis I's 9th year

Further support comes from the fact that the 4th Century Greek mathematician Theon of Alexandria reported that a Great Sothic Year had commenced in the reign of a certain pharaoh "Menophres", and the name Amenophis is certainly not dissimilar to Menophres (both being Greek versions of an Egyptian form). Having observed the many and varied ways in which names can mutate through the centuries, I would put this identification forward for serious consideration. Besides, Theon speaks of "the era of Menophres" and Amenophis I, who was considered a saintly father of the nation, seems an ideal candidate to have an era named after him. Egyptologists will not like this identification one little bit, but the principal reason for that will simply be that I am at least 150 years later than any usually quoted dates for Amenophis I, not to mention being 52 years earlier than the frequently but incorrectly quoted date for the start of a Great Sothic Year!

All Change at Babylon

In 1362BC Babylon had been looted, its gods taken and its walls destroyed by the Hittites. Samsuditana, the last of the line of Hammurabi, disappears from the scene at this point and evidence becomes very sparse indeed. *Babylonian king list A* gives a whole dynasty (over 350 years) of Sealand kings, implying that they stepped straight in when the Hittites left, but this dynasty is now known to be a list of those ruling the southern Iraqi cities in parallel with the kings of Babylon. The only Sealand ruler who has what looks like a genuine claim to have sat, for a short while at least, on the throne of Babylon was a figure called Gulkishar, but with a single document to his name his tenure must have been brief indeed. However, we can be quite sure that not long after the Hittites left it was the Kassite king Agum II who marched into the ruined city and took over governance of the ancient land of Akkad, restoring the gods which the Hittites had earlier removed.[3] Gulkishar may have thought he saw an opening, but it was a short-lived one.

The Kassites had come a long way since being an obscure tribe from the Zagros Mountains. First, they had fallen under the influence of an Indo-European-speaking warrior clan. These natural born fighters had somehow instilled their own thirst for glory into the Kassite population at large and the people had moved out onto the plains of Iraq, seizing the poorly protected region where the city of Mari had once stood. And now they had taken possession of one of the great capitals of the ancient world! The Kassite rulers made themselves thoroughly at home. They soon became almost as Akkadian as the rest of the population; they honoured Akkadian (and Sumerian) gods, they adopted Akkadian language and within one or two generations they had become the natural and rightful rulers of Babylon, at least in their own eyes. They ruled an extensive territory across central Iraq and north-westwards up the Euphrates river. King Burnaburiash I, who succeeded Agum II, drew up a treaty with the Assyrian king Puzur Ashur III (1328-1314BC according to my reading of the *Assyrian king list*[4]) and it seems likely that it was the next king, Kashtiliash III, who sat on the Babylonian throne at the turn of the century. Babylon was under strong leadership and, so far as it is possible to determine, good government.

But Kassite authority still didn't extend to southern Iraq, where the Sealand kings maintained a semblance of the old Sumerian culture. We also know that Elam was still alive and functioning as a state from the handful of economic texts which have been recovered from this period and also from the evidence of a king list which gives the names of rulers throughout this time. However, there is no record of events on the international stage.

The Hittite Empire self-destructs

While Egypt rejoiced in the wise rule of Amenophis I and the Kassite king Agum II was making himself comfortable in Babylon, Mursili I of Hatti returned home to Hattusas as ruler of a very extensive empire. He was doubtless looking forward to a long and happy retirement from the stress of war – but this was not to be. Within a couple of years or so, in around 1360BC, he was murdered and replaced by his brother-in-law Hantili and the whole vast edifice started to crumble. If Hantili thought power was the route to happiness he had another think coming! Mursili's death gave the green light to the Hurrian king to retake lands lost by his predecessors to both Hattusili and Mursili. We don't know exactly how long it took but, within a few years at most, Hurrian armies had pushed the Hittites right back to the original frontier of Hatti. They then launched an attack on Hatti itself, occupied Hattusas for a while and captured Hantili's wife and two of his children, carrying them off to exile in the city of Sugziya, now well within Hurrian territory; Hantili would never see them again. Hatti was thoroughly humbled and it is safe to assume that the lands of northern Syria and southern and western Turkey had by now also thrown off Hittite overlordship. In the end Hantili suffered the same fate as Mursili, murdered at the hands of his nephew Zidanta, who had also been his co-conspirator in Mursili's assassination. But Zidanta didn't last long either. His own son Ammuna killed him, following the example set by his father!

Ammuna, whose violent accession to the throne probably took place around 1335BC, seems to have stabilised things a bit, although a document written a generation later calls his reign a "disaster". He campaigned against the Luwians of Arzawa and Cilicia, and we know that he fought more than one war against the Hurrians. Judging by the cities mentioned (Hahha, Parduwatta), the eastern frontier again lay more or less along the Euphrates river, but northern Syria had long been lost and Hittite power was now but a shadow of what it had once been, under the great kings Hattusili I and Mursili I.

The End of Middle Bronze Age Canaan

Meanwhile a very dramatic change had occurred in Palestine. Kathleen Kenyon's fifth and final archaeological phase at Middle Bronze Age Jericho comes to an end (and a very violent and complete end) within a few decades of the fall of

Hyksos Egypt. Every one of the major Canaanite cities of Palestine, all of which were well fortified, suffered destruction at this time. They included Megiddo, Gezer, Debir, Lachish, Hebron, Hazor and Jericho.[5] Jericho and Debir were abandoned for a long period, more than a century in the case of Jericho. The other cities continued in use but had to be substantially rebuilt. Megiddo seems to have escaped relatively lightly and the culture of Megiddo IX follows on fairly unchanged from that of Megiddo X. Most historians assume that, following his success against the Hyksos stronghold Sharuhen, pharaoh Ahmose launched a campaign of destruction against the cities of Palestine, between about 1388 and 1378BC according to the dates presented in this book. However, the evidence is entirely circumstantial; nowhere has any claim been found in any record, contemporary or otherwise, for such a campaign, and this is most remarkable considering the success of the undertaking, whoever was responsible. It is all the more remarkable since the Egyptians were highly literate and usually extremely keen to trumpet their achievements. Besides, we have reports from more than one army general who served under Ahmose, Amenophis I and the next pharaoh, Tuthmose I, and they make no mention of this campaign whatsoever, even though Tuthmose I clearly passed right through Palestine on his way to Syria. It is a most puzzling mystery – and if the Egyptians weren't responsible, Tuthmose was probably as puzzled as today's historians!

Tuthmose I, not the son of Amenophis I – he died prematurely – but a close member of the royal family, came to the throne in 1357BC. Babylon had fallen to the Hittites five years earlier, Yamkhad a few years before that, and I am sure Tuthmose would have known about both. Trade was still recovering after the economic downturn of Hyksos times but there would most certainly have been travellers who made the journey between Egypt, Syria and Iraq, probably including royal envoys. Tuthmose would also have been aware that many of the cities of Cannan had suffered destruction in recent years, quite apart from Sharuhen and the Hyksos cities annihilated by Ahmose. And it must surely have been news of these events in foreign places which persuaded Tuthmose to investigate in person. The references are brief,[6] but Egyptologists generally take the view that Tuthmose led a short campaign in southern Palestine, establishing a degree of Egyptian control, and then made an unopposed foray into Syria, which is a most surprising thing for him to have done. We can be sure it took place because he actually set up a stela on the banks of the Euphrates river and left a record of his having gone on an elephant hunt in the land of Niy, a city on the Orontes river about mid way between Alalakh and Qatna. The language he uses in relation to this journey is that he "washed his heart" in foreign lands; i.e. he went on holiday! It is only when the true historical context of all this is understood that the event becomes credible. When the Hittites destroyed Yamkhad they left a gaping power vacuum. The land was still inhabited by semi-nomadic Amorites even once the rulers in Aleppo had been dethroned and, after Mursili's death in around 1360BC, it is hard to believe the Hittites would have had much control over the surrounding lands. Syria was effectively leaderless; Tuthmose could lay claim to as much territory as he wished and holiday to his heart's content!

Furthermore, Tuthmose can have found little *en route* in Palestine but ruins or partially rebuilt towns with a reduced and enfeebled population as he travelled north on his way to the elephants of the Orontes valley. No ruler would have been able to contemplate standing in his way. Tuthmose was to claim that he ruled from Ethiopia to the "river that flows upstream", which most take to mean the Euphrates,[7] but of actual rule in Palestine and Syria there doesn't seem to be any evidence. Tuthmose may have planted the Egyptian flag, but that doesn't seem to have meant anything on the ground!

The Empire of Mitanni

The 14th Century BC finally enables us to give a name to the principal Hurrian state; it is 'Mitanni', and we can be pretty sure that it was the Indic Umman Manda tribes who were the real force in Mitannian society. We still don't have any names for the rulers of Mitanni, but we know that their domain was growing. The Hittite records may not be precisely datable but they give a very clear general picture of the frontier between the Hittite and Hurrian empires; it lay along the Euphrates river. The lands to the east of the Euphrates as far as Assyria were under Hurrian (i.e. Mitannian) control. In fact much of our evidence for Hurrian society comes from records found at the city of Nuzu, which lies some 70 miles east of the Assyrian capital Ashur, and which had once been the Akkadian-speaking city of Gasur. White-painted Mitannian pottery (Nuzu ware) can be seen right across the northern half of Iraq and northern Syria as far as the Euphrates. This was a serious empire and it was about to expand further still.

For a start, the internal troubles of the Hittites allowed the Hurrians to push their frontier west such that they held the upper Euphrates valley cities as their own. And at some stage we can be quite sure that they also moved into the leaderless land of Yamkhad. They then absorbed Alalakh, a Hurrian city but hitherto an independent one (when not under Hittite authority). This can be seen in the archaeology of the city as the time, mid way through Level V, when a new temple was constructed, a temple to the Indic god Mithras,[8] and the finding of figurines of similar type to those found in the Mitannian heartland around the modern Turkish city of Diyarbakir. It is also the time that Nuzu ware appears and there is evidence of a siege having taken place mid way through Level V.[9] Since Levels VI and V span the two centuries from about 1500 to 1300BC, the taking of Alalakh by Mitanni must have occurred in about 1350BC plus or minus a decade or so, probably shortly after Tuthmose I and his Egyptian army had left the region. By the way, the discovery in Alalakh V rubbish of part of a bowl

showing an official and the word "scribe" in hieratic Egyptian suggests that Tuthmose may also have included Alalakh in his holiday itinerary!

Hurrian names now start appearing throughout Syria and even Palestine. I
would not go so far as to suggest direct control by Mitanni over Palestine, but I
would certainly suggest that they garrisoned Aleppo and probably also other Syrian cities such as Niy and Qatna.[10] If the pattern which emerges over the next 200
years applied to these times also, they will have entered into treaties with the
local rulers binding these rulers to support the state of Mitanni as and when
called upon to do so. The treaty will almost certainly have involved payment to
the Mitannian king but the local ruler will have received the promise of support
from Mitanni should he ever need it. There is very good reason to believe that
such an agreement was made with the rulers of an emerging city called
'Kadesh'[11] on the Orontes river south of Qatna, and the fact that Hurrian names
appear in Palestine also suggests some form of Mitannian overlordship, perhaps
even Mitannian representation, certainly Mitannian trade. This growth of Mitannian power in western Syria and parts of Palestine took place between about
1350 and 1310BC and it left Mitanni as a true superpower, more than a match for
Hatti and a serious rival to Egypt.

The Mediterranean Lands

Despite the changes which were taking place in western Syria, first under Amorite rule, then Hittite occupation, next a brief visit by Tuthmose I of Egypt and finally control by Mitanni, the coastal cities of Ugarit, Byblos, Tyre and Sidon remained more or less independent. They were part of a different world, a sea-fac-
ing world. They lived by trade and by fishing and, particularly after Amenophis I
of Egypt opened up Egyptian markets once more, they prospered.

The island of Cyprus had by this stage adopted a very similar culture to that
of Ugarit. We can see this, for example, in the pottery type commonly known as
'Cypriot white-slip milk bowls', which is neither particularly Cypriot nor has
anything to do with milk! It is abundant in Cyprus, but the design comes from
Syria and, before that, eastern Turkey. Its appearance in Cyprus during the 14th
Century BC, the start of the Late Cypriot I period, is much later than on the
mainland.[12] There is also some evidence for warfare on Cyprus and mass graves
of this period have been discovered in different parts of the island. This may logically have been the culmination of ethnic conflict between the Semitic (i.e.
Canaanite) culture of the east and an older culture, related to that in south-west
Turkey, in the west – but I am certainly speculating here. If so, the Semitic element came out on top.

But throughout this century, as for the previous seven or so, Crete was the
dominant sea power, and Cretan influence is particularly clear in Egypt.[13] Egyptian paintings, notably from the tomb of an official named Senmut, show Cretan

imports. Crete remained strong despite enduring further natural disasters, the first of which was an earthquake which brought an end to the Middle Minoan III period and ushered in Late Minoan Ia, the pottery type shown in Senmut's tomb. The culture of Greece continued to parallel that of Crete and it is quite possible that there was a very real Cretan empire encompassing many of the islands of the Aegean[14] and with Greek tributary kingdoms on the mainland. It is worth re-calling that this is exactly the picture painted by the later Greek legends of king Minos of Crete and his dealings with the Greek kingdoms, notably Athens. By the close of the 14th Century BC Crete was more powerful than ever and the cul-ture of the island had reached tremendous artistic heights. Cretan designs such as those found by Arthur Evans on walls at the great palace at Knossos are widely admired today and they would have been the envy of the civilised world in the 14th Century BC. Yet one of our finest sources for examples of Cretan artwork of the Late Minoan Ia period also reveals the fact that a further, although rela-tively minor, natural disaster had taken place. It was an eruption of the volcano on the Cretan-controlled island of Thera, which necessitated the hasty evacua-tion of the island as a thick layer of volcanic ash settled over the thriving town known to us as Akrotiri. As at the Italian city of Pompeii, the ash protected Akrotiri from the elements, and this has allowed modern archaeologists to un-cover a breathtaking set of wall paintings in a beautiful and naturalistic style. It is impossible to put a precise date on this eruption but it was some time within the Late Minoan Ia period,[15] probably within the last two decades of the 14th Century BC. It was not a major eruption as such things go, but it was enough to make Thera uninhabitable, at least for a while.

Stability returns to Hatti

King Ammuna of Hatti must have taken to his deathbed more or less as Thera was erupting. Unusually for a Hittite king in these treacherous times, he died of natural causes – quite an achievement! However, his death was to trigger a fresh bout of blood-letting amongst the Hittite royals. A member of the royal family named Huzziya immediately murdered all bar one of Ammuna's young sons and seized the throne, only to be driven out by the one remaining son Telipinu, doubtless with the assistance of powerful friends.

The problem with Hittite records, graphic though they sometimes are, is that they tend to be undated. We have snapshots of events but experts then have to piece the story together from these snapshots, and the result is that we really do not know exactly when this whole episode of history took place. All we know is that Telipinu was approximately of the third generation after Mursili I, since his grandfather's uncle was Mursili I's brother-in-law. So, if Mursili reached his twen-tieth birthday in about 1385BC – already an approximate figure – then Telipinu is likely to have been about twenty years of age in 1315BC,[16] and he probably became king in his early twenties. And finally, in Telipinu, it seems that the Hittite royal family had produced someone who wasn't a pathological murderer! Much of our knowledge of the events of the preceding century comes from a document known as the *Proclamation of Telipinu*, which candidly lists the sins of his fathers as well as some of their achievements. Telipinu's over-riding mission was to put the royal house of Hatti back onto a stable footing and in doing so it seems he brought a fair degree of stability to the country – all of which means that by 1300BC we can leave Hatti in reasonably safe hands once more. The vast empire of Mursili I has long since gone, but the kingdom is again powerful enough to be taken seriously by the other great powers.

Egypt builds an Empire

Egypt certainly considered herself a great power, and equally certainly had ambitions to be greater still. Tuthmose I may have treated his trip to Syria as a holiday, but he was quite serious in his claim to rule as far as the river Euphrates. His son-in-law Tuthmose II was doubtless equally keen that Egypt's claim should be recognized. Unfortunately, however, he only managed to maintain Egyptian control over the southernmost parts of Palestine[17] before his untimely death led to a 21-year power struggle. Let me at this stage give you a full list of the reigns of the 18th Dynasty rulers of the 14th Century BC, dated according to my interpretation of the *Ebers Papyrus*, together with the excellent contemporary evidence for the reign lengths of each monarch:

Ahmose	– 1377BC
Amenophis I	1377 – 1357BC
Tuthmose I	1357 – 1344BC
Tuthmose II	1344 – 1329BC
Hatshepsut	1329 – 1308BC
Tuthmose III	1308 –

According to all the rules of Egyptian succession, Tuthmose II should have been succeeded by his young son, also named Tuthmose – but his widow Hatshepsut had other ideas. She first took the throne in the role of 'protector' of the young Tuthmose, not her own son but the son of a junior wife, and then made it her own, taking on the traditional titles of a pharaoh. Apart from leaving one of the grandest and architecturally most pleasing mortuary temples in all Egypt, Hatshepsut is perhaps best known for her trading expedition to the land of Punt, scenes from which are depicted on the walls of her mortuary temple. Although Egypt remained strong and stable with a sound economy, Hatshepsut never pursued any really aggressive foreign policies; that was left to Tuthmose III once he had the throne to himself (in about 1308BC) following the death, some say assassination, of his step-mother.

One of Tuthmose's first tasks was to have all mention of Hatshepsut removed from the various monuments which she had set up; her name was chiselled out and texts describing her activities defaced. He then set about conquering as if it had gone out of fashion, and he recorded his conquests in some detail in the traditional way on the walls of the temple of Amun at Karnak. In his first campaign, in 1307BC, he laid siege to and captured the Canaanite city of Megiddo;[18] in the following two years he struck north into Lebanon and western Syria, and in doing so he was striking deep into Mitanni-dominated territory. The policy was to make sure that the local rulers were brought into the Egyptian sphere of influence,[19] paying regular tribute and opening their doors to Egyptian trade, and in this he was outstandingly successful. By his energetic tours around the newly-conquered empire he made absolutely sure that city after city became thoroughly dependent on a strong and continuing relationship with Egypt. By 1300BC most of the Canaanite cities were nominally under Egyptian authority and the Lebanese coastal cities were also strongly allied to Egypt. King Parattarna of Mitanni (we have a name at last) now had a real fight on his hands.

Summary

The world has changed a lot in a hundred years and the number of independent sovereign states has been whittled down to just a handful of superpowers. Egypt and Mitanni are now the two greatest powers in the Middle East and they are definitely not on good terms. As far as Mitanni is concerned, the fighting seems to have been principally carried out at arm's length, utilising the forces of vassal rulers such as the king of Megiddo, but the hostility was real and it certainly had a negative impact on economic development. The lands around the eastern Mediterranean enjoyed a continuing prosperity, facilitated by Cretan ships, and the steady supply of gold from the mines of Nubia kept the Egyptian economy buoyant. However, it is clear that times were still not particularly prosperous in Babylonia, nor in southern Iraq, Elam or Assyria. The Sealand kings lived in a state of constant low-level conflict with Babylon. In truth, the world was crying out for peace and stability, but the great rulers were still dreaming of power and glory. Perhaps Hatti was an exception, now under the wise rule of king Telipinu, but it was not an exception that would last!

Finally, if I had any doubts about the correct dating of ancient history, they have practically evaporated. The two absolute dates presented in this chapter, 1362BC for a very rare double eclipse in Babylon and 1369BC for the *Ebers Papyrus*, raise the probability of being correct close to the 100% mark!

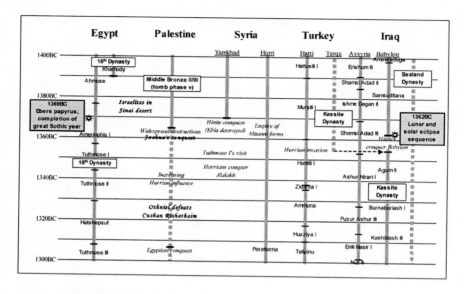

What does the Bible have to say?

The year 1400BC found the Israelites in the desert region south of modern Israel. They moved from campsite to campsite under the leadership of Moses, and on the way they met various other peoples. The first were the 'Amalekites' (Exodus 17:8-16), a people with a particularly bad reputation in the Bible, and a people who are particularly hard to iden-tify. They lived from the Mount Carmel region of western Palestine, south to the Negev desert and east into Jordan; they were clearly a Semitic-speaking people, but they were also clearly distinct from the Canaanites and Amorites.[20] After seeing off the Amalekites and spending a therapeutic 38 years or so in the wilderness, during which time the Hyk-sos were driven out of Egypt by king Ahmose, Moses then led the people east and north. On the way they had to defeat an Amorite army from the southern Palestinian city of Arad (Numbers 21:1-3).[21] Next they skirted the lands of Edom and Moab east of the Dead Sea, the only real information available to history that these lands were already in-dependent of Amorite rule,[22] and then encountered a further set of Amorite kings east of the river Jordan. Amorite kings fit known history well enough – they had dominated the lands east of the Jordan for hundreds of years – but their days were numbered! Moses' generals led the Israelites to victory over king Sihon of Heshbon, not far from Amman the capital of modern Jordan (Numbers 21:21-26), and king Og of Bashan, a country stretch-ing north into southern Syria (Numbers 21:32-35), both Amorite rulers. According to the Bible, these were the first lands to be settled by the Israelites.

Invasion of the Promised Land

I mentioned earlier the destruction which took place right across Palestine within a few decades at most of the collapse of Hyksos power and that most historians attribute this to pharaoh Ahmose despite the fact that no Egyptian claim of responsibility has yet been found. According to the Bible however, the destruction was the work of the Israelites under their new leader Joshua, commencing in 1365BC. Most of the book of Joshua, the 6th book of the Bible, is dedicated to describing the invasion and conquest of Palestine by Joshua and the Israelites and there appears to be pretty much a one-to-one correspondence between the list of cities which Joshua claimed to have conquered and those which archaeology tells us were damaged or destroyed at the end of the Middle Bronze Age. One could debate one or two of them; for example Ai, the second city that Joshua is said to have conquered, is sometimes claimed to show no suitable destruction level, but this depends on the correct identification of Ai and at least one of the possible candidates shows the appropriate evidence.[23] However, the main reason why most historians, and indeed most Biblical scholars, avoid making this seemingly obvious connection is purely one of date. Conventionally, the destruction of these Middle Bronze Age Palestinian cities would be dated to the 16th Century BC, as would pharaoh Ahmose, and there is no way that most Biblical scholars would be prepared to see Joshua and the Israelites entering Palestine at such an early date. But a date of 1365BC on the other hand fits very nicely indeed.

Turning to the archaeological evidence from Palestine, the data fits the picture of an Israelite invasion extremely well. As I intimated earlier, the culture of Palestine was previously Canaanite. It was a highly urbanised and relatively uniform society, with evidence of similar religious beliefs throughout the region as indicated by numerous finds of shrines and cultic objects. Following the destructions, there is actually no significant change in culture in most of the cities excavated; it continues to be Canaanite, although there is evidence for a reduced population and a lower level of economic activity.[24] The

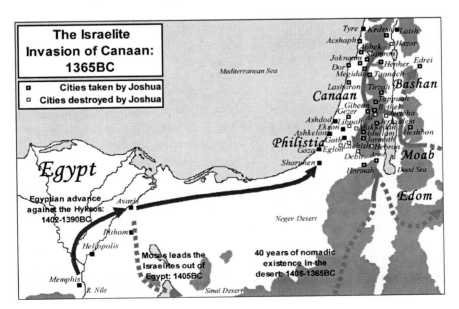

central upland parts of Palestine see an increase in nomadic lifestyle corresponding to the decrease in urban living.²⁵ These trends are exactly what would be expected following an Israelite invasion. The central uplands were the main areas occupied by the Israelites who, at that time, were a nomadic people. The Bible records that they totally failed to dislodge the inhabitants of the coastal lowlands and the plain of Esdraelon, where Megiddo is situated. Among the cities which are recorded in the Bible as having been defeated by Joshua but which are then said not to have been occupied by the Israelites are Jerusalem, Megiddo, Bethshan, Taanach, and Gezer. It is therefore not in the least surprising to see from the archaeology that Canaanite culture recovers quite quickly in most of the cities.

As I reported earlier, the city of Debir was abandoned for some decades and Jericho for well over a century. Jericho in particular ties in with the Bible's record where it is explicitly stated that Joshua put a curse on anyone who re-founded the city, a curse whose fulfilment is also recorded in the Bible but not until the time of King Ahab, some 500 years later.²⁶ There is no way that the archaeology of Middle Bronze Age Jericho can be said to prove the Bible's description of its fall to Joshua, where the walls are said to have fallen down in response to a mighty shout given by the Israelite army (after marching 13 times around the city). However, archaeology does show that the Middle Bronze Age city was violently destroyed and burnt by someone and that it lay unoccupied for a long period of time. Taken together, the correspondence between the picture given by the archaeology of Palestine and that given in the Bible is so close that it would be illogical not to conclude that the cause of this series of destructions was the arrival of the Israelites onto the Middle East scene.

The Peoples of Palestine

The list of peoples living in Palestine at the time of the Israelite invasion is given many times in the Bible (for example Joshua 3:10) although with slight variations. They are listed as: Amorites, Perizzites, Canaanites, Hittites, Girgashites, Hivites and Jebusites. Of these, we can readily identify Amorites, Canaanites and Hittites (i.e. Hattians). Perizzites are found in western parts of the Judean hills.²⁷ Hivites are replaced by 'Horites' in some Bible texts and there is every reason to suppose that these may have been Hurrians. They are described (Joshua 11:3; Judges 3:3) as concentrated in the mountains of Lebanon, north of Palestine, a region which would have seen significant Hurrian (i.e. Mitannian) influence during the 14ᵗʰ Century BC, although Joshua also encountered a Hivite/Horite town, Gibeon, in central Palestine. Jebusites are specific to the city of Jerusalem, then known as 'Jebus'. They seem to be indistinguishable from Canaanites at this distance. The most obscure people are the 'Girgashites'; they are omitted from some lists and I admit I have no idea who they might have been!

Finally, mention should be made of the Philistines. Their territory was the coastal region north of Gaza. They are referred to as being present at the time of Joshua's conquest but only as a people looking on from the sidelines. Their lands were not on Joshua's immediate target list.

<u>Cushan Rishathaim</u> *(Judges 3:7-11)*

It is very difficult to date the events of the book of Judges, the Biblical book which tells several hundred years of history following Joshua's death. However, an early incident, occurring within a generation or so of the conquest, is an 8-year occupation of Israelite territory by a certain Cushan Rishathaim king of 'Aram Naharaim'. Now, Naharaim is the land known as 'Nahrin' by the Egyptians, the stretch of north-west Syria between the Orontes and Euphrates rivers south of Aleppo. Although Aram does not yet appear in other documents, it comprised the semi-desert land southward from Nahrin toward the city of Tadmor. In the context of events at the time (I would estimate 1335-1328BC[28]), Cushan Rishathaim is likely to have been a displaced Amorite ruler, expelled from his homeland as Mitanni took control of Syria. He and his nomadic people apparently came south in search of somewhere to live; they found little opposition from the Israelites and so decided to settle in northern Palestine until a man named Othniel managed to gather enough Israelite support to drive them out. I have absolutely no independent evidence for this identification but it seems a sensible guess now that we know the true context of Othniel's time.

If the passage of time given in the book of Judges is correct, then the closing years of the 14th Century find the Israelites, under Othniel's leadership, living in peaceful obscurity in the uplands of central Palestine[29] and in lands to the east of the river Jordan. Palestine has been conquered, but it is most definitely not under continuing Israelite control. That is clear from archaeology where Canaanite culture recovers and it is equally clear from the Bible. In fact, the century closes with much of Palestine under Egyptian control following Tuthmose III's campaigns.

What was going on in the Rest of the World?

The land of Sheba in southern Arabia (modern Yemen) was a significant early centre of civilisation in the Middle East, but it is not well known yet to either history or archaeology. I mentioned earlier that irrigation schemes were constructed as early as the 3rd Millennium BC and by the 14th Century BC Sheba would have been a significant centre of population and wealth. It was a strategically positioned land with access to the spices grown in the hills of southern Arabia as well as to the exotic produce of Africa. It lay right at the mouth of the Red Sea, almost certainly including territory on the African side as well as in Arabia, and it had firm control over sea-borne trade in and out of the Red Sea.

We know the inhabitants of Sheba as 'Sabeans'. What we don't know because of the lack of records is the political structure in southern Arabia. South Semitic language would by then have spread across the whole southern half of Arabia as far as Oman, and probably to the Gulf coast region. When light begins to dawn in the mid 1st Millennium BC we find Arabia broken into four or so separate states, but that in no way implies the same for the 14th Century BC. Sheba may quite possibly have been the heart of a wide-ranging empire. By the way, it is important to bear in mind that Arabia was much more readily traversable in those days than it is today. The 'Empty Quarter' was much less empty! The giant sand dunes that have swept east from central Saudi Arabia to the Persian Gulf had not formed in those days and so travel between Oman and the Bahrain region would have been quite possible. Oman itself was still a centre of copper production, the land known in ancient times as 'Magan', though whether it was an independent kingdom or in some way linked with either Sheba or other parts of Arabia cannot be known.

But was Sheba 'Punt', the fabulous land visited by Egyptian expeditions from the 5th Dynasty onwards? Majority opinion seems to be that it was. On the murals of Hatshepsut's mortuary temple are depictions of her own expedition to Punt and the mention of "terraces of myrrh", the inclusion of what appear to be Arabian frankincense trees and the mixed Caucasian and African looking population certainly lend support to the theory. The exotic animals (panthers, monkeys) would logically have come from Sheba's African territories. In fact, given that Punt was certainly reached by boat from an Egyptian Red Sea port, I find it hard to see any real alternative.

11

Big Bang: 1300–1250BC

The War between Egypt and Mitanni

King Parattarna of Mitanni was a proud emperor who had no intention of loosening his hold on any of his dominions. King Tuthmose III of Egypt was equally determined that he would secure Egyptian domination over Palestine and Syria. The result, whatever the common people on either side or those caught up in the middle might have wanted, was an inevitably prolonged and bloody war, and we are fortunate to have quite a detailed account from an Egyptian perspective on the temple walls at Karnak.

It was Tuthmose who re-ignited the conflict in 1300BC, his 29th year counting from the day he felt he should have been king, although in reality it was Hatshepsut who had been in charge for 21 of those years. He marched north up the Syrian coast and spent the next four years conquering and pacifying the coastal cities of Ullaza, Ardata and Sumyr and eventually the important inland cities of Tunip and Kadesh. These were all cities whose previous allegiance had been to Mitanni.

Egypt was now a truly great power and there are records of gifts being received from Babylon, from Ashur and from Hatti. But Tuthmose wasn't done yet. In 1296BC he launched a campaign still further into Mitannian territory. He took Qatna and Niy and marched his army to the banks of the Euphrates where he erected a stela next to the one placed there by his grandfather Tuthmose I about 60 years earlier. He then crossed the Euphrates on boats which the army had hauled across Syria and ravaged the Hurrian lands as far north as Carchemish, before returning to Niy.[1] The next nine years saw battle after battle as Tuthmose struggled to ensure the permanence of Egyptian control over western Syria and it culminated in a direct victory over a large Mitannian army somewhere near Kadesh in 1287BC. Alalakh had already been taken and Tuthmose even received gifts from Adana in Cilicia (then known as Kizzuwadna). This was the peak of Egyptian power. The whole Mediterranean coast of Palestine, Syria and a part of southern Turkey was now subservient to Egypt, as were the inland cities of Tunip, Kadesh, Qatna, Niy and Alalakh, and everything to the south. Aleppo was now a front-line city for Mitanni.

History as told by Tuthmose is supplemented by evidence from Alalakh, from Level IV in the city's archaeological record. Here we are fortunate enough to have access to another tablet archive (written in Akkadian), which reveals that Tuthmose set up a significant kingdom in north-west Syria and southern Turkey called Mukis, with Alalakh as its capital and a man called Taku as its king. Egyptian influence is clear from some of the ornamentation found in the ruins of the palace constructed by Taku's successors.

Then, in 1275BC, Tuthmose III died, an old man and a very successful one. In addition to his exploits in Palestine and Syria, he conquered as far south as the 4th Cataract on the Nile, taking the Kushite capital Kerma in the process. And his time was also one of artistic flowering – presumably because wealth bought time and opportunity. Tuthmose was active in supporting a major construction programme, most notably of temples; he is also supposed to have been an accomplished potter, a composer of literary works and a reader of ancient texts – in fact he was a bit of an all-rounder!

In complete contrast, his successor Amenophis II, a man known for his great physical strength, had rather less time for culture and the arts – but he still enjoyed his warfare! He launched three more campaigns into Syria in order to maintain Egyptian control, particularly over the city of Kadesh. But the new

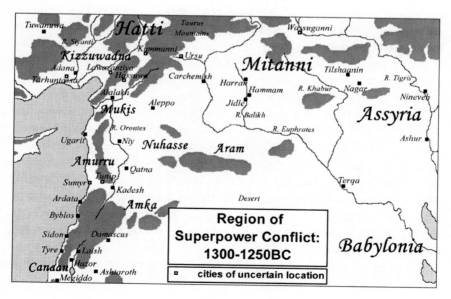

Region of
Superpower Conflict:
1300-1250BC

□ cities of uncertain location

Mitannian king was an energetic man named Saustatar. We know from the text of a later treaty that Saustatar restored Mitannian authority over Assyria, sacking Ashur in the process, and he managed to regain some of the ground Tuthmose had taken. Nevertheless, Egyptian control as far as Tunip and Kadesh seems to have remained intact. Hostilities ceased, so far as we know, in Amenophis II's 9th year, 1266BC. It would be incorrect to say that peace had broken out but neither side was prepared to fight any more. The inhabitants of northern Syria must have been heartily glad of the respite! At some date in the early 1250s Saustatar of Mitanni died and Artatama became king; Amenophis II of Egypt died in 1251BC, replaced by his son Tuthmose IV. To recap, dates for the Egyptian rulers of this period were:

Tuthmose III	– 1275BC
Amenophis II	1275 – 1251BC
Tuthmose IV	1251 –

The State of Mukis

The tablet archive in Alalakh should theoretically allow us to reconstruct the sequence of rulers of the land of Mukis. After Taku, the man Tuthmose III left in charge, the next king we can be sure about was a man called Niqmepa. He is referred to in the archives as 'son of Idrimi', which is confusing since there was indeed a king Idrimi who reigned for 30 years and whose father is named as Ilim Il-imma. However, in the texts Niqmepa gives his father none of the titles of a king and so I am taking the view, not shared by all researchers, that the king Idrimi who ruled for 30 years was a quite different individual, the son of Niqmepa's son Ilim Ilimma.[2] If this assessment is correct, Niqmepa probably came to the throne in about 1280BC while Tuthmose was still in charge of Egypt and Mukis was firmly within the Egyptian fold. When he built himself a magnificent new palace, as kings tend to do, he chose Egyptian decorative styles, and he had Egyptian symbols on his royal seal. But times were changing. Egyptian power weakened under Amenophis II; and it is clear from the tablet archive that at some stage during his reign, Niqmepa started to acknowledge Saustatar of Mitanni as his overlord. For instance one of the citizens of Alalakh brought a civil charge against Niqmepa before king Saustatar. Niqmepa himself had a dispute with Sunassura king of Kizzuwadna (i.e. Cilicia), which was referred to Saustatar for settlement. This is particularly interesting in that it implies that even Kizzuwadna then lay within the Mitannian sphere of influence. Of course, Niqmepa had to walk a very careful line and he also independently signed a treaty with king Irmermer of Tunip, an ally of Egypt.

Niqmepa seems to have successfully steered the state of Mukis through a difficult time and he handed over the kingdom to his son Ilim Ilimma in pretty good shape. From the proportion of the Alalakh archive which dates to Niqmepa's time, his reign must have been a relatively long one, so I suggest that Ilim Ilimma came to the throne in about 1255BC, not long after the time that Artatama took over as king of Mitanni. We then know from the Alalakh archive that Ilim Ilimma was given a much increased kingdom to rule, including Aleppo and Niy, a city recovered by Saustatar from Amenophis II of Egypt. Ilim Ilimma was obviously a willing vassal ruler and in 1250BC he held a large part of north-west Syria on behalf of Mitanni – which naturally meant that he awarded himself a large extension to his royal palace! Alalakh was now a very powerful city and the centre of a considerable kingdom – its rulers would have to watch their backs more closely than ever!

More Chaos in Hatti

One thing is abundantly clear during the period of conflict between Egypt and Mitanni and that is that neither side was in the least worried about the Hittite threat! The stability which Telipinu had brought to Hittite affairs was not destined to long outlast him, despite his efforts at introducing a fail-safe system for ensuring a smooth transition of power. His own reign was reasonably successful and we know from the locations of his storage depots (from Sugziya in the east to Purushanda in the west) that his kingdom was an extensive one. He also conducted a military campaign against the emerging state of Kizzuwadna, where king Isputahsu made a treaty with him. This must certainly have been before Tuthmose III arrived in the region in about 1292BC. But as soon as Telipinu died, probably in around 1290BC, chaos broke out once more.

The next king was Telipinu's son-in-law Alluwamna, but he was ousted almost immediately by a man named Tarhurwaili. He in his turn cannot have lasted long since we have just one seal and the fragmentary remains of a treaty with king Eheya of Kizzuwadna; his name was deliberately left off later lists. However, the next king Hantili II, a son of Alluwamna, must have ruled for considerably longer. I would ascribe an anonymous treaty with the Kizzuwadnan king Sunassura to Hantili's reign, since Hantili clearly reigned in parallel with Niqmepa of Mukis in my reconstruction of events and Niqmepa records dealings with Sunassura.[3] In Hantili's time it is also recorded that a new enemy had appeared on the north-east frontier of Hatti, a people known as the 'Kaskans', and that they had taken the ancient Hittite cities of Nerik and Tiliura. This was a signal to reinforce Hattusas itself which was located dangerously close to the new threat.

Just how much time elapsed between the reigns of Telipinu and Hantili II is hard to know with certainty. Hantili was two generations later, but how old was Telipinu when his daughter Harapseki was born? And how old was she when she gave birth to Hantili? Since both were almost certainly firstborn children we could sensibly estimate 20 year intervals, i.e. a 40 year gap, perhaps 35 years between the deaths of Telipinu and Hantili if, as I suspect, Hantili died aged rather younger than Telipinu, which would place Hantili's death very roughly in 1255BC.

Hatti was not in a particularly strong state when Zidanta II, Hantili's successor, became king. Important territory had been lost to the Kaskans in the northeast; the treaties with Kizzuwadna – and Zidanta added another, this time with king Pilliya of Kizzuwadna – imply alliance but not necessarily overlordship. And Zidanta's reign was another short one judging from the lack of documentation; so was that of his successor Huzziya II, cut short before it had really got going by the murderous attention of a man named Muwatalli. Then Muwatalli was murdered in his turn, quite possibly by sons of Huzziya! The sum total of all three reigns can have been no more than a handful of years, perhaps as little as five. Unsurprisingly, the murders of Huzziya and Muwatalli, clearly the heads of two rival factions within the Hittite royal house, led to all out civil war. Huzziya's blood-line was fronted by a young man named Tudhalya, although we have no real idea how he fits into the family or what connection he may have had with Muwatalli's murder; the line of Muwatalli was upheld by his former steward, a man called Muwa. A full-scale battle took place with chariots and infantry, including a Hurrian force on Muwa's side – but it was Tudhalya who won the day and with it the kingdom, and with Tudhalya Hatti would enter a new age. The year was approximately 1250BC. The Hurrian force which ended up on the losing side had been ordered by king Artatama of Mitanni and because he had backed the wrong horse he now had a new and dangerous enemy to worry about!

The Other Kingdoms of Turkey

The annals of the Hittites give us a glimpse here and there of the political framework across the modern country of Turkey and it is always necessary to remember that just because the rulers of these other kingdoms were not in the habit of writing records that doesn't mean they weren't active in all the normal ways in which a 13th Century BC Middle Eastern state operated. We know something about Kizzuwadna and its kings simply because of the existence of treaties with the Hittites. For example we read in the treaty with king Sunassura that Kizzuwadna had been allied to Hatti in the days of the Hittite king's grandfather, which would be Telipinu in my reconstruction, but that it had then gone over to Mitanni, presumably during the early part of Hantili's reign, while Niqmepa was king in Alalakh and Saustatar was king of Mitanni. Hantili (assuming it was him) then boasts that he has now (probably following the death of Saustatar) restored Kizzuwadna's independence from the evil grasp of Mitanni! Basically, we have a picture of the state of Kizzuwadna as a typical minor kingdom caught between the whims of the bigger players, in this case Hatti and Mitanni. We don't have such a picture during this period for the other states of Turkey, but we can be pretty sure that Arzawa, immediately to the west of Kizzuwadna, would have had a similar constitution. The same would be true for perhaps five or six other states in western Turkey, most famously Troy, already a rich and prosperous city as seen in the archaeology of the long-lasting phase known as Troy VI. And we will shortly be meeting states in the east too, 'Isuwa' north of Carchemish on the upper Euphrates, and 'Azzi' immediately to the north of Isuwa. They all had kings, governments and armies and they would all have maintained some sort of relations with both Hatti and Mitanni, usually diplomatic but sometimes more hostile. In fact the only truly stateless people in the region seem to have been the Kaskan tribes of the north-east.

Disaster in the Aegean

The 13th Century BC had dawned bright and cheerful for Crete and its ruling house, just as the preceding eight or so had done. Cretan naval and economic power held the whole Aegean in its grip, although there were signs that some of the mainland Greek cities were not now far behind in terms of culture and technology. During the first half of Tuthmose III's reign the evidence from tombs is that Late Minoan Ib ware was now accompanied by a certain amount of so-called 'Mycenaean ware', i.e. imports from mainland Greece. And so we come to the famous tomb of Rekhmire, vizier to Tuthmose III, which dates to the second half of Tuthmose's reign. Here on the walls is what many people see as a graphic illustration of something extremely profound which had recently occurred. A group of traders bearing what could be either Greek or Cretan products were clearly originally painted wearing the traditional Cretan kilt, but the painting had then been deliberately altered to show the traders in mainland Greek style clothing. This may seem a petty thing to get excited about, but the fact is that at some time during this period the balance of power in the Aegean swung by 180 degrees. Late Minoan Ib culture in Crete ends dramatically. Every single one of the great centres of Cretan power suffered catastrophic damage with signs of fire everywhere. The succeeding Late Minoan II period, still within the reign of Tuthmose III of Egypt since his cartouche has been found in a Late Minoan II tomb at Knossos, is one of artistic decline but expansion of arms manufacture; it is also one of very visible Greek influence. Most obviously this is seen at Knossos where the Linear A script used to write the language of Crete is replaced by Linear B, known to represent a form of early Greek.

The conclusion of almost every researcher is that this time marks the conquest of Crete by forces from the Greek mainland and the end of one of the most glorious civilisations known to the ancient world. We have little idea what part of the mainland the invaders came from; indeed we have little idea how Greek political life was structured in those days. But it is clear that Greece had, at a stroke, raised its profile on the international stage from a member of the supporting cast to a principal player. Henceforth the king (or kings) of Greece could not be ignored.

But what had caused this shocking change? The answer lies in a layer of ash which is found right across eastern Crete and also on the bed of the Mediterranean for hundreds of miles to the south-east. There had been a moderate eruption of the volcano on the island of Thera some 25 years previously, forcing it to be abandoned; this time Thera literally exploded![4] The present island, known as Santorini, consists of a near circular crater rim sticking up from the sea, with an occasionally still smoking mound of ash rising slowly from its centre once more. It was one of the most violent eruptions known to have occurred anywhere on the planet in historical times – and the prosperous and unsuspecting island of Crete lay just 70 miles away to the south. Evidence for massive tsunamis has been uncovered in the ruins of some of the coastal towns and cities but much longer lasting was the economic ruin (by an estimated 10cm of ash fall) of eastern Crete, accompanied by signs of increased population in western Crete,[5] suggesting that the people had moved *en masse* to escape the worst affected regions. In eastern Crete there is plenty of Late Minoan Ib pottery – but there is no sign of Late Minoan II.

If my overall dating scheme is correct then this disaster occurred some time between 1290 and 1280BC, i.e. late in the reign of Tuthmose III of Egypt – but before his death. Disappointingly perhaps, this matches none of the clear episodes of low tree growth apparent in tree ring records across the world. Nor does it coincide with any of the greatest peaks in acidity from cores through the

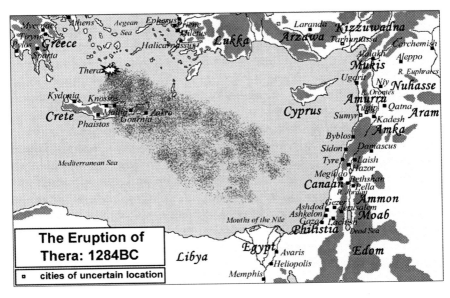

The Eruption of Thera: 1284BC

□ cities of uncertain location

Greenland or Antarctic ice sheets. But it does coincide with a 'lesser' peak; namely 1284BC.[6] I couldn't possibly claim this as a proven date, but if I had to choose one of the acidity peaks on offer then 1284BC (plus or minus a few years) is a much better bet than its nearest neighbours 1120BC and 1327BC.

> **Approximate absolute date: 1284BC**
> Acidity peak from Greenland ice core data, probably
> corresponding to the explosive eruption of Thera

Following the eruption there was some recovery of Cretan culture. The palace of Knossos was rebuilt (although those in the east of the island were not), but the opinion of most is that clear Greek influence had arrived – notably in burial practice as well as in decorative motif[7] – suggesting that by 1250BC Crete had become firmly part of the Greek world. The change which had taken place in the Aegean is also clearly reflected by a change in the pottery evidence on Cyprus some time during the Late Cypriot I period, namely a sudden increase in the quantity of Mycenaean ware from mainland Greece.

All quiet on the Eastern Front

While volcanic eruption reshaped the Aegean world and ferocious warfare raged across Syria, Babylon had settled for an altogether more peaceful approach to life. For the Kassite rulers of Babylon, it seems that conquest of the cultural heart of ancient Iraq was enough; they threw themselves into glorifying Babylon and increasing its wealth. Kashtiliash III, almost certainly king in 1300BC, was followed by Agum III and then by Karaindash. We can't reconstruct the dates with any accuracy here, but we know the period relative to events in Egypt reasonably well. There is plenty of documented evidence for trade with Egypt from Karaindash's reign onwards,[8] which would correspond to the time following the cessation of hostilities between Egypt and Mitanni in 1266BC. From later texts we know that Karaindash maintained an ambassador at the Egyptian court in Thebes and that Amenophis II had a representative in Babylon. Caravans of goods were regularly plying the route between the two countries, probably passing to the south of Mitannian territory through the semi-desert land of Aram. In fact, by acting as an international courier service the Babylonians managed to export their language as well as their produce such that it became the official international language of the day. There are commercial documents from Palestine written in Akkadian; the texts from Alalakh are all in Akkadian, and such meagre written evidence as we have for events in Elam during this time is also in Akkadian.

It is also clear that Babylon finally regained control over the southern Iraqi cities at some stage during this period, probably during the reign of Agum III, putting an end to the long-lasting Sealand dynasty,[9] and archaeology tells us that the Kassite kings then lavished quite a lot of their hard-earned wealth on construction work in places like Ur and Uruk. They most certainly saw themselves as custodians of the glories of ancient Akkad and Sumer and many of their inscriptions in the southern cities were written in the long-dead Sumerian language.

One key document from Karaindash's reign is a record of an agreement with the Assyrian king Ashur Bel Nisheshu (approximately 1253-1245BC) about the location of the Babylon/Assyria border. As well as demonstrating a certain level of Assyrian independence from Mitanni, despite the city of Ashur having been sacked by Saustatar king of Mitanni a few years previously, the text also provides valuable evidence for the historicity of this part of the *Assyrian king list*.

Summary

We have now entered a relatively stable world dominated by a few great powers. These are Egypt, Babylon, Mitanni, Hatti and Greece. There are numerous other states of various sizes but almost all appear to have been forced to ally themselves with one or other of the great powers. The Canaanite rulers of Palestine all owe allegiance to Egypt and, based on later evidence, it looks likely that most do not even bear the title king but only 'governor' on behalf of the pharaoh in Thebes. Further north the kings of Sidon, Byblos, Ugarit, Tunip, Qatna and Kadesh have a greater degree of independence but they are also within Egypt's sphere of influence. Mukis, comprising Alalakh, Aleppo and Niy, is allied to Mitanni; so is Assyria; so, from time to time, is Kizzuwadna, although it looks to have reverted to alliance with Hatti by 1250BC. Although we do not have documentation, Elam probably lies firmly within the orbit of the Kassite rulers of Babylon. The states of western Turkey are more difficult to pin down. The archaeological evidence is that Greek influence at the city of Miletus must have commenced about this time and it may well be that several of the cities and states of the Aegean coast of Turkey were now allied to Greece. This will become clearer as we move into the second half of the 13th Century BC. The peoples who are non-aligned seem to be those with a less defined political structure, people like the Kaskans of north-east Turkey, the Aramaeans of eastern Syria, and the peoples to the east of the river Jordan, or else those with natural protection, notably the island state of Cyprus. However, as Crete has discovered, natural protection is no match for an angry volcano!

Regarding absolute date the evidence continues to mount, with a plausible acidity peak from a Greenland ice core tying in with the Thera eruption. Perhaps I should be worrying about the fact that I am still some 150 years or more ahead

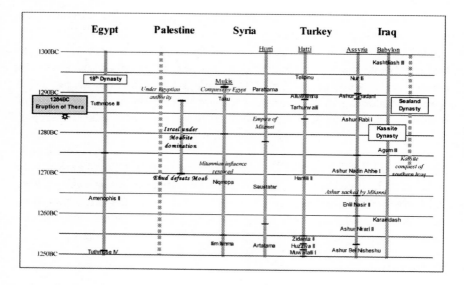

of conventionally quoted dates – but the crunch time is still centuries away so let's not panic yet!

What does the Bible have to say?

These are lean years in terms of Bible history. If my estimated dates for Othniel were right, the Israelites slipped under the control of their neighbours across the river Jordan, the Moabites, in about 1288BC – quite possible since Tuthmose's control was limited to the Canaanite lands of western Palestine. It was only in about 1270BC that Moabite dominance was ended. Judges 3:15-30 tells the story. Needless to say, these events are invisible to archaeology and we find no corroborating records from Egypt or any other literate land. Egyptian records tell us of two Palestinian peoples other than the Canaanites, namely 'Shosu' and 'Apiru'. The Shosu, encountered by both Tuthmose II and Tuthmose III, are mainly found in the south, particularly the Negev desert; the 'Apiru, 3000 of whom were taken captive by Amenophis II, are found in the central hill country. The great majority of historians would equate the word 'Apiru' with 'Hebrew' (and with Akkadian 'Habiru'), which would of course include the Israelites.[10] But for the most part the Egyptian pharaohs were only interested in lording it over the cities of Palestine; neither they nor the Canaanite inhabitants of those cities would have been particularly interested in just who lived up in the hills or on the other side of the river Jordan or the Dead Sea (where Moab is located). Archaeology on the other hand is able to tell us that the hills of central Palestine and the lands east of the river Jordan and the Dead Sea were indeed inhabited, but by semi-nomadic cultures quite different from that of the Canaanites. They could have been Amorite – but they could equally well have been Israelite or Moabite. One possible corroboration of Israelite presence lies in the almost total lack of cultic objects found in the central hill country, contrasting with the highly cultic nature of Canaanite religion.

Anyway, after liberation from Moab we hear nothing. The Bible simply states that the land had peace for 80 years. That may have been true for Israel; the world outside is quite another matter!

What was going on in the Rest of the World?

A new people has appeared on the scene, the 'Kaskans'. What can be said about them, apart from the fact that their culture was rather more primitive than that of the Hittites they threatened? We know they appeared from the north-east and by 1250BC they had clearly moved into territory they had not previously occupied; they were therefore a people on the move – but who were they?

I am going to have to speculate a little here. Caucasian languages come in four flavours, North-West, North-Central, North-East and South, according to their current distribution around the Caucasus Mountain range. The Hurrian and Hattian languages were, in my view, North-Central Caucasian,[11] and they had spread west and north from northern Iran; other North-Central Caucasian languages were probably spoken in Georgia in 1250BC. North-East Caucasian languages were already to be found in the eastern Caucasus, as they are today. The origin of South Caucasian is more obscure, but when the first Georgian state appears in the 4th Century BC (Georgian being the principal South Caucasian language) it is in the east of the modern state of Georgia, suggesting an east to west movement. This leaves North-West Caucasian, a language family which had already been present in the western Caucasus for at least a couple of thousand years by 1250BC.[12] This, I feel, is much the most likely linguistic origin of Kaskan culture, related to today's Circassian people of southern Russia and, possibly, the Colchians, with whom the Greeks did business during the 1st Millennium BC.

The Kaskans were settled farming people and their ancestors had been farmers for thousands of years. They were not so sophisticated as the Hittites or Hurrians – a fact quite evident from their pottery – but neither were they savages. We later find that there was a Kaskan king and their very success, overrunning cities which had been Hittite and, before that, Hattian for a thousand years or more, speaks for a high degree of organisation as well as an ability to handle weaponry. The Hittites despised them – but that is no reason for us to do so.

12

A Golden Age:
1250–1200BC

The Glorious 18th

The 18th Dynasty in Egypt was literally a time of gold. The gold mines of Nubia had been worked for generations already, but in the time of the 18th Dynasty pharaohs they were exploited for all they were worth. Egyptian control over Nubia had often been fragile and it had collapsed completely during Hyksos times. But from the days of pharaoh Ahmose gold flowed in – and out, as Egypt was able to purchase goods from other countries. The 18th Dynasty is one of the best documented periods in all of Egyptian history and the only real room for doubt regarding the succession of pharaohs occurs right at the end of the period, in the next chapter. So, continuing from the dates deduced previously, based largely on the dating of the *Ebers Papyrus* (Year 9 of Amenophis I), the next rulers of the land of the Nile are:

Tuthmose IV	– 1240BC
Amenophis III	1240 – 1202BC
Akhenaten	1202 –

The early death of Tuthmose IV brought his 12 year old son Amenophis III to the throne. This was a time of unparalleled peace for Egypt. The conquests of Tuthmose III had been consolidated and, with the marriage of Tuthmose IV to the daughter of Artatama king of Mitanni, the conflict with Mitanni had come to a permanent end. And all the while the coffers of the Egyptian state were being massively enriched by the flow of gold from the province of Nubia.

Records bearing the name of Amenophis III have been found as far away as Greece, Crete, Assyria, Babylon and even Sheba in the far south of Arabia; Egypt's international standing was very high indeed.

Egyptian-controlled Palestine and Syria

At this point we are blessed with a veritable flood of information stemming from the Egyptian state archives of the period, recovered from Amarna, the Egyptian capital under Amenophis' son Akhenaten, archives containing official correspondence between Egypt and countries right across the Middle East from the reigns of both Amenophis III and Akhenaten. This correspondence, almost all of it written in Akkadian, is known colloquially as the 'Amarna letters', and it represents an invaluable resource to the ancient historian. We have letters from the rulers of city after city in Palestine as they write to the Egyptian pharaoh expressing loyalty, requesting assistance, telling tales on each other and, sometimes, lying through their teeth about this or that matter. Archaeology confirms the close connections between the Canaanite cities and Egypt, for example in the Amarna-style ivories found in Megiddo (Level VIII) and a temple with a plaque of Amenophis III at Lachish (Level VII). The cities of Gath, Megiddo and Bethshan seem to be under direct Egyptian rule with a permanent Egyptian garrison. In other cities a local ruler governs. In Hazor, the ruler calls himself a king; elsewhere simply 'regent' or 'governor'. We find a similar picture to the north, in the Lebanese port cities of Tyre, Sidon and Byblos, and in the Syrian cities of Kadesh, Qatna, Irqata, and Tunip. All profess undying loyalty, many call into serious question the loyalty of their neighbours, and most request assistance from the Egyptian army on a regular basis.

But one particular matter seems to be exercising the minds of many of these rulers and that is the problem of the people known in Akkadian as 'Habiru'. The Habiru seem to be outside Egyptian law, a stateless people and a troublesome one.[1] Several rulers complain of losing land to the Habiru or express suspicion that their neighbours are harming them in collusion with the Habiru. The story seems to be a similar one from Jerusalem to Byblos. Unfortunately the letters are not dated and in many cases it is not even specified who was on the throne of Egypt at the time, but it seems that a similar general picture of life applied during Amenophis III's reign and during that of his son. I'll be saying much more about the evidence of the Amarna letters in Palestine in the next chapter.

The Growing Wealth of Babylon

The Amarna correspondence also gives us a clear view of the situation in Kassite-controlled Babylon. In the Amarna archive are letters between both Amenophis III and Akhenaten and the Babylonian kings Kadashman Enlil I and, particularly, Burnaburiash II. Judging by the somewhat arrogant tone of his letters, Burnaburiash thought of himself as an extremely important world leader, certainly of equal status to the Egyptian pharaoh. He wrote to demand that Egypt send him gold, apparently in exchange for the hand of his daughter in marriage, and complained when the quantity was less than he had hoped for. He also complained about the arrangements for his daughter's travel to Egypt. Whatever we might think of his lack of interpersonal skills, the clear point to emerge is that Babylon was a very rich and powerful kingdom during the Amarna letters period, and there is enough reference back to previous generations to indicate that this had been the situation for some time. The extent of Babylon's connections is illustrated by the finding of a seal of one of Burnaburiash's officials in mainland Greece.

The extensive reconstruction work started in the mid 13th Century BC by Karaindash was continued by his successor Kurigalzu I and then by Kadashman Enlil I and Burnaburiash II. Kurigalzu also founded a new royal capital, Dur Kurigalzu, in the east of the country, as well as continuing the temple building programme in Ur and Uruk. We know about the level of trade from the Amarna letters, but we also have direct evidence, for example an ingot of Mycenaean gold found in Dur Kurigalzu. This period also sees plenty of rich Babylonian graves on the island of Bahrain, for over a millennium a holy resting place for the Sumerian aristocracy. As in Egypt, peace was bringing rich rewards and even the lot of the poorer inhabitants of the land must have been improving steadily.

On the international front, it doesn't look as though Babylon had much to trouble it. Elam was quiet and was probably a vassal state to Babylon; the desert-dwellers of the west were evidently not a significant threat, and Assyria was still in a weak state, under the thumb of the Hurrian rulers of Mitanni. As for Mitanni itself, there were far too many worries closer to hand than Babylon for there to be any likelihood of conflict.

North-western Syria

This region constituted one of Mitanni's more significant headaches. In 1250BC much of north-western Syria was in the hands of Ilim Ilimma king of Mukis with his capital at Alalakh, and he clearly owed his kingdom to his support for Mitanni. However, it is equally clear that he was not a universally popular ruler. In Alalakh itself, his reign ends dramatically with evidence of rebellion everywhere. His nice new palace was burnt to the ground and there are signs that someone made desperate attempts to save the state archives from the blaze. He was partially successful but ironically it is the part which this well-meaning individual failed to save, and which was then baked as hard as concrete in the flames of the palace, that survived the millennia ready for 20th Century archaeologists to uncover.

There is no way to date these events precisely, but the rather limited amount of documentation relating to Ilim Ilimma in comparison with his father Niqmepa suggests that his reign was a shorter one. Since I estimated that he came to the throne in 1255BC, I suggest he probably came unstuck (and lost his life) in approximately 1240BC, leaving his young son Idrimi with no option but to flee the country to avoid suffering the fate of his father. In fact, it is an inscription on a later statue of Idrimi which supplies many of the details of these times. The statue informs us that the rebellion was not restricted to Alalakh; in fact the trouble started in Aleppo before spreading through the rest of the kingdom of Mukis. But what had triggered the unrest? For the answer to this we need to look north, to the unpredictable land of Hatti.

An Empire Regained

Tudhalya I of Hatti was a man of war. His reign had been born in war (in about 1250BC) and so it would continue. He set his sights firmly on regaining the empire which had belonged to Mursili I over a century previously, and much of his early effort seems to have been concentrated in the west. We are most fortunate to have a legible set of military annals and these tell us that Tudhalya launched an attack on the lands of 'Arzawa' (south-central Turkey), the 'Seha river land' (in my view the modern Sakarya river basin in north-western Turkey) and 'Hapalla' (probably between the other two, south-west of modern Ankara). He was clearly successful in bringing these states into vassalship since he then launched an assault still further west into 'Arsuwa', which seems to have been a broad geographical term for much of the west coast of Turkey and probably corresponds to the later Roman province of 'Asia'. Most of the cities he fought against are no more than names to us now, but they include 'Taruisa', which most would equate to Troy,[2] and other names suggest that Tudhalya brought pretty much the whole of western Turkey under his nominal control.[3] The system he used to tame these lands was to translocate large numbers of their inhabitants to Hatti, which appears a dangerous move at first sight, but which seems to have been surprisingly successful.

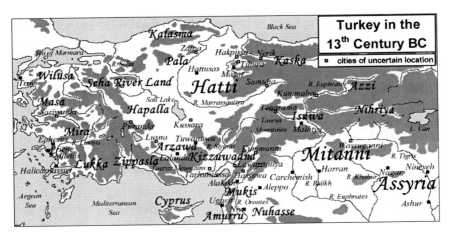

Almost inevitably, with the king so far from home trouble brewed up in the heartland, this time from bands of marauding Kaskans, and we have a number of items of correspondence on the subject from the eastern Hittite city of Maşat, then on the front line against the Kaskans. Tudhalya drove them out again, but the Kaskan problem would be a difficult one. With little state organisation, it was not easy for the Hittites to negotiate with them or to know how to defeat them.

Tudhalya's next problem was with the Hurrians again. The mainly Hurrian-speaking state of Isuwa on the northern bend of the Euphrates river had attacked, probably with the support of Mitanni. The war ebbed and flowed for a couple of years but the end result was that Isuwa became officially a satellite state of Hatti.

Unfortunately, while Tudhalya's conquests may have continued unabated, our level of knowledge doesn't! However, I believe it is possible to reconstruct one other important event, and this was the conquest and sack of the city of Aleppo, coupled with a direct defeat for Mitanni. The story is found in the text of a much later treaty, where we read that the "king of Aleppo" was caught between two superpowers, Hatti and Mitanni. He is said to have first accepted Tudhalya's overlordship but then to have switched sides again and reverted to Mitanni; this is the justification given for Tudhalya's sacking of Aleppo. In the context, the 'king of Aleppo' was clearly Ilim Ilimma of Mukis, in which case it must have been Tudhalya's attack in about 1240BC that encouraged rebellion and brought Ilim Ilimma's reign to an end.[4] You see, a steady demographic change had been taking place across north-west Syria and southern Turkey and it concerned the eastward spread of Luwian speakers. Luwian was the language of Arzawa and Kizzuwadna; we have Luwian hieroglyphic signs on a pot from Alalakh in the days before Niqmepa, and we will eventually find Luwian speech spreading right across the region as far as Carchemish. By the second half of the 13th Century BC, Aleppo would already have had a substantial Luwian population in addition to its more established Hurrian and Semitic residents. So what? Well, the Luwians were closely related to the Hittites and there would still have been a fair degree of mutual intelligibility between the two languages not to mention a lot of commonality between the two cultures. This element of the population of Mukis must have been a real nightmare for Ilim Ilimma's pro-Mitannian admin-istration and they were almost certainly instrumental in bringing about the in-tervention of the Hittite king, an intervention which led to the death of Ilim Il-imma and which, coincidentally or otherwise, also saw the end of Artatama's reign in Mitanni. According to Idrimi of Alalakh's statue, it would be 7 years be-fore Mitannian authority was restored.

The Great Empire of Mitanni

Nevertheless, despite his father's defeat by the Hittites, Shuturna son of Ar-tatama, king of Mitanni, still had every reason to be confident. He had no way of knowing that Hurrian language and culture would end up as dead as Sumerian! From the royal palace in his capital city Wassuganni,[5] he could look out on an empire in pretty good shape, prosperous, secure and, for the most part, at peace. We don't have any detail of the relationship with Babylon but it was certainly peaceful and that equally certainly means that it was one in which commerce thrived. Assyria appears to have been a subservient state, one with a very large Hurrian population. But the rock upon which late 13th Century BC Mitannian foreign policy was based was that of friendly relations with Egypt. Shuturna's sister had married Tuthmose IV of Egypt and now he had given his daughter as a wife to the current Egyptian pharaoh, Amenophis III. It was a high price to pay but it was worth it for the security it bought. Egyptian influence in Qatna, Tunip and Ugarit was recognised in return for Egyptian recognition of Mitannian authority in Alalakh, Aleppo and Niy. This meant that trade could flow between the two power blocks and, via Ugarit, to the lands of the Mediterranean.

But the Hittites still represented a rather annoying problem. His father Artatama had tried to stick his oar in and influence the choice of ruler in Hattusas, backing Muwatalli and then his steward, Muwa, but he had seen his plans come to nothing as the young Tudhalya I took over, driving out a Hurrian army in the process. Worse, Tudhalya had gone on to defeat the armies of Mitanni and take Aleppo, and it had taken him (Shuturna) 7 years to finally expel the Hittites from Syria. If there was one issue which troubled Shuturna's sleep it was the Hittite problem. It would trouble the sleep of his son Tushratta much more deeply still!

A Kingdom Restored

According to the inscription on his statue, Idrimi, son of Ilim Ilimma and heir to the throne of Mukis, escaped the Hittite-inspired rebellion that toppled his father and fled south-east to Emar on the Euphrates, probably just outside the borders of his father's kingdom. But Emar was still too close to danger, so he fled further south and spent the next 7 years living with Habiru tribes in Palestine. There he must have received news that the Hittites had at last been driven out and so he made a bid to regain his throne. The Mitannian king Shuturna[6] was apparently willing to trust him, doubtless on receipt of the standard protestations of everlasting faithfulness to the state of Mitanni, but Idrimi retained barely half the lands his father Ilim Ilimma had once ruled. Niy may still have been part of Idrimi's kingdom but Aleppo remained separate and probably under tight Mitannian control. It seems that Kizzuwadna had also been prised from the Hittites and was now allied to Mitanni once more; we have a treaty between Idrimi and king Pilliya of Kizzuwadna, the king who 20 or so years previously had signed a treaty with the Hittite king Zidanta.

Idrimi ruled Mukis for 30 years; we know that from the information given on his statue, which also speaks of handing over power to his son Adad Nirari. The date would have been about 1203BC. As we shall soon see, the good times were beginning to draw to a close and Adad Nirari would have some serious problems to attend to, but for the moment he remained in charge of a small but relatively well-off kingdom in one corner of Mitannian-dominated territory.

Ugarit was another small but well-off kingdom. It had long been a multi-cultural[7] and independent city state on the Syrian coast, south-west of Alalakh. However, independence had been hard to maintain during the 13th Century BC, with Egytpian and Mitannian armies squabbling over territory just outside Ugarit's borders! In fact, Tuthmose III had certainly been successful in ensuring that Ugarit gave up its neutrality and threw in its hand with the Egyptian cause. Now, while it managed to maintain reasonable relations with its powerful neighbour Mitanni, it still lay more or less within the Egyptian economic and political sphere. King Ammistamru of Ugarit, who reigned around the 1220s BC according to this version of history, made a treaty with Egypt, then under Amenophis III.[8] In fact, we know quite a lot about Ugarit from the documentation recovered from the city relating to this period, including texts written in the Ugaritic language.[9] This was a Semitic language with distinct differences in comparison to Canaanite or Hebrew, written in a cuneiform script adapted to spell out the letters of the Ugaritic alphabet. Ugaritic texts include the famous Epic of Kret.[10]

However the key text for us was written in Akkadian; it is the description of a solar eclipse which I used as an example of astronomical retro-calculation back in Chapter 3. This text was recovered from the burnt-out ruin of a wing of king Niqmaddu's palace (Niqmaddu was Ammistamru's son) and we are fortunate to have a report of a fire in the royal palace at Ugarit from the Amarna letter archive. It is contained in a letter from the king of Tyre, and this fact, together with the archaeology of the Ugarit palace, almost proves that the tablet with the eclipse text dates from the decades immediately preceding the Amarna age, i.e. the second half of the 13th Century BC. The date that I suggested as favourite in Chapter 3, 1223BC, fits in perfectly, whereas no eclipse in the more conventional time frame matches the description given in the tablet at all well.

> **Absolute date: 1223BC**
> The date of a solar eclipse observed at Ugarit and described on a tablet retrieved from the ruins of king Niqmaddu's palace

Meltdown in Hatti

There is no doubt that Tudhalya I was a thoroughly successful king; there is equally little doubt that the far-ranging empire he created collapsed like a house of cards a few years after his death, during the reign of his son-in-law Arnuwanda I. Arnuwanda was probably not many years younger than Tudhalya and he had been a co-ruler with Tudhalya for some time, as proved by several seals and seal impressions. My estimate is that Tudhalya died in about 1225BC and that Hatti imploded in about 1215BC. There were successful rebellions by Arzawa, Kizzuwadna, Isuwa, another eastern state called Azzi, and the inevitable Kaskans. King Idrimi of Alalakh records that he took six Hittite towns himself. One of the Amarna letters is a copy of a message sent by pharaoh Amenophis III to king Tarhundaradu of Arzawa saying that he (Amenophis) had heard that "the country of Hatti was paralysed" and he suggests a marriage alliance between Arzawa and Egypt.

In 1215BC things looked very bleak indeed for the Hittites. The Kaskans had taken virtually all of central Hatti, including Hattusas itself, leaving the remnant of the Hittite army and leadership based at the eastern city of Samuha. What happened to Arnuwanda we don't know but the next we hear is that Samuha is in the hands of his son, another Tudalya. Under this Tudhalya, known as Tudhalya III because of disputed evidence that there may have been a Tudhalya II at some stage during this period, the long slow process of recovery began once more, but it would take many years of warfare before the Kaskans were driven out. By the turn of the century central Hatti had been reclaimed, but the country was still weak and surrounded by unpacified enemies, most notably Arzawa and the Hurrian state of Isuwa.

The Expansion of Greek Influence

All this was music to the ears of the Greeks! The sudden collapse of Crete after the Thera eruption had left the Greeks as the principal sea-farers and maritime traders in the Mediterranean, and unsurprisingly therefore it is at this stage that we first hear mention of a Greek state in annals from other lands, specifically Hatti. The mention comes in a document from Arnuwanda I's reign concerning the rather treacherous activities of a ruler called Madduwatta. He had been a Hittite vassal ruler somewhere in western or southern Turkey under Tudhalya I and we read that he had fled his land under an attack from 'Attarsiya' king of 'Ahhiyawa'.[11] Admittedly there is still a lot of disagreement between experts but majority opinion is firmly of the view that Ahhiyawa is a Hittite version of 'Achaea', the name that Homer uses for Greece. Tudhalya reinstated Madduwatta, who repaid him with several episodes of disloyal behaviour. Another invasion by the Greek king Attarsiya[12] is also recorded. In the end, after Arnuwanda had taken over as king of Hatti, Madduwatta succeeded in extending his rule to include all of Arzawa, plus the so-called 'Lukka lands' in the south-western corner of Turkey. Finally, he joined forces with Attarsiya and the Greeks and launched an invasion of Cyprus! Our information runs dry at this point but the collapse of Hatti in about 1215BC must have left Madduwatta as the most powerful ruler in

Turkey – and he had the Greeks to thank for it. The Arzawan king to whom Amenophis III of Egypt proposed a marriage alliance, Tarhundaradu, was presumably Maduwatta's immediate successor.

The growing economic importance of Greece is reflected in the increasing amount of Mycenaean II pottery found right around the Middle East and also the central Mediterranean lands of Italy and Sicily. This is also the era in which the great palaces of Mycenae, Tiryns and Pylos were built – and in which the last palace at Knossos was destroyed, perhaps as Attarsiya took full control. And this period also sees another new people first making their appearance in the records, the 'Sherden'. They are recorded as having carried out a sea-borne raid on Egypt during Amenophis III's reign, and it is hard to imagine where else they could have come from other than the disturbed region of western or southern Turkey, or possibly Cyprus.[13] The Turkish coast was becoming increasingly well known as a haven for pirates and lawless communities and the activities of Madduwatta and his Greek allies may have driven some of these people to seek new lands in which to settle. The Sherden were unsuccessful this time but we will soon read of them as mercenaries in the service of Egypt, for example in the garrison at Tyre. And this will be by no means their last contribution to history!

Cyprus

I could not really claim that the invasion by Madduwatta of Arzawa and Attarsiya of Greece is proved by Cypriot archaeology, but what is clear is that the previous steady flow of Mycenaean ware into the island now becomes a flood – or, perhaps more likely, Mycenaean pottery starts to be manufactured on Cyprus itself, which is a strong indication that colonisation by Greeks had begun. These were boom times on Cyprus, so if the island was invaded it certainly did no harm to the economy. It seems to have become a natural staging post in the flow of Greek trade between the Aegean and Syria, and all such natural staging posts tend to do very nicely from the profits from that trade! As for the ethnic and linguistic composition of Cyprus during this period, the lack of understandable written materials makes it very hard to know. Cretan influence is still present in the Cypro-Minoan writing system; Greek influence has now appeared in the form of Mycenaean pottery; yet Canaanite influence is still very strong indeed, particularly the cultural connection with Ugarit. And who can say how much Luwian input there might have been from Madduwatta?

Egypt's Cultural Revolution

Amenophis III of Egypt reigned for 38 long and prosperous years and passed the empire on to his eldest surviving son who, in 1202BC, was crowned at the traditional seat of Egyptian spiritual authority, the temple of Amun at Karnak near the capital city Thebes, and who also took the name Amenophis. All should have been well – but it most certainly wasn't! Within a year the new pharaoh started to behave very strangely indeed, promoting a different cult from the traditional worship of Amun, namely that of the 'Aten', a representation of God as the sun disc. In recognition he changed his name to Akhenaten and started the construction of a new capital city, Akhetaten, better known under the name of the later village of Amarna. For Egyptian society it was as if an earthquake had struck and for the priesthood of Amun in Thebes it spelt nothing less than ruin – yet Akhenaten seems to have been quite oblivious to the anger he was generating beyond the walls of his palace and, as the 13th Century BC drew to a close, he wasn't prepared to even think about compromising his firm belief that he was right and the rest of the country – for all he cared the rest of the world – was wrong! Suddenly and quite unexpectedly Egypt was in crisis.

Summary

Until Akhenaten dropped his bombshell, much of the Middle East had been settling into a fairly stable mode of existence. The trade between Babylon and Egypt had enriched both lands as well as those in between. Mitanni was at peace with both and the three great kingdoms had sealed their friendship with various marriage alliances. Palestine had been prospering under Egyptian patronage; so had southern and western Syria. Much of northern Syria had also been prospering under the banner of Mitanni. Whether the changes in Egypt would upset any of this remains to be seen.

But the real problems have been in Turkey. The Hittites have proved to be a rather unfriendly people, particularly to Mitanni. Just at the moment the threat seems to have receded somewhat and the great Hittite empire has burst like an over-full balloon. But Arzawa doesn't appear to be any more stable or trustworthy than Hatti. The Arzawans have encouraged the equally fickle Greeks to enter the scene and the disturbance caused by all this conflict has even meant that some of the Sherden people, probably from western Turkey, have abandoned their own lands and attacked regions controlled by Egypt. And the situation in Turkey has been changing very rapidly indeed, which means that it is very hard to predict what the coming decades will bring.

On the dating front, the Ugarit eclipse tablet inserts another nail into the coffin of traditional thinking and is 100% in line with the dates suggested in this book!

What does the Bible have to say?

One continuing connection between the Bible and other historical documents, which is accepted by a clear majority of researchers, lies in the people known as 'Habiru'. The

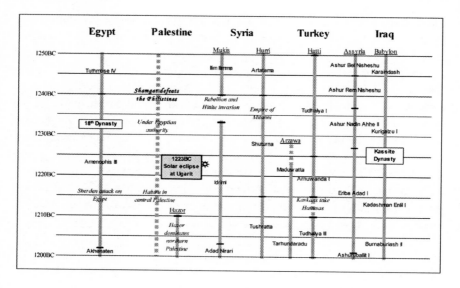

Amarna letters reveal them to have been a stateless people that inhabited the less accessible parts of Palestine, Lebanon and southern Syria. The same people are thought to be represented by the Egyptian term 'Apiru, and the Biblical Hebrews. In Moses' day the Israelites are referred to as Hebrew slaves; much later, in the days of king Saul, Hebrews are fighting for him against the Philistines. However, if the Habiru/'Apiru/Hebrew equation is accepted, it means that the word Hebrew carries no ethnic meaning at all; it simply designates a lifestyle. The Israelites were counted as Hebrews because of how they lived.[14] It is quite logical that Idrimi of Alalakh should have chosen to flee to a people who were outside the control of the great powers when rebellion toppled his father's regime – but these people may or may not have been Israelites.

Jabin king of Hazor

I believe that just four Bible verses (Judges 3:31-4:3) belong to this period. The first simply tells us that a character named Shamgar "saved Israel from the Philistines" – probably in around 1240BC – but adds no historical detail. Otherwise the 80 years of 'peace' recorded following liberation from Moab in about 1270BC take us through to 1200BC and beyond. However, I think it likely that the 20 years of oppression by the kings of Hazor (Judges 4:3) should be dated to the last phase of this period of peace. This ties in with the evidence of the Amarna letters that Hazor is the only city in Palestine whose ruler is called 'king'. Furthermore, the rulers of both Tyre and Ashtaroth complain to the Egyptian pharaoh that Hazor is forcefully taking their territory. The name of Hazor's king in the Amarna letters is 'Abdi Tirshi' rather than 'Jabin', the king mentioned in the Bible – but then the Bible story relates principally to events still in the future.

What was going on in the Rest of the World?

I have mentioned two of the Indo-European peoples of the east. The Indic speakers by now occupied most of modern Pakistan and were beginning to spread east from the Punjab, and other Indic groups had moved into the Middle East and 'energised' the Hurrian and Kassite peoples. I have also mentioned the Iranian speakers of Central Asia. But there is one further sub-group, namely the Armenian speakers. Based on the difference between modern Armenian and the other Indo-European branches, Armenian separated from Iranian speech somewhere in Central Asia some time around the year 2500BC. The next thing we know for sure is the setting up of an Armenian kingdom in 190BC.

However there is plenty of other evidence. A particular type of grey pottery appears in north-western Iran in the Late Bronze Age (1300-1100BC) associated with a culture which looks very Indo-European (militaristic; warrior burials). There are references to 'Armens' in Assyrian annals from about 1100BC (if my dating system is correct). And perhaps of greatest significance, modern Armenians trace their history back to the kingdom known to the Hittites as 'Azzi-Hayasa' (sometimes just Azzi), located around the source of the Euphrates river. The name appears for the first time during Arnuwanda I's reign (1225-1215BC). In fact the modern Armenian name for Armenia is 'Hayastan', although we have to remember that the name of a country can easily be transferred from one ethnic or linguistic group to another, as happened in the case of Hatti. Nevertheless, I believe the evidence is strong enough for us to be fairly confident that the Armenian nation, a nation that would long outlast the Hittites, had now arrived on the stage of the great theatre known as the Middle East.

13

Sunrise Over Hatti: 1200–1150BC

The Heretic Pharaoh

In 1200BC all Egypt was watching nervously to see just how far their new pharaoh Akhenaten would go – and they were right to be nervous! Akhenaten didn't stop at simply promoting his new religion; he decreed in absolute and unquestionable terms that the Aten was the only true god and that he, the pharaoh, was his earthly representative. I apologize if I have misunderstood the theology slightly – it is not easy to understand exactly what was in the king's mind – but the effect was that the old order was suddenly eclipsed, the practical result of which was that the traditional priests of Amun suddenly had their funds cut off. But the word of pharaoh was the word of pharaoh and what the pharaoh said was law. The new capital city Akhetaten, known to us as Amarna, which he set about building some 150 miles downstream from Thebes, reinforced the total and complete separation of the new order from the old. In Akhenaten's day things changed drastically. Gone were all the old traditions of Egyptian art; in their place was a natural and not unpleasing style, tending sometimes to exaggeration of physical features.[1] Gone were all the traditional songs and hymns; in their place were hymns to the Aten, perhaps composed by Akhenaten himself, which suggest to some that Atenism was almost a monotheistic religion with parallels to that of Israel.[2]

Akhenaten and his wife Nefertiti presided over an almost total collapse of Egyptian society as the pharaoh arrogantly forced his religious ideas upon an unwilling populace. He had no interest whatsoever in foreign policy, as is demonstrated by the diplomatic archives known as the Amarna letters. As we have already seen, these 384 documents are of inestimable value in reconstructing the history of the Near and Middle East, containing correspondence with rulers as far away as Arzawa, Hatti, Mitanni, Assyria and Babylon, as well as many in Palestine and Syria, and their single greatest message is the complete inaction of the Egyptian state. It is as if the whole empire was paralysed with indecision and lack of leadership. Akhenaten was interested only in his city of Amarna and in his spiritual role as the representative of the Aten; in short he was completely unhinged. None the less, today's historical researchers have to be grateful to Akhenaten, first for transferring the state archives to Amarna, and then for ensuring he was so hated that the city of Amarna would be abandoned to the elements, never to be inhabited again from that day until now!

Pirates on the High Seas

The time of Akhenaten and Nefertiti brings me to what many believe to be a firm absolute date, a tree ring date determined for pieces of timber recovered from a wreck at the bottom of the Mediterranean off the coast of Turkey, found together with a scarab bearing Nefertiti's cartouche. Interestingly, a letter from the king of Cyprus was found in the Amarna archives referring to a complaint by Akhenaten that Egyptian ships were being attacked by Cypriot pirates. The Cypriot king's reply was that the pirates were certainly not from Cyprus but probably from the Lukka lands of south-west Turkey. Anyway, wherever the pirates came from, the recently-discovered wreck was quite possibly one of those attacked. Regarding the relative dating of the wreck, the pottery finds made put the cargo firmly in the Mycenaean IIIa$_2$ period and exactly similar finds have been made at Amarna itself, together with some from the succeeding Mycenaean IIIb$_1$ phase. The ship therefore dates from the middle of Akhenaten's reign, as one would expect from the Nefertiti scarab. However, the frequently quoted date of 1316BC (sometimes 1318BC) is most certainly not to be believed as I hope I explained sufficiently in Chapter 3. The real date was around 1195BC.

The Egyptian Empire Crumbles

By far the majority of the Amarna correspondence is with the rulers of the various cities and petty states in Palestine and Syria which were nominally under Egypt's control. We have exchanges of correspondence with Jerusalem, Ashkelon, Gath, Gezer, Megiddo, Hazor, Tyre, Byblos, Kadesh and several other cities. Here are a few of the most interesting general points which emerge from Akhenaten's time in office.

i) All the Palestinian rulers continue to be worried about the activities of the Habiru. In one letter there is a complaint that one of the local leaders, Labaya[3] (whose city is not recorded) has given Shechem, a city in central

Palestine, to the Habiru. Complaints about Habiru attacks come from Gath, Gezer, Jerusalem, Shunem, Pella and Byblos.

ii) None of the rulers seem to be getting satisfactory responses from Egypt. They are all asking for Egyptian assistance but this appears to be minimal at best.

iii) There is evidence for rivalry between the different city states. For example, it was not only Labaya who was subject to malicious reports by his neighbours; Milkilu of Gezer seems to be another hate figure,[4] accused of being in league with the Habiru, while Abdi Heba of Jerusalem is convinced that the whole world is against him.[5] A similar picture is found in Lebanon and Syria, where Abdi Ashirta of Amurru (western coastal Syria) is accused of taking territory from others, particularly by Rib Addi of Byblos.[6] He is also accused of being a friend of the Habiru.

iv) All the Syrian rulers refer to a growing Hittite threat. Amurru even jumped ship and backed the Hittites at some stage. The king of Tyre refers to those in the coastal cities being forced to think about abandoning their homes and escaping across the Mediterranean by boat.

Overall we are left with a clear picture of the disintegration of Egyptian control. The cities of Palestine, Lebanon and southern Syria are being left to their own devices and this means that they feel increasingly free to quarrel with each other, knowing that Egypt will not intervene. It also means that they are being left to fend for themselves against an increasing threat from the north, that of the Hittites. It is a classic power vacuum waiting to be filled.

Mitanni in Crisis

Tushratta son of Shuturna must have become king of Mitanni in about 1215BC, and he is another whose letters have been found among the Amarna archive. He corresponded with both Amenophis III and Akhenaten, not to mention directly with queen Tiy, the widow of Amenophis III. It emerges very clearly from these letters that Tushratta was desperate for good relations with Egypt; he wrote repeatedly to Akhenaten reminding him of the friendship which had existed between Mitanni and Egypt during Amenophis III's days. Indeed, Amenophis III had managed to marry both a sister and a daughter of Tushratta, so I guess Tushratta had a right to feel he had bought Egypt's favour!

But it was to no avail. Egypt would not be helping anyone while Akhenaten sat on his throne in Amarna. Mitanni would have to fend for itself.

This Time the Hittites mean Business

It is hard to say exactly when real panic over the Hittite threat started. There is considerable correspondence on the subject in the Amarna archive so it was certainly well before the end of Akhenaten's reign. The Hittite document known as the *Deeds of Suppiluliuma* gives us quite a lot of information on the steady recovery of Hatti after the near-fatal collapse under Arnuwanda I. Tudhalya III, supported by his son Suppiluliuma I, gradually recovered the territory Arnuwanda had lost and, by 1200BC, Hatti itself was safe enough; both Azzi-Hayasa and Arzawa had been pushed back and much of the central Turkish plain was once again in Hittite hands. And 1200BC must have been the approximate year in which Tudhalya III died, leaving his son Suppiluliuma (once he had murdered his own brother) to carry on the fight, an activity which Suppiluliuma seemed to enjoy enormously. In the south the reconquest of Arzawa was soon completed and Hittite rule was also extended over Hapalla, covering the western part of the central plain. We read that it took 20 years to subdue Arzawa, which probably applies to the time from collapse under Arnuwanda I in 1215BC to complete victory under Suppiluliuma.

So, by around 1195BC Hittite territory was once more secure on all fronts. Suppiluliuma was not a man to rest on his laurels however, and he immediately set his sights on the rich lands held by Tushratta of Mitanni. First he took Kizzuwadna, installing his young son Telipinu as priest. He also regained the land of Isuwa, north of Carchemish. We then hear in the Amarna correspondence from Aziru king of Amurru (son of Abdi Ashirta) that the Hittites were in 'Nuhasse', a Syrian state lying east of Amurru. The correspondence with Amurru continues with a report (from Aziru's brothers) that the Hittites were now in 'Amka',[7] a land south of Nuhasse, and we know that they also took Qatna (installing a pro-Hittite vassal, Idanda[8]). A Hittite conquest of Alalakh is also clear in the archaeology of the city, marked by the transition from Level IV to Level III. The date was probably around 1190BC. Adad Nirari, successor to Idrimi of Alalakh, who was one of those who wrote in vain to Egypt for help, had just died, and his successor Takuwa had to flee. Suppiluliuma had Mitanni in his gun-sights and, for Tushratta, the threat had now become frighteningly real.

The Old Order Fights Back in Egypt

Egyptologists disagree over the precise details surrounding the end of Akhenaten's reign – and with good reason since the evidence is most confusing. However, a clear majority is of the view that Akhenaten's reign lasted just over 16 years (to 1186BC in this chronology) and that he was followed for no more than a year by one of his sons-in-law, named Smenkhare. An alternative view, held by a sizeable minority, is that Akhenaten was actually succeeded by his queen, Nefertiti, and that she then reigned under the name Smenkhare.[9] Some Egyptologists suggest a reign of up to 4 years. But, whether we are talking of a male Smenkhare or of queen Nefertiti, whether of months or of years, it was certainly another of Akhenaten's sons-in-law, then known as Tutankhaten, who next rose to the throne in Amarna. He was just nine years of age.

As a child, the young king Tutankhaten was undoubtedly under the domination of the adults who surrounded him, foremost among whom were Ay, vizier of Egypt, and Haremheb, commander-in-chief of the army. They soon persuaded the boy king to throw Akhenaten's policies into reverse. The priests of Amun were restored to their privileged position; Thebes became once more the capital of Egypt and, to signal a complete and irreversible change, Tutankh*aten* changed his name to the more familiar Tutankh*amun*. The whole Aten experiment had endured just 18 years or so – but it had wrecked Egypt as an international force.

Onward March of the Hittites

Suppiluliuma was one of those kings who never seem to tire of conquest and war, rather in the mould of Alexander the Great some eight and a half centuries later. And, like Alexander, Suppiluliuma was a sound military tactician. He could see that Egypt presented no threat at all under Akhenaten. However, he was taking no chances and a letter from him was found in the Amarna archive, referring to the friendship which had existed between Hatti and Egypt in Amenophis III's time, a friendship which may have owed more to Suppiluliuma's imagination than anything else.

But you can't be too careful when tackling a neighbouring superpower and Suppiluliuma decided that a marriage alliance with the remaining great power, Babylon, would be wise, so he callously exiled his first wife to Greece[10] and took a daughter of Burnaburiash king of Babylon as his new chief wife. The net was closing in on Tushratta, the Mitannian king. But Mitannian forces still held all the strategic cities on the Euphrates river, most notably Carchemish, and they were well capable of defending them. Takuwa king of Mukis was still at large (he had fled to Niy) and was still allied to Mitanni. Worse, Suppiluliuma's ally Idanda of Qatna had been overthrown by the pro-Mitannian Akizzi. It would be necessary for Suppiluliuma to use more than just brute force and ignorance if he wanted to break down Mitanni's defences!

Then, in about 1184BC, opportunity knocked. Judging by a treaty document found at Hattusas, Hittite troops had entered Nuhasse in support of king Sarrupsi when he decided to side with the Hittites. Tushratta reacted and successfully invaded Nuhasse – but he had no idea just how close he was to disaster. Suppiluliuma had the military vision to see that Tushratta's forces were now predominantly located in western Syria, in Nuhasse, Aleppo and Carchemish, and that a bold but risky strike in the rear could reap considerable rewards. An uprising in Isuwa gave him the pretext he was looking for. He struck due east from Hatti, gained a quick victory over Isuwa and then kept going, turning south through the mountains and down into the Mitanni heartland, where he sacked

the capital city Wassuganni. Tushratta was completely unprepared for this sur-
prise move and could do no more than withdraw what was left of his eastern
army back west to Carchemish. Meanwhile, Suppiluliuma pushed west again
himself, re-crossing the Euphrates and capturing Aleppo. He then managed to
persuade king Niqmaddu of Ugarit to throw in his lot with the Hittite cause (we
have Suppiluliuma's letters on the subject) and this led to the capitulation of
Takuwa and his allies at Niy and the rapid conquest of all Syria as far south as
Qatna[11] and Kadesh; only the area around Carchemish remained under
Tushratta's control. Technically, Suppiluliuma had infringed Egyptian interests
when he took Kadesh – but Akhenaten had recently died and Egypt was in the
depths of crisis; no-one cared about the fate of far-away lands!

Suppiluliuma then proved that he was no fool at empire building. He rewarded his friends, notably Ugarit, and was not overly cruel to his enemies. The
rulers who had opposed him were deported back to Hatti and replacements were
installed, sometimes from the same ruling house. For instance, Aitakkama, the
son of the king of Kadesh who had opposed Suppiluliuma, was installed as the
new Hittite vassal. As a further measure of the permanence which Suppiluliuma
intended for Hittite control over Syria, he now installed his son Telipinu as direct
ruler over the city of Aleppo rather than allowing a local king to rule. This move
was presumably motivated largely by the knowledge that Tushratta and his army
were still in control of the region around Carchemish and that, unless they were
strictly policed, trouble was certain. Besides, he himself had to return to Hattusas urgently to deal with the troublesome Kaskans who had taken advantage

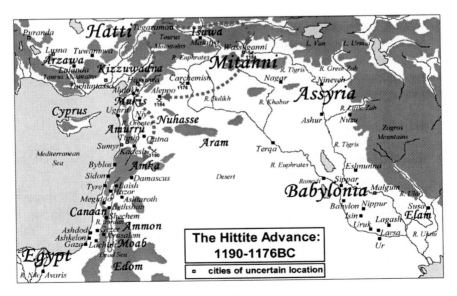

The Hittite Advance:
1190-1176BC

cities of uncertain location

of his absence to help themselves to Hittite lands once more. Some years then passed with Tushratta still controlling Carchemish and the land immediately surrounding the city, carefully watched by Suppiluliuma's son Telipinu. There were all sorts of matters to attend to, not least an attack by Tutankhamun's general, Haremheb, on Kadesh. The Egyptians were repelled and the frontier pushed south into the land of Amka. It would be 1176BC before Suppiluliuma felt free to concentrate his forces on getting rid of Tushratta once and for all.

Babylon and Assyria

Not for the first time, the Kassite rulers looked on with approval as the Hittites brought down a mighty empire. The fact that Burnaburiash gave one of his daughters as chief wife of Suppiluliuma suggests that he would not have been sorry to see Mitanni humbled. However, he also had ambitions of his own and these can be discerned in correspondence from and concerning Assyria. The Amarna archive contains a letter from king Ashuruballit I of Assyria which apparently accompanied a splendid gift to Akhenaten and which declared that Assyria was now a great power and should have independent relations with Egypt. We also have a letter from Burnaburiash to Akhenaten stating that Assyria was actually a vassal state of Babylon and that all dealings should come through him, Burnaburiash! What the truth was we will probably never know but it is certain that Assyria and Babylon came to blows during the reigns of Kurigalzu II of Babylon (Burnaburiash's successor) and Enlil Nirari of Assyria (Ashuruballit's successor), resulting in a redrawing of the boundaries between the two lands, although it is less clear who had gained the advantage. Kurigalzu II also claimed victory over Elam which, from the lack of any evidence to the contrary from Elam itself, was probably true.

For the time of Burnaburiash II onwards, we have a dated Babylonian king list which gives every appearance of being trustworthy so, taking an educated guess at Burnaburiash's dates, the reigns for the remaining Babylonian kings of this period are approximately as follows:

Burnaburiash II	– 1180BC
Kurigalzu II	1180 – 1154BC
Nazi Maruttash	1154 –

Similarly, it is possible to be reasonably confident of the reigns of the Assyrian kings following Ashuruballit, using the data given in the *Assyrian king list*.

Ashuruballit I	– 1165BC
Enlil Nirari	1165 – 1155BC
Arik Den Ili	1155 –

Pleased though Burnaburiash may have been about the demise of Mitanni, the simultaneous collapse of Egypt as an international force must have hit Babylon hard. For a start, the gold supply was cut off! Nevertheless, Babylonia remained a strong and stable kingdom and, whatever the details of the relationship with Assyria, Babylon remained the dominant force in Iraq during the first fifty years of the 12th Century BC.

The Death of Tutankamun

Few people know much about the life of Tutankhamun; indeed his reign lasted just nine years and he was no more than eighteen years old when he died. But everyone knows about his death. Everyone knows that his tomb, discovered in the so-called Valley of the Kings near Thebes in the 1920s, contained a quite breathtaking display of gold and numerous fabulously valuable objects. Yet it has to be supposed that this would have been the norm for all the pharaohs of Egypt during the 18th Dynasty but that accident of history has meant that his particular tomb alone escaped detection under the debris of subsequent excavation. The world is most fortunate that this was the case and that we have a remarkable window onto the wealth of the age.

You may also have come across the ongoing debate as to just how a reasonably healthy teenager managed to meet his end so prematurely and so conveniently for the man who stepped into his shoes, the elder statesman and long time vizier of the land, Ay. Suffice it to say that foul play cannot be ruled out! Ay must have looked longingly at the kingship; he had been within touching distance of the throne right from the day that a young pharaoh Amenophis III had married Ay's sister Tiy. He had then proudly given his daughter Nefertiti in marriage to Amenophis' son Akhenaten. He had bent with the wind and gone along with the Atenist reforms, remaining close to the royal family when they moved to Amarna, even having his own rock tomb prepared (but not used) there. And we can be pretty sure that Ay was the real power behind the young Tutankhamun, perhaps in conjunction with the army general, Haremheb. Did he see his influence slipping as Tutankhamun became a man? Was this enough for him to take the ultimate gamble and possibly engineer a convenient death? We don't know – but many suspect.

What we do know however comes from a truly remarkable and ultimately tragic tale involving Tutankhamun's widow, Ankhesenamun (a daughter of Akhenaten and Nefertiti). The tale is told in the *Deeds of Suppiluliuma*. It was 1176BC and Suppiluliuma was laying siege to Carchemish, the last refuge of Tushratta king of Mitanni, when a message arrived from Egypt purporting to be from the widow of the pharaoh and requesting the hand of one of Suppiluliuma's sons in marriage rather than "having to marry a servant". Although we have no name for the queen, the name given for the dead king is recognisable as

the prenomen (first throne name) of Tutankhamun. Not surprisingly Suppiluliuma reacted cautiously and insisted on further proof that this wasn't simply a
trick; after all Hatti and Egypt had just been at war so it wasn't the sort of request
that he would have expected. But, after sending an envoy to Egypt and receiving
an Egyptian envoy in return, arrangements were put in place for Suppiluliuma's
fourth son, Zannanza, to wed the Egyptian queen (his eldest son, Arnuwanda,
was crown prince; the second, Telipinu, was viceroy of Aleppo and he had just
installed his third, Sarri Kusuh, as viceroy of Carchemish after finally defeating
Tushratta's forces). After all, the possibility that all Egypt could pass into Hittite
hands without a drop of blood being spilt was too good to pass up.

We know nothing of this from Egyptian sources. All we know is that Tutankhamun was succeeded by Ay. However, the Hittite source informs us that
Suppiluliuma's son was assassinated before he ever arrived in Egypt. The inescapable and rather sad conclusion seems to be that Ay simply couldn't let this
marriage take place. Perhaps his reputation is undeserved; perhaps he had no
part in Tutankhamun's death and would willingly have seen Ankhesenamun
marry again, but the prospect of selling Egypt out to a foreign power was just too
much. Whatever the truth, we hear no more of Ankhesenamun, while Ay most
certainly ascended the throne. And, sad though it is, this episode at least provides
an absolutely firm synchronism between the histories of Egypt and Hatti.

This was a messy time in Egyptian history, a time which subsequent generations of pharaohs tried to erase from the records. Accepting the usual identification of Smenkhare as a short-reigning son-in-law of Akhenaten, the last few
rulers of the 18th Dynasty may be dated as follows:

Akhenaten	– 1186BC
Smenkhare	1186 – 1185BC
Tutankhamun	1185 – 1176BC
Ay	1176 – 1172BC
Haremheb	1172 –

Unsurprisingly, Suppiluliuma was not at all pleased at the murder of his son!
His therapy was to carry out further raids into areas of Egyptian-controlled
southern Syria.

Consolidation in Hatti; Recovery in Egypt

The last few years of Suppiluliuma's reign were spent securing his borders. In the
south, an uneasy peace broke out as neither Hatti nor Egypt felt like renewing the
struggle. In the west, so far as we know, the Hittite vassals of western Turkey
were in a reasonably stable condition. However the east was a problem. The sack
of Wassuganni in about 1184BC was not followed up by any serious attempt to

occupy the Hurrian heartland area and this left a gaping power vacuum, a power vacuum which the emerging state of Assyria under its energetic king Ashurubal-lit I was only too happy to fill. The Assyrians soon attacked and installed their own puppet ruler in Wassuganni and caused a serious nuisance to the eastern border region of the Hittite Empire. But, at the time, Suppiluliuma couldn't afford to be diverted. After his campaign against the Kaskans his efforts had to be concentrated on Carchemish and the final defeat of his old enemy Tushratta. Once this was completed there was the little matter of the murder of his son by the Egyptians to avenge, so it was only in about 1174BC that he turned his attention to the deteriorating situation in the east. He took the decision to support a particular claimant to the throne of Mitanni and led a joint Hurrian and Hittite force east where he 'liberated' Wassuganni from the Assyrian faction and installed his chosen vassal Sattiwaza, one of Tushratta's sons. However, the land he gave to Sattiwaza was but a pale reflection of the once glorious empire ruled by his father.

Suppiluliuma had seen the kingdom of Hatti grow from a situation where even its capital, Hattusas, had fallen to enemy attack, to being a vast empire with secure borders. Whilst his conquests were not on the scale of those of Alexander the Great, they were certainly characters with much in common. When he died, in 1171BC according to this chronology, Hatti was the dominant power in the region. Suppiluliuma had not only carved out an empire, he had also taken steps to ensure the real and lasting spread of Hittite culture across the lands he conquered.

Relations between Hatti and Egypt smouldered quietly for a while following the deaths of Suppiluliuma and Ay. Suppiluliuma's eldest son Arnuwanda II died some 18 months after Suppiluliuma himself so, in 1170BC or thereabouts, the throne of Hattusas passed to Suppiluliuma's fifth and youngest son Mursili II, apparently with the full agreement of his surviving elder brothers, the viceroys of Aleppo and Carchemish. In Egypt, meanwhile, it was Haremheb, the general who had led the Egyptian army during Tutankhamun's reign and who had married a daughter of Ay, who now became pharaoh.

With the support of his brothers, Mursili did an excellent job of expanding and consolidating the Hittite empire. He fought two campaigns in western Turkey to keep Arzawa and the Greek colony of Miletus under control; he thoroughly subdued the Kaskan tribes, the people who had actually conquered Hattusas some 40 years earlier, and inflicted another defeat on the ambitious king of Azzi-Hayasa (Armenia). He also had to fight off a serious Assyrian invasion in about 1161BC, during which Carchemish was lost and then recaptured.[12] Meanwhile, Haremheb was more concerned with relaying the foundations of Egyptian society rather than with any thought of conquest. The dislocation caused by Akhenaten's reforms ran deep and needed extensive therapy. Haremheb was a vigorous builder throughout the length and breadth of Egypt and it would be fair to say that he restored Egypt's sense of its own greatness and purpose. He campaigned in Palestine, doing his best to ensure that the local Canaanite rulers understood that they were his vassals, and Kadesh, still on the front line, came in for yet another attack. Mursili reacted however and reclaimed the city but he was in no mood to be any more adventurous; there was too much work to be done maintaining order elsewhere in his realm. Relations between the two great powers continued in a sort of hostile stalemate.[13]

The Situation in Palestine

South of the Hittite border, much of Palestine remained broadly under the thumb of Egypt despite regular rebellions by individual Canaanite cities and the presence of the lawless Habiru in the central hill country, and this is exemplified by the archaeology of Lachish VI, paralleled at Bethshan, Shechem and Hazor, and datable by the presence of Mycenaean IIIa and IIIb pottery. The Lachish VI temple is very similar to those at Amarna with an arrangement of central columns like that at Gaza, a key Egyptian fortress at the time; hieratic Egyptian inscriptions have also been found.[14] But Egyptian control over northern Palestine was now very shaky indeed. The great stronghold of Megiddo had clearly become a very wealthy city during the days of Amenophis III, evidenced by a magnificent hoard of buried treasure found underneath one of the floors of the Level VIII city. Yet the fact that the hoard had been buried at all tells its own story, as does the fact that someone destroyed Level VIII at some stage during the period covered by this chapter. Of even greater significance was the total destruction of Hazor, until that time the greatest city in Palestine, accompanied by the systematic vandalizing of both Canaanite and Egyptian statues. Since the Hittites make no claim for any of this, the finger of suspicion seems to point firmly at the ever-troublesome Habiru tribes.

The Greek World

Hittite annals also shed a certain amount of light on Greece and the Aegean, particularly those from Mursili II's reign, which are excellent. This is just as well since we have no written history at all from Greece itself; although the Linear B script was in use, the few texts we possess are simply lists for record-keeping purposes. Many suspect that the usual material the Greeks were writing on was papyrus,[15] imported from Egypt, a material which would stand no chance of surviving the millennia in Europe (as it has sometimes done in the Egyptian desert). So, it is with interest that we read in Mursili's annals that, in his 3rd year (1168BC), he launched a series of campaigns in western Turkey against the coastal city of Miletus, whose king had joined forces with the king of Ahhiyawa (i.e. Greece). We also read of a king Uhhaziti of 'Arzawa Minor', who was also allied to Greece; his territory comprised the western part of the former state of Arzawa. Mursili needed the support of his brother Sarri-Kusuh in order to defeat Uhhaziti who "fled to the islands", i.e. the islands of the Aegean. Mursili then brought the Seha river land (which had also sided with Greece) and Hapalla under Hittite control.

So, although we have no direct news from Greece itself, it is evident from Mursili's annals that a state called Ahhiyawa had real power in the Aegean such that the kings of western Turkey felt it was a reasonable bet to ally themselves with it, even in the face of known Hittite might. I see no way that Ahhiyawa can be anything less than a country covering much of Greece and the Aegean, reinforcing the equation with Homer's 'Achaea'. The extent of Greek economic ties is also seen in the finding of Babylonian seals in Greece in this period[16] and in Mycenaean IIIa and IIIb pottery finds in Italy and Sicily.

Culturally, Cyprus continued to be closely related to Mycenaean Greece, judging by the pottery evidence. Here too, we have no records other than letters from the king of Cyprus to Akhenaten, but these speak mainly of shipping and trade.

Summary

This has been an eventful 50 years. It has seen the once-dominant state of Mitanni reduced to no more than a small area around its capital city Wassuganni while the Hittites now control all Turkey and much of Syria, including most of the Hurrian lands. Much of their empire is tied in through the use of vassal rulers (for example, Mursili set up several new vassal kingdoms in western Turkey in place of Uhhaziti's realm), but in Carchemish and Aleppo Mursili's brothers, appointed viceroys by Suppiluliuma, have both died and left their own sons in charge. And the population they preside over is now becoming increasingly Luwian-speaking rather than Hurrian.

The other great powers survive. Egypt is beginning to emerge from the crisis generated by Akhenaten's religious reforms and once more has authority over the cities of southern Palestine. However, much of northern Palestine is now outside Egyptian control. Babylon is still the most powerful force in Iraq, maintaining dominance over Elam and Assyria, and in the west Greece is now a major power and a continuing nuisance to the Hittite rulers. In fact, despite one of the major players disappearing from the board, the Middle East still presents a reasonably stable picture of a few great powers dominating a large number of smaller states. It is a situation which once more allows trade and commerce to take place and hope to spring anew – if only the princes of the great powers can be persuaded to refrain from gratuitous warfare!

What does the Bible have to say?

The year 1200BC saw Israel under the oppressive rule of Jabin king of Hazor, perhaps the immediate successor to Abdi Tirshi, the writer of two of the Amarna letters and, if my interpretation of the time periods given in the Bible is correct, this situation continued until about 1190BC. It was the second half of Akhenaten's reign and Egyptian authority

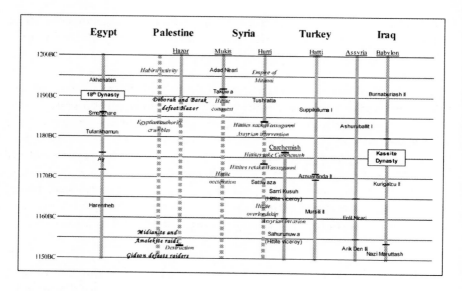

was now all but non-existent. The Egyptians were certainly not going to stop the Habiru taking direct action against Hazor.

The Prophetess Deborah *(Judges 4 and 5)*

The Bible tells us that the particular Habiru who took on the might of Hazor were Israelites under the spiritual guidance of the prophetess Deborah. She encouraged a rebellion, which was led by a man called Barak, and which saw the defeat of Hazor's army and the death of its commander, Sisera, thus ending Hazor's dominance. We then read that the hand of the Israelites grew ever stronger against Jabin "until they destroyed him". Barak and Deborah had won a great victory and Jabin's days were numbered, but the Bible makes no claim for the immediate destruction of Hazor itself. The violent destruction of Level XIII at Hazor, including desecration of both Canaanite and Egyptian statuary and for which the Israelites were almost certainly responsible, probably didn't take place much before 1150BC.

Gideon

Following Deborah's victory, the Bible reports another 40 years of peace, taking us to the year 1151BC – approximately. Haremheb's Egypt was still in re-organisation mode and Egyptian authority over northern Palestine barely existed. The Bible reports *(Judges 6:1-6)* that for 7 years (1157-1151BC) bands of eastern nomads, Midianites and Amalekites, had ravaged the land, taking crops and livestock before departing back east, totally believable for these lawless times. If I had been a Midianite, I would have seen this as a golden opportunity to invade without any real danger of an Egyptian response! Thus it fell to the inhabitants of northern Palestine to defend themselves as best they could and, *in the case of the Israelite inhabitants of the hill country, the task fell to Gideon. The Bible (Judges 6-8) informs us that he succeeded in massacring a large party of invading Midianites, including their leaders, and that he thereby delivered the land for another 40 years. By the way, I have some sympathy with those who make the point that these 40-year intervals look very much like round numbers. However, without information to the contrary, and since by using 40 years I arrive at an appropriate historical setting, I shall continue to use the figures as given. It is undeniable that this approach has given me highly plausible settings for both Deborah and Gideon.*

It is also worth noting that the period of Midianite/Amalekite incursions (1157-1151BC) closely matches another period of worldwide low tree ring width (1159-1151BC), indicating a massive and climate-affecting 'event', quite possibly volcanic, somewhere on the planet, with associated atmospheric dust and reduced sunlight. This could well have been sufficient to destroy the fragile productivity of the Arabian desert and to send the inhabitants in search of alternative food sources.

What was going on in the Rest of the World?

The expansion of Indo-European culture was perhaps a little slower in Europe than had been the case in central and southern Asia. The Greeks and Hittites formed a vanguard as they swept down to the Aegean in the late 3rd Millennium BC before spreading out across the modern states of Greece and Turkey respectively. They had also recently separated from the Albanian speakers, who must have moved into the land which is still Albania today some time before 2000BC. And in Bulgaria those who stayed became the people we know as 'Thracians', linguistically ancestral to today's Slavonic speakers. During the 1st Millennium BC, the Thracians would become a rich and powerful nation. Another related people who must have been just about discernible as a separate group by 1150BC were the Phrygians, although they would not become known to history until the 9th Century BC. On linguistic grounds, their culture was effectively a branch of Thracian culture, and they would soon make the journey from Bulgaria across the Bosphorus and into Turkey, where they will one day emerge as a powerful state around the city of Gordium, not far from present-day Ankara.

But what about the Indo-European tribes of the north? By 1150BC, there would have been a real distinction between Celtic and Italic (i.e. Latin-related) speakers, with the Celts inhabiting the modern lands of Slovakia, Austria and northern Hungary. The culture is still that known as 'Urnfield' after the burial customs used, but it would not be long now before an identifiably Celtic culture named after the archaeological site of Hallstatt would appear in Austria, with its tartan clothing and its own particularly Celtic art style. To the south, most of Hungary, together with Serbia, Croatia, Bosnia, Slovenia and the north-east corner of Italy would have hosted Italic languages and the culture was a remarkably stable and peaceful one, inherited from the pre-Indo-European 'Hungarian Tell' culture. We have no records of any of these people other than archaeological, which means that it is difficult to know just how they were organised, whether in large states or smaller city-based units. But they were most certainly organised. Two-way trade is evident between the Italic and Celtic regions and Greece, with many of the advances in metalwork and sword design being more likely to be Italic/Celtic than Greek.

Moving further north again, the Lusatian culture of the Czech Republic, eastern Germany and Poland was almost certainly Germanic speaking. These people had, like the Greeks, been tamed into practising arable farming rather than the nomadism of their distant ancestors. They too had developed a reasonably wealthy culture with examples of advanced metallurgy and trade with foreign lands. Amber from the Baltic is found in Greece, emphasising the extent of the trans-European trade network.

So, in 1150BC, the Indo-European frontier lay more or less where the Iron Curtain once hung, during the 'Cold War', that is through the middle of Germany and south to the northern end of the Adriatic Sea. To the west of this line Europeans were non-Indo-European speaking and they had a quite different culture. In language terms, only a single descendant remains today from the speech of western Europe in 1150BC, namely Basque, still spoken in the north-east corner of Spain and in south-western France, and it would be unfair to try to base any conclusions about life over 3000 years ago on modern Basque society! What we can say is that western Europe was certainly not a land of cities in those days. Architecturally, the best known remains are the great stone monuments of Britain and France, and the passage graves of Ireland, Britain, France, Spain, Portugal, the Balearic Islands and Italy, although most of today's remains date from significantly earlier times. Nevertheless, there is clear cultural continuity right through the Bronze Age so I think we would be right to see the inhabitants of 1150BC as descended from those who designed and built the great tombs and monuments, and barrow burial was still very much in vogue; the religion would still have been of a similar form. But technologically society had moved on. The second half of the 2nd Millennium BC sees a rapid expansion of population as ever more efficient agricultural practices take hold and more and more land is put under the plough. Western Europe may not have been as sophisticated as some of the states to the east, but it was prosperous enough and there is plenty of evidence of widespread trade by land and sea. The Indo-Europeans were certainly not advancing into a cultural desert!

14

Clash of the Titans: 1150–1100BC

Egypt Rebuilds

As far as Hatti and Egypt are concerned, the documentation for this whole period is once again excellent. There are plenty of records from Hattusas, both in the form of official annals and also numerous treaties, letters and seal inscriptions, and there is also plenty of evidence from Egypt, where the pharaohs were always keen to let posterity know of their achievements by inscribing them in great detail on numerous temple walls and commemorative stelae. Thus, following on from the dates deduced earlier, I have no option but to place the deaths of both Mursili II and Haremheb in 1144BC. Both rulers had laid strong foundations in their respective realms. Mursili had allowed the sons of his brothers, the viceroys of Aleppo and Carchemish, to fill their fathers' positions, thus creating a set of tightly tied dynasties. His own son Muwatalli II filled the position of 'great king of Hatti'. In Egypt Haremheb had selected an army man called Ramesses as his successor and he became the first king of the 19th Dynasty. Unfortunately he only survived Haremheb by a year and it was Ramesses' son Seti I who took on the responsibility of furthering the greatness of Egypt. Once again, the sheer weight of evidence leaves little or no room for doubt as to chronology and, following Haremheb, the first three kings of the 19th Dynasty have to be dated as follows:

	Haremheb	– 1144BC
19th Dynasty:	Ramesses I	1144 – 1143BC
	Seti I	1143 – 1129BC
	Ramesses II	1129 –

The hostility between Egypt and Hatti continued throughout the reigns of Seti and Muwatalli. Whereas Haremheb had not put much of his energies into Palestine and Syria, Seti immediately set about restoring full Egyptian control, at least over Palestine. Several cities had deserted the Egyptian cause over the years and Seti had to fight to regain control. A stela recovered from Bethshan in northern Palestine (where the Level VII city was almost certainly destroyed by Seti) also tells us that he defeated "Habiru from the hills" as well as invaders from across the Jordan. In fact, there is further archaeological evidence that the Habiru were becoming an increasing menace in the hills of Palestine. In addition to the great city of Hazor, probably destroyed shortly before 1150BC, the Canaanite cities of Lachish, Bethel, Shechem and Shiloh all show serious destruction during these times, followed either by abandonment or occupation at a technologically much less advanced level, of the sort associated with the tribes of the interior. Canaanite Jerusalem, also in the central highlands, and where a scarab with a cartouche of Seti I has been unearthed, was beginning to look dangerously isolated.

Nevertheless, under Seti Egyptian control was quickly re-established over the most important Palestinian cities, and he then launched a full-scale attack on the Hittite dependency of Kadesh before pushing on into southern Syria.[1] Muwatalli responded and the subsequent pitched battle is recorded on Seti's war monument but not on any Hittite record, from which one can deduce that it was the Egyptian forces who carried the day. Muwatalli had to acknowledge, at least temporarily, that Syria was no longer entirely under his banner. Both Kadesh and the western state of Amurru were now aligned with Egypt once more.

Hatti Strengthens its Hand

But Muwatalli was playing a long game. He had other concerns to attend to and could not afford to divert too much attention to the defence of southern Syria. For a start the troublesome Kaskans were once more threatening the Hittite heartland and had to be dealt with. This he achieved by assigning his brother Hattusili the task of expanding Hittite settlement into Kaskan areas and re-asserting control over cities which had not been Hittite for generations.[2] At the same time, he moved the capital from Hattusas to a city called Tarhuntassa, further from the Kaskan threat.[3] He then had to fight in western Turkey, subduing Greek supported activity in Troy and on the large Aegean island of Lesbos as well as at Miletus, and in all of these issues Muwatalli was reasonably successful so far as we can tell from his annals. And all the while there was the latent threat from Assyria to the east to counter, for which he relied heavily on the forces of his cousins, the viceroys of Aleppo and Carchemish.

Showdown

In the course of time, after a reign of 14 years, Seti died, leaving the throne of Egypt to his young son Ramesses II. Ramesses was keen to emulate and surpass his father's achievements, so he set about the business of re-establishing Egyptian dominance in Syria, moving his army up the coast as far as Byblos. Muwatalli meanwhile had prepared himself as thoroughly as he knew how and he too took the field to counter the Egyptian threat. In Ramesses' fifth year (1124BC in this chronology) the Egyptian forces advanced north towards the city of Kadesh, nominally their vassal still after Seti's campaigns. However, Ramesses needed lessons in scouting and he had no idea that the Hittite army had made a pre-emptive move south and that they had already reached Kadesh and were waiting, prepared and with a battle plan. The result was the most famous of all the many battles to have taken place at Kadesh, indeed one of the best known and most frequently described battles of the ancient world. And the reason we know so much about it lies in the fact that Ramesses was so inordinately proud of his achievement that he had scenes from the battle depicted at numerous sites up and down the land of Egypt. I have no intention of exposing my lack of military understanding too greatly here; suffice it to say that the Egyptians were caught in an ambush with their army strung out over a great distance and that they lost a large number of troops. However, according to Ramesses' inscriptions he then gained an almost miraculous victory in the most adverse of circumstances; according to the opinion of most historians the battle was at best a draw and, following Ramesses' return to Egypt, Kadesh, Amurru and even Damascus were all in the hands of the Hittites.

However, when Muwatalli died a few years after the battle of Kadesh, in 1120BC, and the throne passed to his inexperienced son Urhi Teshub, this effectively gave the green light to both Egypt and Assyria! Ramesses was quick off the mark; he had just spent a pleasant season reinforcing his hold on Palestine, plundering Jerusalem in the process, and now he advanced east of the river Jordan to Damascus. Over the next two years, he also captured the city of Tunip and, at some stage, Kadesh fell to the Egyptians once more.

Meanwhile an important event had occurred in the east. Sattuara, king of Mitanni, then a vassal of Hatti, decided for a reason which is quite impossible to discern that he would launch an attack on Assyria. One has to suppose that he was counting on Hittite support – but he certainly never received it. The attack probably occurred in the first year or two of Urhi Teshub's reign and it was a total disaster. Adad Nirari I of Assyria won with ease, captured Sattuara, and then reinstated him – with the subtle difference that he was now a vassal of Assyria not of Hatti! Urhi Teshub's inaction had cost him dear. When Sattuara died a year or two later, his son Wasasatta rebelled against Assyrian authority and, once more, no help was forthcoming from Urhi Teshub. Adad Nirari now crushed Mitanni and annexed the entire territory right to the borders of the viceroydom of Carchemish, making a serious situation for Urhi Teshub decidedly worse. Remarkably, we have a copy of a rather rude letter from Urhi Teshub to Adad Nirari of Assyria which barely acknowledges him as a 'great king' and certainly not as a 'brother'. It seems an unbelievably undiplomatic attitude when Assyria was so obviously a dangerous enemy to pick a fight with.

The Balance of Power Shifts in Iraq

The re-emergence of Assyria was a serious blow to the Kassite rulers of Babylon. Their comfortable world was becoming decidedly more chilly and they could no longer automatically assume that they were the dominant force in the land. To make matters worse, Elam was now in the hands of a new and successful dynasty of kings. Both Pahir Ishan and Attar Kittah, whose reigns spanned the period from 1150 to about 1123BC, are called 'plunderers' on inscriptions, which usually means that they had carried out successful raids on the rich farming lands of Babylonia. The next king, Humban Numena, is very well known indeed and the archaeology of Susa and other cities in Elam tells us that his reign was one of great prosperity. Fortunately, and unusually for the Elamites, it seems this prosperity was now largely based on the fruits of peace rather than the more usual plundering!

But Assyria remained a real problem. Under king Adad Nirari I, who reigned from about 1143 through to 1111BC, Assyria grew from an also-ran to become a truly great power, and this could only take place at Babylon's expense. We don't know whether Babylon actually lost any territory at this juncture but she certainly lost prestige and most definitely lost security. The Kassite kings would, from here on, have to be ultra-careful not to upset their neighbours on the throne of Ashur. Following on from the dates suggested in the last chapter, the Assyrian and Babylonian rulers of this period can be dated as follows, using the king list data:

Assyria:	Arik Den Ili	–1143BC
	Adad Nirari I	1143 – 1111BC
	Shalmaneser I	1111 –
Babylon:	Nazi Maruttash	– 1128BC
	Kadashman Turgu	1128 – 1110BC
	Kadashman Enlil II	1110 – 1101BC
	Kudur Enlil	1101 –

Hatti back in safe hands

After enduring 7 years of Urhi Teshub's reign, his uncle Hattusili had had enough. We have a fascinating document from the Hattusas archive which is really a memoir written by (or for) Hattusili, justifying his actions from his youth onwards. He tells us of Urhi Teshub's mismanagement of affairs and how he, Hattusili, had been stripped of many of the privileges he had enjoyed under his brother Muwatalli's rule. Anyway, from his power-base in the Hittite heartland Hattusili gathered support, won a brief civil war, and had Urhi Teshub exiled to Nuhasse. The year was 1113BC. The full dates for the Hittite rulers of this period are as follows:

Mursili II	– 1144BC
Muwatalli II	1144 – 1120BC
Urhi Teshub	1120 – 1113BC
Hattusili III	1113 –

Urhi Teshub had already moved the capital back to Hattusas from Tarhuntassa and now, in a thoroughly diplomatic move, Hattusili installed Urhi Teshub's brother Kurunta as governor of Tarhuntassa. However Urhi Teshub had certainly not given up his claim to the throne of Hatti and he was soon trying to drum up support from Babylon. Hattusili responded by sending him to Cyprus,[4] but from there Urhi Teshub managed to escape to Egypt where Ramesses welcomed him as a potentially useful bargaining counter – but a thorn in the side of relations between Hatti and Egypt for years to come.

In all other respects, however, peace was starting to break out in earnest. When Adad Nirari of Assyria died in about 1111BC Hattusili was careful to write immediately to his successor Shalmaneser I in a friendly way, tacitly acknowledging the fact that Mitanni was now basically an Assyrian dependency. Even when Sattuara II, a cousin of Wasasatta the last king of Mitanni, led an insurrection, Hattusili never lifted a finger to stop Shalmaneser from carrying out severe retribution, destroying several cities and finally extinguishing the life from Mitanni once and for all. But Hattusili couldn't possibly rely on Shalmaneser's good will; he had to hedge his bets. He was therefore careful to seek alliance with Kadashman Turgu of Babylon and, when he died, with his successor Kadashman Enlil II. In fact he even suggested to Kadashman Enlil that Babylon and Hatti should join forces against Assyria – but it seems the Babylonians weren't prepared to trust him any more than they trusted the Assyrians!

Meanwhile in Egypt Ramesses was content with his conquests and was now devoting himself to making sure that the world never forgot him, something in which he was spectacularly successful, creating the greatest number of monuments of the greatest magnificence seen since the days of the great pyramids more than a thousand years earlier. The border between the Hittite and Egyptian spheres of interest in Palestine and Syria had crystallised into a line running just north of Kadesh and the outbreak of peace was formalised by a treaty signed in Ramesses II's 21st year (1108BC in this chronology), copies of which exist both on the temple walls of Egypt and in the Hattusas archive. Some years later this was followed by a royal marriage between Ramesses and a daughter of Hattusili. Both Hattusili and his wife Puduhepa were prolific writers of letters to other heads of state and many were directed at Ramesses. Fascinatingly, the available sources betray the fact that the other great kings liked to remind Hattusili of his dubious right to the Hittite throne and, reading between the lines, it seems that Hattusili was desperate for acceptance![5]

Greeks and Trojans

Once again, we are forced to look to the Hattusas archives for information on Greek activity. I have already referred to Muwatalli's restoring of order in western Turkey; here he ousted a usurper named Piyamaradu from the city of Troy and signed a treaty with the Trojan ruler Alaksandu (i.e. Alexander). For actual Greek activity, our main source is a document known as the *Tawagalawa letter*, written by Hattusili to the Greek king. Tawagalawa was actually a brother of the Greek king, who apparently had his own seat of power somewhere on the west coast of Turkey (we have a fragmentary text which indicates that part of south-western Turkey was at that time recognised as belonging to Greece although we don't know the exact boundaries). The events with which the letter is concerned are not easy to reconstruct, but it seems that the Greeks had been giving their support to Piyamaradu once more and that this time he had been leading a rebellion in the Lukka lands, the most south-westerly of the Hittite dependencies. Eventually, Hattusili had to lead an expedition to quell the uprising, which he succeeded in doing. He also pressured the Greek-allied ruler of Miletus into expelling Piyamaradu, but he never succeeded in stopping raids being carried out from island bases; this was the aim of his writing of a letter directly to the Greek king.

Interestingly, the letter addresses the king as "my brother", which implies equal status; in Hattusili's eyes Greece was a great power and its king deserved the recognition of a great king. If we know nothing else, this is a fact worth knowing! Archaeologically, the breadth of Greek influence remains wide with Mycenaean IIIb pottery appearing from Sardinia to Iraq, Palestine and Egypt. Relations with central Europe are indicated by the widespread adoption of the European flange-hilted sword in Greece as well as the finding of a north Italian winged axe-mould at Mycenae itself.

Summary

The worryingly unstable equilibrium between the great powers continues with relatively minor shifts in the balance here and there. Mitanni is now no more. Her former territory has been divided between the Hittites and the Assyrians, and this has meant that Mitanni's place at the table of great powers has now been officially filled by Assyria, whatever Urhi Teshub king of Hatti may once have thought of the idea. Babylon is weakening but still controls most of Iraq. Egypt is once more a serious force under Ramesses II, one of the greatest pharaohs the land of the Nile would ever see – at least in his own eyes!

The least trustworthy of the great powers are undoubtedly Assyria and Greece. They are both nibbling away at the fringes of the Hittite empire and neither seems to want to commit themselves to the normal diplomatic relations which the others are looking for. This of course has implications for commerce and wealth creation. Egypt hardly needs international relations; it produces plenty of food for its people and its Lebanese allies supply the much needed timber for construction purposes. However, it does need security, and the alliance with Hatti now provides that in good measure. Babylon undoubtedly still enjoys good commercial relations with Egypt and her dependent territories in Palestine and Syria, and trade routes still pass through Ugarit to Cyprus and the Greek territories beyond. In fact, Cyprus is so full of Mycenaean ware these days that the question has to be asked as to whether it might actually have been part of the Greek king's dominion. Similarly, the trade in Mycenaean pottery can be seen throughout the Level III and Level II periods at Alalakh, a time of Hittite control. Thus, it appears that while the Hittites were rightly suspicious of Greek intentions, they were quite prepared to allow Greek imports to continue to flow unabated. In fact, you could be forgiven for being cautiously optimistic about the future. If only Assyria can be persuaded to take a full place at the diplomatic table and if only the peoples on the sidelines (Elamites, Kaskans, Armenians) can be kept under control, then the future of the Middle East looks as bright as it has for many a long year.

	Egypt	Palestine	Syria		Turkey	Iraq	
			Carchemish	Hurri	Hatti	Assyria	Babylon
1150BC	18th Dynasty / Haremheb				Mursili II	Arik Den Ili	
	Ramesses I						
1140BC	War against Libya / Seti I	Egyptian reconquest	Hittite occupation		Hittite vassalship		Nazi Maruttash
			Sahurunuwa (Hittite viceroy)				
1130BC		Increasing Habiru power in central Palestine			Muwatalli II		Kassite Dynasty
	19th Dynasty			Sattuara I		Adad Nirari I	
1120BC	War against Libya	Under Egyptian authority	Battle of Kadesh				
	Ramesses II	Sherden settled in Philistia	Assyrian conquest / Urhi Teshub / Wasasatta / Annexed by Assyria			Kadashman Turgu	
1110BC	Treaty with Hatti	Abimelech destroys Shechem	Hittite/Egyptian occupation		Treaty with Egypt / Rebellion by Sattuara II / Hattusili III		Kadashman Enlil II
			Ini Teshub (Hittite viceroy)			Shalmeneser I	
1100BC							Kudur Enlil

What does the Bible have to say?

Let me start by what the Bible doesn't have to say. In the records of Seti's campaigns we read that there were 'Apiru (i.e. Habiru or Hebrews) in support of the kings of Pella and Hamath, who were resisting Seti's taking of Bethshan. The date in question, about 1142BC, is during Gideon's days as leader, a time during which the Bible reports only "peace". On the other hand, the fact that Seti records battles with invaders from across the Jordan mirrors nicely the conflict between Gideon and invading Midianites and Amalekites just 8 years previously and a few miles to the south. Seti's campaigns were aimed at the Canaanite cities (like Bethshan and Pella) not the hill tribes, and the fact that some Hebrew mercenaries may have assisted a particular city is neither here nor there in the story which the Bible is trying to convey. Nor is the fact that several hill country cities (Shechem, Bethel, Shiloh – possibly also Debir) seem to have passed into Hebrew hands during this period.

The Bible only records an end to 40 years of peace when, after Gideon's death, his illegitimate son Abimelech manages to take control of the city of Shechem and then to murder all but one of Gideon's other sons. This prompted three years of conflict which culminated in the destruction of Shechem by Abimelech's forces, swiftly followed by the death of Abimelech himself (skull smashed by a falling millstone!). You can read the whole unsavoury episode in Judges chapter 9. Following the dates estimated previously, Abimelech would have died in about 1110BC. In the archaeology of Shechem there are two clear destruction levels. One, at the end of the Middle Bronze Age, can be ascribed to Joshua's time; the other is dated to the early Iron Ia period, whereas I am still officially in Late Bronze IIb. My own view of this is that the designation Iron Ia is primarily based

*on the appearance of Israelite-type pottery (rather than iron itself!) and that this partic-
ular pottery phase was already under way in 1110BC. Indeed, using conventional dating
it would have commenced much earlier in the 12th Century BC. I am therefore quite prepared to assign this destruction to Abimelech, including a temple which, according to the
Bible, was burnt down by Abimelech with about 1000 people inside.⁶*

*On a more general matter it is also worth noting that an official of Ramesses II
recorded that the "mountains of Shechem" were inhabited by a Shosu tribe known as
"Isr". The similarity to the name Israel is obvious, though other interpretations have been
suggested,⁷ and I don't think we should read anything into the fact this official called Isr
a Shosu rather than a Habiru tribe.⁸*

What was going on in the Rest of the World?

Egypt has rather fewer frontiers than most lands, which is one reason for its stability as a nation. To the south, tracing the Nile upstream, lies the kingdom of
Kush which, as we have seen, has from time to time represented a problem to
Egypt and necessitated regular campaigns to ensure that the Egyptian frontier is
respected. To the north-east lies Palestine, and it is from this direction that the
most serious problems have arisen, first from the Amorites and then from the
Hyksos. But, with the frontier now right up in Syria, this angle seems well
enough covered!

To the east, after crossing a relatively narrow band of desert, the Red Sea provides protection enough should any adventurous king of Sheba decide to do anything rash. And to the west lies the seemingly endless expanse of the Sahara. But
the Sahara, though virtually endless was actually far from uninhabitable. If you
look at an atlas, you will see a string of oases lying to the west of the Nile, each
of which can (and still does) support a large population. And it seems that the
population of the oases, and of what fertile land there was on the Mediterranean
coast west of the Nile, was becoming ever less Egyptian and more Libyan. Not
only that but these Libyans were no longer simply an interesting ethnic minority
within the borders of the pharaoh's kingdom; they were becoming increasingly
organised for some reason. Seti I had to fight a campaign against them in about
1141BC; so did Ramesses II in about 1123BC, and he actually had a series of
desert forts constructed to keep them under control. So, the questions arise (a)
who were the Libyans and (b) why were they getting so organised?

Well, the Libyans certainly weren't Arabs in those days. The Arab people were
still living in northern Saudi Arabia and wouldn't appear in Africa for nearly 2000
years. The Libyans who fought against Seti and Ramesses were almost certainly
Berbers. Berber-related peoples had spread right across North Africa from the
border of Egypt to the Atlantic Ocean and even beyond, to the Canary Islands.⁹
But what had got into them to make them so keen to invade the land of Egypt
when they had been happy to live in their own lands for so long?

I can think of two likely reasons, one natural and the other man-made. The natural reason concerns the explosive event that must have occurred somewhere on the planet in the year 1159BC and which then caused some 9 years of low tree ring growth worldwide, possibly upsetting the fragile ecosystem of the Sahara. However, I am inclined to give more weight to the man-made reason. This was the arrival in Libya of immigrants from the Mediterranean, including the people known as the 'Libu' who were to give their name to the country of Libya. Ramesses also had to defend himself against the 'Sherden', the same people who had troubled Amenophis III nearly a century earlier, who were also apparently trying to establish themselves in North Africa. His solution to the Sherden problem was to incorporate them into his army and to give them lands on the Palestinian coast, in what the Bible describes as Philistine territory, but his only solution to the Libu problem was to defend Egypt and to try to keep them out.

The origin of both the Sherden and the Libu is something of a mystery and generates endless controversy amongst historians. It can be no coincidence that the Sherden first arrived following the Greek attacks on southern Turkey and Cyprus in Amenophis III's reign and that a second wave arrived at a time of further Greek-supported activity in southern Turkey. So were they Greeks? Their appearance, where they have been depicted, is, according to experts, more Asiatic than Greek.[10] They may have been inhabitants of southern or western Turkey who had been displaced by the wars between the Greeks and Hittites. Some suggest the Sherden came from the region around the city of Sardis in western Turkey, certainly an area right at the centre of Greek-supported activity, and Sardis was already an important city. As for the Libu, they must have arrived in the late 13th or early 12th Century BC, perhaps as a consequence of the war between Mursili II of Hatti and king Uhhaziti, whose kingdom stretched across south-west Turkey, perhaps earlier during the conquests of Tudhalya I. If I had to select a name, I might pick the 'Limiya river land', and I might further surmise (based on other names in Tudhalya's list of conquests) that this was the river the Greeks called the Maeander,[11] the next major valley south of Sardis. The Sherden and Libu may therefore have been neighbouring, and probably Luwian-speaking, peoples prior to their migrations across the Mediterranean.

Of course, this is nothing more than speculation. All we know is that the two peoples arrived on the borders of Egypt and that they seem to have galvanised the existing population into action in a similar way to the Indo-European leaders of the Kassites and Hurrians.

15

Troy: 1100–1050BC

Age of Iron

There can be no doubt about it; in the days of Hattusili III of Hatti and Ramesses II of Egypt some pretty significant changes were afoot. Deep in the hills of Turkey a new wonder material was being produced. For two thousand years bronze had been the premium product and the power of a country was intimately tied to its ability to produce or import bronze. Without bronze, there were no modern weapons, no sophisticated tools, no scientific instruments. Of course, bronze is not just one mineral. It is a blend of copper and tin, sometimes with other minerals added, and the rarest ingredient has always been tin. The need for tin meant that certain lands had a special value to the great powers. For instance, Cornwall in south-west England was at one end of an important international trade network simply because of its tin. But now, so rumour had it, something harder than bronze had been extracted from the rocks of Turkey and that material was iron. The Middle East stood on the threshold of the Iron Age.

In truth, iron had been used for hundreds of years. Meteoric iron, iron from space, had been worked into tools for as long as anyone could remember (a chisel made of meteoric iron being found embedded in Khufu's great pyramid for example) but the supply was clearly rather limited. However, examples have been found of the use of iron from the rocks of the Earth, especially in Turkey, since much earlier times, so the technology was not actually new but it was only now, in the last century of the 2nd Millennium BC, that it had become practical and economic to produce iron for more general use. Prior to this time the value of iron can be measured by the fact that Tutankhamun had an iron dagger buried amongst his fabulous hoard of gold and precious stones, something which today would seem incongruous but which then made perfect sense. Iron vessels appear on the list of tribute received by Tuthmose III in around 1300BC. In the Hittite archives the so-called *Anitta Inscription*, which I suggested earlier dates from around 1500BC, mentions one of the kings of the day giving Anitta a "throne of iron and a sceptre of iron". An iron sword was reported as being present in the so-called 'Dorak hoard' dating from the 23rd Century BC, seen by the archaeologist James Mellart but now lost.[1] Though iron makes only rare appearances in such times, archaeology clearly attests its occasional early use.[2]

But, at the beginning of the 11th Century BC, it was the Hittites who had learnt to produce iron on an economic scale and it certainly gave them a commercial edge over their competitors. A letter from Hattusili III to another unnamed king was found in the Hattusas archive referring to the Hittites' production of iron and stating that now was not a good time for iron production (reason unknown – possibly labour force busy with agricultural issues) but that he would be sending "good iron" when it was available. Quite apart from the light this letter throws on metallurgy, it also demonstrates that the world had re-entered an age where trade was possible and where warfare had taken a rather lower priority.

The Great Hittite Empire marches on

Hattusili III was already mature when he wrested the throne of Hatti from his nephew Urhi Teshub – and he reigned for a further 30 years. It was a stable time and a prosperous time, almost a sleepy time, a time when it was easy for the population of the empire to forget how precarious life really was. By the time Hattusili died, in 1083BC according to this book, the Hittite empire had been more or less the same size for just about 100 years. Generations had come and gone who knew nothing of earlier days; citizens of Aleppo were barely aware that there had ever been a great Hurrian empire of which their city had once been part; similarly citizens of Kizzuwadna and Alalakh would have had no memory or comprehension of independence from Hittite rule. Even the staunchly Hurrian land of Isuwa would by now have grown used to Hittite overlordship. The wealth which this stable time was generating can be seen in the well-built houses of Alalakh II. Hattusili had worked hard for peace; when he died his son Tudhalya IV stepped smoothly into the role of king, largely because of the supreme efforts which Hattusili had made during his lifetime to placate any opposing factions, in particular any supporters of Kurunta, brother to the exiled Urhi Teshub, whom Hattusili had trusted with the job of governor of Tarhuntassa in southern Turkey. Records from Hattusas are excellent and the following dates can be put forward with reasonable confidence – always accepting that I am correct in my deductions for earlier times:

Hattusili III	– 1083BC
Tudhalya IV	1083 – 1055BC
Arnuwanda III	1055 – 1054BC
Suppiluliuma II	1054 –

When Tudhalya IV acceded to the Hittite throne, he was already reasonably experienced in both government and warfare because of the trust previously placed in him by his father. He had been involved in action north and east of Hattusas, controlling the ever-present threat from the Kaskan tribes and, once king, he immediately had to demonstrate to all the Hittite vassals that he would be no push-over. This he succeeded in doing extremely well and, though fighting was required to re-establish Hittite supremacy over the Kaskans, Azzi-Hayasa, the Seha river land and the Lukka lands, he lost none of his empire in the process. In fact a document has been unearthed referring to a successful conquest of Miletus. His loyal cousin Kurunta was promoted from governor to viceroy in Tarhuntassa, equivalent in status to the hereditary viceroys of Aleppo and Carchemish. Basically, all looked to be well with Hatti and its king – and so it might have been if it weren't for the Assyrians!

The Assyrian Problem

Assyria remained a significant problem to all her neighbours. Shalmaneser I had annihilated the remnants of Mitanni and built his kingdom into a great economic and military power; his frontier with Hatti now in places reached the banks of the Euphrates river. However, with Shalmaneser's death in about 1081BC, it seemed that an opportunity existed to develop an improved relationship with his son Tukulti Ninurta I. Tudhalya wrote immediately congratulating him on his accession and speaking respectfully of the achievements of his father Shalmaneser, and Tukulti Ninurta replied cordially enough. The prospects looked good.

But things were not as rosy as they looked – and I am sure that Tudhalya was well aware of it. Tukulti Ninurta was an ambitious young man and his ambition led him to look with envy on Tudhalya's prosperous empire to the west. But the problem for Tukulti Ninurta was that the Hittitte defence of northern Syria was strong and well organised. The viceroys of Carchemish and Aleppo kept considerable armies at their disposal and a frontal attack did not look as though it could possibly succeed. So, when it came, his opening gambit was a modest one; he occupied a series of outlying Hittite towns in the upper Tigris region known as 'Subari', including an important copper-mining centre. Tudhalya's immediate response was economic sanctions. He stopped all trade with Assyria through any Hittite-controlled state.[3] However, this only seems to have fanned the flames – as economic sanctions generally do – and Tukulti Ninurta's next move was to strike north into the land then known as Nihriya, east of Isuwa. This was Tudhalya's opportunity, or so he thought. He drafted a large army from his vassals and, in response to Tukulti Ninurta's initial advance, he marched his army east into mountainous Nihriya. Tudhalya probably hoped to humble the Assyrians once and for all judging from the fact that he ignored Tukulti Ninurta's protestations that a peaceful resolution was still possible. He failed. Even allowing for the ex-

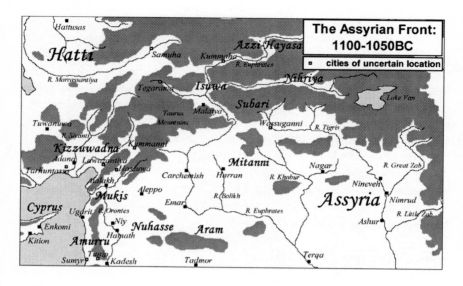

aggerations Tukulti Ninurta may have made when he wrote to the king of Ugarit on the subject, the Assyrians were undoubtedly victorious and most of the lands east of the Euphrates were now most certainly theirs. Tudhalya was left with some serious thinking to do.

The Fall of Kassite Babylon

Tukulti Ninurta was now ruler of a large empire. However, the main Hittite defences were just too strong for him. Besides, there was a serious danger of becoming overstretched and leaving the defences of Assyria itself in a weakened condition, which would hardly be wise since another superpower, Babylon, was lurking to the south and would readily accept any easy pickings. But Babylon was not now the force it had once been. Commercial relations with Egypt and the west were becoming more and more difficult and the semi-desert lands of eastern Syria and western Iraq were becoming increasingly lawless and ever less under Babylonian control. The problem was the growing power of the local nomadic inhabitants, the Aramaeans. The first reference we have to the Aramaean problem is in a letter from Hattusili III to the Babylonian king Kadashman Enlil II, the date of which must have been shortly before 1100BC, and it is clear that the problem had been steadily growing for a while. Unfortunately, records from Babylonia itself are few for this period and we know very little of Kadshman Enlil's successors Kudur Enlil and Shagarakti Shuriash. However, we know that it was the next king, Kashtiliash IV, who had to face up to the ambitions of Tukulti Ninurta I of Assyria. Approximate dates are:

Kudur Enlil	– 1092BC
Shagarakti Shuriash	1092 – 1079BC
Kashtiliash IV	1079 – 1071BC

What Tukulti Ninurta's excuse was we do not know – probably there was none – but we do know from his inscriptions that he attacked and conquered Babylon in his 10th year which, according to the chronology deduced in this book, was 1071BC. Kashtiliash was captured and taken to Ashur and Babylon experienced direct Assyrian rule for the first time. As a city it was devastated. Its walls were destroyed and many of its more important inhabitants were put to the sword (a normal Assyrian practice). Tukulti Ninurta was now in charge of virtually the whole of modern Iraq as well as parts of south-eastern Turkey.

The Elamites stir up Trouble

Meanwhile, the year 1100BC had seen Elam stronger than it had been for centuries. Temple construction, use of the Elamite language in inscriptions (rather than Akkadian), and the sheer wealth of finds from this period testify to a serious resurgence of national identity and strength. And in about 1100BC, perhaps a year or so earlier, one successful king, Humban Numena, had been followed by another, Untash Napirisha, in whose reign the great ziggurat of Choga Zambil was constructed, together with a vast array of other ceremonial buildings.[4] Art was flourishing – but so was the traditional Elamite practice of raiding Babylonia! We have the evidence of a statue looted from the city of Eshnunna in the eastern part of Babylon's realm.

Untash Napirisha had been succeeded in about 1080BC by Unpatar Napirisha, but only briefly. A year or two later another vigorous ruler, Kiten Hutran, was sitting on the Elamite throne. These were dark days for Babylon, under constant threat of assault from Tukulti Ninurta of Assyria – and Kiten Hutran made sure that they got darker still. He was proud of having massacred the population of Nippur, the spiritual heart of ancient Sumer. He also captured Der, another eastern city. Following the Assyrian conquest of Babylon in 1071BC, he continued to raid and cause trouble for the Assyrian vassal ruler; it was simply the way the Elamites did business! But he had chosen the wrong opponent. In about 1070BC Tukulti Ninurta marched swiftly down to the Persian Gulf and inflicted a serious defeat on the Elamites; Kiten Hutran simply disappeared from history and so did the dynasty he represented.

Back in Babylon, the Assyrians ruled either directly or via a vassal king for about 9 years until, in approximately 1062BC, independence was restored. We don't know how; we don't know whether the Assyrians were simply not strong enough to hold onto the city or whether a deal had been worked out. However, we do know that Adad Shuma Usur, a son of Kashtiliash IV, regained the throne of his father and reinstated a time of relative stability.

Trouble in Hatti

Compared to the devastation suffered by Babylon at Assyrian hands, you might imagine that the relatively modest losses suffered by the Hittite empire would be little more than a minor inconvenience. But the economic reality of the day was that Subari, the land which Tukulti Ninurta had captured, had been one of Hatti's main sources of copper and, while the Hittites led the world in iron production, bronze (which is 90% copper) was still the common metal and one of the mainstays of the economy. Tudhalya simply had to do something about this to prevent economic meltdown and, since recapture of Subari from Assyria was beyond him, he took the easier option of invading and occupying the island of Cyprus. There was no excuse of which we are aware; Cyprus had given no offence to the Hittites. The reason was purely the fact that Cyprus is rich in copper. In fact its very name today comes from the Latin word for copper. Tudhalya's invasion, which must, according to this chronology, have occurred some time between 1075 and 1070BC, is matched archaeologically by the presence of destruction levels in several Cypriot cities datable to this approximate period.[5] Yet despite securing copper supplies, something was badly amiss in the state of Hatti. A seal has been found in Hattusas bearing the inscription "Kurunta, Great King" and the only plausible explanation offered is that Tudhalya's cousin, whom he had generously made viceroy of Tarhuntassa, did indeed try and briefly succeed in seizing the throne. Although Tudhalya regained power, this was a clear sign that all was not well.

But from Egypt comes the message which most truly indicates Hatti's plight. Ramesses II's son Merneptah records the fact that he was then (around 1060BC) shipping grain to Hatti to keep the population from starving. This was not a sustainable long-term position and disaster would be inevitable if the Hittites failed to turn the situation around.

The Greeks march off to War

The Greeks seem frequently to have gone to war! Tudhalya's annals reveal that it was Greece that was behind an insurrection in the Seha river land; it seems they were continually on the look-out to secure influence amongst the states of western Turkey. However, Tudhalya had been remarkably successful in limiting their activities, even bringing the city of Miletus into a vassalship agreement. In fact, a treaty between Tudhalya and Sausgamuwa of Amurru in western Syria throws further fascinating light on the subject. The treaty lists the kings which Tudhalya recognised as being of comparable status to himself, namely the kings of Babylon, Assyria, Greece and Egypt – except that the king of Greece had been ruled through with a line! The context of the treaty is the war between Hatti and Assyria, which fixes the date to between about 1080 and 1075BC, and the implication is that Tudhalya thought Greece was effectively finished as a great power. Yet, despite Tudhalya's opinion, in about 1070BC the Greeks launched a very serious war indeed. The Hittites' most loyal vassal state in western Turkey had always been the land known as 'Wilusa' with a capital city named 'Taruisa', identified by virtually all experts with 'Ilion' and 'Troy'. And from Tudhalya IV's reign comes an incomplete piece of correspondence which speaks of Tudhalya reinstating a certain king 'Walmu' as his vassal in Troy, presumably because he had been ousted by an anti-Hittite (and therefore pro-Greek) faction.

Archaeologically, this is the period during which Troy VIh comes to an end with a mighty destruction. Sceptics will continue to sneer at the idea, but I see no realistic alternative to this being the era of the famous Trojan War, the subject of Homer's *Iliad* and many a subsequent play or film. There has of course been endless debate about the historicity of the Trojan War for as long as Homer's epic tales have been in circulation, which is since about 700BC! There was a long period during which the respectable academic position was that the whole story of the Trojan War was just so much Greek imagination. That respectability was shattered by Heinrich Schliemann's discovery of the actual site of Troy on the west coast of Turkey and, since then, there has been confirmation after confirmation that the story really has a strong foundation in truth. Recent excavation at Troy[6] has shown that the Level VIh city, which had previously been thought to be rather small, was actually vast. The area which archaeologists had initially thought to represent the entire city has now been found to be only the citadel area, the rest of the city lying on the surrounding plain, including a large outer defensive wall.

The fact is that someone destroyed Troy and, given the Hattusas archive evidence that generations of Greek kings seem to have been trying to gain a foothold in Turkey, the Greeks are much the most likely culprits. Furthermore 'Walmu', the king that Tudhalya reinstated, may quite plausibly be 'Priam', the king of Troy in Homer's story. This may look unlikely at first glance, but the consonant sounds *p, b, v* and *w* are known to interchange readily with either time or translation; the same is true of *r* and *l*[7]. And vowel sounds appear and disappear readily enough in most languages. Of course Walmu may not be Priam – but linguistically he could be. We have already come across the name Alexander as a king of Troy some 50 years earlier, and Priam's son, according to Homer, was 'Alexander Paris'.

Quite simply, the Trojan War shook the world. If the story told by Homer has a shred of truth then the war effort would certainly have depleted the resources of the Greek cities very seriously indeed.[8] To have so many key economic producers away from their farms and businesses for so long must have cost the country dear – and all for the sake of a kidnapped woman (Helen of Troy) who, according to Homer, may not have wanted rescuing at all! By such accidents of history are the fortunes of the world changed. Perhaps as the smoke rose from the ashes of Priam's city in about the year 1060BC the idea that this war would have a dramatic impact right across the Middle East might have looked a little far-fetched. But it would; and the impact would be felt very soon indeed.

The Self-destruction of Mycenaean Greece

The story goes that Agamemnon king of Mycenae was murdered on his return from leading the victorious Greek forces at Troy and archaeology tells us that the problems which engulfed Greece were not restricted to a single man or a single city. The pottery type known as Mycenaean IIIb had been in use since the first half of the 12th Century BC and the single sherd (plus a few local imitations) recovered from Troy VIIa, the level immediately following the destruction of the Level VIh city, tells us that Mycenaean IIIb fashions did not long outlast the city's fall. Yet the evidence from mainland Greece is that several of the major Greek cities (Mycenae, Tiryns, Zygournis, Berbati) suffered serious destruction while Mycenaean IIIb styles were still current; this can only have been in the years during or immediately following the Trojan War. In fact the general level of insecurity in Greece can be seen in the massive fortifications which had already been thrown up around all the major cities over the preceding few decades. Furthermore, a second round of destructions can be seen in the Argolid plain of southern Greece a few years later, more or less at the Mycenaean IIIb/IIIc transition. It seems most unlikely that this was the work of outsiders; the destructions are too selective. For instance Attica, the region around Athens, seems to have escaped. The signs are that civil war was raging across Greece, undoubtedly fuelled by the breakdown of the commerce upon which the Greek economy depended, and not helped by the fact that so many people had just spent so many years doing nothing other than fighting; they knew no other trade!

With the total break-down of central authority and an economy in tatters, it was left to local city states, notably Athens, to survive as best they could. Mycenae, previously the seat of the great king, was still an inhabited city, but its power had gone for good.

Egypt is Attacked

More than half a century has now passed since a young ambitious Ramesses II acceded to the throne of his father Seti, eager to make sure that his reign wouldn't be forgotten. He couldn't wait to wage war on Hatti and to conquer new lands. Then, as a great statesman, he enjoyed his prestige amongst the lesser rulers of Palestine and Syria. He enjoyed his place at the head of the great power league. Back in Egypt he set up monuments to his own greatness, many in his magnificent capital city of Piramesse in the eastern Nile delta, built close to the site of the earlier city of Avaris. He was probably popular, a ruler whose achievements the country could be proud of. But the trouble was he refused to die! And so the monuments kept going up. Crown prince Khaemwaset died; one by one Ramesses' sons and heirs predeceased him but still he kept going. The land was at peace, there was no particular problem, but such a long reign inevitably brings with it growing uncertainty regarding the succession. At last however, in 1063BC, after 66 long years as pharaoh, he finally breathed his last and his thirteenth son Merneptah could step into his shoes.

Merneptah was himself no longer young, and it had only been in the last 10 years or so that he had realised he might one day be pharaoh. But in his 5th year (1058BC) he had to face up to an unprecedented attack from the west, from Libya. There was no warning; Libya had been peaceful throughout most of Ramesses' reign. When Merneptah eventually recovered from the shock and sent his army to resist the invaders, he had to fight a serious battle in which 6000 of the enemy were killed and a further 9000 captured. But just who were these invaders? According to Egyptian texts they are given the collective name "Peoples of the Sea" and are listed as: Libu, Meshwesh, Ekwesh, Shekelesh, Teresh and Lukka. As you may be aware, there is endless discussion as to the identification of these peoples and I give the following with a mixture of confidence and speculation.

Libu	*people from the Limiya (or Maeander) river land, western Turkey*
Meshwesh	*people from the land of Masa, also western Turkey*
Ekwesh	*Ahhiyawans (or Achaeans), i.e. Greeks*
Shekelesh	*people from the Seha (or Sakarya) river land, north-western Turkey*
Teresh	*people from Taruisa (or Troy), i.e. Trojans*
Lukka	*people from the Lukka lands (classical Lycia), south-western Turkey*

It can, of course, be no coincidence that these assorted peoples arrived on Egypt's western frontier immediately following the Trojan War. The lands of western Turkey were exhausted. No-one had planted crops so there was no harvest. The inhabitants had become accustomed to fighting and they naturally tried to fight their way out of their predicament. The Greek lands had exploded into civil war and consequent economic collapse. Displaced people were everywhere and it only needed a strong voice of leadership to suggest that a new life awaited them on the other side of the Mediterranean and many would follow. By far the largest number of Merneptah's prisoners were 'Ekwesh', i.e. Greeks, so this looks to have been a Greek-inspired adventure. But it failed; the Libu and the Meshwesh had already made their home in North Africa and Merneptah could do no more than drive them back west. The other 'Peoples of the Sea' were expelled; they would have to look elsewhere for a land to call their own.

Who knows how many mass movements of displaced peoples there may have been during these troubled days, movements which have gone unrecorded but which were very real at the time? However, one further tale needs to be told. It is the story told by the Greeks of a character named Mopsus. He fought at Troy and, after the war, headed south through western Turkey, gathering an army of supporters as he did so. The story is that he founded the city of Aspendos, now Antalya, in the Lukka lands (Lycia), before moving on to Kizzuwadna (Cilicia) and fathering a whole dynasty of rulers! You might be disposed to treat the tale as nothing more than myth if it were not for the finding of an 8th Century BC inscription of king Asitawanda (a good Hittite/Luwian name) of the "house of Mopsus" at Karatepe in Cilicia. We also see the archaeological evidence that someone using Mycenaean IIIc pottery destroyed the Hittite temple at Tarsus (Tarhuntassa?) in Cilicia. The whole of western Turkey was obviously in total chaos following the Trojan War, and there were rich rewards to be had for the adventurous – and for the very lucky!

Hatti under Real Pressure

Tudhalya IV of Hatti was quite unable to stem the tide of anarchy which had taken hold in the western regions of his empire; nor was his son Arnuwanda III, who succeeded him in about 1055BC. We read of open rebellion in Hatti and factionalism.[9] Upon his early death, Arnuwanda was replaced by his brother Suppiluliuma II, who set about doing what he could to restore order. But it was an uphill struggle. Hittite vassals were refusing to swear allegiance (we have a letter from Suppiluliuma II to the king of Ugarit on the subject) and the scant evidence we have reveals that Suppiluliuma fought extensive campaigns in western Turkey to maintain some degree of order there; we also know that he fought a naval battle off Cyprus. Indeed we have a letter which he sent to Ugarit asking for increased naval support. We also have a letter to the king of Ugarit demanding a ship to transport grain to one of his southern ports. The year 1050BC, therefore, finds Hatti beset by problems. It is still a great empire, controlling territory throughout central Turkey and much of northern Syria, but the surrounding kingdoms, Isuwa, Azzi-Hayasa, the Kaskans, Arzawa and the Seha river land are all more than usually restless. Suppiluliuma will need to summon the abilities of his great great grandfather Suppiluliuma I if he is to preserve Hatti's great power status!

Revolt in Alalakh

Alalakh seems to have been a typically rebellious Hittite vassal. The prosperous Level II city had come to an end much earlier in the century, probably while Hattusili was still on the throne of Hatti, with what looks like a civil uprising. The fact that this uprising was accompanied by smashing of Hurrian-style pottery suggests that it was the growing Luwian element of the population who were responsible, strongly allied to the Hittite cause. This is confirmed by the fact that the first phase of the succeeding Level I city has revealed Luwian hieroglyphs on a seal and a seal impression, and decorative motifs reminiscent of Luwian and Hittite art. A stone relief of Tudhalya IV has also been found. However, the second phase represents a dramatic change. The Tudhalya relief was turned upside down and used as a step in front of a new temple building, a building whose architecture was nevertheless still Luwian in style. The inference is that Alalakh, though now a predominantly Luwian city, had thrown off Hittite authority, and the finding of a seal reading "Paluwa, son of the king" suggests that the king in question was no longer the great king in Hattusas. Alalakh was apparently amongst those many vassals who were refusing to swear allegiance to Suppululiuma II.

Cyprus is Overrun

The archaeology of Cyprus tells a clear story of the times. The destructions of Enkomi and Kition during Tudhalya IV's invasion of about 1075BC are followed by rebuilding on a grand scale using ashlar masonry techniques very similar to those used at Ugarit just across the sea on the Syrian coast. The rebuilding clearly took place while Mycenaean IIIb styles were still in vogue; for example, so-called 'lion craters' were popular in IIIb times and examples have been found both at Ugarit and also in the rebuilt city of Enkomi. Both Ugarit and Cyprus were still economically strong; they were key Hittite vassals and vital to the struggling Hittite economy.

Then, right at the beginning of the Mycenaean IIIc period, in about 1055BC, we see evidence of fortified settlements appearing at coastal locations in Cyprus, usually on promontories which could be readily defended from land attack. A similar example is seen at Ras ibn Hani on the Syrian coast near Ugarit. Nothing is proved, but the obvious candidates for the inhabitants of these coastal settlements are the same 'Peoples of the Sea' who had tried to colonise northern Egypt a year or two earlier. And it seems this time they were more successful. Both Enkomi and Kition went on to suffer destruction during the early Mycenaean IIIc period, in roughly 1050BC, and when they were rebuilt the style was much more Aegean in appearance. We have a telling letter from the Hittite appointed governor of Cyprus to king Ammurapi of Ugarit referring to "the enemy" having 20 ships off the mountainous regions of the island. Fortunately on this occasion they left; but it seems that it wouldn't be long before the enemy, who were surely displaced persons from Greece and western Turkey, were successful. We read that king Suppululiuma II of Hatti fought three battles against ships from Cyprus, as well as fighting the same enemy on land.

The Destruction of Ugarit

We also know without question that the same enemy destroyed Ugarit; a sword bearing the cartouche of pharaoh Merneptah was found in the ruins. The fire which destroyed the whole city such that it would never be inhabited again was also responsible for preserving cuneiform tablets including the letter from the governor of Cyprus. Another preserved letter, which may also be from the governor of Cyprus, talks of enemy ships having been sighted and urges Ugarit to "stand firm". But the most poignant letter of all was found still in a kiln ready to be fired (to a suitable hardness for normal preservation). It was written by king Ammurapi of Ugarit to someone he calls the "king" of Cyprus, and it speaks of the enemy having landed and that they were burning his towns. He states that Ugarit's fleet is away, stationed off the Lukka lands far to the west, and that his army is away fighting in Hatti. The silence which follows is deafening. A year or two before 1050BC, Ugarit was no more.

The Sun sets on the Egyptian 19th Dynasty

The days of pharaoh Merneptah, the man who was unlucky enough to be faced with the fall-out from the Trojan War, provide me with one last check on absolute date. As I'm sure you remember, the dates I have been deducing are some 150 years later than you will usually read and, although I am very happy with the weight of evidence found already in support of these dates, I will not pass up the opportunity for a further check. During the war of words between Kenneth Kitchen, supporting the conventional view of Egyptian history, and David Rohl, proposer of a dramatically revised chronology, Kitchen drew attention to a brief piece of graffiti next to a path near Thebes, which he believed referred to the return of the Nile flood taking place on Day 3 of Month 3 of the flood season in Merneptah's first year.[10] With Year 1 of Merneptah in 1063BC as I have suggested, Day 3 of Month 3 should have been the 8th of July, 11 days before the heliacal rising of Sothis and the officially expected start of the flood season. In fact, since the tie-up between the heliacal rising of Sothis and the first signs of the flood season originally stems from the ancient capital of Memphis, and since the flood used to reach Thebes four or five days before Memphis, the mismatch is reduced to 6 or 7 days – not bad.

Now I must admit that there have been significant differences from year to year as to exactly when the flood arrived in Egypt, so I would allow that the true date could have been anywhere from about 1150 to 1030BC, but this nonetheless represents another indicator that I may well be on the right track. To arrive at a more conventional date for Year 1 of Merneptah (1213BC) it is necessary to apply a different interpretation and to assume that the inscription refers to the Nile bursting its banks or, in the opinion of Kitchen himself, reaching the high water point. Nothing is impossible, but the first sign of flooding (water changing colour and starting to flow faster) seems to me to be a more likely interpretation of the flood 'returning'.

> **Absolute date range: 1150-1030BC**
> Graffiti at Thebes dated to Day 3, Month 3 of the flood season, Year 1 of Merneptah, describing the return of the Nile flood

For reasons which are not evident today, when Merneptah died in 1053BC he was not followed by his son Seti but by an individual named Amenmesse, apparently a usurper from a different line of the huge family of Ramesses II's descendants. We know little of his reign, not least because those who came after him were at pains to erase his name from the records, but according to this chronology it was Amenmesse who sat on the throne of Egypt in 1050BC.

Palestine and Lebanon

The treaty between Ramesses II and Hattusili III of Hatti seems to have remained in force throughout this period, meaning that the cities of Palestine continued to be nominally within the domain of the pharaoh and that Egypt continued to station troops in key centres. Egyptian authority had become accepted as a fact of life. This being the case, it is interesting to read on one of Merneptah's victory stelae that "Ashkelon has been carried off, Gezer has been seized upon, Yanoam (in the Galilee region) has been made as if it didn't exist and Israel's seed is no more", all pronounced in the context of Egypt entering a time of great peace and security! We have no further details as to what the nature of the problems might have been but, unless this was all just poetic license, Palestine can hardly have been entirely peaceful.[11] It is also noteworthy that the Israelite people were now recognised as a separate entity, contrasting with earlier evidence which only spoke of the Canaanite cities, the Habiru and the Shosu. One particular find also throws light on Israelite culture; it is a large stone altar discovered on the slope of Mount Ebal in central Palestine and the combination of Ramesses II scarabs and Iron Ia pottery discovered in the infill material is a potent piece of relative dating evidence – and not one that supporters of the traditional dating of Ramesses II want to see![12]

Further north, Byblos remained firmly allied to Egypt, and Ramesses II's cartouche has been found on fragments of vases from the tomb of king Ahiram of Byblos. In fact, the evidence from this particular tomb has been tossed back and forth many times amongst those arguing for particular versions of ancient history and much of the problem stems from the fact that an example of Canaanite alphabetic writing was also found adorning the king's sarcophagus, writing which was not dramatically different from 10th Century BC examples. It is another small point but it adds yet more weight in support of the dates proposed in this book.

Summary

The first half of the 11th Century BC has seen a serious descent from a world of stable great power politics, trade and, by and large, peace, to a situation where endemic warfare now makes commercial relations next to impossible! The blame can be divided between the power-hungry Assyrians in the east, who first attacked Hatti and then conquered both Babylon and Elam, and the Greeks, whose thirst for glory has led them into an ultimately disastrous war against Troy and a whole confederation of states from western Turkey. In this war, victory and defeat mean very little as there seem to be only losers. There are whole populations on the move, looking for lands where they can settle and live in peace, but there are also those whose intentions are anything but peaceful, men like Mopsus who are seizing the opportunity that chaos provides and carving out their own little empires. This can be seen in parts of Turkey, in Cyprus and also on the Syrian coast, and Merneptah's Egypt has barely managed to defend its borders against a massive army of displaced persons. Hatti has been caught between the violent attentions of Tukulti Ninurta of Assyria and the mounting anarchy in western Turkey and now finds itself in a very difficult position indeed, having lost both Cyprus and Ugarit to invading Greeks and others; worse still, the country doesn't seem to be able to grow sufficient food to feed its own population!

Egypt is at a safer distance from trouble, but memories of the glory days of Ramesses II are fading fast and family feuding now seems to be engulfing the Egyptian royal house. The country is not in any mortal danger yet – but it will be unless the ruling house can get its act together. Palestine is under control for the moment, but Merneptah's inscriptions prove that the region is far from peaceful. In short, the situation right across the Middle East is spiralling out of control.

What does the Bible have to say?

Following Abimelech's death in 1110BC – if my reading of the Biblical dates is correct so far – we read (Judges 10:1-5) of two further leaders, Tola and Jair, with 23 and 22 years respectively, but in neither case are any specific events recorded. Then, in about 1066BC, comes Jephthah (Judges 10:6-12:7). For 18 years (i.e. since about 1084BC) Israel had been oppressed by both Philistines and Ammonites and the task fell to Jephthah to sort out the Ammonite problem. This he duly did, including in his ultimatum to the Ammonite king

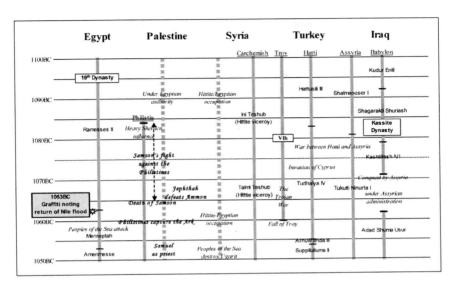

the observation that Israel had occupied the lands east of the Jordan for 300 years (Judges 11:26). With Joshua's conquest in 1365BC and occupation of Transjordan a few months earlier, Jephthah's words look impressively precise!

Samson and the Philistines

After 6 years Jephthah was followed by Ibzan (7 years), Elon (10 years) and Abdon (8 years), which should take us well beyond 1050BC, in fact down to about 1038BC, and it is only then that we read of the famous strong-man Samson and his struggle against the Philistines. However, I am quite certain that Samson did not follow Abdon. In the first place the language is different here – the words "after him" are not used – and then there is the odd anomaly that although both Philistines and Ammonites are said to have oppressed Israel from about 1084BC, Jephthah only dealt with the Ammonite problem, east of the Jordan river. So what about the Philistines? The most plausible answer I can see is that Samson's 20-year struggle against the Philistines should also be dated to this period of oppression; his ill-fated marriage to a Philistine girl (Judges 14:1-15:8) would therefore have taken place in about 1084BC.

For nearly three centuries since the initial Israelite invasion of Palestine the Philistines had lived in relative peace with Israel; only a single conflict is mentioned, in the days of Shamgar (around 1240BC). In archaeological terms, the Philistine cities (for example Ashkelon) were indistinguishable from those of their Canaanite neighbours. Philistia was very much part of the Egyptian empire and we read that Ramesses II had settled his Sherden mercenaries in exactly that region some time in the last quarter of the 12th Century BC, something which cannot have failed to have an impact. May I suggest *that the impact was a similar one to that of the Libu on the Berber tribes of Libya. The Philistines were suddenly energised into becoming a thoroughly aggressive people. At this range, this is a very difficult phenomenon to understand. It had happened to the Kassites of western Iran and to the Hurrians also and the common factor always seems to be these meddlesome Indo-Europeans. If, as seems likely, the Sherden were Luwian speakers from western Turkey, then their culture was also Indo-European. The immediate effect seems to have been that the Philistines started to dominate their neighbours. This probably included neighbouring Canaanite cities such as Gezer but the Bible tells us that it certainly included the Israelites of the central hill country.*

Samson grew up during this period of Philistine dominance. The bloody aftermath of his marriage represented the start of Israelite resistance to the Philistines (Judges 15:9-16:3). For 20 years Samson was a serious thorn in their side, until the day he was betrayed by his Philistine mistress Delilah into the hands of the so-called 'Seren' of the Philistines (Judges 16:4-21). The word 'Seren' is usually translated 'rulers' but the real meaning is not known; I suggest it should be rendered 'Sherden', the ruling class with origins in Turkey, settled in the region by Ramesses II. The Sherden were simply carrying out the job which Ramesses expected them to do, namely keeping Palestine in order and taking whatever measures they thought necessary to do so! By the way, there is plenty of mention of 'Apiru (Hebrew) slaves in Egypt in Ramesses II's time, emphasising Israel's subservient position.

From Samson to Samuel

Following Samson's death in Philistine custody in about 1065BC, we read of the migration of the Israelite tribe of Dan, previously neighbours to the Philistines, to the far northern Canaanite city of Laish (Judges 18). Logically, this took place immediately after the death of Samson, who had been leader of the tribe of Dan. Archaeological investigations at the site of the city of Laish (renamed 'Dan') have revealed extensive evidence for its conquest around this time[13].

The next episode (Judges 19-22) is a destructive civil war between one tribe, Benjamin, and the rest of the Israelite people, and one of the key events is the total destruction of the Benjaminite city of Gibeah. A massive destruction is attested in the archaeology of the site and is datable to this approximate period – say 1060BC.

The final and greatest disaster in the sequence given in the Bible is the defeat of an Israelite army by the Philistines and the (temporary) capture of the Ark of the Covenant, the most sacred symbol of the Israelite religion (1 Samuel 4), an event which also resulted in the death of the entire priestly family in charge of the Ark. To any outside observer it would appear that Israel was now a spent force. One such outside observer was the Egyptian pharaoh Merneptah and his statement of 1058BC that "Israel's seed was no more" becomes thoroughly understandable! The Egyptian enforcers in Palestine, the Sherden-led Philistines, had seemingly snuffed out any threat that Israel might itself emerge as a force in the land. If the Merneptah stela is factual then we have to assume that Philistine/Sherden forces also inflicted a defeat on Gezer and another on Yanoam. The reference to Ashkelon, itself a Philistine city, being "carried off" is admittedly rather harder to interpret, but at this distance we have no idea of the factionalism and civil war which may have raged.

So, by 1050BC Israel was well and truly under Philistine/Sherden dominance. On Merneptah's stela Israel is given the hieroglyphic sign for a people – but not a state. They had no king and no government, just the rather ineffective leadership of Elon from the northern tribe of Zebulun and the spiritual guidance of a young priest called Samuel.

What was going on in the Rest of the World?

I'd like to remind you that the Middle East was not the only corner of the world where civilisation had taken hold. By 1050BC the Indo-European speaking Aryans had occupied Pakistan and parts of north-west India, and both Indian culture and the Hindu religion were already taking the form that they have today. It was in many ways a rich culture, but the trouble for the historian is that writing was not one of its riches. The hieroglyphic script used by the earlier Indus valley people had fallen out of use and the Aryans had nothing to replace it. They had a quite remarkable oral tradition however, the evidence for which lies in the various Hindu sagas and tales, some of which clearly have a high degree of historical validity, and the oral transmission of the *Vedas* over more than 3000 years certainly puts the survival of Homer's *Iliad* and *Odyssey* over a few hundred years into perspective.

Another great centre of civilisation was China. For about 500 years, northern China had been under the authority of the Shang emperors, ruling from their capital city of Anyang, 300 miles south of Beijing, but in this approximate period they were finally ousted by the Chou.[14] This was a very major change. The Shang rulers came from the north-west of the country and, personally, I am doubtful as to whether their roots were 'Chinese' at all. Of course, they lived in China and their descendants are now modern Chinese, but their cultural affinities seem to lie at least in part with South-East Asia or even Polynesia. Their art had no antecedent in China, but plenty of parallels in South-East Asia and also in Central and South America! However, that is another story.[15]

In contrast to the Shang, the Chou were most definitely 'Chinese', by which I really mean 'Sino-Tibetan', the language family which includes Chinese. They had adopted the latest in chariot warfare just as the armies of the Hittites and Egyptians had, and they proved technologically just too advanced for the Shang forces. Interestingly, the origin of certain Chinese terms relating to horse-riding and chariotry has been traced back to Indo-European roots and the path by which horse culture reached China is thought to have been via the Indo-European 'Tocharian' people, at that time living in western China.

Writing developed fast in Chou times and, despite the First Emperor's book burning edict of the late 3rd Century BC, a few records survive from throughout the Chou period in a language and script which is clearly related to those of modern Chinese. It is true that a similar looking script was in use under the Shang dynasty, as seen on the famous 'oracle bones' for instance, but it is hard to say just how similar the language really was.

16

Peoples of the Sea: 1050–1000BC

The Break-up of the Hittite Empire

It is impossible to say exactly when the end came. The archives of Hattusas are excellent – but when they cease, some time during the reign of Suppiluliuma II, we are suddenly cut off from our source of knowledge. Archaeology informs us that the city of Hattusas was destroyed; so were numerous other Hittite cities in the old heartland area. We don't know when exactly, but it cannot have been long after 1050BC (if my overall dating is correct). We also know that the next inhabitants of Hattusas were not Hittites. They were a people whose material culture was much more basic, a people who did not yet use the fast wheel for pottery manufacture, and whose architecture was crude – one might say uncivilised. The evidence points straight at the Kaskans. The Kaskans did not write so we have no direct record, but it is hard to see that it could have been any other people, particularly since we will soon be finding Kaskans inhabiting territory as far south as the Euphrates river.

But it wasn't the Kaskans who destroyed Hattusas. The careful torching of all the public buildings, the fact that all valuables had been removed, these can only mean one thing; this was a deliberate and planned operation! The logical inference is that life had simply become unsustainable in the hills of central Hatti. The endemic warfare in western Turkey, together with the loss of territory in Cilicia and western Syria to the 'Peoples of the Sea', had brought Hatti to a state where it could no longer secure the food supplies it needed. Suppiluliuma had no choice; he and his people took the desperate decision to abandon their ancestral home and to join the already swollen ranks of the homeless, heading south in search of more hospitable lands.

The great empire was at an end – but Hittite civilisation definitely wasn't! The empire simply split up into sizeable chunks, each with its local Hittite king, probably the previous governor or viceroy. It may well be that Suppiluliuma himself survived and continued to rule as 'great king' from the lands of south-central Turkey, the region we know as the Konya plain and which the Hittites called the 'Lower Land'. We know that this would later be the location of a so-called 'Neo-Hittite' kingdom and it is reasonable to assume, even without any written record, that this kingdom was formed when the empire collapsed. Besides, several inscriptions have been found, from Cilicia right across the Konya plain, referring to a certain "Hartapu son of Mursili, great king of the Hittites". The old empire was gone, but Hittite culture was alive and well. We also know that the viceroydom of Carchemish became a separate kingdom and that Kuzi Teshub, great great grandson of the original Hittite viceroy Sarri Kusuh, was another who styled himself "great king of Hatti"; Aleppo became another independent kingdom and, further south, so did Hamath. The lack of records means we have no idea what sort of political relationship there may have been between these various Hittite states, but it is hard to imagine that there wasn't any.

The culture of these states was Hittite, exactly matching the culture of pre-conquest Hattusas, but the dominant language in all these lands was now Luwian. In fact, Luwian speech had already become widespread at Hattusas itself.[1] As we have seen, Luwians had also been a growing element of the population of northern Syria, and their dominance is demonstrated by the fact that inscriptions of this era, from locations as widely separated as Troy and Hamath, are all in hieroglyphic Luwian.[2]

So, loss of heartland territory, yes; total extinction, most certainly not!

The Mustering of the Peoples of the Sea

Refugees from the Trojan War and its aftermath had been a major factor in Hatti's downfall – and they weren't finished yet! The walls of the great temple at Medinet Habu near Thebes are liberally inscribed with both pictures and texts and many of them relate to the activities of the so-called 'Peoples of the Sea', the same name as that given to the people who attacked in Merneptah's day. We read that the "northern islands and coasts were on the move and scattered in war", a very good description of the situation following the Trojan War. Then: "no country could stand before their arms; Hatti, Cilicia, Carchemish, Arzawa and Cyprus, they were cut off"; again, a good description of what we saw in the last chapter with sea-borne invaders conquering Cyprus and Ugarit while Mopsus and his land-based army took Arzawa and Cilicia. For all we know, they may also have defeated an army from Carchemish. And now, according to the Medinet

Habu inscriptions, a confederation of these peoples had set up camp in Amurru, just south of Ugarit, and was advancing on Egypt.

OK, but why? No record exists unfortunately, but the fact that "Hartapu, great king of the Hittites", would soon be acknowledged in parts of Cilicia suggests that the Hittites were still strong enough to exercise considerable authority and to make life very uncomfortable for Mopsus and those who had settled with him in Cilicia. The same was true in Syria since Aleppo and Carchemish were still strong centres of Hittite power. Cyprus had been taken, that is true, but there were still leaders looking for lands to rule and populations looking for fields to plant. As a consequence, a large group of these people mustered in Amurru (desolating the land according to the Egyptian inscriptions, although that may have been a slight exaggeration) and headed south.

The Fall and Rise of New Kingdom Egypt

In 1050BC Egypt was in the hands of Amenmesse – a usurper. However, Merneptah's son Seti II had his own power-base somewhere in the country and he eventually gathered enough support to oust Amenmesse. Seti then died, leaving his young son Siptah under the protection of queen Twosre, Seti's widow but not Siptah's mother. This, of course, was a recipe for disaster, and it was compounded when Siptah himself died shortly after reaching manhood. Power lurched back to Twosre and her chancellor, a man called Bay.[3] The mess was only cleared up when another claimant to the throne, Setnakht, was able to oust Twosre and Bay, and to usher in a new dynasty and a restoration of order.[4]

Some of our principal sources of information here are the records of the town of Deir el Medina near Thebes, which had been specifically constructed to house those working on the royal tombs in the Valleys of the Kings and Queens, and fortunately these records are sufficient to establish the continuity and approximate duration of this rather obscure period. Opinions differ slightly, but here are my suggested dates for the Egyptian rulers down to the close of the millennium.

	Amenmesse	– 1048BC
	Seti II	– 1047BC
	Siptah	1047 – 1041BC
	Twosre	1047 – 1039BC
20th Dynasty:	Setnakht	1041 – 1039BC
	Ramesses III	1039 – 1007BC
	Ramesses IV	1007 – 1001BC
	Ramesses V	1001 –

The major ruler of the 20th Dynasty in Egypt was Ramesses III, son of Setnakht. His authority is attested in Palestine both by Egyptian documents and by the discovery of various artefacts with his name on them, notably at Megiddo and Bethshan.[5] We know plenty about the reign of Ramesses III, partly from the official records on the walls of his mortuary temple at Medinet Habu and from official papyri, but also from other chance finds. In the magnificent *Harris Papyrus*, we have a complete record of the income received by the pharaoh from all parts of Egypt and also from towns in Palestine over 31 years of his reign; we also have full records of expenditure, much of it on the various great priesthoods of Egypt, particularly the priests of Amun at Karnak. In the 5th year of his reign we read that he successfully defended Egypt from another attack from Libya by the Libu and the Meshwesh and the depictions of the battle show that his army included Sherden mercenaries. But Ramesses' real challenge came in his 8th year, 1031BC.

Showdown with the Peoples of the Sea

The texts state that, in Ramesses' 8th year, a powerful confederation of Peoples of the Sea launched an attack on Egypt, this time from the east, from Philistia. In Philistia itself the archaeology of Ashkelon, Ashdod, Ekron and Gath tells us that these cities were all captured, accompanied by varying amounts of destruction. Previously the culture had been Canaanite with plenty of evidence of Egyptian and Egyptian-style artefacts, as one would expect from an area which had long been part of the Egyptian empire. But now Canaanite culture became amalgamated with evidence of a quite different people, a people who brought Mycenaean IIIc pottery and Mycenaean building practices.[6] They also brought a very different cuisine judging by the relative numbers of bones of different domestic animals, and the closest parallels are with Greece. The very obvious deduction is that the Peoples of the Sea had arrived. The Mopsus legend speaks of him finally conquering the southern Palestinian coastal city of Ashkelon, where he 'retired' and died. It seems that legend and archaeology speak with one voice on this occasion. The Philistines were certainly not totally destroyed, but they were now under the authority of another dominant people. From the evidence of Egyptian finds immediately before these events, the date was some time early in the reign of Ramesses III. In point of fact, it was probably between his 5th and 8th years since the Sherden, who mainly lived in Philistia, were still fighting on the Egyptian side against the Libyans in Year 5.

There are plenty of texts from Egypt about the invasion of Ramesses III's 8th year. On the walls of Ramesses' mortuary temple at Medinet Habu, the invaders are listed as "Peleset, Tjekker, Shekelesh, Weshesh and Denyen"; the *Harris Papyrus* adds the Sherden. The major force this time seems to have come from the 'Peleset' and experts are united in identifying these people with the more familiar Philistines. Ramesses III's inscriptions speak of the "towns and orchards of the Peleset", which implies that they were a settled people.[7] The Sherden we know had been living amongst the Philistines for many decades. The Shekelesh

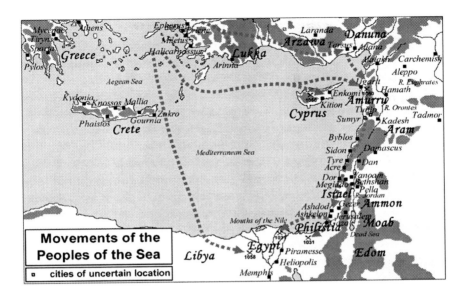

had also fought against Merneptah in 1058BC and they are next spotted in ships off Cyprus; Suppiluliuma II of Hatti asked the king of Ugarit who they were. It is therefore quite logical that a contingent should have joined Mopsus on his journey south. The Denyen are often identified with Homer's 'Danaeans', a word he seems to use interchangeably with 'Achaeans' and which might therefore logically represent the Greeks. The alternative, which I would certainly favour, is that the word refers to inhabitants of Cilicia, also known as 'Danuna'.[8] The most rational explanation of the Tjekker is that they are 'Teucri' a people from the Troy area and followers of a certain semi-legendary character named 'Teucer'. Teucer is supposed to have founded Salamis on Cyprus, which is un-provable but quite possible, and this would certainly put the Teucri into the same area as the Shekelesh. The Weshesh are the most problematic of all, but the most plausible suggestion I have seen is that they are from the land known as 'Wilusa' by the Hittites (Ilion by the Greeks) which was the name of the state with Troy as its capital. The Weshesh would therefore be from the same area as the Tjekker; both could be seen as Trojans.

To cut a long story short, Ramesses won. There was fighting on the Egyptian border and also in the Nile delta following a sea-borne invasion, but he won and the Peoples of the Sea were forced to flee. Ramesses then brought the Philistine cities under his control once more, although the Tjekker managed to hold onto the Palestinian coastal city of Dor. Sherden are found settled in various places in Egypt (many probably remained loyal to Ramesses throughout). The rest fled where they could, many doubtless managing to remain in Philistia.

Cyprus under the Peoples of the Sea

The dominant pottery during this period of Cypriot history was of Mycenaean IIIc type. It was evidently a boom time and Cyprus was clearly a major stronghold for the Peoples of the Sea. There is textual evidence that these people conquered Cyprus, archaeological evidence in that the major cities of Kition and Enkomi were both destroyed in the Mycenaean IIIc period and both rebuilt with a distinctly different architecture showing Aegean elements, and the evidence of depictions found on Cyprus, which exactly parallel those of the Peoples of the Sea at Medinet Habu in Egypt. However, while the dominant culture on the island was now Aegean, it is also clear that the older Semitic element was still present and that the two co-existed. This is evident, for example, in the continuing use of two different weight systems, one from the Aegean and the other with an older history on Cyprus.⁹

At some stage Enkomi was destroyed again, this time for good, and our total lack of written records means we cannot know who was responsible. It may quite possibly have been elements from the armies defeated by Ramesses and forced to flee from Palestine. Nevertheless, there is no doubt that Cyprus was still prospering materially and was a real centre of technical excellence, for example in metalwork.

The Lands of the Aegean

And, despite its troubles, Greece was not yet dead! In Mycenae itself archaeology has revealed that the city continued to exist even after suffering significant destruction on two occasions in the mid 11ᵗʰ Century. The palace and city of Pylos, located right at the far south-western extremity of the Peleponese, continued to thrive and we have evidence from both cities that the writing system known as Linear B was still in use for record keeping. Unfortunately, the only records we have are lists of commodities and the like, but they at least demonstrate that the occupants of Pylos were there for the long haul; they were not anticipating any sort of terminal decline in their fortunes! Indeed, Mycenaean IIIc pottery is still found as far afield as Italy and Sardinia although on a much reduced scale compared to Mycenaean IIIb times.

But terminal decline there was. At some stage during the Mycenaean IIIc phase, the palaces of Pylos, Mycenae and Tiryns were all destroyed for the last time (preserving the Linear B tablets in their ruins). Conventional wisdom among the later Greek authors was that the perpetrators were a people known as 'Dorians', who derived from the north-western hills – but many researchers have their doubts. Most are more inclined to blame the continuing endemic warfare which had taken hold since the Trojan War and this is supported by the fact that the destructions were localised. It could well be that returnees from the

Egyptian campaign against Ramesses had a hand in the matter. They were by that time desperate people and totally outside the standard conventions which most citizens may have felt obliged to maintain. The date is about right, probably some time in the 1020s BC.

In the history books, the final destruction of the great palaces sees the onset of the 'Dark Ages', and this is fair enough in the sense that we have no records and so the period is dark to our eyes. But it was not particularly dark for those who lived through it! Athens was still a thriving city and Ramesses III records trade in metal (perhaps chromite) with Attica, the region around Athens. Many of the Greek cities of western Turkey were being founded, places like Smyrna, Phocaea and Ephesus. The cities already existed but this is the period during which the Greeks took full control. However, one important political change had certainly taken place; whereas in Homer's picture of the Greeks during the Trojan War there is a definite 'great king' with overall authority over the Greek nation, and this is supported by continual reference in Hittite documents to the king of Ahhiyawa (Achaea), the situation following the final destruction of the Mycenae palace was one of numerous independent city states. Just as the Hittite empire had disintegrated into its component parts, so had Greece. The so-called Dorian invasion must surely have a grounding in truth,[10] but it seems unfair to blame the Dorians for the collapse of Mycenaean authority; like the Kaskans in Turkey, they simply moved in and picked up some of the pieces.

And what of Troy itself, the epicentre of the chaos which had gone on to engulf the whole eastern Mediterranean? The city was rebuilt and Troy VIIa was a sturdy enough town inhabited by people who used a certain amount of Mycenaean IIIc-style pottery. Gone was the wealth of Troy VI, largely built on trade, but life would have been quite bearable for those who remained behind.

The Syrian, Lebanese and Palestinian Coasts

The upheaval caused by the 'Peoples of the Sea' led directly to the birth of a new civilisation, the civilisation we know as 'Phoenician' which, archaeologically, can be said to be a blend of Aegean and Canaanite cultures. When the Peoples of the Sea and their armies were driven back north by Ramesses III, some would certainly have been admitted by the principalities of Tyre, Sidon, Byblos and some of the smaller ports of Amurru – after all, in manageable numbers these people were useful economically – and the cultural blend which this created would turn out to be a particularly potent one.

So, though our records are zero, that is just accident of archaeology. The coastal cities right down the eastern end of the Mediterranean were doing very nicely thankyou, and they were developing their own particular hybrid civilisation. The indigenous Canaanite element was the stronger, which means that the language and religion remained the Semitic language and cultic religion of the region, but the benefits of Greek technology and Greek enterprise were not lost. These city states would go on to become leading lights in trade and commerce for many hundreds of years.

Right at the northern end of this coastal region, although it is not quite on the coast itself, lies Alalakh. The final phase of the city after the casting-off of Hittite authority was relatively long, judging by the amount of housing construction and re-flooring of the temple. It was not a wealthy time, it has even been de-scribed as a decadent time, but it was a time in which vast amounts of Myce-naean IIIc pottery were used, which puts the city squarely in the cultural orbit of the Peoples of the Sea. The ethnic mix of the population must have been a heady brew of Aegean, Luwian and Hurrian. However, this experiment in cross-cul-tural interaction came to a violent end when the city was destroyed some time towards the end of the 11th Century BC. The perpetrators may well have been from one of the Hittite states (probably Aleppo) as part of a pro-active defence against possible further aggression by the Peoples of the Sea. Whoever it was did a thorough job and the city was thereafter only sparsely inhabited, little more than a village. A latest possible date is given by the finding of a scarab with Ramesses VI's cartouche on it in a burial which took place after the destruction of the city. Ramesses VI would reign early in the 10th Century BC.

To the south, in Palestine, the extent of Egyptian control is far from clear. Ramesses III still kept Egyptian forces at the strategic strongholds of Megiddo and Bethshan but there is little indication as to how much authority he had over the rest of the country. There is only one record of an Egyptian campaign in the region and that was against the land south and east of the Dead Sea, the land which the Bible knows as 'Edom', and this certainly implies a degree of con-trol over southern Palestine; Egyptian influence further north was probably much weaker.

The Aramaeans

As the great powers suffered so Aram thrived. I have mentioned the semi-no-madic Aramaeans in passing already and they are now beginning to play a major role in the affairs of several states, so it is worth checking in on them again. One of the Amarna letters, dating from around 1200BC, mentions the land of 'Ahlamu' although the text is in very poor condition so we know nothing more than that the same letter refers to the king of Babylon. Ahlamu also appears as a land conquered by Shalmaneser I of Assyria (in about 1100BC) and Tukulti Nin-urta I is reported to have conquered Mari, Hana, Rapiqum (all on the middle Eu-phrates) and "the mountains of Ahlamu". Basically, we have enough sightings to know that Ahlamu meant the region around Tadmor, the city which would be-come known as 'Palmyra' in Greek and Roman times, south-west of the Eu-phrates river, the same region which we now find referred to as 'Aram'.

To be honest, we have little idea what the Aramaeans were up to during this particular period. The archaeology of Qatna suggests Aramaean occupation from the early 11th Century BC, which means they must have wrested it from the Hittites. They may also have been responsible for the destruction of Emar, about 50 miles east of Aleppo. What we do know is that they would shortly be active on a much wider front, so it is a fair bet that, records or no records, they were already moving in on the settled lands of Syria and Iraq. Tellingly, an Egyptian text dated to Ramesses III refers to Damascus by its Aramaean name 'Damasek', implying that the Aramaeans were now in charge of that city too.

The End of an Era in Iraq

But it wasn't the Aramaeans who put an end to Kassite Babylon. Kassite kings had sat on the throne of Babylon since the mid 14th Century BC, a period of well over 300 years, with just a 9-year interruption following Tukulti Ninurta's conquest in 1071BC. And during the reign of Adad Shuma Usur it must have seemed that things were almost back to normal. Peace had broken out with Assyria (we hear of Assyrian merchants operating in Babylon), Elam was also in a relatively friendly mood and the Aramaeans were not yet a serious threat, just a disruptive nuisance. Babylon again ruled the whole of southern Iraq and sea-borne trade across the Persian Gulf was taking place once more.

But in reality the land was dangerously weak, having suffered dreadfully during the Assyrian wars and also from the effects of Elamite raids and conquests. If Babylon was ever to regain her former greatness it would take many decades of rebuilding. Fortunately for Babylon, Assyria was herself in a weakened condition after her many wars and also due to a crisis brought about by the murder, in about 1044BC, of Tukulti Ninurta by one of his own sons. In fact, Assyria is now entering a very confused period for which the various versions of the king list do not agree as to reign lengths. Some researchers even suggest that the country was divided. This deduction is based on a letter from Adad Shuma Usur of Babylon addressed to "Ashur Nirari and Ili Hadda, kings of Assyria". Ashur Nirari III we know well enough from the king lists as the second ruler after Tukulti Ninurta; the identity of Ili Hadda is a complete mystery. But the letter certainly implies that Assyria was no longer in the hands of a single personality. So, while the long and nearly invisible reign of king Ashur Dan I of Assyria probably began in about 1029BC (following two of the three versions of the king list[11]), we cannot be at all sure that he was in sole charge of the country. There is no suggestion that there was any civil strife, but Adad Shuma Usur's intriguing letter warns of the possibility that Assyrian kingship may have been shared;[12] if so, it must have been with an even more anonymous personality than Ashur Dan!

But despite the reduced threat from Assyria, in 1007BC (accepting the reign lengths in the *Babylonian king list*) the death knell rang for Babylon and its king,

Marduk Apla Iddina I. As had been the case for the glorious 3rd Dynasty of Ur nearly 800 years previously, the fatal blow was delivered by an Elamite army, this time under one of their most successful rulers Shutruk Nahhunte; 350 years of Kassite rule came to an abrupt end as Shutruk Nahhunte captured Babylon and installed his son Kutir Nahhunte as governor. In fact, Shutruk Nahhunte conquered the whole of Babylonia and imposed a large tribute on the land, enforced by regular military action, and because he was such an avid 'collector' of antiquities we can have a fair idea of the extent of his conquests. For example, he 'liberated' a statue of Manishtushu and a stela of Naram Sin, dating from a thousand years earlier, from the ancient city of Sippar north of Babylon. As ever, the Elamites were not particularly interested in promoting the welfare of their conquered subjects but rather tended to bring what they could back to Susa or one of the other Elamite cities, which of course means that this was a very difficult time indeed for the population of Babylonia, and it ensured that the Elamites got a very bad press in later years. The only ray of sunshine on the horizon for the hard-pressed citizens of southern and central Iraq as a new millennium dawned (not that they knew that of course!) was that the city of Isin had rebelled against the Elamites and was now a centre of resistance, albeit not as yet a very successful resistance.

Egyptian Authority Ebbs Away

Babylon has fallen; Assyria is enfeebled; the Hittite empire has collapsed; Greece is in turmoil; and Ramesses III was the last of the great pharaohs of New Kingdom Egypt. After his success against the Peoples of the Sea he had another assault from Libya to contend with (in 1028BC) but his reign then continued in peace and prosperity. Basically, Ramesses III was a pharaoh in charge of his country, with an international profile and who enjoyed reasonable success. True, Egypt was much less wealthy in his day than it had been when the gold mines of Nubia were producing more freely, but Nubia still remained under his control, as did parts of Palestine. He certainly failed to prevent the widespread settlement of Libyans but he kept them under some sort of control. Relatively speaking, Egypt remained a beacon of light in a world where the lights were going out at a frightening rate.

But at the close of his reign that beacon began to flicker! We have extensive records, official and otherwise, of a palace revolt which probably brought Ramesses' reign to an end and resulted in the execution of conspirators from among his closest advisers, his harem and even one of his sons. And Ramesses III really was the last powerful Egyptian pharaoh for some time. The order and approximate reign lengths of the remaining 20th Dynasty pharaohs (all called Ramesses) are pretty well attested, both from the workman's village at Deir el Medina near Thebes and from several other documents and inscriptions.

Ramesses IV, a son of Ramesses III, became king in 1007BC but he died after just 6 years in the job. He was then succeeded by a cousin (how this occurred is unclear), Ramesses V. Both kings were ambitious in their intentions but struggled to fulfil their ambitions. There is little evidence by now of any real authority in Palestine but records from the economically important turquoise mines in the Sinai desert between Egypt and Palestine can still be found. Nubia also seems to have remained firmly under Egyptian control. But the documents tell a story of continuing decline; papyri from Elephantine on the southern border tell of fraud and theft throughout the country in the days of Ramesses IV and V; texts from Deir el Medina tell of times when wages were not paid and work stopped on the royal tombs in the Valley of the Kings. A long papyrus of Ramesses V's time (the *Wilbour Papyrus*) lists the lands and taxes due over a large part of middle Egypt, but the opinion of most experts is that the main beneficiaries of the taxes would have been the priesthoods rather than the secular state. Danger does not appear imminent, but the steady decline of royal authority must have worried many in the Egyptian administration.

Summary

We are nearing a critical stage in this journey through time, and I am still about 150 years adrift of orthodoxy in most respects. For example, Ramesses III's battles against the Peoples of the Sea would conventionally be dated to about 1185BC rather than the date of 1031BC which I have suggested here. However, I will soon be entering times for which dates are genuinely known. I will soon have to account for my missing 150 years. Can such a vast discrepancy really be accommodated?

Whether it can or not, I am leaving the Middle East in a rather sorry state as I move from the 2nd to the 1st Millennium BC. The problem is that where there used to be four or five great powers, making for a stable world where trade could thrive, we now have a myriad of smaller kingdoms jostling for position. Greece has exploded into numerous small city states, including newly founded Greek cities on the Turkish mainland. There are now several small Hittite states rather than one large one. Assyria and Egypt have been severely weakened; Babylon has been overrun. This has meant that lesser powers such as the Kaskans, Armenians, Aramaeans, Philistines, Israelites, Libyans and Elamites have been able to take advantage. The Middle East has suddenly become a much more complex place than it was just 50 years previously, and much of the cause can be traced back to a single war, the Trojan War, and thence to a single event, the kidnapping of Helen of Troy from her home city of Sparta in Greece. No historian would credit the story with much truth – but that doesn't mean it's actually untrue; mankind has been known to fight over much less important matters! That single event, leading to the disastrous Trojan War, has produced a thorough destabilising of the region,

	Egypt	Palestine		Syria		Turkey	Iraq	
		Philistia	Israel	Carchemish		Hatti	Assyria	Babylon
1050BC	Amenmesse / Seti II		Samuel as priest	Damascus		Suppiluliuma II	Tukulti Ninurta I	
	19th Dynasty					Hattusas abandoned	Ashur Nadin Apli	
1040BC	Siptah / Setnakht			Kuzi Teshub			Ashur Shuma Usur	Adad Shuma Usur
						Kingdom of Tugal	Ashur Nirari III / Ili Harida	
	Libyan attack — Peoples of the Sea conquer Philistia		Canaanite cities remain under				Enil Kudurri Usur	
1030BC	Peoples of the Sea attack		Egyptian authority				Ninurta Apla Ekur	
	Libyan attack	Egyptian authority restored	Saul	Neo-Hitite rule			Dual kingship (see Chapter 18)	Meli Shipak
	Ramesses III		Saul defeats the Philistines					Kassite Dynasty
1020BC				Aramaean conquest			Shalmaneser I	
	20th Dynasty						Ashur Dan I	
							Adad Nirari IV	Marduk Apla Iddina I
1010BC								
	Ramesses IV	Battle of Mt Gilboa					Ashur Rabi II	Elamite conquest
		David						Elamite
1000BC	Ramesses V	David conquers Jerusalem						rule

destroying trade networks and thereby strangling the economic life out of the whole Middle East. The consequence of economic downturn has been military weakness and this has now led to the demise of both Hatti and Babylon and a tremendous reduction in power for both Assyria and Egypt. What next?

What does the Bible have to say?

According to the Bible, as Egyptian control in Palestine weakened so Israelite power expanded. In 1050BC, the Israelite lands were disorganised and weak, relying on the spiritual leadership of the prophet Samuel, although security improved significantly following a series of Israelite victories over the Philistines (1 Samuel 7:7-14), bringing to an end some 40 years of Philistine (and Sherden) dominance. But the people wanted more; they wanted a king and the apparatus of state which all the surrounding peoples had. We have no figure for the length of Samuel's time in office and only a corrupted text (1 Samuel 13:1) indicating a reign length for Saul, the man Samuel eventually anointed as king, but I suggest the year in which the first kingdom of Israel was born was actually 1038BC, coinciding with the end of Abdon's term as 'judge' if the dates given in the last chapter were correct.[13]

Saul

Saul's kingship began with a dramatic victory over the Ammonites, Israel's eastern neighbours (1 Samuel 11:1-11), but much of the history of Saul's reign reported in the Bible concerns conflict with the Philistines. In particular, we read of two further remarkable victories. The first (1 Samuel 14:1-46) happened when Saul's son Jonathan was a young man, which suggests a date some 10-15 years into his reign, say 1025BC. The

Philistines had recently suffered defeat by Ramesses III and they were now once more loyal Egyptian vassals, Ramesses' 'enforcers' in Palestine. They were confident of their superiority over Israel and had every reason to be. They controlled the metal industry in the region (1 Samuel 13:19-22) and by that means they controlled what Israel could and could not do. Nevertheless, if the Bible is to be believed Saul and his son Jonathan scored a resounding victory, driving the Philistines back to their coastal cities. This was followed a few years later by the most famous of all the battles against the Philistines (1 Samuel 17), in which David, then just a teenager, managed to slay the Philistine champion Goliath[14] using just a slingshot.

Years of simmering hostility followed between the two peoples, sometimes erupting into minor battles, but the status quo seems to have been maintained throughout Saul's time as king, which means during the reign of Ramesses III of Egypt.

Then came a seemingly decisive battle. Perhaps the Egyptian administration had become fed up with the Israelite problem and had decided to tackle it once and for all. The Bible tells us (1 Samuel 28:1-4) that the Philistines marched north to Shunem in the plain of Esdraelon, near to the Egyptian strongholds of Megiddo and Bethshan. Saul gathered his army to resist this move and the battle (1 Samuel 31) took place on Mount Gilboa, overlooking the Esdraelon plain. It was a complete victory for the Philistines. Saul and Jonathan were killed and their bodies hung on the walls of Bethshan. The date was 1007BC[15] and it seemed that Egypt and her allies had finally put paid to the Israelite problem.

David

David had been out of favour with Saul for years, which meant that the Philistines saw him as a useful ally, so they had given him a small territory in southern Palestine to look after (1 Samuel 27). In fact, as Saul was being defeated in the north, David was away chasing an Amalekite war party which had raided his territory and carried off his womenfolk (1 Samuel 30)! In the power vacuum which followed Saul's death the fledgling state of Israel became factionalised between the tribe of Judah, who turned to David as their leader, and the tribe of Benjamin, who took Saul's remaining son, Ishbosheth (2 Samuel 2-4). After about 3 years of civil war it was David who won, taking charge of a shattered land, firmly under Philistine domination (2 Samuel 5:1-5; 1 Chronicles 11:1-3). The date was 1004BC. Ramesses III of Egypt had recently died and Egyptian power was very much on the wane.

In his 7th year (1001BC) David conquered the Canaanite stronghold of Jerusalem and made it his capital (2 Samuel 5:6-10; 1 Chronicles 11:4-9). The archaeology of Jerusalem has never been easy because, like Aleppo and Damascus, it has been under continuous occupation. The back-fill to a great terrace system on the slopes to the site includes Mycenaean IIIa pottery, which dates it to around 1200BC, long before David's time. However, the terrace system was then repaired and extended several times during the Iron Ia and

Iron II periods and this structure may therefore plausibly be identified with the so-called 'Millo' described in the Bible (2 Samuel 5:9; 1 Chronicles 11:8) and attributed there to king David.[16]

So, while Egypt faltered, Israel now had a new and vigorous leader. The Philistines and their Egyptian friends had a new and vigorous enemy to contend with. Jerusalem has fallen, but Megiddo and Bethshan are still in Egyptian hands, and the Philistine cities, together with the Canaanite city of Gezer, are still intact.

What was going on in the Rest of the World?

One of the most remarkable legacies of this particular period of history in the Mediterranean stems from the scattering of the Peoples of the Sea. The strange-looking names of these people recorded in Egyptian texts now appear in all sorts of places. In Sicily, a people known as the 'Sikels' were recorded by the Greek colonists of the 8th Century BC, a people whose culture descends from that known to archaeologists as 'Pantalican'. Pantalican culture originated in the late Mycenaean IIIb period – we know because of the numerous Mycenaean artefacts recovered from Sicily – which means just about the time of the war between the Peoples of the Sea and Merneptah's Egypt. The closeness between the names 'Sikel' and 'Shekelesh' positively invites the suggestion, made by most re-searchers, that the two are in fact the same and that some at least of the displaced people known as the Shekelesh found a new home on Sicily.

Then there are the Sherden. The Sherden were one of the first of the dis-placed peoples, making a nuisance of themselves since the time of Tudhalya I's wars in western Turkey, and then accepted as part of the Egyptian army, based mainly in southern coastal Palestine. But many observe that the name 'Sardinia' looks very like the word 'Sherden'. In Sardinia, as in Sicily, there is plenty of Mycenaean evidence from the IIIb period. But there is also the evidence that someone brought in a bronze technology very similar to that in use on Cyprus. Nothing is provable but, once again, majority opinion seems to favour the view that some of the Sherden did indeed set up home on Sardinia.

Finally and most dramatically, there is the phenomenon of Etruscan civilisa-tion in Italy. Ancient tradition is strongly of the view that the Etruscans arrived in Italy from western Turkey and this is supported by archaeology in that Etr-uscan culture is clearly a mixture of indigenous Italian and so-called 'Oriental' cultures. It arose shortly before 1000BC – that is as close as archaeology can get – and it was a very advanced culture, easily a match for the Greeks. Then we have the language evidence. The Etruscans were highly literate and, helpfully, they adopted the Canaanite/Phoenician script but, unfortunately for us, we don't yet understand their language! There are large numbers of inscriptions and texts, some of them bilingual inscriptions in both Greek and Etruscan, so we know enough to realise that the language isn't Indo-European. But one quite remarkable finding is that a text from the island of Lesbos, just off the Turkish coast south of Troy, almost exactly parallels certain Etruscan texts; we can't read either of them with any confidence but we can say that the two are very similar languages indeed. The evidence seems hard to refute. The Etruscans were immigrants into Italy from western Turkey and they arrived in the 11th Century BC, just after the time of Merneptah's defeat of the Peoples of the Sea. My view is that the Etruscans were undoubtedly the 'Teresh' and that they were Trojans. Their first settlements were right along the western coast of Italy and it was only later that they consolidated their position as a specifically north Italian power. Coincidentally, the Indo-European-speaking Latin people had also just started to arrive in Italy from the north-east, spreading down the eastern side of the country. The stage was set for one of history's most dramatic power struggles; the Etruscans started as clear favourites but the Latins would be the winners in the end.

17

Chaos and Darkness Reign: 1000–950BC

The Dying Days of New Kingdom Egypt

As the 20th Dynasty drags on so our sources of information become ever scarcer – and Manetho isn't much help; he simply reports "12 kings for 135 years".[1] We have a few papyri, some building inscriptions and, most usefully of all, texts from Deir el Medina, the town of the tomb-builders. It isn't as much as we would like but it is enough to be reasonably sure of the reign lengths of these kings, plus or minus a year here or there.

Ramesses V	– 997BC
Ramesses VI	997 – 989BC
Ramesses VII	989 – 981BC
Ramesses VIII	981 – 978BC
Ramesses IX	978 – 960BC
Ramesses X	960 – 957BC
Ramesses XI	957 –

A problem throughout this period was lack of continuity. Ramesses V died young – of smallpox apparently – and was followed by Ramesses VI, another son of Ramesses III, who was already an old man. His son Ramesses VII also died young and so yet another of Ramesses III's sons took over, though he too was old and wouldn't last long. It was only with the accession of Ramesses IX, whose connection to the family is unclear, that things could begin to settle down.

In terms of influence abroad, there doesn't seem to have been much! The last references to the turquoise mines of the Sinai come in the reign of Ramesses VI; similarly the last significant evidence from the Palestinian cities, although Ramesses IX's cartouche was found on a scarab in Gezer. Nubia seems to have remained under Egyptian control until the reign of Ramesses X according to inscriptions.

These were uncertain times. At Deir el Medina there are increasing references to unrest and to the unwelcome presence of foreigners, specifically Libyans, in the Thebes region. The tomb of Ramesses VI was broken into by robbers and subsequently resealed in Ramesses IX's 9th year and, in his 16th year, a group of tomb robbers was put on trial at Thebes, several different papyri recording aspects of the story.[2] The increasing power of the Amun priesthood also becomes graphically evident during the reign of Ramesses IX from the fact that high priest Amenhotep had himself depicted of equal size to the pharaoh on one of the walls at Karnak in the king's 10th year. This innocuous seeming act would have been unthinkable in earlier times, given the strict conventions of official Egyptian art. Ramesses IX himself was probably based mainly at Heliopolis in the Nile delta, where many of his building works are to be found, so he may have been rather out of touch with matters in Thebes and Karnak. Nevertheless, evidence of his construction activities has been found from the Nile delta to Nubia, which tells us that his authority was acknowledged right across the country.

However, after Ramesses IX's death (960BC by my reckoning) all certainty evaporates. Almost nothing is known from Ramesses X's reign, presumed to be only 3 years long because of the lack of any inscription with higher date. All we really know is that he occupied his tomb! But even this is more than can be said for Ramesses XI. His existence is betrayed by a handful of debatable texts and a part-finished tomb in the Valley of the Kings which he never occupied; he is referred to by others, pictured on temple walls, but we really have little idea what he actually did! I will return to Egypt in a while, but first let's peer through the gathering gloom at the other lands of the Middle East.

Palestine slips out of Egyptian control

The complete lack of texts from Palestine (other than the Bible) means that we are thrown back on archaeology – but this tells us that a major change was afoot. Megiddo and Bethshan were both important Canaanite cities and had long been key Egyptian strongholds, and Level VII at Megiddo displays these Egyptian connections in the form of an ivory pen case of Ramesses III and a statue base of Ramesses VI. But both cities were violently destroyed by someone some time during or shortly after the reign of Ramesses VI. The subsequent Level VI city at Megiddo is divided into two phases, each lasting some 30 years. The first phase

(VIb) is relatively unimposing, whereas the Level VIa city includes plenty of new construction and was clearly a major centre. The culture is still largely Canaanite except that Iron I pottery typical of the central highlands (collared rim storage jars etc) appears alongside the Canaanite remains. Highland style buildings are also evident.[3] A similar occupation pattern can be seen at Hazor, and at Kinneret near the Sea of Galilee, the latter also including an Egyptian 20th Dynasty type seal. It is also possible to correlate these cities with the Philistine pottery sequence. After the expulsion of the Peoples of the Sea in 1028BC, monochrome 'Philistine ware' soon replaces Mycenaean IIIc. This only lasts for a couple of decades, which means that the next phase, bichrome ware, commenced in around 1010BC,[4] and bichrome ware is found in Megiddo VIb, tending toward a more degenerated phase of bichrome ware in Megiddo VIa.

So what does all this mean? Firstly, Egypt had clearly lost its Palestinian dominions by the end of Ramesses VI's reign, 989BC. Secondly, someone was powerful enough to destroy Megiddo and Bethshan, two of the strongest cities in Palestine. Thirdly, highland culture, usually associated with the Israelites, is now found in the lowland cities. Fourthly, the second phase of Megiddo VI indicates significant power and prosperity. It very much looks as though the Israelites have seen a significant upturn in their fortunes. Approximate dates would be 990BC for the conquest of Megiddo and 960BC for the start of the major construction phase. Incidentally, a recent set of fifteen C14 dates for Megiddo VIa averaged out at 970BC,[5] which fits reasonably here but is disturbing to some.[6] This period should theoretically mark the point where C14 dates become more trustworthy as the upwelling of stagnant (low C14) water in the eastern Mediterranean was by then drawing to a halt.

The Phoenician Coast

North of the Israelite and Philistine lands lived the Phoenicians. They were a literate people – but unfortunately they didn't use their literacy very widely. This was an early phase of Phoenician culture, a period when the cities of the coast were regaining their strength after the migrations of the Peoples of the Sea. The seas themselves were undoubtedly still swarming with pirates. For Greeks, piracy was to become a respectable profession and it would have been rife throughout the Aegean. However, Phoenician influence was certainly being felt out in the Mediterranean. The Greeks had abandoned their Linear B script, which was not well suited to their language anyway, and at some stage they adopted the Phoenician alphabet, the forerunner of our own. So did the Etruscans of Italy. These facts alone lead one to deduce that Phoenician ships were already plying their trade across the Mediterranean. It wouldn't be too long before they would think in terms of colonies overseas.

Cyprus

On Cyprus, archaeology sends out a very clear signal. While the Phoenician civilisation of the Syrian and Lebanese coasts grew out of a happy blend of Aegean and Semitic cultures, that same blend on Cyprus produced an explosive cocktail! The prosperous Mycenaean IIIc period on Cyprus was brutally extinguished not too far into the new millennium; almost all the cities on the island were destroyed and abandoned and there was massive depopulation. After a while new cities were founded, but there was a very clear cultural break and, even where a city was rebuilt over the ruins of its predecessor, it was often built to a completely new plan. One has to suspect warfare on a devastating scale, and the most likely cause is civil war between Aegean and Semitic elements of the population, between the north and south of the island. The Greeks (with other Peoples of the Sea) were in charge during the Mycenaean IIIc period yet, when light finally shines once more in the form of historical records, we find the Semitic speakers in charge. Clearly something caused the change and it is a fair bet that plenty of violence was involved!

Greece

Far to the west, Greece has now entered the depth of the 'Dark Age' with no records and little sign from archaeology that the country is anything more than a series of small states. The pottery style known as proto-Geometric, a development of Mycenaean IIIc, now appears and the fact that a similar style also appears on Cyprus demonstrates that even in these dark days there was a certain amount of trade,[7] perhaps carried on Phoenician ships. But overall this was an age of poverty or, at best, hard graft. It was, presumably, also the time during which the Dorians started to settle in numbers, arriving in Greece from the north-west.[8] The former times were not forgotten however, and the epic tales of the Trojan War and the journey of Odysseus would have grown in the telling as they were sung out in halls across the length and breadth of Greece.

Troy

The archaeology of Troy is interesting here. The rather plain but well-built city comprising Level VIIa was burnt to the ground less than 100 years after the end of the Trojan War, perhaps around 970BC, and the succeeding culture included elements which were clearly foreign and, apparently, of Balkan origin. The inference is that peoples were moving into Turkey from the west, peoples who were at a lower technological level, and the obvious suspects are the people we know as Phrygians.

Phrygia

I have mentioned the Phrygians in passing already. According to Homer they fought with Troy against the Greeks and at some stage during this period they must have completed their resettlement in Turkey (from Bulgaria), more or less in what was once the Seha river land. Their capital, Gordium, had once been a Hittite city or at least its archaeology mirrored that of Hattusas and the Hittite lands.

Lydia

To the south of Troy, the Lydians had their capital at Sardis, from where many believe the Sherden once fled. We have no record of the language of the Sherden, but we know that the Lydians spoke a close relative of Luwian, the language which had become the *lingua franca* of the Hittite world. They were therefore not a new people to Turkey; in effect they were stay-at-home Sherden. The earliest Lydian kingdom was probably founded in the 10th Century BC.[9]

The Hittite Lands

Lydia may have grown out of one corner of the Hittite world, but its language was already distinctly different from that of the other Hittite states, where Luwian speech dominated. We have a few Luwian hieroglyphic inscriptions from these times but not many. We know that the grandsons of Kuzi Teshub of Carchemish, self-styled great king of the Hittites back in about 1040BC, now ruled in Malatya. The south-central Turkish region known as Tubal, which had been ruled by Hartapu following the loss of Hattusas and the old heartland cities, must still have been in existence since we find it again in later centuries, but the complete lack of records means that it is impossible to say more than this, and Assyrian texts (see below) tell us that the Kaskans still controlled the region around Hattusas. Meanwhile, the kingdoms of Carchemish, Aleppo, Hamath, Cilicia and other smaller Hittite states were apparently prosperous; we have a name for the king of Carchemish, king Sukis I, and a reference to the existence of a 'great king', perhaps someone other than the king of Carchemish himself. But, whether there was any overall Hittite leader or not, it is apparent that the Hittite lands still formed a significant power-block during these dark days.

The Years of Elamite Terror

Babylonia, however, was not weathering the years of chaos at all well! Babylon was in Elamite hands, and Elamite records and inscriptions recovered from Susa tell of numerous victories over the various Iraqi cities. These are supported by later Babylonian texts, which imply that Elamite policy, so far as it existed, was to keep the land under a regime of terror. Yet this is the period that saw the greatest flowering of Elamite civilisation during all their long history. Numerous records have been found in the ruins of Susa, the Elamite capital, from the reigns of

Shutruk Nahhunte, Kutir Nahhunte and Shilhak Inshushinak, spanning a period of some 60 years during which Elam flourished. They controlled Babylonia for around 40 years, although how much of this was actual government and how much was raiding and pillage is unclear – but it is certain that no city in southern Iraq could defeat them. There are also records of Elamite raids north into Assyrian territory during Ashur Dan I's long and not particularly glorious time in office.

The principal independent Babylonian city was now Isin, and we have a king list which names rulers right through from the time of the Elamite conquest in around 1007BC (according to the last chapter). Isin had suffered as much as any from Elamite oppression; in fact the third king of the so-called 2nd Dynasty of Isin, Ninurta Nadin Shumi, was captured and dragged off to Elam. However, matters changed markedly for the better under the next ruler, king Nebuchadnezzar I (not to be confused with his better-known namesake, Nebuchadnezzar II, responsible for the destruction of Jerusalem in 586BC). In his early years Nebuchadnezzar did all he could not to antagonise the Elamites and was clearly subservient to them, particularly after suffering a serious military defeat. But in the end it was Nebuchadnezzar who had the last laugh. He took the risky decision to take the war to Elam, opting for the bold strategy of marching his army through the summer heat to the Elamite capital Susa, where he fought the 'battle of the Ulai canal' and defeated the Elamites once and for all. The year was 967BC. Nebuchadnezzar had thus, at a stroke, liberated the region and he duly took over as king of Babylon and undisputed master of Akkad and Sumer. Unfortunately, it seems that this was the highpoint of his career and the economy continued to suffer the effects of Aramaean incursions, but at least the Elamite problem had been dealt with.

The Long March of the Assyrians

Assuming we can trust the reign lengths in the *Assyrian king list*, the long-lived Ashur Dan I of Assyria had died in about 983BC, replaced by Ashur Resha Ishi.[10] Records are still very sparse, from which it seems fair to assume that Assyria was still weak and unable to challenge Elam's position as ruler of southern Iraq. However, when Tiglath Pileser I ascended the Assyrian throne in approximately 965BC things changed dramatically. Nebuchadnezzar of Isin had recently taken care of the Elamite threat and this meant that Tiglath Pileser felt secure enough to embark on one of those conquest sprees which ancient rulers seem to have enjoyed so much. He gathered his not inconsiderable army around him and headed off into the unknown.

Fortunately, since he was quite successful in his enterprises, Tiglath Pileser left us a reasonably full, though hard to interpret, record of his achievements at his capital city of Ashur. The records are thought to relate to campaigns during the first five or six years of his reign (965-960BC) during which he conquered in several directions. First, numerous battles are recorded in the region of the old

Hurrian heartland around the upper reaches of the river Tigris. Tiglath Pileser then claims that he was attacked by Kaskans (also called "tribes of Hatti") whilst undertaking his noble work of expanding the kingdom, and the location must have been somewhere on the upper Euphrates. Next we find him campaigning to the east of Ashur, conquering 'Khirikhi'[11] in the Zagros Mountains of Iran, before setting his sights once more to the north. He and his army ventured far into the depths of eastern Turkey, defeating the 'Nairi' kings (23 in number – probably Armenian[12]), reached the Black Sea[13] and returned via the Hittite city of Malatya. Having subdued lands to the north and east, he next headed south, to the "country of the Aramaeans" where he reports that he pursued the enemy across the Euphrates and destroyed six of their cities. Most ambitiously of all, he tells us of his conquest of the lands of 'Muzri' and 'Comani', from where he brought back a selection of two-humped camels, indigenous to Central Asia! He had clearly reached Azerbaijan or the Caspian Sea region of Iran.[14] Everywhere he went he demanded and received tribute.

The military annals continue with further lists of unknown kings and lands but conclude with the statement that the whole land from "beyond the river Zab (east of the Tigris) to beyond the river Euphrates, the country of Hatti and lands to the Black Sea" had been brought under his government. The frequent use of the word *Hatti* and the mention of Kaskans and Aramaeans place these annals very clearly in a time after the occupation of the Hittite heartland by the Kaskans, a time of fragmented Hittite city states, and a time when the Aramaeans were encroaching east of the Euphrates. The contrast between the world of Tiglath Pileser I and that of his predecessor Tukulti Ninurta I is stark.

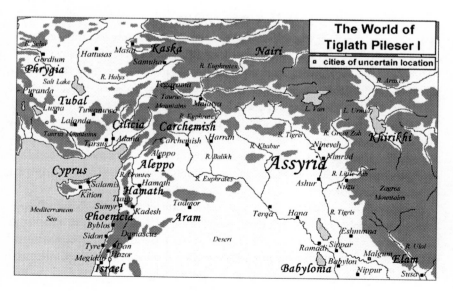

Gone is the extensive network of international trade between great powers; there were no 'great kings' standing in Tiglath Pileser's way, simply a record of numerous petty kings ruling small territories. It is as if Tiglath Pileser is setting off to explore unknown regions, regions which a century earlier would have been very well known indeed. The flow of information across the Middle East had simply ground to a halt since the collapse of the Hittite Empire and the problems which had also beset all the other great nations over the same period. The only character who seems to have been accorded a status equal to that of the Assyrian king was the pharaoh of Egypt, then Ramesses IX, from whom, so we read, Tiglath Pileser received the unusual gift of a crocodile. All in all, we have to be most grateful to Tiglath Pileser and his army for affording us this rare view of a difficult age for the historian!

Aram

At least Tiglath Pileser's annals give us independent witness that Aram existed! We also have reports that the countryside of Babylonia was being seriously ravaged by Aramaean invaders. Tiglath Pileser says that he defeated Aram "as far as Carchemish, belonging to Hatti", which tells us that the Aramaeans were right on the Hittite frontier in the north-west, presumably in possession of Emar and Qatna. As I noted in the previous chapter, they had also taken over the southern Syrian city of Damascus.

The Priests take charge in Egypt

And so back to Egypt: it is 960BC; the New Kingdom is fading fast; this is the phase of Egyptian history known as the 'Third Intermediate Period'. Ramesses IX of the 20th Dynasty, who had recently donated a crocodile to Tiglath Pileser's botanical collection, is on his deathbed, and we now make the acquaintance of a man who will be a key player in the drama which marks the start of the appallingly convoluted 21st Dynasty, namely the high priest Herihor. Herihor followed in his predecessor Amenhotep's footsteps (indeed, on the basis of the titles given to Herihor's wife Nodjme, many suggest that he was Amenhotep's son-in-law) by depicting himself liberally on walls and columns of the temple of Chons at Karnak pretty much interchangeably with the pharaoh, at that time Ramesses XI. He is even shown wearing the ultimate symbols of power, the uraeus, a sort of decorative snake worn on the forehead of pharaohs, and the double crown of Upper and Lower Egypt. In these temple inscriptions his name is written in a cartouche in the manner of a pharaoh and he also awarded himself a so-called 'Horus' name, a prerogative of pharaohs. Herihor clearly considered himself at least the equal of the pharaoh, but the question here is: exactly when did he hold high office?

In point of fact there are two possibilities – and this is where it gets a bit complicated. In Herihor's time a new system of dating events was introduced (presumably by Herihor himself) termed 'Repetition of Births', the exact meaning of which is not at all clear. What is clear however is that those who had used the expression previously (Amenemes I and Seti I) had inaugurated new eras of Egyptian history and it seems Herihor considered he was doing likewise. Anyway, we have a document, *Papyrus Mayer A*, which refers to "Year 1 of the Repetition of Births" and it is a document which spells out the misdeeds of certain tomb robbers. We also have another document, *Papyrus Abbott*, which mentions exactly the same tomb robbers but which is dated to "Year 1, corresponding to Year 19", and the question is: whose reign does the "Year 19" refer to? Only three 20th Dynasty kings are eligible for consideration, Ramesses III, IX and XI. Ramesses III is clearly not a serious candidate – he had the high priests under some sort of control – but the other two are both possible. Although Ramesses IX is generally assigned an 18-year reign, it is quite possible that he survived into his 19th year.[15] The conventional answer, however, is Ramesses XI, justified by the fact that the officers who presided over the trial of the tomb robbers in *papyri Mayer A and Abbott* are quite different from those presiding in Ramesses IX's 16th year, at the trial of earlier robbers. Nevertheless, I am proposing here that the pharaoh in question was actually Ramesses IX, possibly at that time already dead, and I have the following principal reasons:

i) The inauguration of the period known as the Repetition of Births implies a dramatic new start. A change of pharaoh would be the least one might expect, yet Year 19 of Ramesses XI does not appear to be in any way special.

ii) There was an event termed the "war of the high priest", referred to in a document known as the *Testimony of Hartenufe*, which speaks of the "suppression" of the high priest Amenhotep for 9 months, as well as the overrunning of Thebes by "barbarians". This war seems likely to have ended with Herihor's accession as high priest and the start of the 'Repetition of Births' period and, since we only hear of high priest Amenhotep during the reign of Ramesses IX, then Year 19 of Ramesses IX looks the more plausible date.

iii) The death of the pharaoh, a barbarian occupation lasting several months, a new regime in the office of high priest – these are reasons enough for the total change of personnel at the second set of tomb robber trials.

The identity of these barbarian occupiers can be guessed from *Papyrus Mayer A*, which speaks of an invasion by "Pinhasi" from the province of Nubia, still nominally a dependency of Egypt.[16] We know Pinhasi came from Nubia – he had a tomb prepared there – and Egyptologists suspect that he was the Egyptian governor of the province.[17] It seems that, probably late in Ramesses IX's 18th year, all hell broke loose. As the king lay dying, probably at his palace in Heliopolis in the Nile delta, there was some sort of coup; Pinhasi invaded, the high priest Amenhotep was imprisoned, and there was war. After some months Herihor re-conquered Thebes, and Pinhasi and his rebels were driven back south into Nubia. These events were sufficient for Herihor to declare a new age and to usher in his 'Repetition of Births'. The date was 960 or 959BC – according to this dating scheme.

The pharaoh during the first three years of the Repetition of Births period was Ramesses X, then followed by Ramesses XI, and it would have been early in Ramesses XI's reign that Herihor had himself depicted as the equal of the pharaoh on the walls of the temple of Chons, since by Year 7 of the Repetition of Births the high priest named in an item of correspondence was Piankh.[18] Herihor's insubordinate attitude to Ramesses' authority was continued by Piankh who remarks in one of his letters: "as for pharaoh, how shall he reach this land; who still serves pharaoh?" We begin to get a very clear picture from these odd clues that the high priests were more or less running the show now and that they had little respect for Ramesses XI. Piankh, whose relationship with Herihor is unknown,[19] disappears from the scene in Year 9 of the Repetition of Births, 951BC, to be followed by his son Pinudjem I.

Manetho's 21st Dynasty

Though Herihor, Piankh and Pinudjem were very powerful men, undoubtedly more powerful than pharaoh Ramesses XI himself, they do not appear in any of Manetho's dynasties. To find those he did mention we must travel north down the Nile and fortunately history gives us the ideal travelling companion. The *Tale of Wenamun*, envoy of the high priest Herihor, is a powerful piece of evidence as well as giving a graphic illustration of Egypt's low standing in the world at this time. Let me paraphrase it for you. Wenamun was charged with purchasing some high quality timber, cedars from Lebanon, for the royal barque of Amun at Karnak. He duly set off (in Year 5 of the Repetition of Births – about 955BC) and travelled downstream to the city of Tanis in the Nile delta, where he was received by a character by the name of 'Nesbanebded', who seems to have been Herihor's opposite number in northern Egypt.[20] Nesbanebded duly provided a suitable ship and provisions and sent Wenamun on his way to Byblos in Lebanon. The tale is worth a read. I am particularly struck by Wenamun's religious attitude, that the world is ordered and governed by Amun and Amun alone, to the extent that Zakarbaal, king of Byblos, should have been grateful for the opportunity of serving the great god of the universe! Zakarbaal was a little less than grateful however and insisted on hard cash, which was a problem since Wenamun had been robbed on the way when he called in at the Palestinian port of Dor! The papyrus as we have it is not complete, but we know that Wenamun received his timber (and Zakarbaal his cash) and that he then fled to Cyprus under the threat of pirates.[21] You have to assume Wenamun made it home somehow otherwise we wouldn't have the story, but we are left wondering how.

This evidence is important because linguists have worked out that the Egyptian name 'Nesbanebded' is actually one and the same as 'Smendes', the first of seven kings listed by Manetho in his 21st Dynasty.[22] Smendes, then, was in office at Tanis at the same time that Herihor was high priest in Upper Egypt, and also at the same time that Ramesses XI was nominal head of state. In fact the *Tale of Wenamun* speaks of "the other great ones of Egypt", which is usually taken to be a veiled reference to Ramesses and his court.[23] But the question is: did Smendes already consider himself to be a pharaoh? We have just one inscription of Smendes; it is at a quarry site and records his commissioning of stone cutting for the repair of one of the temples of Karnak which had suffered flood damage. In it he has all the titles of a pharaoh but, significantly, his seat of power is given as Memphis rather than Tanis. You see, since the days of Ramesses II the capital of northern Egypt had been Piramesse, built on the site of the former Hyksos capital Avaris, but a major shift in the course of the Pelusiac branch of the Nile is blamed for causing the abandonment of the city around this time. Smendes is the man credited with constructing the new northern capital of Tanis, about 20 miles north of Piramesse,[24] and Tanis was obviously in use in 955BC when Wenamun arrived. The quarry inscription, titles and all, was therefore probably created earlier – which means that yes, Smendes did indeed already consider himself a pharaoh in 955BC. Manetho gives 26 years for Smendes, but of course we now have absolutely no idea from which year he counted his 'reign'. My guess, and it's just a guess, is that he had originally been appointed vizier of Lower Egypt under Ramesses IX, but we simply have no information on the subject.

Summary

I have spent some time on the details of Egyptian history for two reasons. Firstly, there isn't much information from anywhere else! Secondly, as I said right at the outset, the dating of Egyptian history has always been absolutely crucial to assigning dates to the rest of the Middle East. And if I am right in my deductions about Herihor and Smendes then I am at last beginning to eat into my 150 year problem.

As far as the Middle East scene goes, the picture is one of fragmentation and strife. Egypt appears to be sinking ever deeper into a paralysis similar to that when Akhenaten was on the throne and the Aten cult was flavour of the month; it is so bad that the country even finds it hard to buy timber from the small Phoenician city state of Byblos. Greece, Turkey and Syria are now a patchwork quilt of small states, with Hittite kingdoms forming a relatively powerful economic block stretching from Carchemish to the Konya plain in south-central

Turkey. To the east, the Assyrians have once more taken to conquering, although one has to suspect that such distant conquests cannot possibly be sustained. If I was a minor Armenian king, I wouldn't be expecting to see another Assyrian army for many a long year!

Southern Iraq is just beginning to recover from four decades of Elamite rule, a rule which seems to have been more of an organised plundering session than anything else. Nebuchadnezzar I has regained the throne of Babylon and his immediate successor now rules the whole of southern Iraq once more. But there is trouble to the west. Aramaean raiders have become increasingly bold, crossing the Euphrates and striking deep into both Babylonia and Assyria. Damascus has been under Aramaean control for the past several decades.

In Palestine, now free of Egyptian control, the Israelites appear to be playing an ever increasing role, while the coastal cities are still in the hands of the Philistines or, in the case of Dor, the Tjekker. To the north, the Lebanese and Syrian coast is the scene of an increasingly confident Phoenician civilisation, and Phoenician ships are heading out across the Mediterranean, trading with the Greek cities and, probably, lands further to the west also.

As a footnote, Cyprus appears to have self-destructed on a massive scale, probably due to civil war between two culturally quite different elements of the population.

What does the Bible have to say?

The Bible supplies much missing information concerning these times. From outside sources and archaeology we know that the Egyptians lost control of Palestine in about 990BC and

	Egypt	Palestine	Syria	Turkey	Iraq
		Philistia Israel	Damascus Carchemish	Assyria	Babylon Isin
1000BC	Ramesses V	Canaanite cities under Egyptian authority		Dual kingship (see Chapter 18)	
	Ramesses VI	David		Ashur Dan I	Marduk Kabit Ahheshu
990BC	Ramesses VII	under Israelite authority	Egypt abandons Canaan Hadadezer	Ashur Rabi II	Elamite rule
		David defeats Aramaeans		Phrygian kingdom in west	Itti Marduk Balatu
980BC	Ramesses VIII		Aramaean rule Neo-Hittite rule	Kaskians in the north	Ninurta Nadin Shumi
	20th Dynasty		Suks I	Neo-Hittite kingdom of	Ashur Resha Ishi
970BC	Memphis/Tanis Ramesses IX			Tubal in south	Nebuchadnezzar I
	Smendes (vizier)	Solomon			
960BC	Thebes War of the high priest Ramesses X Herihor Smendes I		Assyrian campaigns in Turkey and Syria		Nebuchadnezzar I
	Ramesses XI	Temple completed		Tiglath Pileser I	
	Piankh Smendes I Voyage of Wenamun to Byblos	Rezon			
950BC	Pinudjem I 21st Dynasty				Enlil Nadin Apli

229

that someone was then able to conquer the strongholds of Megiddo and Bethshan. Turning to the Bible, we learn that king David is on the throne and that he has the land firmly under his control. Two victories over the Philistines are recorded (2 Samuel 5:17-25), probably some time in the 990s and he is then reported to have waged war against Aramaean forces (2 Samuel 8:3-12). His main enemy is Hadadezer of 'Aram Zobah', who has command of Damascus. Indeed, Zobah may be derived from Aba, the name used for Damascus by the Egyptians. And, of course, this is exactly as it should be. We know that the Aramaeans have been spreading out from their homeland in the east and already have evidence that they have taken Damascus; the Bible adds confirmation to what would otherwise be mere surmise. David's campaigns also involve Tou king of Hamath, an enemy of Hadadezer and therefore an ally of David. Hamath was the centre of an important Hittite-ruled kingdom; the Bible supplies the name of one of its kings.

The Bible does not specifically record the taking of Megiddo or Bethshan, although David could hardly have fought his campaigns against Aram without having control of these important cities. And once Solomon became king in around 968BC, we read that both Megiddo and Bethshan were in his hands. He is specifically reported to have built up Megiddo as one of his store cities (1 Kings 9:15) and the relatively impressive architecture of Megiddo VIa supports this. What is of considerable interest is the degree to which the culture of the city is still Canaanite. Clearly Solomon ruled over a mixed society.

Solomon's reign also brings us a highly satisfying tie-up between Egypt and Israel. Solomon is reported to have married a daughter of the Egyptian pharaoh – name unstated – and it is further recorded that the Egyptian king attacked and destroyed the Canaanite city of Gezer, donating it to Solomon as a wedding present (1 Kings 9:16). With the dates above, the pharaoh concerned could only have been Ramesses IX, and it so happens that a rare example of this pharaoh's name outside Egypt was on a scarab discovered in the ruins of the city of Gezer. Coincidence? I might add that even those sceptics who have taken the view that it would have been inconceivable for an Egyptian pharaoh to marry his daughter to a foreigner would have to concede that the times of Ramesses IX were hardly days when Egypt could afford to be too haughty. Solomon, the most powerful ruler in the Palestine/Syria region at the time, would have been a most desirable ally, particularly since Ramesses had his hands full with problems closer to home.

The claims made for Solomon's empire are one reason why historians sometimes hold the Bible in low regard. According to the Bible Solomon ruled not only over Palestine but also over swathes of Lebanon and as far north as the territory of Hamath in southern Syria (2 Chronicles 8:3). He is even said to have built in Tadmor, in the heart of Aramaean territory (1 Kings 9:18; 2 Chronicles 8:4). In the context of the story told in the Bible this is perfectly logical however, since David had thoroughly subdued the Aramaeans. Israel may well have been granted rights to build and also to station troops both in Aramaean territory and in the Hittite kingdom of Hamath; we have absolutely no hard information from either Hittite or Aramaean sources. However, archaeology tells us that this was a period of peace and prosperity for the Philistine cities (for example Ashdod XI, paralleling Megiddo VIa) with no need for defensive fortifications, suggesting that they were now at peace with Israel and therefore, if not actually part of Solomon's empire, strongly allied to it.[25]

What was going on in the Rest of the World?

Let me take you somewhere quite different now. I guess you are well aware that the civilisations of Central and South America lagged behind those of the rest of the world, but by 950BC there were serious signs of high culture. In South America, intensive agriculture using irrigation had been the norm in northern Peru for about 1000 years and it had spread gradually south along the near-desert coastal strip, making use of water from the rivers flowing down from the Andes. The settled life which this allowed had meant that there was time and energy for things other than farming which, in human society the world over, means that rulers started ruling and organising themselves, and religions started to assume an importance beyond the immediate matter of a relationship between individuals and God! In Peru, this development of the trappings of human civilisation can be seen in the monumental architecture and temple mounds, not to mention the appallingly gruesome art (dismembered bodies etc) of the time. With no writing we of course know nothing of political structure, but you can be quite sure that kings ruled in Peru as surely as they ruled throughout the Middle East; you can be equally sure that they made war in the time-honoured human fashion.

Inland, on the high altiplano of the Andes Mountains, around the great lake of Titicaca, farming had also been practised, although using a quite different technique, for several hundred years, and by 950BC the first efforts at copper smelting had proved successful. In this respect South America was about 3500 years behind parts of Europe and the Middle East.

Moving far to the north, the large settlement of Poverty Point, Louisiana, in the southern United States, was near the end of 500 years of successful life, representing a remarkably impressive culture considering the almost total lack of farming at that time in North America.

But it is perhaps the Olmec people of Central America who are the New World's most advanced citizens in 950BC. Olmec culture can be found right across central Mexico. It was a culture which produced cities such as La Venta on the Gulf coast of Mexico, as well as a not unpleasing form of art, much more pleasant than that in vogue in Peru at the time. It also produced one of the wonders of the ancient American world, a set of magnificent carved stone heads, some weighing many tons. But the most culturally significant achievement of the Olmecs was to develop a system of writing which would go on to form the basis of Mayan and Mixtec glyphs in later times. By 950BC Olmec culture was at its height (although writing was yet to develop) and was spawning other spin-off cultures such as that of Monte Alban in the south-east corner of Mexico, Kaminaljugu (now Guatemala City) and the Mayan cities of Tikal and Nakbé. The Olmecs may have lacked the metal technology of Lake Titicaca but in other respects they were not so very far behind the Old World civilisations of Europe, the Middle East, India and China.

18

Judgement Day: 950–900BC

The day of reckoning has finally come! In just a few years' time, in 911BC, Adad Nirari II will be crowned king of Assyria and history will start to become genuinely known. There is no way to avoid the issue; the requirement to tie in with this date – and with all those dates in other lands which have been deduced from it – is an absolute one. This chapter should therefore settle the dating issue once and for all. Let me remind you how the evidence stacks up so far.

The case for the defence of the traditional chronology of the Middle East was initially based on the *Ebers* and *El Lahun papyri*, with support from C14 dating and a tree ring date. In the case of the *Ebers* and *El Lahun papyri*, however, it was first noted that the wrong great Sothic year length had been used (1461 years instead of 1507) and then that Egyptologists now no longer seem to trust the original interpretation of the texts. In the case of C14 dating, reason was given to believe that low C14 water in the eastern Mediterranean was leading to a significant error in dates for all surrounding lands from the 5th Millennium BC to the end of the 2nd Millennium BC. Finally, the tree ring date, for timbers from a wreck in the Mediterranean, has been found to be at best unproven and, in my opinion at least, utterly without foundation. Not a particularly impressive-looking start!

More embarrassing still for the defence team, one of its original star witnesses, the *Ebers Papyrus*, has now been called to support the prosecution! Sothic dating has also provided firm date ranges for the reigns of pharaohs Djer (1st Dynasty), Sobekhotep VIII (13th Dynasty) and Merneptah (19th Dynasty), all of which support the prosecution's case, namely that 3rd and 2nd Millennium BC history needs a downward shift of about 150 years. And this evidence has been supplemented by astronomical retro-calculation relating to two solar eclipses, two lunar eclipses and a set of month length data. On paper, the weight of evidence looks impressive.

But now comes the sternest test. Traditional chronology inserts some 150 years at this point, a view underpinned by Manetho's list of Egyptian pharaohs, the *Assyrian king list* and, to a lesser extent, by a *Babylonian king list*. This could go either way!

The Assyrian Dark Age

Following Tiglath Pileser I's recorded campaigns (965-960BC according to the last chapter) information is scarce. An inscription fragment lets us know that he defeated Babylon at some point during the reign of Nebuchadnezzar I's brother and second successor Marduk Nadin Ahhe, retaliating after a Babylonian raid into Assyrian territory. It is also clear that Aramaeans still represented a real problem in Iraq and that they were raiding into Assyria itself. More serious still, there was a severe famine towards the end of Tiglath Pileser's long reign (39 years according to the *Assyrian king list*), perhaps caused in part by the Aramaean incursions. In Babylon the famine was even worse – we read of cannibalism![1]

The *Assyrian king list* then tells us that Tiglath Pileser's son Asharid Apal Ekur only outlived his father by two years, to be replaced (in 925BC in this chronology) by his brother Ashur Bel Kala. We read that Ashur Bel Kala fought campaigns against Aramaean settlers, who were now pitching their tents deep inside Assyrian territory, and of a meeting with the Babylonian king Marduk Shapik Zeri.

And that's it; for the next nine kings on the *Assyrian king list* we have just a few inscriptions, no external reference and no discernible archaeology! The dates for Ashur Bel Kala in this chronology are 925 to 907BC; the 7th Century BC Assyrian document known as the *Synchronistic History* jumps clean over the next nine kings, straight from Ashur Bel Kala to king Adad Nirari II, crowned in 911BC, the man who revived Assyrian fortunes by clearing Aramaean settlers from the Tigris valley.

So what about the nine missing kings? And how can I explain a 4-year overlap between Ashur Bel Kala and Adad Nirari II? Well; perhaps the letter I quoted a couple of chapters ago from Adad Shuma Usur king of Babylon to two different kings of Assyria, apparently ruling simultaneously, holds a clue. I am also struck by the fact that the names 'Ashur Resha Ishi' and 'Tiglath Pileser' occur twice in sequence in this part of the *Assyrian king list*. Oddly, the second Tiglath Pileser, grandfather to Adad Nirari II, is referred to by his descendants as a mighty monarch – yet we know nothing of him!

May I put forward what I believe to be a logical solution to these conundrums? It is that the dual kingship evident from Adad Shuma Usur's letter of about 1040BC actually continued throughout the time of Ashur Dan I and also into the reign of Ashur Resha Ishi, and that Ashur Dan's co-rulers were Shalmaneser II, Ashur Nirari IV and Ashur Rabi II, three of the most obscure names on the king list.[2] Ashur Rabi, given 41 years, is not even attested at Ashur at all, only in the west of the country. The king list names Ashur Rabi's successor as Ashur Resha Ishi and I suggest this signifies a return to single ruler status during the last 5 years of Ashur Resha Ishi's life, 970 to 965BC.[3] Unified rule continued through the successful reign of Tiglath Pileser until his 32nd year, 933BC, the year of the appalling famine that also brought the rule of Marduk Nadin Ahhe of Babylon to an end. In this year and probably in response to the crisis, Tiglath Pileser appointed his eldest son Ashur Dan II as co-ruler, reinstating the system of dual kingship. This is why the king list gives just 32 years for the character Assyriologists refer to as Tiglath Pileser II, the father of Ashur Dan II, but 39 years for Tiglath Pileser I. I suggest that the two Tiglath Pilesers are one. When Tiglath Pileser himself died, in 927BC, his second son Asharid Apla Ekur became Ashur Dan's co-ruler, replaced after his early death by Ashur Bel Kala. We know of Ashur Dan from inscriptions recording his construction activities and economic policies because that was his role in the dual kingship; we know of Ashur Bel Kala because his role was to fight off the Aramaeans.[4]

If this explanation of the Assyrian riddle is correct, then dual kingship continued through the reign of Adad Nirari II, son of Ashur Dan II. His almost invisible co-rulers would have been Ashur Bel Kala's son Eribu Adad II, for 1 or 2 years, followed for 3 or 4 years by the last of Tiglath Pileser's sons, Shamsi Adad IV, and then Shamsi Adad's son (and Adad Nirari's cousin) Ashurnasirpal I. The only signs of the existence of these characters are building inscriptions and, in the case of Ashurnasirpal, three prayers to the goddess Ishtar about the troubled times he was living through, understandable since Aramaeans still filled much of the land. Here is my suggested list of Assyrian rulers for this period.

Tiglath Pileser I/II	– 927BC		
Ashur Dan II	933 – 911BC	Asharid Apla Ekur	927 – 925BC
		Ashur Bel Kala	925 – 907BC
Adad Nirari I	911 –	Eribu Adad II	907 – 905BC
		Shamsi Adad IV	905 – 901BC
		Ashurnasirpal I	901 –

The evidence has been circumstantial – that is undeniable. The fact that the *Synchronistic History* jumps from Ashur Bel Kala to Adad Nirari II doesn't prove anything on its own; nor does Adad Shuma Usur's letter; nor Adad Nirari's grandfather's reputation; nor the sparse evidence for the missing kings. Even the fact that the compiler of the *Assyrian king list* 'has form' for inserting extra kings into his list – and for making up non-existent father-son relationships – none of these things prove the case.[5] But they all contribute to my finding that, on the balance of probability, the traditional chronology is wrong and that this shortened version is right! You will have to make up your own mind of course.

The Phantom Rulers of Babylon

The history of Babylon under the rulers of the 2nd Dynasty of Isin is tied by inscriptional evidence to that of Assyria. Marduk Nadin Ahhe was the king who suffered defeat by Tiglath Pileser; Marduk Shapik Zeri was the ruler who travelled to Ashur to meet with the Assyrian king Ashur Bel Kala; and the next king on the *Babylonian king list*, Adad Apla Iddina, is named as an Aramaean usurper. He seized power in about 920BC according to this version of history. In his time it is recorded that an Aramaean-related people known as the Sutu plundered Sippar near Babylon.

But that is as far as we can go. The three remaining kings listed under the 2nd Dynasty of Isin are completely unknown. The *Babylonian king list* then gives a '2nd Sealand Dynasty' (containing 3 kings), a 'Dynasty of Bazi' (3 kings), an 'Elamite Dynasty' (1 king) and the so-called 'Dynasty E' – the cryptic identification given by the compiler of the king list. In all the histories written about Babylon that I have come across, this period, which is said to have lasted well over 100 years, is covered in a line or two, basically to admit that we have absolutely no idea what was happening! The first king for whom we have any corroborative evidence at all is Nabu Mukin Apli, the first king listed in Dynasty E, in whose time it is recorded that the New Year festival of Marduk, involving public processions of the god's statue, could not take place for nine successive years because security was so bad due to heavily-armed Aramaean settlers – exactly the same conditions as those applying under Adad Apla Iddina, supposedly more than 100 years previously. Possible? Yes. Likely? No!

The lack of contemporary evidence throws serious doubt on whether the last few kings of the 2nd Dynasty of Isin actually ruled Babylon at all. We also know that the 'House of Bazi' were high officials during the Isin period, plausibly accounting for the 'Dynasty of Bazi' in the king list. And the king list document concerned (*King list A*) has already listed about 350 years worth of kings from a 1st Sealand Dynasty, almost all of whom are known to have reigned in parallel with other dynasties (the Amorite and Kassite dynasties), so there is every reason to suspect that the same thing applies to the 2nd Sealand Dynasty. Finally, the single king of the Elamite Dynasty may signify no more than a period of Elamite control over the east of the country. If we were to rely on real contemporary evidence, then we would have no hesitation in placing Nabu Mukin Apli of Dynasty E not many years after Adad Apla Iddina of the 2nd Isin Dynasty. The chronology of Babylon would certainly be easier to understand if the poor security induced by Aramaean raids in Nabu Mukin Apli's reign followed directly from the marauding Aramaeans and Sutu raids of Adad Apla Iddina's reign. In contrast, the conventional chronology for both Babylon and Assyria implies a dark age of incomparable obscurity to the extent that one wonders how such skills as writing Akkadian and Sumerian came to be carried through it! I know which interpretation I find the more plausible.

Elam bows out

The Elamite king list tells us of two further kings following Hutulutush In-shushinak, defeated by Nebuchadnezzar in about 967BC. Despite the lack of contemporary evidence, both were famed in later times as great rulers, particularly the second, Humban Nimena, and it may be that the 'Elamite Dynasty' in the *Babylonian king list* reflects his authority in eastern Babylonia.

But Humban Nimena's reign only takes us to around 920 or 910BC, and the lack of subsequent information either from contemporary inscriptions or later histories tells its own story. Other than records of Assyrian raids, we hear nothing more from Elam until the reign of Humban Tahrah in about 760BC. Even at 150 years, this is an uncomfortably long 'dark age'; under the conventional chronology, it becomes a deeply disturbing 300 years.

The Kingdoms of the Hittites

The archaeology of Carchemish shows continuing prosperity and clear continuance of Hittite culture in art, architecture and religion throughout this period, however long it was – and you might note that I am comparing the situation immediately prior to the retreat from Hattusas to a time that archaeologists universally allocate to the late 10th Century BC. The Hittite kings of 900BC presided over a culture very similar to that of the last emperor Suppiluliuma II. Some of the last artwork from Hittite empire days is found at the site of Yazilikaya, just a short walk from Hattusas and an important ceremonial centre. It shows a procession of Hittite gods in distinctive garb and it has been noted by many that exactly the same gods turn up in 10th and 9th Century art from Carchemish, prompting the strong feeling that not too many decades have passed; the extra 150 years imposed by conventional chronology looks highly implausible. It is just unfortunate for us that the Hittites of this period wrote so little about their activities or, if they did write, the records have not been preserved.

The Mediterranean Lands

The evidence against the conventional chronology, circumstantial though it is, is stacking up uncomfortably, and the evidence from Phoenicia does nothing to alter this. The Phoenicians were another reticent people when it came to historical records, a trait which persisted throughout their history. However, archaeology tells us of suspiciously little change (for example in Canaanite writing style) between the time of king Ahiram, a contemporary of Ramesses II, and the 10th/9th Century BC Byblos kings Abibaal and Elibaal.[6]

The late 10th Century BC saw a steady increase in Phoenician trade. It was probably also the period during which the Phoenicians started to exert authority in Cyprus, eventually bringing order to the absolute chaos which had engulfed the island over the previous few decades, a chaos which has to be extended to an uncomfortable 200 years according to conventional thinking!

In Greece itself, excavations at Lefkandi on the large island of Euboia have revealed a degree of prosperity during this period, which makes sense since Euboia will turn out to be one of the earliest centres of classical Greek civilisation. Euboian proto-Geometric pottery from this approximate phase has been found as far afield as the Palestinian city of Dor. And there is a clear line of descent from Mycenaean IIIc pottery through proto-Geometric to 9th/8th Century BC Geometric designs. According to the timescale in this book, proto-Geometric designs have a life of just over a century; under conventional thinking, the time gap which proto-Geometric is being asked to plug seems quite unbelievably large. Overall, therefore, the archaeology of Phoenicia, Cyprus and Greece tells a consistent story – and it isn't the story currently told in the history books!

The Palestinian Story

Palestine has the potential to be another key witness. At Megiddo, the 60 years or so which experts usually assign to Level VI come to an end in about 930BC (according to the dates in the last chapter) with yet another terrific destruction. The remains of the next level, Vb, were largely obliterated by rebuilding in the Va/IVb period, but such evidence as there is shows a sharp decline in the material culture; the pottery types are now predominantly those associated with the Israelites during what is known as the Iron IIa period. Gezer likewise suffered a significant decline in its fortunes at about the same time. There is ongoing debate over C14 evidence,[7] but the view that the Megiddo Va/IVb structures date to the early 9th Century BC, the time of kings Omri and Ahab, is now very widely held – which means that a continuous archaeological record at Megiddo appears to take us from the days of Ramesses VI (Level VII) to those of king Omri (Level Va/IVb) within about a century. There is absolutely no room at all for the extra 150 years demanded by conventional thinking unless a period of abandonment is allowed – and I can detect no reported evidence for this.

On the evidence so far, therefore, the case in defence of the traditional chronology of the Middle East looks decidedly thin. Not only have several absolute dates been produced which contradict it, but archaeology also strongly supports a considerably reduced timescale during the confused years conventionally known as the 'dark ages'. Even the king lists from Assyria and Babylon have proved fickle friends, giving plenty of reason to doubt their conventional interpretation. But the cornerstone of the defence's case has always been Egypt. I still have a whole dynasty to account for, the 21st, before the first king of the 22nd Dynasty, Shoshenq I, who is usually thought to have come to the throne in 945BC! It's easy to see why the arguments of archaeologists have been ignored in the face of such a persuasive witness.

The Reign of Amun

If I interpreted things correctly in the last chapter, the year 950BC saw Egypt theoretically under the rule of the last 20th Dynasty king, Ramesses XI, then in his 7th or 8th year, but actually in the hands of high priest Pinudjem in Thebes and Smendes, the first king named in Manetho's 21st Dynasty, in the delta city of Tanis. According to Manetho, Smendes was followed by Psusennes I, who reigned for either 41 or 46 years depending on which version is believed, and then by five other much shorter-reigning pharaohs, Nephercheres, Amenemophthis, Osochor, Psinaches and Psusennes II. Turning to documentary and inscriptional evidence, we find plenty of reference to the activities of an "Akheperre Psusennes", including dates as late as his 48th year, and almost all experts agree that he was Manetho's Psusennes I – but there is precious little evidence for his five successors, nor for Smendes for that matter.

Psusennes I was much the most visible figure among the 21st Dynasty rulers. His building activities are evident at Tanis; his tomb, containing his body, richly encased in a set of coffins 'borrowed' from earlier Egyptian rulers, was found at Tanis in the 1930's.[8] And experts are pretty certain that he was the eldest son of Pinudjem, high priest of Amun in Thebes.[9] Oddly, Psusennes I is himself also named as 'high priest of Amun' in many of his inscriptions, and I suggest the most likely interpretation of this is that Pinudjem appointed him as his representative in the north shortly after he (Pinudjem) stepped into Piankh's shoes in Thebes, i.e. in around 951BC. Although Smendes was still secular ruler of northern Egypt (technically vizier under Ramesses XI, but in his own and Manetho's eyes a genuine pharaoh), Pinudjem had thus ensured that the priests of Amun (i.e. his family!) had an increasingly firm grip on the whole land.

So far so good; if these deductions are correct, Psusennes I started his reign (initially as high priest) in Ramesses XI's 7th year. However, the next of Manetho's rulers, Nephercheres, presents real problems. His name (Amenemnisu Nepherkare) appears on a well-known list recording the high priests of the god Ptah, recovered from Memphis. The pharaoh of the day is noted against some of the priests' names and Nephercheres is listed only two names after the last of four appearances of Ramesses II. Admittedly the limestone slab upon which the list is recorded is broken and it is possible to argue that two or even three further names should be inserted[10] – but even as the fifth name after Ramesses II the gap is still a short one. With Ramesses II dying in 1063BC, the fifth high priest of Ptah after this is unlikely to be more than about 125 years later (938BC), allowing 25 years each. To complicate matters further, evidence has been put forward for periods of parallel rule between Psusennes I and both Nephercheres and Manetho's next ruler, Amenemophthis![11]

Let me cut a long story short. The Ptah priest list evidence points firmly to Nephercheres having been appointed co-ruler with Psusennes I quite early in his reign. My guess is that when Smendes died (I estimate 943BC) Psusennes needed a replacement to look after the day-to-day management of northern Egypt (another glorified vizier in fact) and Nephercheres was the man chosen for the job. Nephercheres himself then died in 939BC (if Manetho's 4 years are correct), so Psusennes needed yet another co-ruler. However, we now have a problem. There is real evidence that the next king on Manetho's list, Amenemophthis, actually co-ruled much later in Psusennes I's reign,[12] which suggests that Manetho's order may need revising and that Nephercheres may actually have been followed by Osochor, a man for whom we have no direct evidence at all! Never mind; if true, and accepting Manetho's 6 years, Osochor would himself have died in about 933BC, bringing another unknown, Psinaches, to the 'throne', followed in about 924BC by Psusennes II. Finally, after Psusennes II's death in around 911BC, we should logically insert the 9-year reign of Amenemophthis. Whether I am right to have messed around with Manetho's reign order is open to question, but the key point is that this view of the evidence has all five of these rulers, as well as Smendes, reigning in parallel with Psusennes I, the high priest in Tanis and very much the senior figure in northern Egypt.[13] In their roles, they were all in effect viziers, despite their adoption of royal titles.

Meanwhile, in Year 16 of Ramesses XI, 941BC, Pinudjem had also followed the trend and admitted himself to the ranks of royalty,[14] relinquishing the post of high priest of Amun in Thebes to his second son Masaharta and then, when Masaharta died a few years later, to a third son, Menkheperre.[15] Pinudjem continued to act as pharaoh in Thebes until his death in around 926BC,[16] despite the fact that Ramesses XI may also have been alive somewhere in the country until about 930BC.[17] Menkheperre then had a long spell as high priest (and effectively ruler of Upper Egypt) and his relationship with his elder brother Psusennes I was clearly a friendly one; bricks have been found at El Hiba in middle Egypt bearing both their names. He died about a year before Psusennes,[18] in around 903BC.

This interpretation of the data appears logical. It matches the available evidence (the Ptah priest list, evidence for co-rule, the year dates found on the monuments) and it explains why all but one of Manetho's 21st Dynasty are so invisible to us today; they may have been pharaohs in name, but in their actual jobs they were viziers under the authority of Psusennes I, while southern Egypt was ruled first by Pinudjem and then by Menkheperre. The last defence of conventional chronological thinking looks to be crumbling!

A New Dynasty is Born

When Amenemophthis died in about 903BC, the long-lived priest-king Psusennes I looked around for his seventh co-ruler. His choice was a man named Shoshenq. There is strong evidence linking Shoshenq with Amenemophthis' predecessor Psusennes II; we have the record of an official who was promoted first under Psusennes II and then under Shoshenq, a statue dedicated by Shoshenq to Psusennes II, and we also know that Shoshenq's son Osorkon married Psusennes II's daughter Maatkare. And the accession of Shoshenq I, named as the first king of Manetho's 22nd Dynasty, marks the fact that a momentous change had occurred in Egyptian society over the course of about a century. He was a Libyan, a chief of the Meshwesh, descended from immigrants who fled western Turkey after the Trojan War.[19] Merneptah had succeeded in keeping them out of Egypt. Ramesses III had fought them but with rather less effect and the records from the reigns of the next several kings who bore the name Ramesses contain numerous references to Libyans settling in Egypt itself. Now, some 27 years after the death of the last Ramesses (and about 42 years later than conventionally thought!), a Libyan pharaoh was ascending the throne, albeit a throne made for a vizier rather than a genuine king.

However, the balance of power was about to shift. Psusennes I died within the year (902BC) and was buried in the tomb at Tanis he had had prepared many decades earlier, a tomb which was discovered intact and which also contained the remains of Amenemophthis, Psusennes II and an otherwise unknown army general, Wendjebaendjed. The tomb was sealed by a character called Siamun.[20] Siamun was another priest-king, whose name is found on the sarcophagi of many of the great pharaohs, signalling that he was responsible for their re-interment, and the seemingly obvious deduction is that he was Psusennes I's chosen successor as high priest of Amun at Tanis, a position which carried much greater power than that of Shoshenq I, at least initially.[21]

You might have been wondering why our records for this period are so confused. The problem is that the great northern capital of Tanis in the Nile delta is a barren wilderness today as far as textual evidence goes, with the exception of many of Ramesses II's inscriptions and of buried texts such as those found in tombs or on building foundations. The reason is that the magnificent city was built largely of limestone, a perfectly good building material and one ideally suited to the carving of walls, obelisks and stelae, but also a material of great value in later times for the production of lime. As poverty closed in on the land of the pharaohs during and after Roman times, one way to make a living was to turn limestone into lime and, rather than face the difficult and energy-sapping task of extracting the limestone from a quarry, an obvious move was to 'recycle' the useless ruins at Tanis with their peculiar signs and symbols which no-one could understand. The result: Tanis has not merely been destroyed as so many

other cities have, it has been physically consumed, leaving just the scattered granite monuments of Ramesses II which Smendes I had rescued from the former
capital of Piramesse and those underground structures which the lime-burners
couldn't find. For the historian it is a tragedy – but then life would be tedious if
we knew everything!

Summary

This has been an enormously important 50 years for a proper understanding of
ancient history. It marks the join between the chronology which I have deduced
based on a number of pieces of absolute dating evidence and the accepted
chronology of the 1st Millennium BC and, personally, I would say the join between the two chronologies has been remarkably painless. No-one can deny that
this has been a sort of 'Dark Age', and it has certainly been a time of fragmentation and of relatively small kingdoms. However, the degree of continuity of language and archaeological culture across the period strongly suggests that it was-
n't all that long. Furthermore, both the Assyrian and Babylonian king lists have,
on closer inspection, proved much less certain in their support of conventional
thinking than is often claimed.

But Egypt has always been the real sticking point. In this chapter, I hope I
have demonstrated the likelihood that the kings of Manetho's 21st Dynasty
reigned in parallel rather than in sequence, a version of Egyptian history which
you will not read outside this book (at least not at the time of writing). But the
bottom line is that the year 900BC saw Egypt at a time of transition, whether the
main protagonists realized it or not. Power was divided between the high priests
of Amun and Shoshenq, the new secular ruler of the north, and only time would
tell which way the wind would blow. And all of this now leaves me with a mere
42 years to 'explain away', although my personal view is that it is proponents of
the conventional chronology who have the explaining to do. The remaining 42
years should vanish easily enough, since they never really existed in the first
place!

Leaving the dating issue aside, the Middle East is now showing flickers of revival after a century and a half of difficulty, all sparked by the tragedy of the Trojan War. The epic tales of the *Iliad* and the *Odyssey* are still being sung out around
the camp-fires of Greece, gaining embellishments each time they are retold, tales
which will become top-grade literary classics when Homer puts pen to paper in
about 200 years time. But the actual legacy of the war has been massive disrup-
tion to international trade and therefore to development across the whole region, and this has led to a series of invasions, rebellions and civil wars, sending
civilisation on a seemingly endless downward spiral. Now however things are beginning to stabilise. The Phoenician cities are growing in prosperity, a sure sign
that trade is on the increase, and this will soon be awakening the seeds of future

	Egypt		Palestine	Syria		Turkey	Iraq	
	Thebes	Tanis	Israel	Damascus	Carchemish	Assyria		Babylon
950BC	20th Dynasty	Smendes I						Enlil Nadin Apli
940BC	Ramesses XI / Pinudjem I	Nephercheres / Osochor	Solomon	Rezon		Tiglath Pileser I		Marduk Nadin Ahhe
930BC	Psinaches / Psusennes I		Judah	Aramaean rule	Neo-Hittite rule	Phrygian kingdom in west / Dibál kingship / Neo-Hittite kingdom of Tubal in south	Severe famine in Iraq / Ashared Apal Ekur / Aramaeans settle intra	Sealand Dynasty
920BC	Shishak attacks Jerusalem / Rehoboam / 21st Dynasty	Psusennes II	Jeroboam I				Ashur Bel Kala / Adad Apla Iddina	Marduk Shapik Zeri
910BC	Menkheperre / Amenemophthis		Abijah / Nadab				Adad Nirari II / Eriba Adad II	Nabu Mukin Apli / Dynasty E
900BC	Smendes II / Pinudjem II / Siamun Shoshenq I		Asa / Baasha / Attack by Zerah the Cushite				Shamsi-Adad IV / Mar Biti Ahhe Iddina / Ashurnasirpal I	

greatness in Greece and, further west, in the Etruscan area of western Italy. Assyria is once more a strong nation, although this may not necessarily be a good thing for the health of others! The Aramaeans are still a menace and have briefly been able to take over Babylon; they have also settled in the west and rule several kingdoms, one based at Damascus. And in Palestine archaeology reveals that the Israelites are now firmly in charge.

What does the Bible have to say?

The Bible informs us that in 950BC king Solomon was at the height of his powers. His riches were immense and growing yearly as a consequence of his far-reaching trade links. He is said to have bought horses and chariots from Egypt and to have sold them on to the Hittites and the Aramaeans (1 Kings 10:28-29). He had links with various Arabian rulers, most famously with Sheba, now Yemen (1 Kings 10:1-13; 2 Chronicles 9:1-12). His close connections with the Phoenician kingdom of Tyre meant that he could call upon a sea-faring expertise and this led to trading expeditions to the completely unknown land of 'Ophir' – some say India[22] (1 Kings 9:26-28; 2 Chronicles 8:17-18). And the truth is that if there was one era in which Solomon could have reigned without leaving any evidence in the outside world, this was it. Egypt was torn between the fading power of Ramesses XI and Pinudjem I, high priest of Amun in Thebes. The Nile delta was in effect the fiefdom of Ramesses IX's former vizier Smendes. The pathetic journey of Wenamun to Byblos had recently taken place. In short, Egypt was in the grip of an appalling crisis and had no interest in what was happening beyond its borders. And to the north of Israel the kings of the Phoenicians, Hittites and Aramaeans ruled their own lands but refused to leave us any written indication of what was going on! One day we may find

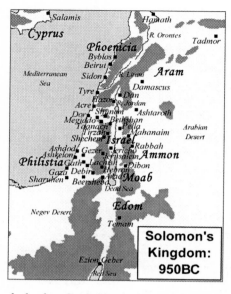

Solomon's
Kingdom:
950BC

a further Hittite archive, but that day is yet to come.

It is true that archaeology has unearthed none of Solomon's fabulous wealth – but then neither has it unearthed any of the fabulous wealth of Persepolis, the capital of the Persian Empire until it was conquered by Alexander the Great. The problem at Persepolis was that the Greeks looted the great city with a ruthless efficiency. And the problem at Jerusalem may have been similar. The Bible tells us (1 Kings 14:25-26; 2 Chronicles 12:1-9) that four or five years after Solomon's death, in around the year 925BC according to most commentators, the Egyptian pharaoh 'Shishak' invaded the by then divided land of Israel, attacked Jerusalem and carried off "everything". The treasures of the temple and the royal palace are specifically included. Solomon's son Rehoboam, who had just lost the greater part of his kingdom to his great rival Jeroboam (1 Kings 12:1-24; 2 Chronicles 10:1-11), now found his remaining realm impoverished and subservient to the awakened power of Egypt. Israel's glory days had been brief and they were now well and truly over.

The kingdom remained divided into a southern state (Judah) with its capital at Jerusalem and a northern state (taking the name Israel) with its capital first at Shechem and later at Tirzah about 5 miles to the north-east. And it was not a peaceful division. The Bible tells of almost continual low-level warfare between the two states throughout the remaining decades of the 10th Century BC.

As so often before, the most useful archaeological evidence comes from Megiddo. After the reign of Solomon the city is not mentioned in the Bible for some time, and there was good reason not to mention it! Someone had destroyed the impressive Level VIa, the city of Solomon, and it had been replaced with a much more impoverished looking city. Gone were the Canaanite elements in the population and gone too were the impressive structures of the past. Nothing is stated, but it would make sense that Megiddo was a victim of the division of the kingdom in around 929BC. Rehoboam would have inherited it as one of his major centres and, when he tried to restore his authority in the rebellious north, it would hardly have been surprising if Jeroboam and the northerners had torched Megiddo as part of their destruction of Rehoboam's power base. The rather warlike outlook of Jeroboam and the state of Israel would also explain the massive defences which the rulers of Ashdod suddenly saw fit to construct.[23]

Pharaoh Shishak

This is all very well and reasonably consistent with the evidence but for one thing: who was pharaoh Shishak? Conventional wisdom is that he was Shoshenq I – but I have just suggested that Shoshenq I didn't come to any sort of power until 903BC! Besides, you may remember that in Chapter 2 I highlighted the very major differences between the campaign of Shoshenq I described on a temple wall at Karnak and the Bible's description of Shishak's attack on Jerusalem. I am afraid I cannot possibly identify pharaoh Shishak with Shoshenq I.

There is only one possible contender according to the version of history which I have been laying out, and that is none other than the underrated Psinaches, co-ruler of northern Egypt from 933 to 924BC. I suggest that Manetho's name 'Psinaches' is almost certainly a corruption of 'Shoshenq', as 'Osochor' is a corruption of 'Osorkon' and 'Amenemophthis' is a corruption of 'Amenhotep'. The Egyptian script does not mark the vowels, so 'Shoshenq' (often written 'Sheshonq' in the literature) may actually have been pronounced 'Shishanq'. If so then the Bible's 'Shishak' is easily understandable and Manetho's 'Psinaches' becomes distinctly plausible. Those who may wish to rubbish this idea might like to ponder the fact that the academic world is currently content to equate the names 'Psinaches' and 'Siamun'!

Under Psusennes I Egypt was beginning to feel its strength once more. The last Ramesses had died in 930BC and, when Pinudjem I died in 926BC, this left his son Psusennes I with real power. The news that Solomon had died and that his kingdom was more divided than Egypt ever had been must have sent a delighted shiver down spines throughout the court at Tanis. Psusennes' response was to send his number two, Psinaches, with his general, Wendjebaendjed, on a mission to restore Egyptian authority in the land that Ramesses VI had abandoned some 70 years previously. They succeeded brilliantly and I have no doubt that their triumph was emblazoned all over the limestone walls of Tanis, walls which, of course, have since fallen victim to the lime-burners' kilns. Wendjebaendjed was rewarded with a place in Psusennes' tomb – and Psinaches may, I believe, have had a similar honour. I find the traditional explanation of the magnificent silver coffin of 'Heqakheperre Shoshenq' found in the tomb's antechamber to be rather unsatisfactory to say the least. Most suppose it to bear the body of a son of Osorkon I and grandson of Shoshenq I, which is extremely odd considering the time that would have elapsed since the deaths of the other inhabitants of the tomb. I see no fundamental reason why Heqakheperre Shoshenq should not be identified with Psinaches, despite the coffin style suggesting a rather later date to most.[24]

Zerah the Cushite

The Bible (2 Chronicles 14:9-15) reports yet another invasion of Judah, this time during the reign of Rehoboam's grandson Asa. The date is not specified but it must have been in about the year 900BC. The invader's name is given as 'Zerah the Kushite' and his army is also composed of Kushites, i.e. people from the land of Kush south of Egypt and, though it is described as "vast", the 300 chariots he brought is only a quarter of the number fielded by Shishak/Psinaches 25 years earlier. According to the Bible, Asa king of Judah managed to repel this invasion and inflict heavy losses. Unsurprisingly there is no record of such an invasion in Egypt, but this certainly doesn't mean it didn't happen! As a failure it would hardly have been plastered all over the temple walls, even if those walls hadn't since been burnt to nothing. However, a Kushitic force is certainly reasonable as a division of the Egyptian army – Shishak was also reported as having Kushites in his invasion force.

So, if the story is true it means that Egypt was beginning to look outside its borders once more. Siamun may have been a priest-king, but he is shown smiting an enemy like any other warlike king on a relief fragment found at Tanis. His scarab has also been found at Sharuhen in southern Palestine. As senior ruler of Egypt, he may well have been keen to match the achievements of his forebears, inscribed on the many monuments of Tanis. The attack by Zerah the Kushite is therefore most certainly plausible.

What was going on in the Rest of the World?

It's time to take a last look at the Indo-Europeans as they make their seemingly rather slow progress across Europe. By 900BC, as we have already seen, the Latin people had reached Italy, having brought the tradition of cremation urn burial with them from Hungary. To some extent they blended with the other new arrivals, the Etruscans from Troy; but the eastern side of the country soon became a Latin stronghold.

Further north the Celts, close kin to the Latins, now inhabited Austria and were moving into southern Germany and Switzerland. This particular phase of Celtic culture is known as Hallstatt A, the first of several phases which have become particularly well known from the site of Hallstatt near Salzburg in Austria. Neither the Celts nor the Latins seem to have been particularly warlike at this time and their slow progress across the continent is simply what one might expect due to a certain cultural advantage over the existing population, but nothing more. This is unsurprising when one considers who the existing population were. They were a people who had known 5000 years of agricultural life; they were capable metal-smiths; they built sturdy constructions and had done so since the 'long-house' period many thousands of years earlier. We don't know what languages they spoke, but I personally am confident that they were relatives of modern Basque.[25] So what cultural advantage might the Celts and Latins have possessed?

Despite the non-warlike nature of Celtic and Latin society in 900BC, the people still retained a typically Indo-European social structure, based on clans and chieftains and, whatever you think about the merits of such a structure, it seems that it enabled a more effective and cohesive society to develop than was possible under other social regimes. It meant that Indo-European groups tended to rise to prominence in a mixed society, giving them control of wealth and power. Unsurprisingly, the next generation would have tended to speak the language of the powerful even if their own parents had not, and so the language and culture spread inexorably westward across the land.

A similar story could be told (if only the evidence was greater) north of the Carpathian Mountains where the Germanic-speaking peoples were also spreading their language and culture across the north German plain. The existing population would have been of a similar type to those who stood in the path of the Celts – and the pattern of a slow change to Indo-European culture was also similar.

19

The Seeds of Revival: 900–800BC

This will be the final leg of my journey through the labyrinth of ancient Middle Eastern history and much of it will once more be spent in the land of the Nile. It is not that the story is complete by the year 800BC, but the controversy will be over. In fact, the only remaining discrepancy between the story told in this book and that more conventionally found in the history books is a 42-year mismatch at the start of the Egyptian 22nd Dynasty. However, before tackling this issue, let's take a final trip around the other lands of the Near and Middle East as they emerge from the chaos which developed in the aftermath of the Trojan War.

The Years of Assyrian Conquest

The story of 9th Century BC Assyria can be read in several excellent books from recognized experts and the only point I wish to make is that, if the deductions of the last chapter are correct, the dual kingship system ended with the death of Ashurnasirpal I in about 884BC, more or less the time that his namesake Ashurnasirpal II took charge.[1] The full list of 9th Century BC rulers is as follows.

Adad Nirari II	– 891BC	*co-ruler Ashurnasirpal I*
Tukulti Ninurta II	891 – 884BC	*co-ruler Ashurnasirpal I*
Ashurnasirpal II	884 – 859BC	
Shalmaneser III	859 – 824BC	
Shamsi Adad V	824 – 811BC	
Adad Nirari III	811 –	

Basically, this was a century of warfare and empire-building. Adad Nirari II took the first steps by clearing the Tigris valley of Aramaean intruders, defeating the forces of Babylon on two occasions, and annexing a large chunk of formerly Babylonian territory east of the Tigris. His successor Tukulti Ninurta II died young, so it was left to the impressively vicious Ashurnasirpal II to take empire-building a stage further. He really laid into the Aramaeans, massacring freely as far as the Euphrates and resettling the area with Assyrian citizens. Then, in 877BC, he went on the rampage right to the Mediterranean. During this period of their history the Assyrians' rationale for war seems to have followed the Elamite principle of 'smash and grab'; conquer, massacre, loot and return to base with the booty! When Shalmaneser took up the noble cause of enriching the treasuries of Ashur, he spent a remarkable 31 consecutive seasons campaigning north, south, east and west. He conquered north against Armenians, Hurrians, Georgians and Parthians;[2] he went south against the Chaldeans, a nomadic people who had been settling across southern Iraq; he went east and fought Medes, Persians and Elamites and he went west and won victory after victory (according to his annals) against Aramaeans, Hittites and Phoenicians. He crossed the Euphrates so many times that he must have lost count and regularly pushed west into Cilicia and even into the Hittite kingdom of Tubal in south-central Turkey. But the fact that he seems to have had to conquer the same cities and lands time after time speaks volumes for the impermanence of his conquests. Shalmaneser's reign ended in a 5-year civil war between two of his sons but, once Shamsi Adad V was in full control, the conquests continued and Babylon was almost annihilated. And the century ends with Adad Nirari III once more marching at the head of an Assyrian army, capturing Aramaean-ruled Damascus, ravaging the Hittite lands and, in the east, the lands of the Medes and Persians.

On the fringes of the Empire

Babylon was now much the weaker of the two main states of Iraq. The southern parts of the country had been lost to Chaldean tribes, the Chaldeans being yet another Semitic people from the deserts of Arabia. But it was Shamsi Adad's conquest which really did the damage. He invaded Babylonia, slaughtered the Babylonian army and pushed the country into another and even worse episode of chaos, one which historians are still trying to sort out!

Times were also becoming increasingly tough for both the Hittites and the Aramaeans. Shalmaneser's campaigns in particular must have wrecked the Hittite economy. Time and again he crossed the Amanus Mountains into the Hittite/Luwian state of Cilicia and, less frequently, across the Taurus and into Tubal. Everywhere he went he demanded and received tribute, with or without bloodshed. Malatya and Carchemish are also among the cities that submitted to him; Hamath was defeated more than once, and the inference is that the Hittite kings of Hamath were acting in concert with the Aramaean kings of Damascus (named as Rimmon Idri and then Hazael). There was some respite following the civil war of 827-823BC, but when Adad Nirari III started campaigning again in about 806BC there was clearly more trouble on the way. They didn't know it, but both Hittite and Aramaean rulers were about to enter their final century of statehood. For the Hittites, the future led to extinction; for the Aramaeans, it would lead to linguistic domination over the entire Middle East.[3] There are Aramaic-speaking communities in Syria to this day!

The Emerging Kingdoms of Turkey

Beyond the Hittite states of southern Turkey, the 9th Century BC saw the Phrygians of the west coming increasingly to the fore. We can see from archaeology that they spread east and eventually settled in much of the former Hittite heartland east of the Marrassantiya river (known to the Greeks as the river Halys), dislodging or perhaps absorbing the Kaskan tribes. Many consider that a people known as 'Mushki' in Assyrian records were actually Phrygians. They are first mentioned in the annals of Tiglath Pileser from the 10th Century BC and they reappear in the record of Ashurnasirpal's conquests as a people who paid him tribute. Whether this identification is correct or not, it is certain that a Phrygian state was in existence in the 9th Century BC with its capital at Gordion.

Another significant state, which would continue to grow in power, was 'Urartu' (the name has the same root as 'Ararat'). This was a Hurrian-controlled state, although Armenians may have made up a significant proportion of the population, and it was situated in the mountainous country of eastern Turkey.

For completeness I should also mention the Greek city states of the Aegean coast, which were growing in strength as Aegean commerce began to revive itself, and also Lydia, centred on the ancient city of Sardis.

The Phoenician Coast

The Phoenicians were not exempt from Assyrian attention; Byblos, Tyre and Sidon all paid tribute to Ashurnasirpal and to Shalmaneser III. The problem for the Phoenicians was that they were not set up to fight land wars. When trouble came they just shut themselves up in their cities, all on islands or promontories, and hoped that it would pass them by! Their strength was on the high seas. Here they reigned supreme. They were a century or more ahead of the Greeks and at sea their greatest rivals were now the Etruscans. The Phoenicians were traders. They bought and sold; sometimes they transported, sometimes they contracted out, but always they made a profit. And as they ranged ever further out across the Mediterranean, they would have had agents in many of the coastal cities and states of Greece, Italy and the islands of Sicily, Sardinia and Corsica. Cyprus they had already commandeered. We don't know what the political arrangement was on Cyprus but the culture of the island was now Phoenician – with some Greek influence. And tradition has it that the city of Carthage, 1500 miles away on the Tunisian coast, was founded in 810BC by emigrants from the Phoenician port of Tyre. The Phoenicians were taking their long-distance trade very seriously indeed.

Greece

The Greeks may have ceded control of sea trade to the Phoenicians, but Greek culture was still alive and well. Particularly on the island of Euboia and in Attica (where Athens is situated), archaeology has revealed that the economy was still active if not at a particularly wealthy level. A 9th Century BC Greek crater has been found as far away as Galilee in northern Palestine, probably carried on a Phoenician ship. Significant contact with the Phoenicians was certainly occurring, but the fact that it would be the Greeks who adopted the Phoenician way of writing tells us that it was the Phoenicians who were the dominant force. The bottom line is that Greece was still not a significant power in 800BC.

Palestine

South of the main Phoenician territory lay the Tjekker city of Dor, with the Philistine cites further south still. These continued to survive throughout the 9th Century BC – although Gath suffered a catastrophic destruction some time toward the end of the century.[4] Inland from the Philistine coast we see a considerable amount of construction work in cities throughout Palestine during the first half of the century, the Iron IIa phase. The rather poor standard of Level Vb at Megiddo, for instance, is replaced by a much more substantial building phase in Level Va/IVb. This is also the time that the hill-top site of Samaria was first occupied, with very similar structures and a very similar material culture – even identical masons' marks on the stones. The same is true of the adjacent city of Jezreel. Strong parallels are also found at Hazor, Bethshan and Beth Rehov.[5] Gezer also has a very similar form of construction to Megiddo.[6] Most historians would attribute this construction activity to king Omri of Israel, with a date around 880BC. Shalmaneser's annals then tell us of Omri's son Ahab, who contributed a considerable force to a coalition, including a small consignment from Egypt, which faced Shalmaneser in his 6th year (853BC). Israel was therefore very well aware of the danger faced by any country within striking distance of an Assyrian army. A further inscription dated to 841BC tells us that a later king of Israel, Jehu, submitted to Shalmaneser's authority and paid the required tribute.

The Egyptian 22ⁿᵈ Dynasty

And so to Egypt once more: we pick up the complex story of Egyptian history in 900BC, with power divided between three principal players. Siamum, anointed successor to the powerful priest-king Psusennes I, reigned in Tanis in Lower Egypt; in Thebes the high priest was now Pinudjem II son (or grandson) of Menkheperre, and he controlled Upper Egypt. Finally, the weakest member of the triumvirate was Shoshenq I, also based in Tanis, whose role was little more than that of vizier of Lower Egypt. These three were supposed to work as a team,[7] but human nature being what it is this was never going to be entirely straightforward! Then, in 892BC, Year 10 of Siamun and Year 11 of Shoshenq I, Pinudjem II, high priest of Amun in Thebes, died and was buried in a tomb at Deir el Bahri near Thebes. We know all about this because Pinudjem's tomb, when it was uncovered late in the 19th Century, also contained dozens of other coffins holding the mummified remains of the great and the good of Egypt, characters like Seti I and Ramesses II.[8] But a key point is that on the wrappings of one of the mummies[9] the name of the high priest of Amun is given as 'Iuput', a son of Shoshenq I. The logical inference is that Shoshenq had taken the opportunity afforded by Pinudjem II's death to impose his son Iuput on Upper Egypt (where he was made governor and commander-in-chief of the armies of the south as well as high priest of Amun!). Siamun was still Amun's senior representative on Earth but Shoshenq had thereby expanded his power base very considerably.[10] In fact, the appearance of Iuput's name in a tomb which inscriptions tell us was sealed in Siamun's 10th year is a significant piece of evidence in support of the parallel reigns which this book has suggested.

Pinudjem's death and Iuput's accession as high priest would certainly have left Shoshenq with a much strengthened hand. Nevertheless, it was only when Siamun himself died in 884BC that Shoshenq felt free to do what he had always wanted – to invade Palestine! The famous wall at Karnak detailing his Year 20 (884BC) campaign tells us that Shoshenq bypassed most of the kingdom of Judah – he must have secured the submission of the Judean king – and captured most of the major cities of Israel, including Megiddo, Taanach, Bethshan, Shechem and the capital at that time, Tirzah. In Megiddo a stela of Shonshenq's was found and, although it was not found *in situ*, notes taken at the time suggest that the spoil heap from which it was recovered had been dug from the remains of either Level Vb or else the succeeding Level Va/IVb city,[11] and I have just dated the transition from Level Vb to Level Va/IVb at Megiddo to approximately 880BC. This was a very significant conquest, and a mark of Shoshenq's standing in the wider world can be seen in the fact that a statue with his name on it has been discovered at Byblos; it had been presented to king Abibaal of Byblos.

Shoshenq I's Year 20 Campaign: 884BC

□ cities listed on Shoshenq's commemorative wall

Shoshenq died a year or so after his Palestinian campaign, his life's ambition fulfilled! It was 883BC, 41 years later than the conventionally quoted date. My discrepancy has shrunk by one year since I have chosen to believe that the 21-year reign quoted by Manetho simply means 'more than 20 years'. Be that as it may, Shoshenq's son Osorkon I quickly set about spending the money which Shoshenq had squeezed out of Israel, dedicating literally tons of gold to the various temples of Egypt – according to an inscription found in the delta city of Bubastis (Shoshenq's home city). Manetho then tells us that Osorkon I reigned for 15 years, which ties in with the lack of inscriptional evidence beyond Year 12.[12] Yet this contrasts with the conventional view among Egyptologists, which is that Manetho is quite wrong and that his reign should be extended to about 35 years. This I believe to be a mistake for the following reasons:

i) A 23-year long lack of inscriptions is highly unlikely considering the number of inscriptions found either side of this period.

ii) Osorkon I married a daughter of Psusennes II, who died over 20 years before Osorkon's coronation. The implication is that Osorkon was at least middle-aged when he became king.

iii) The 35 year reign believed by so many is obtained indirectly from the mummy of an individual named Nakhtefmut, which was found wearing a bracelet with Osorkon I's prenomen 'Sekhemkheperre' on it, and one of whose wrappings includes a *Year 33* mark. However, there is no direct tie between the bracelet and the wrapping.[13]

As far as I can see the real justification for awarding Osorkon such a long reign stems from the need to fill non-existant years and without this driving force Manetho's 15 years look to be perfectly reasonable – and 20 years of my 41-year discrepancy go up in smoke!

Unfortunately, however, Osorkon I is the last king of this period for whom Manetho gives a reign length, so we are forced back on the evidence of inscriptions, which means there is plenty of scope for uncertainty. The following list is my best estimate. The '3 unknown kings' are Manetho's words and I am not aware of hard evidence for the reign lengths of any of them (or indeed who they all were); in the cases of Takelot I and Osorkon II, I am broadly following majority opinion, although I am giving Osorkon three more years than most would. You can check the notes if you wish to know my reasoning on any of these. If these dates are approximately correct, the small Egyptian force in the coalition which faced Shalmaneser III in 853BC at the battle of Karkar on the Euphrates was sent by a young Osorkon II, keen to have a hand in international affairs.[14]

Shoshenq I	– 883BC
Osorkon I	883 – 869BC
3 unknown kings	869 – 867BC[15]
Takelot I	867 – 858BC[16]
Osorkon II	858 – 825BC[17]
Takelot II	829 – 804BC
Shoshenq III	825 –

So, with no further significant re-dating, I am still 21 years adrift of conventional thought[18] as I come to the reign of Takelot II. Now, as it happens, the solution to this 21-year mismatch, which is the 21-year period of co-rule shown between Takelot II and his son Shoshenq III, is now accepted by many Egyptologists.[19] However, it gives me an excuse to introduce a further remarkable and powerful source of evidence.

The Cult of Apis

For hundreds of years, sacred Apis bulls were buried in an underground mortuary complex known as the Serapeum, at Saqqara near Memphis. The cult of Apis may seem a little strange to us; it involved the deification of a young bull calf, which would then be looked after and worshipped until the day it died, after which it would be replaced by another calf. The dead bull would be buried in its own sarcophagus with the honour befitting a god and numerous gifts would be presented by the most important dignitaries in the land. Fortunately for us, these gifts often referred in their inscriptions to the current pharaoh and sometimes even to the year of his reign or the age of the bull at death. By linking up such inscriptions, it has been possible to deduce quite a lot about the reigns of the kings of the period and evidence from the Serapeum has been one of the main tools used by Egyptologists in reconstructing the 22nd Dynasty. In the relevant part of the Serapeum, the so-called 'Lesser Vaults', 21 bulls have been found and at least 3 more were observed by the original excavator, Auguste Mariette, but have never been recovered – numbers 10-12 in the following plan.[20] These 24+ burials covered the time from Ramesses II's reign right through to the 26th Dynasty pharaoh Psamtek.

Clearly an ornate, honorific chamber was prepared for the first burial, with a long access corridor and, thereafter, additional chambers and corridor extensions were created as necessary. When times were hard (during Ramesses XI's reign and after), multiple use was made of individual chambers. Burials 10, 11 and 12 were observed by Mariette in a chamber beneath the main level of the vaults, which is currently inaccessible due to continuous infilling by desert sands. The assignation 'Ramesses XI' simply means that his name was the only one found in the complete mess of debris which Mariette first discovered in the chamber with Burials 7, 8 and 9.

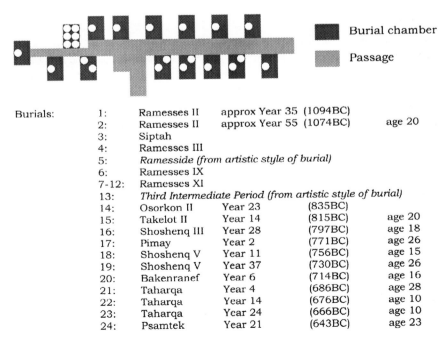

Burials:	1:	Ramesses II	approx Year 35 (1094BC)	
	2:	Ramesses II	approx Year 55 (1074BC)	age 20
	3:	Siptah		
	4:	Ramesses III		
	5:	*Ramesside (from artistic style of burial)*		
	6:	Ramesses IX		
	7-12:	Ramesses XI		
	13:	*Third Intermediate Period (from artistic style of burial)*		
	14:	Osorkon II	Year 23	(835BC)	
	15:	Takelot II	Year 14	(815BC)	age 20
	16:	Shoshenq III	Year 28	(797BC)	age 18
	17:	Pimay	Year 2	(771BC)	age 26
	18:	Shoshenq V	Year 11	(756BC)	age 15
	19:	Shoshenq V	Year 37	(730BC)	age 26
	20:	Bakenranef	Year 6	(714BC)	age 16
	21:	Taharqa	Year 4	(686BC)	age 28
	22:	Taharqa	Year 14	(676BC)	age 10
	23:	Taharqa	Year 24	(666BC)	age 10
	24:	Psamtek	Year 21	(643BC)	age 23

Now let's take a look at the rather unfortunate gap in the first part of the sequence. Between Burials 2 and 14, 12 bovine lifespans should have passed over a period of 239 years (1074-835BC), an average of about 20 years each if my overall chronology is correct. Since the ages at death recorded for later burials range from 10 to 28 years (averaging 19 years), 20 years clearly represents a pretty normal life expectancy. Conclusion number one, therefore, is that all burials are present and correct and that the findings from the necropolis basically make sense – which is not something I have ever read elsewhere! Furthermore, there are no anomalies in individual burials. The order looks logical on the plan; the lifespans look sensible. Here, then, is powerful confirmation that both the overall timescale and the detailed sequence of rulers are approximately correct for the period from Ramesses II right through to 800BC and beyond. And the specific detail which gave me the excuse to present this evidence is that Burial 16 died aged a perfectly normal 18 years, whereas without the 21-year co-rule between Takelot II and Shoshenq III the age would be an unlikely 39 years. The whole 42-year discrepancy with which I started this chapter was nothing more than a mirage!

Summary

And so I reach the end of my journey. I am now fully satisfied that this re-dating exercise has been 100% successful. The evidence of astronomical retro-calculation, Sothic dating, tree rings and even C14 dating, combined with the documentation available, has pointed a very clear path, a revolutionary and controversial path but a path which has genuinely led to the truth!

As far as the Middle East is concerned, there is now (800BC) but one super-power, Assyria. Egypt under Shoshenq I looked for a moment as though it might put in another challenge, but is now subsiding. Unfortunately for the well-being of the inhabitants of much of the Middle East, the Assyrian model of empire building is not one of peace and expansion of trade but rather one of conquest, slaughter, robbery and destruction, which means that all the lands bordering Assyria are in trouble! Babylon has felt the full force of Assyrian conquest once more and, although it will manage to recover, it will remain a relatively minor player in an Assyrian world for the next 200 years. Elam will also raise its head again – but only to have it removed once and for all by Assyrian conquest. Elam will not survive as a nation after defeat by Ashurbanipal in the 7th Century BC. And in the north, the Hurrian kings of Urartu will also come up against an implacable foe in Sargon II of Assyria; Urartu will be crushed by Assyrian military might before being wiped from the map by the Medes and Persians. The Hurrian language, once spoken in many parts of Assyria itself, will soon vanish for ever. A similar fate awaits the Luwian language spoken in the Hittite kingdoms of northern Syria and southern Turkey. Within a hundred years, Assyria will have swallowed the Hittite and Aramaean worlds whole. Israel too will be absorbed. Only the tiny kingdom of Judah will outlive the Assyrian threat!

However, Assyria is not a maritime power and never will be. Assyrian armies will reach the Mediterranean many times but they will never be able to extinguish the life from the Phoenician cities, barricaded behind their defensive walls on their secure promontories and islands. Phoenician power will continue to expand across the Mediterranean for many centuries to come. The Greeks, another Mediterranean power, have already shown the first signs of recovery; within a couple of decades (776BC), the first Olympic Games will be run and Greek colonies will start to spring up alongside those of the Phoenicians. Greek influence will grow once more in Cyprus, the Greek emporium of Al Mina will soon be founded at the mouth of the Orontes river in Syria, and it will be the Greeks who lead the way in opening Egypt up to international trade again, setting up commercial centres in cities in the Nile delta. And many would argue that ancient Greek culture forms the basis of western civilisation to this day.

What does the Bible have to say?

In the 9th Century BC the history in the Bible meets and agrees with the history told elsewhere, specifically Assyria. The substantial building phase during the Iron IIa period in Palestine, visible archaeologically, matches the reigns of Omri and Ahab. Omri, an army general, had seized the throne of Israel after a year of chaos during which two kings came and went in quick succession (1 Kings 16:8-22). Although the Bible doesn't say so, the correspondence in date (884BC) with Shoshenq's campaign tells us exactly what had caused this year of chaos. Omri had clearly got himself on the right side of the Egyptians and, with their backing, he marched on the capital, Tirzah, and torched the royal palace with king Zimri inside. Zimri himself had only seized power 7 days earlier when he murdered the previous ruler, Elah! Omri proceeded to stamp his authority on a devastated land and, under Egyptian patronage, he soon built up the major cities once more, founding Samaria as his new capital (1 Kings 16:23-24). So, as you can see, a knowledge of Shoshenq I's true dates throws new light on Bible history.

Omri's son Ahab is mentioned in Assyrian annals, as is the later Israelite king, Jehu. Ahab's enemies, the Aramaean kings of Damascus, Ben Hadad II and his son Hazael, are identifiable in Shalmaneser's campaign records. Indeed, the name of king Hadad has been found on a controversial stone slab from Dan in northern Israel, which may also refer to Joram king of Israel and Ahaziah king of Judah.[21] And Hazael's reported attack on the Philistine city of Gath (2 Kings 12:17), probably in about 820BC, matches the archaeological evidence for a destruction of the city about this time.[22] Finally, Adad Nirari III's report of his conquest of Damascus in 806BC reveals the identity of the "deliverer" who was responsible for Ben Hadad III (Hazael's son) ceasing his attacks on Jehoahaz of Israel (2 Kings 13:5). In short, we have entered a time for which there is plenty of independent corroboration of Bible history. There will always be those who claim that the whole Bible is a Jewish myth of course – but for the serious investigator the story it tells is clearly compatible with known events and therefore likely to be historically trustworthy from the 9th Century BC onwards.

What was going on in the Rest of the World?

I have already mentioned the Medes and the Persians as enemies of Ashurnasirpal II and Shalmaneser III of Assyria. They are new arrivals in Iran, where once Gutians and Kassites lived, and we can be quite sure from the way that similar 'Iranian' languages (most now extinct) were distributed across Central Asia that they had come from the Aral Sea region.[23] The journey was not a rapid migration however, but more of a steady spread of a successful culture. Personally, I would put much of the success down to the art of horse-riding, something which the Medes and Persians delighted in. Despite their initial defeats by Assyrian armies, it wouldn't be long before they were able to hold their own. Neither would it be long before the Persians turned up on the borders of Elam, turning initial defeat into victory and lasting dominance. The Persians would continue to treat Elamite learning with respect, just as they would that of Babylon, but from the 7th Century BC onwards the fate of the Elamite nation was sealed.

This successful sweep of Iranian culture south from Central Asia into Iran was matched by movements north, east and west also. Horse culture swept across the Tien Shan Mountains along the Silk Road into western China, where Iranian language would be spoken for many hundreds of years. It also swept north into southern Russia and then west across the Steppe to the Ukraine and beyond. These Iranian-speaking peoples are known to history as the Cimmerians and the Scythians. They would have a dramatic influence on eastern Europe and their interaction with the Celts of central Europe would be at least partly responsible for turning them from a relatively peaceful nation into the warlike people we associate with the Celts of old. Of more immediate consequence for the Middle East, Cimmerian invaders also crossed the Caucasus Mountains into Turkey, where they would eventually destroy the Phrygian kingdom.

History never stands still!

20

Setting the Record Straight

This book has set out a scheme of history which, whether you were aware of it or not, is highly controversial. You may read many versions of ancient history, but you will not read this one elsewhere, at least not at the time of writing. The main theme has been a shift in dating for much of the 2nd and 3rd Millennia BC of around 150 years, rather more in some parts of the region and at some periods. I hope I have presented sufficient evidence to persuade you that the proposal is worth taking seriously. I hope also that it has been an interesting experience to see just how the history presented in the Bible fits in with this new chronology; in my view it fits very well indeed and demands that the Bible is treated with respect as a historical source no matter what you think of it as a spiritual guide.

When I first started on this adventure I was expecting the issue of the join between an adjusted chronology for the 2nd Millennium BC and conventional dates back to 911BC in Assyria to be a tricky one. Instead, I find evidence after evidence that the 150 year reduction proposed for 2nd Millennium dates makes much more sense than the conventional view.

This is important.

In the rarefied world of ancient historical research it is important to make sure that the foundation upon which one is building is sound. This has not been the case and the consequence has been serious error by otherwise eminent scholars.

But the real importance for many will be that the Bible becomes once more a trustworthy document. Perhaps you always knew it was! But believe me there are many who will be very upset at this conclusion and who will do anything to deny it. Let me refresh your memory as to the most significant ways in which this adjusted chronology now makes the Bible just that much more believable – to those without unquestioning faith.

i) Abraham now wanders across Canaan during the days of occupation by the Amorites, for whom nomadism was the standard way of life.

ii) The four kings from Iraq defeated by Abraham are given a highly plausible historical setting as an army under the authority of the 3rd Dynasty of Ur.

iii) Joseph's time as vizier in Egypt coincides with the reign of Amenemes III and with both records of high Nile floods (abundant harvests) and also 7 years of worldwide poor growth (famine).

iv) The time of Israelite oppression in Egypt corresponds to the period of Hyksos rule, a time also remembered by Egyptians as one of great oppression and hardship.

v) Joshua's invasion of Canaan and his destruction of all the major cities are matched by destructions revealed by archaeology at all the major sites. No-one else has claimed responsibility for these destructions.

vi) Specifically, the abandonment of Jericho following Joshua's conquest is matched by the archaeology of the site.

vii) The 'Habiru' mentioned in numerous Late Bronze Age texts correspond to the Israelites (Hebrews) during the days of the Judges when they were still only a semi-settled people.

viii) Pharaoh Merneptah's recording of 'Israel' on his stela now corresponds to the days of the prophet Samuel shortly before the formation of an Israelite state.

ix) The wars between Israel and the Philistines now cover the period during which Ramesses III also fought a war against the Philistines.

x) The reigns of David and Solomon now take place immediately following Egypt's loss of Palestine under Ramesses VI, during a time when Egypt was extremely weak and divided between the monarchy and the priesthood.

xi) Solomon's father-in-law is revealed as Ramesses IX, whose scarab was found at Gezer, the city he donated to Solomon as a wedding gift.

xii) The campaign of Pharaoh Shoshenq I does not now have to be forced to fit an attack on Jerusalem. It corresponds to a time of anarchy and chaos in Israel rather than Judah.

Good. I hope you have enjoyed the trip. Many questions remain to be answered of course, but at least with a right appreciation of the historical sequence we will be asking the right questions!

TIMETABLE OF ANCIENT HISTORY

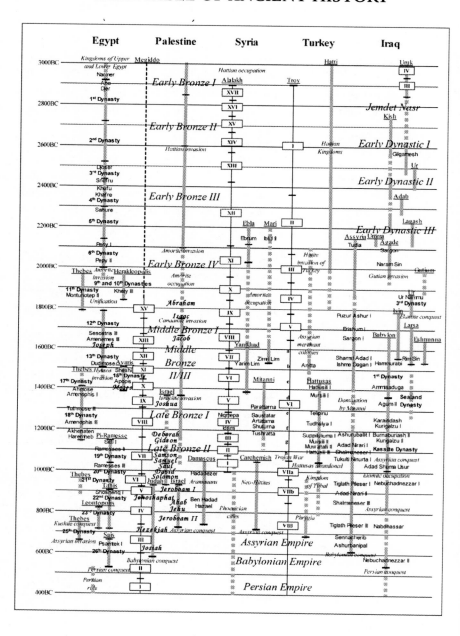

Notes

Chapter 1. Introduction

1. For Britain the war started at 11.00 on 3rd September 1939 when Hitler failed to respond to the British ultimatum over withdrawal from Poland. In Europe, 23.01 on 8th May 1945 saw the command to all German forces to cease fire.
2. The land sighted on that day was actually an island of the Bahamas group.
3. For an excellent overview of Mayan history I recommend Drew (1999).
4. We have no direct evidence for this date. However, archaeology tells us that Rome was certainly a city by the 8th Century BC.
5. Classical Greek characters developed from those of the Phoenicians and the first brief texts appear during the 8th Century BC. However, an earlier generation of Greeks, the so-called Mycenaeans, were writing using a quite different script known as 'Linear B' back in the 2nd Millennium BC. This died out completely, requiring the Greeks to start again from scratch on the path to literacy.
6. My principal source for Egyptian history is Nicolas Grimal's *A History of Ancient Egypt*. However, I also note the dates cited by Kenneth Kitchen in *The Third Intermediate Period in Egypt*, by Charles Freeman in *Egypt, Greece and Rome*, and to those referred to as 'orthodox' in David Rohl's *A Test of Time*.
7. I believe it is fair to say that the current orthodox view of Egyptian history is little altered from that spelt out by Gaston Maspero in the 1890s and by Henry Breasted, the best known of the translators of the texts of ancient Egypt. It is true that debate raged at that time as to whether an extra millennium and a half should be added in, but the majority view prevailed and has since been proved, albeit in my view only approximately, to be correct. Velikovsky (1977) points out that as early as 1819, before Champollion had even deciphered Egyptian hieroglyphs, the Scottish author J.C. Pritchard assigned dates not dissimilar to those conventionally believed today.
8. Courville (1971) came up with a scheme in which the Egyptian 6th and 12th Dynasties were one and the same. His solution is rightly ignored by Egyptologists.
9. Kitchen, 1996.
10. See Manning (1999).
11. Manning suggests a re-dating of the pottery found on Thera, arguing that it represents a very early phase, but this has not been generally accepted.
12. Both Peter James and David Rohl have highlighted the disparaging tone of Kenneth Kitchen's letters on their respective websites (www.centuries.co.uk and www.nunki.net), as well as providing full refutations of the criticisms made. David Rohl has published one of the letters in full.

Chapter 2. Winding back the Clock

1. Suetonius, Plutarch, Vergil, Tacitus and Cassius Dio are among those who wrote extensively on the quarrel between Mark Anthony and Octavian. It is true that there is some

263

disagreement between sources, but not enough for us to doubt the dates involved. See Wells (1984).

2. Many authors wrote about Alexander's exploits. These include Arian's *Anabasis of Alexander* and Plutarch's *Life of Alexander* and several others still extant. However, the original sources used by these later authors (Ptolemy, Aristobulus, Callisthenes, Nearchus and Cleitarchus), all eyewitnesses to all or part of the adventure, are now lost. See Walbank (1981).

3. Much the most important source for the earlier part of the Persian Empire period is Herodotus' *Histories*, which is well worth reading as a travelogue besides being a useful historical work. However, Diodorus Sicilus and Cornelius Nepos, not to mention Xenophon, the Athenian general who marched his army from Babylon to the Black Sea, all contributed valuable information.

4. I shall continue to use the traditional form, Nebuchadnezzar, because it is more widely known, although the preferred reading nowadays seems to be Nebuchadrezzar.

5. The principal sources for the Babylonian era are from a few contemporary inscriptions, notably those relating to Nabonidus' reign found at the city of Harran in northern Syria (Oates, 1986), and from Greek writers.

6. I have adopted the well-known Greek names for several Egyptian cities including Thebes – which the Egyptians actually called 'Niwt-rst'.

7. In *The Bible is History*, Ian Wilson gives a useful overview of the various tie-ups between Bible texts and Assyrian records, notably those of Sennacherib and Shalmaneser III.

8. See, for example, Wilson (1999).

9. The black obelisk of Shalmaneser III was recovered from the ruins of the city of Nimrud by Henry Layard in the 1840s, Nimrud being the Assyrian capital at the time.

10. Egyptian pharaohs regularly took a number of honorific names. Besides the principal name or 'nomen', for example *Ramesses*, there would commonly be a 'prenomen' and a further 'cognomen'. In the case of Ramesses II, his prenomen *Usermaatre* was the name used by the Hittites in their copy of a famous treaty between Ramesses and the Hittite king of the day, Hattusili III; in fact the prenomen seems to have been the name commonly used in correspondence.

11. Manetho is undoubtedly the key historical reference for the pharaohs of Egypt. Although others wrote earlier (notably Herodotus), Manetho was the first to attempt a serious history of the whole of dynastic Egypt. He was a priest who lived in the 3rd Century BC, during the reigns of the Ptolemies, and he clearly had access to a number of ancient priestly sources. Before the decipherment of Egyptian writing, Manetho's history enabled a reasonable guess to be taken regarding the sequence and duration of events. Unfortunately, we no longer possess a copy of Manetho's work today. However, much of it has been preserved in the writings of three other classical authors, namely Josephus, Africanus and Eusebius, unfortunately not always agreeing with each other!

12. Grimal's *A History of Ancient Egypt* and El Mahdy's *The Pyramid Builder* are two recent examples where respected Egyptologists continue to quote 1461 (or 1460) years for a Great Sothic year. This has also been widely adopted by broader historical reference works such as Grun's *The Timetables of History*.

13. It should be acknowledged that the readings of both the year and the king's name have been subject to dispute. The reading I am quoting, however, definitely reflects current majority opinion. (Also note that the traditional name 'Amenophis' is often read as 'Amenhotep', a more accurate rendering of the Egyptian signs)

14. Here too, there was plenty of initial dispute as to the king's identity and, although Egyptologists do not appear to challenge this identification much nowadays, it cannot be seen as secure. (Also note that the traditional name Sesostris is often and more accurately rendered Senwosret or Senuseret)

15. The *Ebers Papyrus* is illustrated fully in Rohl (1995).

16. Read (1970) noted 12 lunar observations on other documents from the same source at El Lahun, from which he determined a most likely date of 1549BC, over 300 years later than that traditionally given. However, I suggest that 12 observations is simply not enough for this sort of analysis.

Chapter 3. The Dating Game

1. Kenyon, 1970.
2. Carbon 12 is the natural state of carbon. However, atoms of Carbon 14 are created continually in the upper atmosphere due to the impact of cosmic rays on atoms of Nitrogen 14 (the natural state of nitrogen).
3. Arnold and Libby, 1949.
4. The chief reason for the preservative powers of peat bogs is the anoxic nature of stagnant water.
5. I recommend M.G.L. Baillie's book *A Slice through Time* for a useful overview of tree-ring dating.
6. Pulak, 1994.
7. Keenan (2005) gives a very thorough critique of so-called Anatolian tree-ring studies. He points out deficiencies in the ways in which the data has been handled mathematically as well as providing direct evidence of the lack of match to be expected between trees of different species or growing in different climatic zones.
8. Kuniholm et al, 1993.
9. Ussishkin, 1978.
10. The Pyramids Radiocarbon Dating Project (Bonani et al, 2001) was originally intended to answer the question as to whether the pyramids may have been many thousands of years older than is conventionally thought. This question was answered emphatically – but the project has certainly not increased the general level of confidence in C14 dating.
11. See Keenan (2002).
12. The evidence for stagnation comes from analysis of sediments (e.g. Troelstra et al, 1991). The likely reason seems to be a large increase in fresh water in-flow from the Black Sea (which had previously been a separate lake) and the river Nile.
13. Note that the Middle Kingdom sites sampled during the Pyramids Radiocarbon Dating Project were located south of the Gebel Qatrani hills, whereas the Old Kingdom sites were slightly to the north. A much lower influence of Mediterranean air south of the hills may explain the closer date matches at Middle Kingdom sites.
14. Richard Alley's *The Two-Mile Time Machine* is an excellent introduction to ice-core science.
15. Horgan, 1987.
16. Baillie, 1995.
17. There is no argument regarding the fact that Late Minoan 1a pottery is found at Akrotiri and that Late Minoan 1b is not. The argument solely concerns the correlation between these pottery phases on Thera (and on Crete) and the dynasties of Egypt. Sturt Manning proposes that the time period covered by Late Minoan 1a and 1b is much longer than has conventionally been assumed (perhaps 100 years for 1a), which just about allows his 1b phase to reach the reign of Tuthmose III. Most others would argue that the Egyptian evidence, both pottery and also depictions of Minoan traders, favours the 1a period extending at least close to Tuthmose III's time.
18. Zielinski et al, 1994.
19. Zielinski and Germani, 1998.
20. Hardy and Renfrew, 1991.
21. Schultz and Paul (2002) compare several of the climatic indicators, including deep sea deposits and ice core records.
22. Mitchell, 1990.

23. The word is rendered *b-t-t* here because the Akkadian language of the tablet, in common with many ancient Middle Eastern languages and with modern Arabic and Hebrew, did not mark the vowel sounds.
24. The identification of Hiyaru as February/March according to an Egyptian-based system was argued by de Jong and van Soldt (1989) with reference to other calendrical texts. As the second month of the modern Jewish year, Hiyaru is much better known as April/May.
25. de Jong and van Soldt, 1989.

Chapter 4. Let there be Light: 3000-2500BC

1. See Wilkinson (2003). Interestingly, these early sightings of the red crown are not confined to northern Egypt but also appear in central and southern regions.
2. Rohl (1999) notes the appearance of headgear similar to the white crown on a seal impression from Iraq.
3. Bard (1994) summarises the evidence. A series of C14 dates from Hierakonpolis in Upper Egypt gave dates of 3760BC for Naqada I, 3600-3300BC for Naqada II and 3025BC for Naqada III. On the other hand, four C14 dates from Maadi in Lower Egypt during Naqada II times average 3650BC, giving support to the theory that Lower Egyptian dates are erroneously high.
4. The difference in culture is quite evident from archaeology. The difference in language cannot be proven but see Thom (2006) for relevant evidence.
5. The site of Nabta Playa, about 50 miles east of the Nile and just downstream from the second cataract, provides evidence for occupation by a pastoralist people from around 6000BC. See Wendorf and Close (1992).
6. Although the Bronze Age started in around 3000BC in the Middle East and copper had been used for over 2000 years previously, metals were still rare commodities.
7. The donkey is descended from the African Ass and was domesticated during the 4th Millennium BC. Egypt is one of the places where the earliest evidence for domesticated donkeys has been found.
8. Throughout this book there will be reference to the phases of occupation at various cities. These are determined from archaeology. Unfortunately, there is no one common numbering standard. This means that a phase sometimes refers to a single level of building construction, typically representing about 100 years, while at other cities it denotes a much longer period which is then broken down into sub-phases. Uruk III represents a single construction level and therefore only lasted around 100 years. The other variable is the numbering order. In most cases, Level I is the uppermost and therefore most recent level, this being the most convenient system for archaeologists who do not know when they start an excavation how many levels they are going to find. However the order is reversed at some sites, in this book most notably Troy.
9. There are no obvious systemic similarities between the writing systems adopted in Egypt and those in Iraq, which means that only the general idea of writing can have been transmitted from one culture to the other.
10. See Bard (1994).
11. The tablet shows the cow goddess Sothis with a plant between her horns, thought to represent the year (Drioton and Vandier, 1962). Experts appear to be in agreement that this tablet represents the link between Sothis and the solar calendar.
12. The alternatives are the 62 and 57 years quoted by Africanus.
13. C14 dates for the time of Djer are typically in the 3200-3000BC range although a group of dates from a piece of fabric from Tarkhan average 2990BC (Weinstein, 1980). The fact that Tarkhan is just south of the Gebel Qatrani hills and so was less affected by low C14 Mediterranean air may be relevant here.
14. Narmer's name was found on a famous slate pallette, which I think I am right in saying all historians agree symbolises the forceful unification of the country. Most believe that

Narmer was the real unifier of the land and that Aha was his immediate successor. Narmer's name has been read at Tell Areini near Gaza, implying control of northern Egypt and beyond.

15. This is a very approximate estimate based on the evidence in Thom (2006). Some linguists believe that Semitic language originated in Asia rather than Africa and that it therefore never made the journey from Egypt.

16. Woolley, 1929.

17. The Persian Gulf has been steadily receding for the last 6000 years or so due to the build-up of silt from the Tigris and Euphrates rivers.

18. Since its founding in the 6th Millennium BC and until Uruk's rise to power, Eridu had been much the largest southern Iraqi city. In Sumerian legend, kingship descended first to Eridu.

19. Oates, 1986.

20. Money as we know it wasn't invented until the 1st Millennium BC. In earlier times business was carried out in a similar way, but weight of silver was the standard measure of value.

21. The Jemdet Nasr period is more typically dated to about 3000 to 2800BC.

22. The northern tomb, situated at Saqqara near the capital Memphis (or 'White Wall' as it was then known), was always the largest and most prestigious, and was presumably the actual burial site. However, the southern tombs at Abydos were substantial monuments and also included numerous subsidiary burials. See Emery (1961) for a full description.

23. Not all Egyptologists agree that Nebka was the first 3rd Dynasty ruler since the sources for this period are limited in number and also contradictory. I am following Grimal's opinion here.

24. Bard (1994) draws attention to similarities between the pottery cultures of Palestine and Lower Egypt and to the fact that imported Palestinian and Syrian wares have been found at Maadi near Cairo and Buto in the eastern Nile delta, all in late 4th Millennium BC contexts.

25. Note that typical C14 dates for the Early Bronze II/III horizon are in the range 2950-2850BC, for example Arad II and Ai V (Weinstein, 1980).

26. Kenyon, 1970.

27. This is a slightly controversial statement although I believe it now represents majority opinion. The alternative view is that the Hittites arrived via the Caucasus Mountains. Thom (2006) gives some of the linguistic arguments against this.

28. The archaeological culture which dominated the lands south of the Caucasus Mountains in the 4th and early 3rd Millennia BC is known as Kura-Araxes. It was an advanced metal-using culture with clear links to Uruk. In the second half of the 4th Millennium BC Kura-Araxes culture spread steadily west into central Turkey and south into northern Iraq and northern Syria, displacing Uruk-related cultures as it progressed. The change is very distinct and was often violent (Kavtaradze, 2004). The principal pottery type associated with Kura-Araxes sites is known as Karaz ware and it is directly ancestral to Khirbet Kerak ware.

29. Woolley (1953) excavated the site of Tabara al Akrad on the lower Orontes plain. Here, four construction levels contained Khirbet Kerak ware (overlying Uruk pottery levels) and the latest also contained pottery typical of Alalakh XVII, the oldest level at the nearby Hurrian city of Alalakh.

30. Grey 'Ninevite 5' ware, dating to the early 3rd Millennium, can be found both in northern Iraqi sites like Chagar Bazaar and also at Iranian sites like Sialk and Hissar. This pottery type seems likely to represent Hurrian culture.

31. See Woolley (1953) for details.

32. Woolley's excavations showed that the founding of Alalakh brought wheel-made pottery to the region and that it was followed by the end of Khirbet Kerak ware (Woolley, 1953).

33. That Greek language arrived in Greece from the north is agreed by almost all linguists. However, the relatively close relationship with Hittite suggested here is controversial and reflects my own analysis of the evidence (Thom, 2006).

34. About 210 letter-like signs have been noted on artefacts from Vinča culture sites, notably Tordos and Tarteria in Romania, dating to around 4000BC (Rudgley, 1998). Of these, 50 have direct parallels in the 2nd Millennium BC Linear A script from Minoan Crete (Haarmann, 1989). Others have noticed similarities to signs found at Troy on the Turkish coast. For the archaeological evidence for a north to south cultural movement in the Balkans see Renfrew (1973).

35. Cyprus was actually first inhabited as early as the 9th or 10th Millennium BC, but occupation came to an end around 6000BC and was only resumed in about 4500BC.

36. See Peltenburg (2006). C14 dates suggest about 2800BC for this cultural change but, allowing for the likelihood of distorted results in the eastern Mediterranean, the true date was probably nearer 2500BC.

37. Many linguists link Elamite with the Dravidian tongues of southern India, a view with which I would agree. Nevertheless, the differences are still very great and a separation date as far back as 13000BC seems to fit the evidence (Thom, 2006).

38. The *Sumerian king list* is a most useful document, compiled from 15 different fragments of cuneiform tablet and relating the history of Sumer from semi-mythical times through to the 2nd Millennium BC.

39. Greece is denoted by 'Javan' in the Bible.

40. Arpaxhad is likely to be Arrapha (or Arrapachitis), modern Kirkuk (Unger and Larsen, 1984).

41. Lud is most commonly identified with Lydia in western Turkey.

42. Leick, 1997.

43. This deduction is based on the current and past distribution of the language family known as Austro-Asiatic, stretching from eastern India through parts of Burma, Malaysia and Thailand and into Cambodia and Vietnam. For the logic behind the deduction see Thom (2006).

Chapter 5. Pyramids and Ziggurats: 2500-2000BC

1. The place of origin of the Palermo stone (fragments of which are housed in museums in Palermo, Cairo and London) is unknown, which means that, though further pieces may be awaiting discovery, no-one knows where to look.

2. My principal sources for Old Kingdom Egypt are Emery (1961), Grimal (1992) and El Mahdy (2003).

3. Egyptian pyramids developed from the imposing rectilinear mausoleum-like tombs which the rulers of the first two dynasties built for themselves. The first pyramid, the step pyramid, was basically a series of mausoleum-like structures one on top of the other. Egyptian tomb history can be traced still further back in time to the relatively simple raised table-top tombs, known as 'mastabas', in use in predynastic days.

4. This information is from El Mahdy (2003), who gives an excellent account of the pyramid age.

5. The large number of richly dressed bodies found arranged neatly within the enormous royal graves at Ur has given rise to quite a lot of heated discussion. Leonard Woolley, who excavated the tombs, was firmly of the opinion that they had been sacrificed (probably poisoned) deliberately to accompany the king or queen concerned into the next life. Others since have held equally firm views that the individuals concerned would have been dead already. The problem, of course, is that neither position is provable.

6. Pettinato, 1981.

7. I include Aleppo here on the assumption, accepted by most, that it is to be identified with 'Armi', a city mentioned often in the Ebla tablets and also referred to in texts from Iraq.

8. In reality all we know is that Mesalim predated the war between Umma and Lagash, records of which have been found at Lagash and which is generally estimated to have taken place some 70 years before the end of the Early Dynastic III period. We know he predated this war because the resulting boundary stone refers to Mesalim's stela having been restored to its former place (Roux, 1966).

9. The problem seems to be that Agade only existed as a major city for the duration of Sargon's dynasty, less than 200 years, and this is not long enough for much accumulation of debris. Today the site may therefore be as flat as the surrounding land. An alternative favoured by many is that Agade actually lies deep beneath the modern water table at the site of Babylon.

10. The practice of naming individual years was also introduced during Sargon's reign, making life much easier for the historian.

11. For example, see Gadd (1963).

12. Elamite trade is evidenced by the distribution of artefacts of chlorite, produced at Tepe Yahya in southern Iran; also copper axes, compartmental stamp seals, and various precious stones from Afghanistan.

13. The *Sumerian king list* reports that Elam was subjugated by king Enmebaragesi of Kish, rival to Gilgamesh of Uruk. The country then regained independence and managed to defeat Kish during the supremacy of the 1st Dynasty of Ur. However, this didn't last either and Kish dominated again.

14. This evidence relies on the integrity of archaeologist James Mellart, who reports that he was shown this particular collection of illegally excavated royal grave goods (Mellart, 1959).

15. Kenyon, 1970.

16. Kenyon, 1970.

17. Troy is one of those sites where the levels are numbered from bottom to top, i.e. from oldest to most recent.

18. The people who took Purushanda are named as 'Umman Manda', a term which was certainly applied to Indo-European invaders in later centuries (see Chapter 9). According to Naram Sin, he retook the city as well as several others in the area.

19. There has been plenty of debate over the years (e.g. Piggott, 1973) as to whether the similarities of sites such as Los Millares in southern Spain and Vila Nova da São Pedro in Portugal to Aegean settlements is coincidental or not. Superficially, the similarities in the city walls appear significant, as does the sudden arrival of copper technology in Spain, so some form of Minoan influence does indeed seem likely. A C14 date from Los Millares came out at 2340BC and, remote from the low C14 atmosphere of the eastern Mediterranean, this date is likely to be fairly reliable.

20. The chief archaeological site of this period on Cyprus is Philia, although many more have been found with similar culture. The parallels with southern Turkey are exemplified by identical forms of copper dagger and a close similarity between sets of gold ear-rings from Philia and from Tarsus in Turkey (Herscher and Swiny, 2006).

21. Two of the months of the Eblaite calendar were named after Hurrian gods.

22. In fact, the 17 kings were spread right around the corners of the Middle East from Turkey to southern Iran and Arabia, so they were in no sense a coalition. They are presumably a list of all the rulers which Naram Sin had to fight.

23. Naran Sin's campaigns are discussed fully by Gadd (1963). Neither Purushanda nor Ulisum have been located as yet. However, Purushanda I suggest was in south-western Turkey, the later Roman province of Pisidia – the name *Pisidia* may even be descended from *Purushanda*; Ulisum I would equate to Ilion, the province where Troy is located, known as Wilusa to the Hittites. Yet another distant city which Naram Sin famously subdued, Apishal, could plausibly be Ephesus on the Aegean coast.

24. The levels are Anau II and Hissar II; the typical pottery is a plain grey/black ware and the production technique represents a total change in comparison with earlier levels. Relative

dating is made easier by the presence of Sumerian style tools and weapons from the Early Dynastic period.

25. Pryor (2003) gives an excellent overview of British prehistory, emphasizing the degree of continuity across the millennia.

Chapter 6. Ur of the Chaldeans: 2000-1800BC

1. The *Admonitions of Ipuwer* is an undated document in a form of language used two or three hundred years after the end of the 6th Dynasty. However, its content leads Egyptologists to believe that it relates to this period. As well as telling us of cities being destroyed, plague, blood etc, Ipuwer also speaks of the poor becoming rich and of gold and lapis lazuli being worn by female slaves, which suggests that there was some sort of people's revolution as well as an Amorite invasion. At this distance, it is not possible to know which was cause and which was effect.

2. The Lullubi inhabited the territory immediately north-west of Elam, in what is now Luristan.

3. Hinz, 1972.

4. The document is known as *Enuma Anu Enlil* and was preserved in the library of the 7th Century BC Assyrian king Ashurbanipal. The actual collecting of the data took place in the late 2nd Millennium BC.

5. Mitchell, 1990.

6. Only five out of the 21 Gutian kings in the *Sumerian king list* have left us inscriptions (Roux, 1966).

7. At Jericho, Kenyon (1970) found evidence, largely pottery, for a long period of occupation by a people who did not build houses. This was then followed by construction of a relatively low standard using a soft, greenish-coloured brick, in a haphazard pattern across the site. At Megiddo, the evidence is less clear, but it seems likely that various phases of temple construction in Level XV have to be dated to Amorite times.

8. I have adopted Grimal's estimate of about 120 years from the end of the 8th Dynasty to reunification under Montuhotep II. From Inyotef II's time onwards reign lengths are pretty well established.

9. It is impossible to be confident about the length of Gutian rule. The *Sumerian king list* states "21 kings for 124 years" but the reign lengths actually given only total 97 years, even if two kings which only appear in one of the source texts are included. Furthermore, it is to be expected that a quoted reign length such as *6 years* actually implies *between 5 and 6 years*, i.e. that the king died (or was deposed) in his 6th year; hence my reduction to 'approximately 85 years'.

10. Woolley, 1929.

11. Much the greatest number of texts from the 3rd Dynasty of Ur come from the city of Umma, with an important set of judicial documents from Lagash (Oates, 1986).

12. There is ongoing debate as to the actual linguistic origin of the earliest Assyrian kings' names.

13. The extent of the so-called Anatolian languages (Hittite, Palaic and Luwian) is impossible to judge with certainty because of the lack of written records. However, an inscription from the island of Lemnos proves that there at least a non-Indo-European tongue survived. Others almost certainly survived on the adjacent Turkish mainland.

14. The Bible's figure of 430 years is stated as precise "to the very day". An alternative figure is the 400 years for which Abraham was told his descendants would wander through lands not their own, which has a very uncertain start point and a very uncertain end; I therefore take it to be a round number rather than a precise figure.

15. The word *Perizzite* is simply asking for speculation. For a start, it has effectively the same consonant group as *Philistine*, although it is true that the Bible makes a distinction between the two peoples. It is also remarkably similar to *Pelethite*, and the Pelethites formed one of a pair of mercenary armies who later fought for king David. The other mercenary

group were the Kerethites, whose name many (including the prophet Ezekiel – Ezekiel 25:16) would equate to Cretans. To complete the circle, the Bible reports that the Philistines came from Crete. Thus Philistines, Perizzites, Pelethites and Kerethites may all originally have been of Cretan (or wider Aegean) origin.

16. Sodom is most commonly identified with the archaeological site of Bab edh-Dhra, east of the Dead Sea in Jordan. Documentary evidence for this comes from the Ebla archive where a geographical text lists cities which some identify with 'Admah' and 'Sodom' as lying on a route north along the eastern side of the Dead Sea (Shea, 1983). Gomorrah is usually identified with the site of Numeira, not far from Bab edh-Dhra. However, while Bab edh-Dhra was inhabited over a period of centuries, Numeira only had about 100 years of life, explaining why it was not mentioned on the 22nd Century BC Ebla tablet (Wood, 2006). Both cities were destroyed by fire some time after the end of the Early Bronze III period. Wood argues strongly that the evidence points to fire from above and that the cause of the destruction can be found in the massive geological fault line which passes immediately underneath. He also makes the case that the real date of the destruction was during the Early Bronze IV phase, coinciding with Amorite occupation elsewhere in Palestine.

17. The name *Ashur* has several variant forms in ancient texts, one of which is 'Lál-sar' (Hallo, 1956).

18. Rohl (2002) dates this battle to the time of Shulgi's son Amar Sin and argues that the names *Amar Sin* and *Amar Piel* are alternative versions of the same name. I would agree that Amar Sin is likely to be the king mentioned in the Bible but that he was then still crown prince; in common with many ancient kings (e.g. Tutankhaten / Tutankhamun) he may well have changed his name when he came to the throne, in his case reflecting allegiance to the moon god Sin rather than to El.

19. If Ellasar is indeed a corruption of Ashur, then contemporary records provide a possible identity for 'Arioch' king of Ellasar; he is Zari'iq, named as governor of Ashur in Shulgi's last year, 1816BC (Hallo, 1956). The dates don't quite match – but we have no proof of exactly when he was first appointed; he may already have been in office during the 1820's BC. Regarding Tidal king of Goiim, the name is given as "Thurgal" in the often more reliable Septuagint version of the Bible and this name is reminiscent of Tirigan king of Gutium who was defeated by Utu Hegal of Uruk in 1889BC. The king of Goiim mentioned in the Bible may therefore have been one of his successors on the Gutian throne, at that time a vassal king under the authority of the Ur empire.

20. The Arabah region to the south of the Dead Sea was an important centre of copper production throughout the 3rd Millennium BC and down to the close of the 3rd Dynasty of Ur (Levy et al, 2004).

21. The Indo-European culture of the Ukraine is known as 'Tripolye', and the Tripolye people were a mixed arable farming and herding society. Their pottery and art betrays their Indo-European affiliation. They apparently maintained a relatively peaceful existence for about 1000 years but something disrupted this stability in approximately 2000BC. I suspect this to have been the time when Germanic speaking people took over, pushing the ancestral Celts and Italics westward into Hungary (see Thom, 2006).

Chapter 7. Middle Kingdom: 1800-1600BC

1. For example, Bur Sin of Isin, who reigned from about 1664BC according to this chronology, was able to erect a monument at Ur in which he is called "king of Akkad and Sumer" and "ruler of the four quarters of the earth".

2. A further piece of astronomical retro-calculation which some have used to date the 12th Dynasty relates to a useful-looking set of lunar month length records in documents dated to the reigns of pharaohs Sesostris III and Amenemes III. David Lappin of Glasgow University (Lappin, 2002) suggests that an apparently outstanding match (37 out of 39 correct) is found when the coronation date of Amenemes III is assumed to be 1678BC, 21

years earlier than I am proposing. However, I do not believe we can regard this particular absolute date as trustworthy. The problem lies in the fact that the sequence of lunar month lengths in a given year, whether 29 or 30 days, will always be closely matched 13 years later, and again after 21 years. The technique really only becomes trustworthy when discriminating between date options which have been derived by other techniques. In this case I note that Lappin himself admits that an alternative date of 1802BC provides almost as good a match as 1678BC, which would comfort those wedded to a more traditional chronology!

3. The dates quoted take the view that reigns were only counted from the date of sole ruler-ship with the exception of Amenemes III who overlapped with his father Sesostris III for 18 years.

4. There is also evidence of 12th Dynasty influence at Ugarit (Grimal, 1992), including a temple containing a 12th Dynasty style offering (Kenyon, 1970).

5. The Cretan Linear B script was famously deciphered in 1952 by Michael Ventris and was found to be an early version of Greek. Its predecessor Linear A uses substantially the same character set and it is therefore logical to assume that the sound values of each character were similar in the two scripts.

6. Khirbet Iskander in central Jordan is the only known site in the region to have remained a fortified settlement during the Amorite 'Early Bronze IV' period, albeit much reduced in scale relative to the preceding Early Bronze III town. Three building phases have been identified during Early Bronze IV, suggesting a duration of about 300 years.

7. In addition to these specific finds, a scattering of 12th Dynasty scarabs has been found from sites right across Palestine; 12th Dynasty pottery has also been found extensively in tombs at Byblos (Kenyon, 1970).

8. We read something of the relationship between city and tent-dwelling Amorites in the letters of the 16th Century BC Amorite king Shamsi Adad of Ashur to his son in Mari (Oates, 1986).

9. It seems very likely that the trade policies of Gungunum of Larsa in southern Iraq and possibly even Sesostris II of Egypt were being felt right across the Middle East, and Erishum did not want Assyria to be left out in the cold.

10. There has been some debate as to whether this iron was exclusively 'meteoric', that is derived from meteorites which are nearly 100% iron, or whether it could have been extracted from the rocks of the Earth. I have the impression that there is growing acceptance of evidence that some of it was, even at this early date, extracted from the Earth. This is quite possible; although it would be several hundred years before the official start of the Iron Age, iron smelting doesn't require any technological advance other than the ability to increase furnace temperature and this would have been feasible since the earliest days of copper smelting. It would not, however, have been economic. Iron extraction would therefore remain a luxury until furnace technology improved significantly. The rarity of iron is reflected in its price – more than that of gold!

11. Syrian names appear in the Kanesh tablets. There was also a merchant colony at Ursu on the Syrian border (Orlin, 1970).

12. This date is based on the fact that texts from this phase of the Kanesh colony tie into the reigns of kings Erishum I, Sargon I and Puzur Ashur II of Assyria (Bryce, 1998). Puzur Ashur II's reign ended in about 1624BC according to the dates in this book.

13. One possible cause which should not be ignored is the significant worldwide down-turn in agricultural production from about 1628 to 1622BC, the evidence for which is seen in narrow tree rings both in America and in Europe (Baillie, 1995). Hungry people can easily turn into desperate fighters.

14. Grimal, 1992.

15. It is noticeable how many names of foreign (mainly Asiatic) workers appear in late 12th Dynasty texts. The strength of the Egyptian economy clearly led to large-scale immigration to supply the labour market.

16. Genesis 10:14 makes a distinction between the Cretans (Caphtorites) and Philistines (descended from Pathrusites and Casluhites), but they are mentioned consecutively as sons of Mizraim grandson of Noah.

17. One further name can be added to the Philistine/Perizzite/Pelethite debate – see note 15 of Chapter 6 – and that is 'Pelasgian'. The Pelasgians were the non-Greek inhabitants of the Aegean according to various classical Greek authors and it is stated that Pelasgians lived on Crete, among other places. It seems quite possible that all these names stem from a common original.

18. The Aramaic language separated from its closest West Semitic relatives (Eblaite, Ugaritic) in roughly 2000BC according to my evaluation of the language evidence, probably following the collapse of the empire of Ebla.

19. The word Aram may also be linked to Armi, the city usually identified with Aleppo. Refer to note 7 of Chapter 5.

20. The evidence of later times, during the days of the kings of Israel and Judah, is that when the Bible quotes a period of time in years, for example '60 years', this means more than 59 years but less than 60; hence it is not realistic simply to sum the numbers given. The same applies, if my reading of the evidence is correct, to the *Assyrian king list*, and probably to many other similar documents.

21. See Baillie (1995).

22. Schiestl, 2001.

23. See Agarwal (2005) for a balanced assessment of the arguments.

Chapter 8. The Rise of Babylon: 1600-1500BC

1. The *Assyrian king list* gives a list of "ancestors" who appear to have lived in parallel with the Assyrian kings from about the time of Puzur Ashur I. King Hale is the first of these ancestors and so should be dated to the mid 18th Century BC according to the chronology of this book.

2. We rely on a few sentences in the *Assyrian king list*.

3. Roux, 1966.

4. The *Sumerian king list* covers both the 3rd Dynasty of Ur and the Isin Dynasty and this part of the list gives every appearance of being reliable since it ties in well with evidence from other sources (monuments, tablets). However, it should be admitted that there are several differences between source texts; here I have followed Oates (1986).

5. No-one knows where Mama was but mention of the city of Sibuha (surely the same place as the later Samuha) suggests that it lay to the north-east of Kanesh. Although Samuha/Sibuha has not been definitely located, the obvious match today is with the city of Sivas, about 120 miles north-east of Kanesh. Whether the equation of names is correct or not, the location cannot be far out.

6. Only 250 tablets have been recovered from the second phase of the Kanesh colony out of a total of 15000.

7. The site of Acem Höyük about 10 miles from Aksaray is often suggested as the location for Purushanda (for example Bryce, 1998). However, both the geography and the correspondence between the names *Aksaray* and *Kussara* suggest otherwise to me. Let us hope that continuing excavation provides the answer.

8. Pithana stresses that he was a benevolent conqueror and that he brought no destruction to the city of Kanesh. However, it seems logical to date his conquest to the Level 1b/1a transition, since this marks an archaeologically noticeable change, which suggests a date in the mid 16th Century BC by the chronology of this book.

9. An inscribed dagger of Anitta was found in Level 1a at Kanesh.

10. The actual site of Ulamma (or Ulma) is unknown. However, it is associated with a later military campaign by the Hittite king Hattusili I, who defeated Kanesh before proceeding to Ulamma, from which we can be fairly certain that it lay south-east of Kanesh.

11. In the Mari archives, the rulers of Ursu and Hassuwa, both in southern Turkey, have Hurrian names, as does the king of Laish in northern Palestine.

12. The location of Hassuwa is certainly somewhere north of Alalakh and probably in the forested region of the Amanus range since "timber from the mountains of Hassuwa" is mentioned in a later text about a siege of Ursu. The best match today is with the Turkish town of Hassa.

13. The clearest evidence that the king Yarim Lim of the Alalakh VII archive dates to this period and no later is seen in a tablet which details a request from the king of nearby Ugarit that Yarim Lim organise a visit to see the famously magnificent palace at Mari, a palace which was destroyed during Hammurabi's reign (Woolley, 1953). Thus, the currently fashionable opinion that the Yarim Lim of the Alalakh archives is a much later ruler than the Yarim Lim of the Mari archive seems to me to be untenable.

14. The Middle Minoan II/III earthquake reveals one slightly shocking aspect of Cretan society, namely the fact that they practiced human sacrifice. We have direct evidence for this from the site of Arkhanes, where the earthquake had entombed both victim (on a stone platform with a bronze knife across his body) and would-be sacrificers. Whether the victim died under the knife or in the earthquake is unclear, but the meaning was crystal clear. See Sakellarakis and Sapouna-Sakellaraki (1981), quoted by Wilson (1999).

15. Grimal (1992) assigns 44 years to the early 13th Dynasty, prior to Neferhotep I's accession.

16. See Williams (1975), who quotes von Beckerath (1964). We know of a vizier named Ankhu who had inherited the title from his grandfather and who was succeeded by two of his sons.

17. Williams, 1975.

18. The point has been made by several defenders of traditional Egyptian chronology that the Sobekhotep stela is still just about compatible with a date in the early 17th Century BC, the traditional time of the last few 13th Dynasty rulers, if the flood occurred late in the season, some time in October.

19. The extent of Hammurabi's conquests can be gauged by the finding of a stela at Diyarbakir in southern Turkey (Roux, 1966). Also, the text of his famous law code claims that he was master of the Assyrian cities of Ashur and Nineveh.

20. There are grounds for thinking that the Kassite people may have been related to the Elamites. The language structure was agglutinative (Roux, 1966), their original territory must have been immediately adjacent to Elamite lands, and the name *Agum* occurs in the king lists of both Elamites and Kassites.

21. Grimal places Hornedjeratef (known as 'the Asiatic') 30 years into the dynasty. The extent of his fame is revealed by the fact that his name has also turned up on a mace-head from Ebla.

22. This was the century which saw the founding of the lower city at Hazor, representing a massive expansion of the site.

23. The word *Hyksos* is used to describe a group of Asiatic dignitaries bearing tribute depicted in the tomb of Khnumhotep, who served under Sesostris II of the 12th Dynasty. There is also a text from the reign of Sobekhotep III of the 13th Dynasty which speaks of "Hyksos servants" (Phillips, 2002). The people, whoever they were, had therefore been known to the Egyptians for some time.

24. The Tell ed Daba excavations have spawned a massive literature. The information quoted here is taken from Schiestl (2001).

25. The mass graves at the end of Stratum G at Avaris contained bodies which had been thrown in haphazardly, followed by signs that the Egyptian population had abandoned the city (Bietak, 1979, discussed in Rohl, 1995).

26. A key military innovation of Hyksos times seen at Avaris was the plastered revetment, a smoothly sloping bank created immediately outside a city's defensive walls. These are common at other Hyksos cities.

27. If *kings of the desert uplands* is a correct translation then the origins of the Hyksos have to be looked for in Arabia, a location which would also fit the interpretation *king shepherds*. The Egyptian word *shosu*, meaning *shepherd* (*hyk* is king), was later applied by the Egyptians to a nomadic people inhabiting the Negev desert, southern Palestine and southern Jordan. Indeed, Velikovsky (1977) reports strong Arab tradition (e.g. Masoudi, 1861-77) that the Hyksos were 'Amalekites' and that they were originally from the Mecca region of Arabia. However, majority opinion still seems to favour the Hyksos being an organised Palestinian confederation, possibly under the leadership of Hazor.

28. Schiestl, 2001.

29. The date at which the Arabian camel was first domesticated is still a subject of debate. The Bactrian camel of Central Asia had almost certainly been domesticated by the 3rd Millennium BC but I am not aware of hard evidence related to the Arabian camel earlier than the late 2nd Millennium BC. Nevertheless, many experts (e.g. Afshar, 1978) suggest that it too was domesticated in the 3rd Millennium BC.

Chapter 9. The Lights Go Out: 1500-1400BC

1. The principal source is *Babylonian king list A*, which traces kings from Hammurabi's dynasty through to the 6th Century BC.

2. His name, Kashtiliash, is not actually of Kassite root but Indo-European, but it is typical of the names of later Kassite rulers.

3. The planet Venus was surprisingly important to a variety of ancient cultures. For example, the Mayan calendar is largely based on the Venus cycle, as the planet is first one side of the sun (from the Earth's perspective) and then the other. Since five Venus cycles takes almost exactly eight years, the motion of Venus can be readily linked to the solar calendar. The observations contained in the *Venus Tablets* of Ammisaduga actually fail to match those evident today, and no convincing explanation that I am aware of has yet been put forward, but the overall length of the cycle was the same – indeed it would be astounding to find otherwise.

4. Mitchell, 1990.

5. Manetho's 14th Dynasty consists of an amazing 76 kings. Numbers 1 to 41 have normal Egyptian-style throne names; the remainder do not and it is thought by most that these later kings were Hyksos rulers, governing the eastern delta on behalf of the Hyksos 'great king'. The sheer number of kings means that each had only 6 months to a year in charge since the duration of the first 41 reigns is generally estimated at no more than about 25 years. The system was clearly one of bureaucratic appointment rather than hereditary monarchy, as in the parallel 13th Dynasty.

6. It was certainly the 15th Dynasty names which were prominent internationally. The name of pharaoh Khyan has turned up on objects from Crete (an alabaster lid) to Iraq (a stone lion in the Baghdad museum).

7. Grimal, 1992.

8. I am principally following Vendel (2004).

9. The sheer number of Hyksos finds throughout Palestine does suggest that the local rulers at least acknowledged the overlordship of Avaris in some way.

10. A single 17th Dynasty text suggests that Thebes was, at least for a time, subject to the Hyksos (Williams, 1975). Bricks have also been found in Upper Egypt (at Gebelein) bearing the names of both Khyan and Apopis. Apopis himself is described as "king of Upper and Lower Egypt" in several inscriptions, although there is no direct evidence that he was ever acknowledged in Thebes. Several texts suggest peaceful relations with Thebes in Apopis' time although the strongest evidence appears to be the absence of any sign of hostilities.

11. By far the most common scarabs (394 in total) are those of Sheshi, whose position in the list of Hyksos kings is disputed. The fact that these scarabs have been found in relatively early levels at Sharuhen suggests an early reign. Rohl (1995) points out that one has also

been found late in the Jericho tomb sequence and uses this to adjust history considerably. However, with 394 scattered around, it would hardly be surprising if some had a long life as valuable artefacts, particularly amongst a people who couldn't even read the hieroglyphs inscribed on them.

12. Hattusili I's annals were recorded on a small golden statue found at Hattusas and appear to relate to a six year period, presumably early in his reign. However, some suppose that the text actually represents edited highlights from a much longer period.

13. *Umman Manda* seems originally to have been an Akkadian expression meaning 'terrible people', with a reference during Agade times (see note 18 of Chapter 5), probably to the first Hittite invaders. It is also used much later (7th Century BC) to refer to the Medes of eastern Iran. However, in this period of history we read that Ammisaduga of Babylon fought a battle against the Umman Manda and that they were also fighting for the Hurrians against Hattusili I of Hatti at Hassuwa.

14. The inscription referring to a Hurrian king as a king of the Umman Manda dates to the 13th Century BC (in this chronology) and it comes from Alalakh. Coming from a mainly Hurrian city, this makes sense; the Hurrians would have looked on the Umman Manda as foreigners long after the rest of the world had accepted them as Hurrian.

15. The text concerned was on the subject of chariotry, which seems to have been an Indo-European speciality (Piggott, 1950).

16. Hattusili's annals make it clear that Yamkhad and the Hurrians (plus the "officers of the Umman Manda") were acting in concert.

17. Extracts from Hammurabi's law code were even found in the 7th Century BC palace of king Ashurbanipal of Assyria.

18. The age of 40 is not actually given in the book of Exodus but is found in the words of Stephen in Acts 7:23. Stephen was presumably quoting from another text, no longer in our possession.

19. We know something of Artapanus' work from quotations by Eusebius (Rohl, 1995).

20. Khyan's reign represents the high-point of Hyksos power and the bricks with his name on them found at Gebelein just south of Thebes indicate that the regime at Thebes was at least friendly and probably subservient. It is just possible, therefore, that a campaign against Kush could have been fought, involving forces from both the Hyksos and Upper Egypt, although we have no other record of such a campaign.

21. Midian is never pin-pointed in Bible texts but it is consistently portrayed as lying to the east or south-east of Palestine.

22. We know nothing of the fate of Khamudy; nor can we be 100% sure that he was the direct successor to Apopis. It is therefore not impossible that a pharaoh of Egypt died at the time the Israelites left. However, I do not believe that this is directly stated anywhere in the Bible.

23. Some suggest that Rephidim, where the Israelites camped *en route* from Egypt to Mount Sinai, should be identified with Serabit.

24. The Serabit El Khadum inscriptions are presumed by most researchers to have been made by Canaanite employees working the mines – which could be true. The inscriptions are subject to various translations; many seem to describe the purpose of stone enclosures, including metallurgical terms, so there is no definite link to the Israelites. Nevertheless, the date has been narrowed down to this specific period (Beit-Arieh, 1984). It is also noteworthy that similar (but possibly later) inscriptions have been found dotted across the Negev Desert, a large percentage of which mention the names used for God in the Bible, *Yahu* and *El* (Harris and Hone, 2006).

25. Egyptian, like the Semitic languages, is of the Afro-Asiatic language family, whose origin most linguists would place in East Africa somewhere.

26. The dominant language in Yemen today is the North Semitic language Arabic, but there are still a few communities in both Yemen and Oman where South Semitic tongues are spoken.

Chapter 10. The Growth of Empire: 1400-1300BC

1. Mitchell (1990) identifies several possible dates for eclipses which, according to the tablets, relate to the fall of Gutium, the death of king Shulgi of Ur, and the fall of Ur under king Ibbi Sin. However, in my opinion there are simply too many eclipse date options to choose from. Rohl (2002) selects 1908BC, 1835BC and 1793BC for these three events, all some 10 to 20 years earlier than the dates I have suggested.

2. Mitchell, 1990.

3. The fact that the Kassites were able to restore Babylon's gods provides further evidence that they had been acting in concert with the Hittites. The gods had presumably been left with the Kassite king in Terqa.

4. The *Assyrian king list* is an exceptionally useful document. The reign lengths are listed for every Assyrian king following Shamsi Adad I except two, and they appear to correlate very well with the histories of other countries over a period of many hundreds of years. In proposing dates in this book, I have made the assumption that the reign length quoted means that the monarch in question had at least started that particular year of his reign. I have assigned 15 and 10 years respectively to the two missing reigns (Ashur Rabi I and Ashur Nadin Ahhe I).

5. Williams (1975) detects evidence that the city destructions of southern Palestine (he highlights Jericho, Bethel, Debir and Gibeon) occurred a decade or so earlier than those of northern Palestine (including Hazor). This is based on the archaeology of the sites.

6. We only have a few lines of Tuthmose I's annals, most of which are concerned with a campaign in Nubia. He simply states that he "overthrew the Asiatics" before journeying to Syria.

7. To the Egyptians a conventional river flowed from south to north, like the Nile. The Euphrates therefore flows the 'wrong way', which they expressed as 'flowing upstream'.

8. The deduction that the Level V temple was dedicated to Mithras comes from Woolley's (1953) observation of a sunken sanctuary, which is very unusual in the Middle East but became common in Mithras temples of the Roman Empire period.

9. The siege evidence is again based on Woolley's (1953) observations. It reflects his interpretation of the presence of a grain silo and burials of women and children within the city's citadel, which someone had then deliberately demolished.

10. Qatna is currently under excavation. However, a funerary complex has been unearthed which served the royal family over a period of some hundreds of years, suggesting cultural continuity. Mitannian control may therefore have been relatively loose.

11. The 'good reason' stems from the campaign reports of king Tuthmose III of Egypt, who fought long and hard against both Kadesh and Mitanni. The clear inference is that the two were allied.

12. For example, so-called white-slip milk bowls appear throughout Levels VI and V at Alalakh, that is from about 1500BC in this chronology (Woolley, 1953).

13. The city of Avaris has revealed evidence of Cretan-style wall frescos showing typically Cretan scenes of bull-leaping. These could date from either Hyksos times or the early 18th Dynasty.

14. Evidence of direct Cretan influence can be seen on the islands of Aegina, Kea, Melos, Thera and Phylakopi, in the shape of Linear A texts. On Phylakopi, there appears to have been a Cretan quarter.

15. At Knossos Hutchinson (1962) reports an ash layer with Late Minoan 1a pottery both above and below it.

16. The subject of the length of an average generation always raises controversy. For better or worse, I have assumed 25 years as an average and 20 years for a first-born generation. In this case, just one of the three generations in question is likely to have been a first-born generation.

17. Tuthmose II's campaign brings the first mention of which I am aware of the Shosu (*shepherd* in Egyptian) people of the Negev and southern Palestine, possibly to be identified with Palestine-based Hyksos clans.
18. Megiddo was in alliance with Kadesh, so Tuthmose informs us, and we can be pretty sure that both were in alliance with Mitanni (see note 11).
19. It is interesting that Tuthmose III justified his conquest as far as the Euphrates with reference to the claims of his grandfather Tuthmose I. The fact that Tuthmose I had erected a stela on the banks of the Euphrates was enough for his grandson to consider all of Palestine and western Syria to be rightfully Egyptian. In Tuthmose III's eyes, Megiddo and Kadesh were rebel cities.
20. The distribution of Amalekites according to the Bible (Negev desert and southern Palestine/Jordan) approximately matches the distribution of the Shosu people encountered by the Egyptians. They may therefore be Hyksos groups (see note 17 and Chapter 8, note 27).
21. Arad is one of those cities where archaeology does not appear to support the Bible. The site known today as Tell Arad, a few miles west of the southern end of the Dead Sea, shows no evidence of occupation during this period at all. However, Aharoni (1976) suggests that nearby Tell Malhata, which was occupied throughout the Middle Bronze Age, is the real location of ancient Arad.
22. It is only relatively recently that archaeological evidence has emerged for a sedentary population east of the Jordan during these times (Andrade, 2002).
23. Traditionally Ai has been identified with the mound of Et Tell about 3km east of Ramallah, and the fact that this site was certainly unoccupied during the whole of the Middle and Late Bronze Ages has frequently been used to discredit the Bible's account of Joshua's campaigns. However, the nearby site of Khirbet el Maqatir appears to many to be a much more likely candidate for the Biblical Ai. See Andrade (2002).
24. This reduction in urban population is highlighted by Williams (1975).
25. The non-urban lifestyle of the period was dramatically evident from a study of the central highland area carried out by Adam Zertal and reported by Wilson (1999).
26. It is clear from the Bible (2 Samuel 10:5) that Jericho was occupied in the early 10th Century BC, i.e. well before the time of Ahab. The archaeology also suggests no more than about 200 years of total abandonment (Kenyon, 1970). The re-founding during the days of Ahab may therefore represent the turning of a modest town into a walled city once more.
27. Refer to note 15 of Chapter 6.
28. The dates quoted assume that Joshua survived for 30 years following the conquest, dying in about 1336BC. The Bible reports that he died aged 110, and it also reports that his close colleague Caleb was 80 years of age at the time of the conquest (1365BC).
29. Archaeology (Finkelstein, 1988) reveals a dramatic fall in the number of towns occupied in upland Palestine during the Late Bronze Age in comparison with the Middle Bronze Age (25-30 compared to nearly 200). This implies a complete change to a much more nomadic, or at least tent-dwelling, culture.

Chapter 11. Big Bang: 1300-1250BC

1. Physical evidence of this 'ravaging' of the land east of the Euphrates can be seen in the destruction of the Balikh valley sites of Jidle and Hammam (Mallowan, 1956). These destructions were of levels containing white-painted Mitannian ware.
2. In fact, most researchers now seem to disagree with the view I am taking, which is based on Woolley's initial assessment of the archaeological evidence (Woolley, 1953) and Sydney Smith's original translation of Idrimi's statue (see note 6 of Chapter 12).
3. Because of the rather different view of the sequence of kings of Mukis taken by most researchers, implying a rather different time-frame for Sunassura of Kizzuwadna, this treaty is not normally ascribed to Hantili II. However, Hantili is usually awarded another equally anonymous treaty with a king Paddatissu of Kizzuwadna (e.g. Bryce, 1998). Both may be correct of course since Hantili's reign was longer than many.

4. The sequence of eruptions on Thera can be determined approximately from the various ash and pumice layers. It seems that a relatively modest eruption, accompanied by lava flows, caused abandonment of the island and that this was followed 10-30 years later by the 'big one', spewing 10 cubic miles or so of ash into the sky and leading to catastrophic tidal waves due to under-water collapse of the sides of the volcano. See Heicken and McCoy (1984).

5. Hood, 1967.

6. See Zielinski et al (1984). Thera is a very similar volcano to Krakatoa, with evidence for a very similar pattern of eruption, based on the evidence of ash and pumice. This means that the eruption of Thera would have been of similar or probably greater violence but, as at Krakatoa, the overall volume of ash was still insufficient to cause the worldwide climatic effects of larger but less violent eruptions such as that of Tambora in 1815 (Luce, 1969).

7. Mainland Greek influence is claimed for Late Minoan II stemmed drinking cups and palace-style vases; similarly, shaft graves where single warriors were buried accompanied by rich grave goods.

8. Amenophis II records gifts from Babylon; there is also reference in the later Amarna correspondence to trade relations which must have stretched back to well before 1250BC.

9. *Babylonian king list A* gives 368 years for the Sealand Dynasty, which seems an impossibly high figure even allowing for considerable overlap with other dynasties. True independence for the Sealand region (southern Iraq) was only achieved some time during Samsu Iluna's reign, less than 150 years before the fall of Babylon to the Hittites. Archaeology then tells us unequivocally that Karaindash of Babylon was in charge again within 100 years of the Kassites taking over. The implication is, therefore, that the neat linear progression of Sealand kings given in the king list conceals something more complex, presumably that there was at least one period when more than one of the recorded Sealand kings ruled at the same time. This is a timely warning that a king list, whether Egyptian, Babylonian or Assyrian, can never be relied upon in the absence of other supporting data.

10. The word *Habiru* appears as a Sumerian logogram from the days of Shulgi king of Ur, where it refers to a tent-dwelling class of people who live entirely outside the jurisdiction of the state. Similar references are found throughout the Isin period and then the rule of the Amorite dynasties, and it is clear that the Habiru could be from any ethnic group. It is only during the reign of Tuthmose III that the 'Apiru are found in Egyptian records. It therefore seems likely that the Israelites were designated Habiru/'Apiru/Hebrew by surrounding states in recognition of their stateless and semi-nomadic lifestyle rather than because of their ethnic origin.

11. This reflects my own analysis (Thom, 2006). However, others have come to the view that Hurrian was a North-East Caucasian language and that Hattian may have been North-West Caucasian.

12. This statement is based on the large differences between the modern North-West Caucasian languages Circassian and Abkhaz.

Chapter 12. A Golden Age: 1250-1200BC

1. See note 10 of Chapter 11.

2. Bryce (1998) reports the publication of a text written in hieroglyphic Luwian on a silver bowl in the Ankara museum. The text refers to the conquest of "Taruisa" by a king "Tudhalya".

3. Tudhalya I's second campaign in western Turkey, according to his annals, was in response to a declaration of war by a confederation of 22 kings from "Arsuwa" (Asia). The first name may be "Lukka" (the text is damaged), in the far south-west, classical Lycia, and the last name is certainly "Taruisa" (Troy), in the far north-west; the implication is that the remaining 20 names, most of which are otherwise unknown, relate to places in between, i.e. along the western coast of Turkey.

4. The information is contained in a treaty between Muwatalli II of Hatti and Talmi Sar-rumah viceroy of Aleppo, dating to the second half of the 12th Century BC (in the chronology of this book). After Tudhalya's conquest of Aleppo, it is stated that the population had to deal with a king of Hatti named "Hattusili", who is otherwise unattested. I suggest that this individual (known to historians as Hattusili II) looked after Tudhalya's Syrian possessions, while Tudhalya and his other co-ruler Arnuwanda I ruled the rest of the empire.

5. Most commentators favour a location for Wassuganni somewhere near modern Di-yarbakir in south-east Turkey, based on the contexts in which the city is mentioned, no-tably the campaigns of the Hittites and Assyrians.

6. My mention of Shuturna directly contradicts the opinions of most commentators. The problem is that there have been variant readings of the relevant name on Idrimi's statue. Sydney Smith, who originally read the text for Leonard Woolley not long after it had been found, read it as *Shuturna* (Woolley, 1953), but the same symbols read slightly differently could also be *Parattarna*, and most since (for example Bryce, 1998) have gone with *Parat-tarna*. I am sticking to Smith's original reading here for the simple reason that the place-ment of Idrimi's reign at this juncture rather than two generations previously seems to me to make much better historical sense.

7. Tablets from Ugarit include many in the Hurrian language, suggesting that Ugarit, like Alalakh, was originally a Hurrian city, although for much of its history it clearly lay right on the border between the Semitic and Hurrian worlds.

8. Gurney, 1954.

9. Ugarit's relations with the Egyptian-controlled lands to the south can be seen in the find-ing of Ugaritic texts in Palestine (at Taanach, Bethshemesh and on Mount Tabor) but nowhere else outside Ugarit itself.

10. The *Epic of Kret* has been shown to have similarities with the epic tales of Mycenaean Greece and to deal with similar themes. There are also those who believe that it shares a common heritage with some of the stories in the Bible, notably those of the patriarchs. Whether this is accepted or not, it is clear that many of the poetic expressions in the *Epic of Kret* are paralleled in some of the psalms of the Bible, suggesting some commonality between Hebrew literary culture and that of Ugarit. See Gordon (1975).

11. The document, known to researchers as the *Indictment of Madduwatta*, goes on to tell us that Tudhalya of Hatti intervened and put Madduwatta on the throne of 'Zippasla' and (later) the 'Siyanti river land', which I suggest was the southern coastal region of Turkey and the Seyhan river area of Cilicia (previously part of Kizzuwadna).

12. The resemblance between the name 'Attarsiya' and 'Atreus', known in Greek mythology as the father of Agamemnon, has been pointed out by numerous investigators.

13. See Chapter 14 under *'What was going on in the rest of the world?'*

14. Most Biblical commentators make the assumption that the word *Hebrew* is related to Abraham's ancestor Eber. However, this is no more than supposition and I do not believe the evidence supports it (see note 10 of Chapter 11).

Chapter 13. Sunrise over Hatti: 1200-1150BC

1. Tyldesley (1998) presents a full description of the art of Akhenaten's time, including dis-cussion of the apparently distorted body shapes sometimes used when depicting Akhen-aten himself.

2. The 'Great Hymn of the Aten', found on the walls of an Amarna tomb, has been com-pared many times to Psalm 104 in the Bible. The general form of expression used is cer-tainly similar.

3. There is extensive reference to Labaya in the Amarna correspondence, including three let-ters from Labaya himself denying the wrongdoing which others are accusing him of, but referring to the fact that he had "entered Gezer". Biridia of Megiddo refers to Labaya's plans to take his city, then to Labaya being defeated and captured. Later we read from

Shuwardata, possibly of Gath, that Labaya had died. In several letters (for example from Abdi Heba of Jerusalem) we read that Labaya's sons were consorting with the Habiru, referred to many times as "the enemy". Rohl (1995) identifies Labaya as king Saul of Israel, and he has recently highlighted the finding of a cylinder seal of Labaya's at Bethshan, the city on whose walls Saul's body was hung after his defeat by the Philistines.

4. Milkilu of Gezer was a rival of Labaya. However, it is later reported by Abdi Heba of Jerusalem and Addu Qarrad (city unknown) that he became strongly allied to the sons of Labaya.

5. The series of letters from Abdi Heba of Jerusalem makes fascinating reading. He complains that the Habiru are taking the cities, that Milkilu is conspiring to isolate Jerusalem, that there are enemy troops in Bethshan and, most regularly of all, that the pharaoh sees nothing and does nothing! Of course, one has to assume a large dose of exaggeration, but the picture which is painted is one of a general breakdown of Egyptian authority and a marked increase in the influence of the Habiru.

6. Rib Addi of Byblos was the most prolific of the Amarna letter writers with nearly 70 to his name and his letters paint a very similar picture of events in Lebanon and southern Syria to those in Palestine. Rib Addi accuses Abdi Ashirta of Amurru of allying himself with the Habiru in order to achieve his aim of taking Byblos. On the other hand we read from Abdi Ashirta himself that all he was doing was looking after the interests of the pharaoh – by occupying Rib Addi's towns! Egyptian authority was clearly evaporating very fast indeed.

7. It is tempting to identify the land called 'Amka' in the Amarna letters with the country known as 'Aba' by the Egyptians, with its capital at Damascus. However, this remains speculative.

8. The archive material which has recently been emerging from the excavation at Qatna includes a letter from Suppiluliuma to Idanda concerning preparations for war as well as orders from Idanda for the manufacture and distribution of swords.

9. This dispute has produced very entrenched views on either side. Tyldesley (1998) presents a discussion of the evidence and concludes that Nefertiti predeceased Akhenaten, based largely on the lack of any evidence for her existence during the last couple of years of Akhenaten's rule.

10. The deduction that queen Henti was exiled to Greece is based on a fragmentary tablet and is still unproven (Bryce, 1998).

11. King Akizzi of Qatna is among those who pleaded for assistance from Egypt, stating that his city along with Niy and Tunip were in grave danger of being overrun.

12. We read about this invasion both in the annals of Mursili I of Hatti and also in a text from Adad Nirari I of Assyria but relating to the time of one of his predecessors, presumably Enlil Nirari. The timing of it seems to have been prompted as much as anything by the death of Sarri Kusuh, Mursili's brother and viceroy of Carchemish. Assyrian occupation doesn't seem to have lasted long before Mursili restored Hittite control.

13. The fact that a degree of mutual tolerance existed can be seen in that Niqmaddu of Ugarit, who had become a Hittite vassal, also married a daughter of Haremheb (Rohl, 2002). However, the status of Ugarit was rather higher than that of most vassals. Suppiluliuma had rewarded Niqmaddu with as much territory as he could lay his hands on during the war against Mitanni so long as he remained firmly on the Hittite side in that conflict – we have Suppiluliuma's letter on the subject. Niqmaddu was clearly able to determine his own foreign policy on matters other than the Mitanni conflict.

14. Interestingly, the same Level VI at Lachish produced an example of proto-Canaanite writing, the script which was directly ancestral to Hebrew, Phoenician, Greek and, eventually, Latin (Ussishkin, 1978).

15. This deduction is based on the finding of threads of fabric in sealing wax (Hutchinson, 1962).

16. Oates, 1986.

Chapter 14. Clash of the Titans: 1150-1100BC

1. Seti justified this campaign by claiming that he was attacked by the combined forces of Hamath and Pella. Hamath was a Hittite dependency; Pella was a Canaanite city and had presumably rebelled against Egyptian authority.

2. Hattusili tells us all about his successes against the Kaskans in his autobiography. He was immensely proud of having restored the sacred cities of Nerik (seat of the storm god) and Tiliura to Hittite control.

3. Tarhuntassa has not been identified. On grounds of phonetic similarity, Tarsus in Cilicia, which we know from archaeology was an important Hittite city, seems an obvious choice, but there doesn't seem to be any other evidence for this.

4. Cyprus was not, so far as we know, part of the Hittite empire at this stage. It was presumably a close ally, with strong cultural ties to Ugarit, Hatti's strongest ally in Syria.

5. Ramesses II sent a letter to Hattusili reminding him of the words of the king of Assyria (probably Adad Nirari I) that he was no more than a "substitute for a great king" (Bryce, 1998).

6. Some have noted that the Late Bronze Age temple at Shechem wasn't large enough to hold 1000 people. I suspect that the solution to this riddle, however, lies in finding the true meaning of the archaic Hebrew word transcribed, re-transcribed and then translated as *a thousand*.

7. See Wilson (1999), who refers to the opinion of some that *Isr* may be *Asher*, one of the tribes of Israel. However, the location (the Shechem area) is quite different from the coastal territory ascribed to Asher in the Bible.

8. Note also that an inscription dating to Amenophis III in a temple at Soleb, now in northern Sudan, refers to "Yahu of the Shosu". Yahu is clearly the same as Yahweh, the name used for the God of Israel (Redford, 1992).

9. The Guanche people of the Canary Islands have now disappeared from history under the weight of six centuries of Spanish occupation. However, those fragments of their language that were recorded are clearly related to the Berber languages of North Africa (Thom, 2006).

10. For example, Sandars (1978).

11. The list of cities and lands conquered by Tudalya is far from crystal clear and numerous individuals have speculated as to the locations. Allied to Arzawa, Hapalla and the Seha river land were Sariyanda (Sardis?), Uliwanda (Alabanda?) and Parsuhalda (Purushanda/Pisidia?). If these identifications are correct, the region of these three cities centred on the upper reaches of the Maeander river. Tudhalya then reports that he fought the Limiya river land, Akpuisa (Ephesus?), Pariyana (Priene?), Arinna (Alinda?), Wallarima (Euromos?) and Halatarsa (Halicarnassus?) clustering around the lower Maeander valley. Thus, the Limiya river of the Hittites seems most likely to be the Maeander of the Greeks.

Chapter 15. Troy: 1100-1050BC

1. See note 14 of Chapter 5.

2. The earliest claimed usage of non-meteoric iron of which I am aware comes from a find at the site of Chagar Bazaar in northern Syria, dating to the Jemdet Nasr or Early Dynastic I period, i.e. before 2500BC (Mallowan, 1956).

3. The clearest evidence we have is in the wording of a treaty between Tudhalya and Sausgamuwa king of Amurru. Here it is explicitly stated that Hatti is at war with Assyria and that no Assyrian goods are to be allowed through Amurru.

4. Even today, Choga Zambil rivals the great pyramids of Egypt (see Hinz, 1972). In fact, its multi-layer construction means that it greatly resembles a step pyramid. However, as a ziggurat it was never just a tomb but a great temple to the Elamite gods Humban and Inshushinak at the heart of a new city, Dur Untash. It is powerful testimony to the wealth of Elam at the time.

5. Both Kition and Enkomi, the two largest cities on the island, show destructions datable to late in the Mycenaean IIIb period, the time window during which Tudhalya IV invaded.
6. Excavation at Troy is proceeding today under the direction of Manfred Korfmann of the University of Tübingen.
7. The clearest illustration of this effect that I can think of comes from the Bantu languages of southern Africa, which have all diverged from a common ancestor less than 3000 years ago. The word for *two* is *piri* in the Shona language of Zimbabwe and *wili* in the Yao language of neighbouring Mozambique and virtually every combination of *b, p, v,* or *w* followed by *r* or *l* can be found in one Bantu language or another.
8. Homer lists nearly a thousand ships from Greece, each of which would have held at least 50 men. He also describes contingents as coming from all corners of the Greek world. On the Trojan side, contingents are listed from right across western Turkey, from Lycia in the south-west to the Bosphorus. According to Homer the war lasted fully 10 years.
9. Suppiluliuma II refers in his coronation oath to widespread rebellion against his brother Arnuwanda (Bryce, 1998).
10. Several authors have referred to this piece of graffiti, notably Janssen (1987). Rohl disputes the interpretation and prefers Month 2 of Year 2 rather than Month 3 of Year 1 but, as some have pointed out, this actually damages his case rather than assisting it. I am no expert on Egyptian short-hand but it looks more like Month 3 of Year 1 to me. Rohl also prefers the reading that the flood 'started to go down' rather than 'returned'. Unfortunately, this damages the case he makes for his own chronology still further! See Rohl's web-site www.nunki.net to view the inscription.
11. In the context of the history emerging from this book, the most likely explanation is that Egypt's allies in Palestine, the Philistines and Sherden, had been stamping their authority on any part of the region which failed to acknowledge Egyptian overlordship.
12. See Zertal (1985), quoted by Wilson (1999).
13. The destruction of Stratum VI at Tell Dan saw the end of Canaanite occupation and the arrival of a people using typical Israelite pottery (collared rim storage jars etc). The date is conventionally given as early 12th Century BC, which translates to the mid 11th Century BC in this chronology.
14. Accurate dates for the Shang Dynasty have not been agreed by historians. Estimates for the defeat of the Shang range from about 1122BC down to 1027BC.
15. For a suggested explanation for this link to America, see Thom (2006).

Chapter 16. Peoples of the Sea: 1050-1000BC

1. For example, the well-known rock inscriptions at Yazilikaya near Hattusas, dating to the reign of Tudhalya IV, are in hieroglyphic Luwian.
2. In fact it was the mystery of hieroglyphic Luwian which first led researchers to talk in terms of a great Hittite empire. Only with the later discovery of the tablet archive at Hattusas was it realized that the hieroglyphic script actually post-dated an earlier cuneiform means of writing Hittite.
3. The *Harris Papyrus,* dating from the reign of Ramesses IV, refers to these times as "empty years" with no universally acknowledged leader, no central government and a consequent breakdown of law and order.
4. A stela which Setnakht set up at Elephantine in southern Egypt declares that he "rid the land of foreigners". Bay may have been of non-Egyptian origin.
5. A silver pen case of Ramesses III was found at Megiddo; an inscription of the 'Great Steward' of Ramesses III was found at Bethshan.
6. For example, the round hearths found at Ekron parallel examples found at Mycenae and Pylos (Wilson, 1999).
7. I consider the current majority view that the Peleset/Philistines were just another 'People of the Sea', arriving in Philistia early in Ramesses III's reign, to fly in the face of the evi-

dence. Besides the references to towns and orchards, the fact is that these people are never mentioned in connection with any location other than Philistia itself.

8. It is clear that the inhabitants of Cilicia came to be known as 'Danunites', a word with the same root as the major city of the region, Adana. This we read on a Luwian rock inscription at Karatepe (Gurney, 1954). Furthermore, it seems this region was known as Danuna by some as far back as the Amarna letters period since Abi Milki king of Tyre refers to the "death of the king of Danuna". The situation is complicated by the evidence that refugees from the Trojan War set up their own state in Cilicia and, of course, many of these may have been of Greek origin.

9. See Landau (2003).

10. The presence of Dorians is often linked to that of 'cist graves'. They were used in northwest Greece during Mycenaean IIIb times and subsequently spread steadily across the country (Hood, 1967).

11. Three copies of the *Assyrian king list* exist, known as A, B and C. King lists B and C agree but give shorter reigns for two of the kings of this period than king list A. I have opted to believe king lists B and C since the reign lengths given tie in with the history told in this book.

12. The idea of shared kingship is unusual but not unique. The Greek city state of Sparta was famous for its dual kingship system.

13. 1 Samuel 13:1 appears to give a 2-year reign for king Saul, something which is quite impossible if the rest of the history of Saul told in the Bible is to be believed. Scholars therefore assume that something is missing due to transcription error and that the actual number was originally 12, 22, 32, 42 or 52. Since Acts 13:21 (Saint Paul's words) quotes a reign of 40 years, most Biblical commentators therefore suggest *42 years* as the original for 1 Samuel 13:1. My view is that *32 years* fits the evidence of the events in Saul's life better; it also ties in better with the dates which I have already deduced for Samuel and Abdon.

14. Goliath's armour is of historical interest. He is said to have worn bronze 'greaves', i.e. lower leg protection, which was a typically Greek form of battle-wear.

15. This date is principally derived by counting backwards from the relatively confidently dated reigns of Omri and Ahab in the 9th Century BC, using the reign lengths given in the Bible. However, it also ties in with my suggestion in note 13 that Saul reigned for 32 years and followed directly on from Abdon.

16. The reason the archaeology of Jerusalem is so difficult is that the majority of it has been destroyed over the centuries as subsequent building phases levelled the ancient hill-top site of old Jerusalem. The information used in this book is taken from Kenyon (1974).

Chapter 17. Chaos and Darkness Reign: 1000-950BC

1. Eusebius quotes 178 years rather than 135.

2. It seems likely that a document known as the *Testimony of Amenpnufer* dates from this time, since Amenpnufer speaks of "habitually robbing tombs" and that "many others are engaged in similar activities".

3. Harrison, 2003.

4. Philistine pottery parallels Phoenician styles throughout this period, both going through a monochrome and then a bichrome phase.

5. Mazar and Carmi, 2001.

6. Gilboa and Sharon (2001) have also published 10th Century BC dates for a contemporary level at Dor. Boaretto et al (2005) summarise the cumulative dating evidence, suggesting that the history of Philistia and Phoenicia should be lowered in date significantly compared to the conventional view (in line with the suggestions made in this book).

7. Both proto-Geometric and Cypro-Geometric styles are clearly derivative from Mycenaean IIIc.

8. According to Thucydides, the Dorians arrived 80 years after the Trojan War (Murray, 1993), which would be 980BC according to this book.

9. We can only be confident about a Lydian state from about 685BC when the house of Mermnadae took charge. However, writers such as Herodotus imply that earlier kings ruled, and the culture and language of Lydia when it emerges is directly derived from Hittite/Luwian.

10. As stated in note 11 of Chapter 16, I am following the shorter version of Assyrian history (by 12 years) given in king lists B and C.

11. Nothing is known about the Khirikhi people other than repeated Assyrian conquests. Some suggest that they were Indo-European tribes like the Medes and Persians; I consider it much more likely that they were the ancestors of today's Georgians (or Kartvelians) who, on language evidence (Thom, 2006), reached the Caucasus via western Iran.

12. The word *Nairi* is used by modern-day Armenians as a poetic name for their country. The fact that Tiglath Pileser reached Armenia is proved by an inscription at Melazgerd.

13. The expression used here is 'Upper Sea', which in many ancient texts clearly means the Mediterranean (the 'Lower Sea' being the Persian Gulf). However, in this case the geography of Tiglath Pileser's campaign strongly suggests that the Black Sea is meant. In the eyes of ancient Assyrians, there is no reason to think that these two bodies of water would have been thought of as separate.

14. Azerbaijan still holds many secrets for archaeologists. The ancient trading centre of Mingethaur on the Kura river was certainly established by the 2nd Millennium BC. Whether this was one of the lands known to Tiglath Pileser as Muzri and Comani remains unknown however.

15. Manetho does not quote the reign lengths of the 20th Dynasty rulers so it is necessary to deduce them from contemporary texts. Although no other text has been found from Ramesses IX's 19th year, he may still have lived through at least part of it.

16. In *Papyrus Mayer A* it is said that some of the tomb-robbers were "killed by Pinhasi" and others "killed in the war in the northern district". If Pinhasi had time to dispense justice to tomb-robbers this implies that he was in charge of Thebes for a period of some months at least.

17. We have a record of an order sent to Pinhasi in Year 17 (of Ramesses IX if my deductions are correct) to arrange the procurement of special furniture and also precious stones for one of the temples.

18. Piankh is known chiefly from several items of correspondence with a certain Dhutmose and his son. Dhutmose was apparently looking after affairs in Thebes while Piankh was away with the army in the south. The obvious assumption is that he was pursuing (ultimately unsuccessfully) the war against Pinhasi and his break-away state of Nubia.

19. Many suggest they may have been father and son, but there is no hard evidence for this.

20. Just as Herihor was, among other things, vizier of Upper Egypt, Nesbanebded seems to have filled the role of vizier of Lower Egypt.

21. This particular group of pirates were the Tjekker, one of the 'Peoples of the Sea', now living in Dor.

22. Bennett (1996) is among those who suggest that Smendes was a son of Herihor.

23. Another personality mentioned in the tale is "Khaemwise" in whose days an earlier expedition evidently arrived at Byblos and, judging by the words of Zakarbaal, it was even less successful than Wenamun's. In this reconstruction he is to be identified with Khaemwise, vizier of Upper Egypt during the days of Ramesses IX, who was one of the presiding authorities at the tomb robber trials in Ramesses IX's 16th year.

24. For this he physically caused many of the monuments and even entire buildings of Piramesse to be transported and re-erected at Tanis, where many inscriptions of Ramesses II have been found, much to the confusion of archaeologists.

25. Hagens (1999) illustrates the archaeological connections between the various cities of Palestine and Lebanon during this period. He argues that the overall picture points strongly to a much reduced chronology compared to conventional opinion.

NOTES

Chapter 18. Judgement Day: 950-900BC

1. An Assyrian chronicle tells us that the inhabitants of Babylonia were reduced to eating human flesh and that this occurred at the end of Marduk Nadin Ahhe's reign, 933BC according to this book (Oates, 1986).

2. This means that I am 'cutting' the *Assyrian king list* between Ashurnasirpal I and Shalmaneser II and I suggest that all references to Shalmaneser being a son of Ashurnasirpal should be ascribed to Shalmaneser III, son of Ashurnasirpal II. The two parts of the king list are then overlapped by about 146 years.

3. Documents relating to Ashur Resha Ishi I refer to his being a son of Ashur Dan I, whereas later documents and the *Assyrian king list* name Ashur Rabi as the father of a second Ashur Resha Ishi. It is of course possible that there were two Ashur Resha Ishis, but the more likely scenario seems to me to be that an erroneous assumption was made in non-contemporary documentation.

4. Ashur Dan II's annals tell us that he provided ploughs throughout the land. Thus, as well as letting us know that Ashur Dan II was a real ruler, this also gives information on the state of the agricultural economy. Something had prevented normal farming from taking place and the obvious cause is Aramaean invaders. The contention of this book is that as Ashur Bel Kala fought military campaigns against the Aramaeans so his brother and co-ruler Ashur Dan did his best to restore the economy of the country after the terrible famine which had caused his father Tiglath Pileser to appoint him in the first place.

5. Eight ancestors of Shamsi Adad I are also inserted into the king list and fictitious father-son relationships added. Fortunately, our records are good enough for us to spot that one! The propensity of the compiler to invent father-son relationships is also seen in the case of Ashuruballit I, whose father according to the king list is Eriba Adad I but whose father on contemporary monuments is Ashur Nadin Ahhe.

6. King Ahiram's tomb at Byblos is datable to Ramesses II's time by the presence of pottery with his cartouche; kings Abibaal and Elibaal are datable to the times of pharaohs Shoshenq I and Osorkon I by inscription evidence. However, the Canaanite script associated with all three kings is similar, suggesting the passage of much less than the 300 years which conventional chronology would demand.

7. Refer to notes 5 and 6 of Chapter 17.

8. In most cases the identity of the previous owner of the various funerary goods had been carefully obscured, but the name of pharaoh Merneptah had accidentally been left in a corner of the pink granite sarcophagus which Psusennes had decided to use.

9. There is plenty of reference to Psusennes I being a king's son and, despite not being on any of Manetho's lists, Pinudjem I definitely took over kingship in Thebes. Furthermore, Psusennes I took as his Horus name 'The star which arose in Thebes', which indicates that his ancestry did not lie in northern Egypt where he reigned.

10. The list is in four rows; the slab is broken at one end. The size of the missing end-piece can be estimated from the fact that at the unbroken end of one row we have a priest with no pharaoh named, preceded by one who was installed under Amenophis I; at the broken end of the next row we have a priest who was installed under Tuthmose III. Amenophis I reigned for 19 years and was followed 49 years later by Tuthmose III who reigned for 33 years. Obviously it is impossible to be certain how many priests of Ptah there should have been over this period, hence the point that there may be up to three columns missing at the broken end of the slab. Inevitably very strong opinions have been expressed on this matter, either based on the shape of the broken slab edge or on historical evidence, but personally I cannot see that certainty is possible. Rohl (1995) gives an excellent illustration of the slab.

11. There is strong reason to believe that the reigns of Nephercheres and Psusennes I overlapped since the two names are found together on a set of bow-caps recovered from Psusennes I's tomb. Kitchen (1996) has added an argument for joint rule between Amenemophthis and Psusennes I, although this is based on an unattached mummy bandage

which has unfortunately since been lost. It is reported to have given the name of *Amenemophthis* together with a *Year 49* mark, which can only refer to Psusennes I in this context. The presence of four items in Amenemophthis' tomb with Psusennes I's name on also strongly suggests a close association between the two rulers.

12. See note 11.

13. On the Ptah priest list, the priest who was installed in the reign of Nephercheres was followed by one who served under a certain 'Akheperre', the next two served under a 'Psusennes', there is then one with no pharaoh's name, and he is followed by a priest against which is inscribed the name 'Hedjkheperre', the prenomen of Shoshenq I. Logically, 'Psusennes' refers to Psusennes II and 'Akheperre' refers to either Osochor or Psinaches; either is possible since we don't know any names other than those Manetho gives. The entry with no name would probably fall in Amenemophthis' reign. Overall, therefore, I conclude that the Ptah priest list makes good sense – which is not a conclusion that you will see expressed too often!

14. Pinudjem is known for the active role he played in re-interring several of the mummies of earlier kings, presumably following the wide-spread tomb robbing which, as we have seen, was rife during the reign of Ramesses IX. We know of his role in this because, when the mummies were eventually unearthed toward the end of the 19th Century, stashed away in hidden rock tombs, many had little dockets attached proclaiming that they had been transferred from one resting place to another under the authority of a certain high priest. Some had more than one, proclaiming more than one movement. These included the mummies of the great kings Seti I and Ramesses II, with dockets showing that Herihor had first reburied them, in Year 6 of the Repetition of Births (his last year). We know from some of the dockets found on the coffins in one particular cache that Pinudjem had been responsible for their reburial in Years "6" to "15", although the name of the pharaoh is omitted. In the reconstruction I am offering here, this refers to Years 6 to 15 of Ramesses XI, still nominally the head of state (951-942BC). From Year 16 onwards, however, Pinudjem took his own *prenomen* and *nomen* and wrote his name in a cartouche like any genuine pharaoh.

15. Documents with the name of high priest Masaharta are dated between Years 16 and 19; I assume these year dates to refer to Ramesses XI. The first year date referring to high priest Menkheperre is Year 6; this I take to refer to the reign of his father Pinudjem I, who had by then (935BC) effectively superseded Ramesses XI. A Year 8 reference to Pinudjem (as king, not high priest) also implies that he had by then started counting his own rather than Ramesses' years.

16. I base this date on the *Maunier Stela* of high priest Menkheperre, which suggests that Menkheperre had recently become effective ruler of Upper Egypt following the death of his father. It is dated to Year 25, and this is logically the 25th year of his brother Psusennes I's reign, since subsequent dates of Menkheperre's time in office use this system.

17. This is based on a single inscription at Abydos dated to Year 28. However, Ramesses XI never occupied his tomb in the Valley of the Kings and the second half of his reign is shrouded in mystery.

18. We know that Menkheperre predeceased Psusennes I because Menkheperre's son Smendes managed to donate a pair of bracelets to Psusennes in memory of his father. These bracelets were found among a collection in Psusennes' tomb at Tanis. However, there can only have been a few months between their deaths since we have two *Year 48* inscriptions of Menkheperre, and Psusennes I is thought to have died in his 49th year (refer note 11).

19. We have a full genealogy of Shoshenq I, recorded on a stela by one of his descendants, Pasenhor. It traces Pasenhor's royal ancestry back through kings Takelot I, Osorkon I and Shoshenq I to a founding father of the dynasty, Buyuwawu, a chief of the Meshwesh. With a middle-aged Shoshenq I (his son married a predecessor's daughter) acceding to the throne in 903BC, the six generations before Shoshenq would give me a date of roughly 1050BC for Buyuwawu which, since the Meshwesh settled in Libya after the Trojan War,

i.e. from about 1060BC, is perfectly reasonable. The point is hardly a precise one but it adds to the very considerable pile of evidence in favour of the foreshortened chronology in this book.

20. This statement is based on the fact that Siamun's scarab was found at the entrance to the tomb.

21. This interpretation is supported by the fact that Shoshenq I is only referred to as "Chief of the Meshwesh" in his 2nd year, but as "Pharaoh" in his 5th year (Montgomery, 2003).

22. Gold of Ophir is mentioned several times in the Bible, not only during Solomon's day, which suggests a location rather closer than India. A further clue comes in the listing of Ophir as one of the grandchildren of Eber, an ancestor of Abraham. Putting all this together with the fact that a long Red Sea voyage was necessary in order to reach Ophir suggests southern Arabia as a likely location.

23. The archaeology of Ashdod reveals that a period of peace, security and prosperity (Level XI, paralleling Level VIa at Megiddo) was replaced by one in which massive fortifications were required (Level X), fortifications which faced inland, toward Israel.

24. The silver coffin of Heqakheperre Shoshenq speaks of real wealth, since silver was considered more valuable than gold to the Egyptians. The style is unique but reminds most people of later examples. However, it also bears strong similarities to Tutankhamun's gold coffin. None of the accompanying goods bears the name of Osorkon I, which leads an increasing number of Egyptologists to reject his being the son of Osorkon I otherwise known as Shoshenq C. There are items with the name of Shoshenq I however, both as Chief of the Meshwesh and also as king, which suggests a burial some time in the early years of Shoshenq I's reign. On the other hand, this was a reburial, as presumably were the interments of Amenemophthis and Psusennes II, and it is not possible to know whether the Shoshenq I items related to the coffin of Heqakheperre Shoshenq or to one of the other occupants, notably Shoshenq I's former close colleague and relative by marriage Psusennes II. Taking the evidence as a whole, I feel the possibility that Heqakheperre Shoshenq was Manetho's Psinaches deserves serious consideration.

25. See Thom (2006) for an analysis of the history of Basque language and culture.

Chapter 19. The Seeds of Revival: 900-800BC

1. It is logical, and in my view quite reasonable, to suggest that the two Ashurnasirpal's are one and the same person and that he simply moved from being co-ruler to sole ruler on the death of Tukulti Ninurta II. However, I am not aware of direct evidence to support this.

2. By 'Georgians' I mean the Khirikhi people (see note 11 of Chapter 17); the Parthians were an Iranian- speaking people whose homeland was modern Turkmenistan, and who would later rule a vast empire and compete with Rome for domination over the Middle East.

3. By the time the Assyrian Empire reached its height in the 7th Century BC, Aramaean (or Aramaic) had already become the dominant language, and when the Persian Empire took charge in the mid 6th Century BC Aramaean was chosen as the *lingua franca* of that empire.

4. As well as the destruction evidence, Maeir (2003) reports on the presence of a siege trench which matches the description (in the so-called *Zakur inscription*) of a siege of the city of Hadrach by Aramaean forces.

5. C14 dates for this phase at Beth Rehov have produced mid 9th Century dates (Mazar, 2001).

6. The strong similarities between the city gates of Megiddo, Hazor and Gezer in this period, together with their excellent construction quality, prompted many early archaeologists to claim that they must date from the reign of king Solomon, i.e. the 10th Century BC. It is unfortunate to say the least that the rush to find evidence for the Bible seems to have led many to listen to their hearts rather than the weight of evidence. This battle is still being fought, but I have the impression that a majority is now prepared to date Megiddo Va/IVb to the 9th Century BC.

7. We may have a portrait of two members of the team. Shoshenq is shown on a funerary stela for his father Nimlot alongside (and of apparently equal status to) another unnamed king of Egypt (Bennett, 1996). The so-called Neseramun family tree also provides support for Shoshenq and Siamun being of the same generation (Jansen-Winkeln, 1999) since a man named Hor was initiated as priest in Year 17 of Siamun and his grandson (also named Hor) married a granddaughter of Shoshenq I.

8. Dockets attached to the coffins proclaim that many were transferred from one tomb to another on a certain day in Year 10 of Siamun (892BC), the very same day as the burial of Pinudjem II (presumably providing cover for the coffin transfers). An argument rages as to whether the coffin transfers made on that day were actually to Pinudjem II's tomb, where they were eventually found, or elsewhere, but the issue is only of importance to those wishing to defend the traditional chronology of Egypt; it doesn't affect the history told in this book.

9. The mummy concerned was that of Djedptahefankh, a second prophet of Amun. He has been the subject of controversy because his wrappings were marked with Years 5, 10 and 11 of Shoshenq I, whereas conventional chronology would suggest that he should have been interred long before Shoshenq's reign.

10. Many Egyptologists list a Psusennes III as successor to Pinudjem II in the role of high priest of Amun at Thebes. However, Bennett (1996) points out that this identification is entirely based on a misreading of the journal of archaeologist Gardiner Wilkinson.

11. Harrison, 2003.

12. Some independent confirmation of the general dates of Osorkon I can be found in the genealogy of Nespaherenhat. It is found on a statue which refers to Osorkon I as king and it goes back 9 generations to a second prophet of Amun called Roma. Roma's son is named as Ipuy, "Sem priest of the Temple of Baenre" and the name *Baenre* points firmly to the time of Merneptah, one of whose throne names was Baenre. Taking 20-25 years between generations, this gives an interval of 160-200 years between Ipuy and Nespeherenhat – and therefore between Merneptah and Osorkon I. The chronology in this book gives 180 years between the coronations of these two monarchs and 184 years between their deaths.

13. I suggest the truth is that the *Year 33* mark relates to the reign of Osorkon II (and the *Year 3* mark on another wrapping either to Takelot II or Shoshenq III) and that the bracelet with Osorkon I's prenomen was simply a treasured heirloom. I realise this is the standard explanation of archaeologists when their theory doesn't match the facts – but it can happen! I have plenty of trinkets from my parents and grandparents.

14. Modest support for this comes from Samaria, the capital of king Ahab of Israel, where Osorkon II's cartouche was found on a jar fragment from Ahab's palace.

15. Manetho simply notes "three kings" between Osorkon I and his son (by a lesser wife) Takelot I. Discounting Heqakheperre Shoshenq (see Chapter 18, note 24), whom I have assigned an earlier role, we have evidence (a stone block from Tanis and a piece of pottery from Abydos) for a 'Tutkheperre Shoshenq', together with indirect evidence that a king Shoshenq reigned about two generations before Shoshenq III based on an inscription of vizier Nesipaqashuty. Who the other two kings may have been and if they really existed at all is anybody's guess – but they certainly couldn't have lasted long.

16. Takelot's 9 years reflect the highest dated inscription, a stela from Bubastis. A *Year 14* inscription on an Apis bull burial I assign to Takelot II, whose *nomen* and *prenomen* were identical.

17. Majority opinion now assigns at least 30 years to Osorkon II based on a *Nile Level text* (Year 29) and a damaged inscription from the great hall at Bubastis (Year 30 in the view of many). I would also assign a *Year 33* mark on a mummy wrapping (see note 13).

18. By 'conventional thought' I am referring to the dates suggested by Kitchen (1996).

19. Takelot II is unattested at Tanis or elsewhere in the Nile delta; he was therefore basically a Theban ruler. I suggest in common with many Egyptologists (e.g. von Beckerath, 1997) that Osorkon II appointed his son Takelot II as his co-ruler in Thebes. He in his turn then

appointed his son Shoshenq III as ruler of Tanis following Osorkon's death. We have evidence that Year 5 of Takelot II was also Year 1 of Shoshenq III (Aston, 1989).

20. I am indebted to Rohl (1995) for details of the Serapeum burials.
21. The Tell Dan inscription, which is of keen interest because of its mention of the "house of David", has attracted cries of "forgery" from the moment it was unearthed in 1993. However, my reading of the state of the argument at present is that these claims have not been substantiated.
22. Refer to note 4.
23. See Thom (2006).

Bibliography

A. Afshar, "Camels at Persepolis", *Antiquity*, Vol 70, 1978.

D.P. Agrawal, *The Indus Civilisation = Aryans equation: Is it really a problem?*, http://www.infinityfoundation.com/mandala/h_es/h_es_agraw_indus.htm, accessed August 2005.

Y. Aharoni, "Arad", in *The Interpreter's Dictionary of the Bible*, Supplementary Volume, Abingdon Press, Nashville, 1976.

Richard Alley, *The Two-Mile Time Machine*, Princeton University Press, 2000.

Phillip Andrade, *An Historical Geography of the Exodus/Conquest Period*, http://home.earthlink.net/(neatoguy/conquest.html, accessed November 2003.

J.R. Arnold and W.F. Libby, "Age determinations by radiocarbon content: checks with samples of known age", *Science*, Vol 110, 1949, pp678–680.

David Aston, "Takeloth II – a king of the Theban 23rd Dynasty?", *Journal of Egyptian Archaeology*, Vol 75, 1989, pp139–153.

M.G.L. Baillie, *A Slice through Time*, Batsford Ltd, 1995.

Kathryn Bard, "The Egyptian predynastic: a review of the evidence", *Journal of Field Archaeology*, Fall, 1994.

Jürgen von Beckerath, *Unterzuchungen zur Politischen Geschichte der zweiten Zwischenheit in Ägypten*, Glückstadt, 1964.

Jürgen von Beckerath, *Chronologie des Pharaonischen Ägypten*, Verlag Philipp von Zabern, Mainz am Rhein, 1997.

Itzhaq Beit-Arieh, "Fifteen years in Sinai: Israeli archaeologists discover a new world", *Biblical Archaeology Review*, No. 1014, 1984, pp26–54.

Chris Bennett, *Temporal Fugues*, Journal of Ancient and Mediaeval Studies 13, 1996.

Manfred Bietak, *Avaris and Piramesse: Archaeological Exploration of the Eastern Nile Delta*, London, 1979.

Elisabetta Boaretto, Timothy Jull, Ayelet Gilboa and Ilan Sharon, "Dating the Iron Age I/II transition in Israel: first intercomparison results", *Radiocarbon*, Vol 47, No 1, 2005, pp39–55.

Georges Bonani, Herbert Haas, Zahi Hawass, Mark Lehner, Shawki Nakhla, John Nolan, Robert Wenke and Willy Wölfi, "Radiocarbon dates of Old and Middle Kingdom monuments in Egypt", *Radiocarbon*, Vol 43, No 3, 2001, pp1297–1320.

Trevor Bryce, *The Kingdom of the Hittites*, Oxford University Press, 1998.

Donovan Courville, *The Exodus Problem and its Ramifications: a critical examination of the chronological relationships between Israel and the contemporary peoples of antiquity*, Challenge Books, Loma Linda, California, 1971.

David Drew, *The Lost Chronicles of the Maya Kings*, Weidenfeld & Nicolson, London, 1999.

Étienne Drioton and Jean Vandier, *L'Égypte; des origins à la conquête d'Alexandre*, 4ᵗʰ edition, Paris, 1962.

Christine El Mahdy, *The Pyramid Builder*, Headline Book Publishing, 2003.

Walter Emery, *Archaic Egypt*, Penguin Books, 1961.

I. Finkelstein, *The Archaeology of the Israelite Settlement*, Israel Exploration Society, Jerusalem, 1988.

Charles Freeman, *Egypt, Greece and Rome*, Oxford University Press, 1996.

C.J. Gadd, *The Dynasty of Agade and the Gutian Invasion*, Cambridge University Press, 1963.

Ayelet Gilboa and Ilan Sharon, "Early iron age radiometric dates from Tell Dor: preliminary implications for Phoenicia and beyond", Radiocarbon, Vol 43, No 3, 2001, pp1343–1351.

Cyrus Gordon, *Forgotten Scripts*, Thames & Hudson, 1975.

Nicolas Grimal, *A History of Ancient Egypt*, translated by Ian Shaw, Blackwell, Oxford, 1992.

Bernard Grun, *The Timetables of History*, 3ʳᵈ Edition, Simon & Schuster, 1991.

O.R. Gurney, *The Hittites*, 2ⁿᵈ Edition, Penguin Books, 1954.

Harald Haarmann, "Writing from old Europe to ancient Crete: a case of cultural continuity", *The Journal of Indo-European Studies*, 17/3–4, pp251–275, 1989.

H. Haas et al, "Radiocarbon chronology and the historical calendar in Egypt", *BAR International Series*, 379, Lyon, France, CNRS, 1987.

Graham Hagens, "An ultra-low chronology of Iron Age Palestine" *Antiquity*, Vol 73, 1999, pp431–439.

William Hallo, "Zariqum", *Journal of Near Eastern Studies*, Vol 15, No 4, 1956, pp220–225.

D. Hardy and Colin Renfrew (eds), *Thera and the Aegean World III, Vol 3, Chronology*, Thera Foundation, London, 1991.

James Harris and Dann Hone, *The Names of God*, http://www.lib.byu.edu/~imaging/negev/main/s.html, accessed May 2006.

Timothy Harrison, "'The battleground (Who destroyed Megiddo? Was it David or Shishak?)", *Biblical Archaeology Review*, 29/6, 2003, pp28–35.

G. Heicken and F.W. McCoy, "Caldera development during the Minoan eruption", *Journal of Geophysical Research*, Vol 89:B10, 1984, pp8441–8462.

Herodotus, *The Histories*, translated Aubrey de Sélincourt, Penguin, London, 1954.

Ellen Herscher and Stuart Swiny, "Defining Philia in the south: material culture and Chronology", International workshop on the Philia Culture and the transition from Chalcolithic to Early Cypriot, University of Cyprus, 2002.

Walther Hinz, *The Lost World of Elam: recreation of a vanished civilisation*, translated by Jennifer Barnes, Sidgwick & Jackson, 1972.

Homer, *The Iliad*, translated by Robert Foyles, Viking Penguin, 1990.

Sinclair Hood, *The Home of the Heroes*, Thames & Hudson, London, 1967.

J. Horgan, "Volcanic winter", *Scientific American*, 1987, Vol 2, pp 83–84.

R W Hutchinson, *Prehistoric Crete*, Penguin Books, Middlesex, 1962.

P. James, I.J. Thorpe, N. Kokkinos, R. Morkot and J. Frankish, *Centuries of Darkness*, Jonathan Cape, 1991.

Carl Jansen-Winkeln, "Dating the beginning of the 22nd Dynasty", *Journal of the Ancient Chronology Forum*, Vol 8, 1999.

Jac Janssen, "The day the inundation began", *Journal of Near Eastern Studies*, Vol 46, 1987, pp129–136.

T. de Jong and W.H. van Soldt, "The earliest known solar eclipse record redated", *Nature*, Vol 338, 1989, p239.

Giorgi Kavtaradze, "The chronology of the Caucasus during the early metal age: observations from central trans-Caucasus", in "AView from the Highlands: Archaeological Studies in Honour of Charles Burney", ed. Antonio Sagona, *Ancient Near Eastern Studies*, Supplement 12, 2004, pp539–556.

Douglas Keenan, "Why early-historical radiocarbon dates downwind from the *Mediterranean* are too early", *Radiocarbon*, Vol 44, 2002, pp225–237.

Douglas Keenan, *Anatolian tree-ring studies are untrustworthy*, http://www.informath.org/ATSU04a.pdf, accessed July 2006.

Kathleen Kenyon, *Archaeology in the Holy Land*, 3rd Edition, Earnest Benn, London, 1970.

Kathleen Kenyon, *Digging up Jerusalem*, Ernest Benn, London, 1974.

Kenneth Kitchen, *The Third Intermediate Period in Egypt*, 2nd Edition, Aris and Phillips, Warminster, 1996.

P.I. Kuniholm, S.L. Tarter and C.B. Griggs, "Dendrochronological report". *Tille Höyük 4*, British Institute of Archaeology at Ankara, Ankara, 1993.

Assaf Landau, "The many faces of colonisation: 12th Century Aegean settlements in Cyprus and the Levant", *Mediterranean Archaeology and Archaeometry*, Vol 3, No 1, 2003, pp45–54.

D. Lappin, *The decline and fall of Sothic dating: El Lahun lunar texts and Egyptian astronomical dates*, Journal of the Ancient Chronology Forum 9, 2002.

Gwendolyn Leick, *Mesopotamia*, Penguin Books, 2001.

Thomas Levy, Russel Adams, Mohammad Najjar, Andreas Hauptmann, James Anderson, Baruch Brandl, Mark Robinson and Thomas Higham, "Reassessing the chronology of Biblical Edom: new excavations and 14C dates from Khirbat en-Nahas (Jordan)", *Antiquity*, 302, 2004.

J.V. Luce, *The End of Atlantis*, Thames & Hudson, London, 1969.

Aren Maeir, "Notes and News: Tell es-Safi/Gath: 1996–2002", *Israel Exploration Journal*, No. 53, 2003, pp237–246.

M.E.L. Mallowan, *Twenty-five years of Mesopotamian Discovery*, The British School of Archaeology in Iraq, London, 1956

Sturt W. Manning, *A Test of Time: the Volcano of Thera and the Chronology and History of the Aegean and East Mediterranean in the mid Second Millennium BC*, Oxbow Books, Oxford, 1999.

Masoudi, *Les Prairies d'Or*, Paris, 1861–77.

Amihai Mazar and I Carmi, "Dates from Iron Age strata at Tel Beth-Shean and Tel Rehov", *Radiocarbon*, Vol 43, No 3, 2001, pp1333–1342.

Colin McEvedy and Richard Jones, *Atlas of World Population History*, Facts on File, New York, 1978.

James Mellart, "The royal treasure of Dorak – a first and exclusive report of a clandestine excavation which led to the most important discovery since the royal tombs of Ur", *Illustrated London News*, 28 November 1959, pp 754 ff.

Wayne Mitchell, "Ancient astronomical observations and near eastern chronology", *Journal of the Ancient Chronology Forum*, Vol 3, 1990.

Alan Montgomery, *A Chronological Model for the Bible*, http://www.ldolphin.org/montgochron.html, 2003, accessed October 2003.

Oswyn Murray, *Early Greece*, 2nd Edition, Fontana Press, 1993.

Joan Oates, *Babylon*, revised edition, Thames and Hudson, London, 1986.

Louis Orlin, "Assyrian colonies in Cappadocia", *Studies in Ancient History*, Mouton, The Hague, Vol 1, 1970.

Edgar Peltenburg, "Broadening the Philia Debate: chronology, consumption and climate", International workshop on the Philia Culture and the transition from Chalcolithic to Early Cypriot, University of Cyprus, 2002.

Giovanni Pettinato, *The archives of Ebla*, Doubleday, 1981.

Graham Phillips, *The Moses Legacy*, Sidgwick & Jackson, London, 2002.

Stuart Piggott, *Prehistoric India*, Penguin, London, 1950.

Stuart Piggott, *Ancient Europe*, Edinburgh University Press, paperback edition, 1973.

Francis Pryor, *Britain BC*, Harper Collins, London, 2003.

Cemal Pulak, "1994 Excavation at Uluburun: the final campaign", *The Institute of Nautical Archaeology Quarterly*, Vol 21.4, 1994, pp 8–16.

John Read, "Early 18th Dynasty chronology", *Journal of Near Eastern Studies*, Vol 29, 1970.

D.B. Redford, *Egypt, Canaan and Israel in Ancient Times*, Princeton, 1992.

Colin Renfrew, *Before Civilisation*, Penguin Books, 1973.

David Rohl, *A Test of Time*, Century Press, London, 1995.

David Rohl, *Legend: the Genesis of Civilisation*, Arrow Books, London, 1999.

David Rohl, *The Lost Testament*, Century Press, London, 2002.

Georges Roux, *Ancient Iraq*, Pelican Books, 1966.

Richard Rudgley, *Lost Civilisations of the Stone Age*, Century Press, London, 1998.

Yannis Sakellarakis and Efi Sapouna-Sakellaraki, "Drama of death in a Minoan temple", *National Geographic*, February 1981.

Nancy Sandars, *The Sea Peoples: Warriors of the Ancient Mediterranean*, Thames & Hudson, London, 1978.

Robert Schiestl, "Some links between a late middle kingdom cemetery at Tell ed Daba and Syria-Palestine: the necropolis of F/I, Str. d/2 and d/1 (= H and G/4)", Proceedings of the International Middle Bronze Age Conference, Vienna, 2001.

Michael Schultz and André Paul, "Holocene climate variability on centennial-to-millennial time scales: 1. Climate records from the north Atlantic realm", in *Climate Development and History of the North Atlantic Realm*, eds, G. Wefer, W. Berger, K.-E. Behre and E Jansen, Springer-Verlag, Berlin, 2002, pp41–54.

W.S. Shea, "Two Palestinian segments from the Eblaite geographical atlas", in C.L. Meyers and M. O'Connor (eds), *The Word of the Lord shall go forth*, Eisenbrauns, Winona Lake, Indiana.

Nick Thom, *The Origin of Tongues*, Grosvenor House, Guildford, 2006.

Joyce Tildesley, *Nefertiti*, Penguin Books, 1999.

S.R. Troelstra, G.M. Ganssen, K. van der Borg and A.F.M. de Jong, "A late Quaternary stratigraphic framework for eastern Mediterranean sapropel S1", *Radiocarbon*, Vol 33(1), 1991, pp15–21.

Merrill Unger and Gary Larsen, *The Hodder Bible Handbook*, Hodder & Stoughton, London, 1984.

United Nations, *The World at Six Billion*, http://www.un.org/esa/population/publications/sixbillion/sixbilpart1.pdf, 1999.

David Ussishkin, *Excavations at Tell Lachish 1973–1977*, Tel Aviv University Institute of Archaeology, 1978.

Immanuel Velikovsky, *Ages in Chaos*, Sidgwick and Jackson, 1977.

Ottar Vendel, *Second Intermediate Period (SIP) Dynasties 15–17*, http://www.nemo.nu/ibisportal/0egyptintro/6egypt/6main.htm, accessed March 2004.

F.W. Walbank, *The Hellenistic World*, Fontana Press, 1981.

James Weinstein, "Palestinian radiocarbon dating: a reply to James Mellart", *Antiquity*, Vol 54, 1980, pp21–24.

Colin Wells, *The Roman Empire*, Fontana Press, 1984.

Fred Wendorf and A.E. Close, Early Neolithic food-economies in the eastern Sahara" in R. Friedman and B. Adams (eds), *The Followers of Horus: Studies dedicated to Michael Allen Hoffman*, Oxbow Monograph 20, Egyptian Studies Publication Association No 2, Oxford, 1992, pp155–162.

Toby Wilkinson, *Genesis of the Pharaohs*, Thames & Hudson, London, 2003.

Bruce Williams, *Archaeology and Historical Problems of the Second Intermediate Period*, PhD Dissertation, Oriental Institute, Chicago, 1975.

Ian Wilson, *The Bible is History*, Weidenfeld & Nicolson, London, 1999.

Bryant Wood, "The Discovery of the Sin Cities of Sodom and Gomorrah", *Bible and Spade*, 1999, pp67–80.

Leonard Woolley, *Ur of the Chaldees: seven years of excavation*, Penguin Books, 1929.

Leonard Woolley, *A Forgotten Kingdom*, Penguin Books, 1953.

Adam Zertal, "Has Joshua's altar been found on Mount Ebal?", *Bulletin of Archaeological Research*, Jan/Feb 1985, p35.

Adam Zertal, "Israel enters Canaan", *Bulletin of Archaeological Research*, Sept/Oct 1991, p32.

G.A. Zielinski et al, "Record of volcanism since 7000BC from the GISP2 Greenland ice core and implications for the volcano-climate system", *Science*, Vol 264, 1994, pp948–952.

G.A. Zielinski and M.S. Germani, "New ice core evidence challenges the 1620s BC age for the Santorini (Minoan) eruption", *Journal of Archaeological Science*, Vol 25, 1998, pp279–289.

The Holy Bible, New International Version, Hodder & Stoughton, 1979.

The Epic of Gilgamesh, translated by Andrew George, Penguin Press, London, 1999.

Lightning Source UK Ltd.
Milton Keynes UK
25 February 2010

150622UK00001B/118/A